The Collaborative Turn

The Collaborative Turn

Working Together in Qualitative Research

Walter S. Gershon
Kent State University

SENSE PUBLISHERS
ROTTERDAM/BOSTON/TAIPEI

A C.I.P. record for this book is available from the Library of Congress.

ISBN 978-90-8790-958-1 (paperback)
ISBN 978-90-8790-959-8 (hardback)
ISBN 978-90-8790-960-4 (e-book)

Published by: Sense Publishers,
P.O. Box 21858, 3001 AW
Rotterdam, The Netherlands
http://www.sensepublishers.com

Printed on acid-free paper

Cover artwork by Dena J. Gershon

All Rights Reserved © 2009 Sense Publishers

No part of this work may be reproduced, stored in a retrieval system, or transmitted in any form or by any means, electronic, mechanical, photocopying, microfilming, recording or otherwise, without written permission from the Publisher, with the exception of any material supplied specifically for the purpose of being entered and executed on a computer system, for exclusive use by the purchaser of the work.

CONTENTS

Acknowledgements   vii

Foreword   ix
JANICE KROEGER AND MARIE-FRANCE ORILLION

Introduction: Working Together in Qualitative Research: *The Many Faces of Collaboration*   xvii
WALTER S. GERSHON

PART I: EXPANDING QUALITATIVE METHODOLOGIES THROUGH COLLABORATION

1. Troubling the Angels Redux: *Tales of Collaboration Towards a Polyphonic Text*   3
   WALTER S. GERSHON, PATTI LATHER AND CHRIS SMITHIES

2. Co-optation, Ethical Dilemmas and Collective Memory: *A Writing Story*   35
   BRIAN D. SCHULTZ AND PARIS BANKS

3. What we Know First: *Interrupting the Institutional Narrative of Individualism*   55
   PAM STEEVES, MARNI PEARCE, ANNE MURRAY ORR, SHAUN M. MURPHY, MARILYN HUBER, JANICE HUBER AND D. JEAN CLANDININ

4. Partnerships for Participatory Action Research: *The Case of Recent Immigrant Women in Toronto, Canada*   71
   AMOABA GOODEN AND DENISE GASTALDO

5. Translational Research in Education: *Collaboration & Commitment in Urban Contexts*   89
   JOSHUA S. SMITH AND ROBERT J. HELFENBEIN, JR.

PART II: EMERGING QUALITATIVE METHODOLOGIES AND THE ARTS: COLLABORATION AS QUALITATIVE METHODOLOGY

6. Restorying Work Inside and Outside the Academy: *Practices of Reflexive Team Research*   105
   ALETTE WILLIS AND JANET SILTANEN

7. Duoethnography: *Articulations/(Re)Creation of Meaning in the Making*   127
   RICHARD D. SAWYER AND JOE NORRIS

CONTENTS

8. Collaboration Without Compromise: *Reflecting on Collaborative Discensus in Action*   141
WALTER S. GERSHON, AMANDA PEEL AND CARRIE BILINOVICH

9. Ethnodramatic Playwriting as Collaborative Work   165
DIANE CONRAD, KIM MCCAW AND MATTHEW "GUS" GUSUL

10. Imbed/In Bed: *Two Perspectives on Dance and Collaboration*   185
MELANIE GEORGE AND JOAN MEGGITT

11. Improvisation and Collectivity: *Practical Applications for Research*   209
RENEE T. COULOMBE

Contributors   223

Endnotes   231

Index   233

Author Index   239

ACKNOWLEDGEMENTS

I would like to thank those people without whom this book would not have been possible. First, I would like to thank the contributors for the depth, strength, and timeliness of their work, time and effort even more laudable given the their personal commitments and the ever-increasing demands of their professional lives. In addition to these named contributors, several people served as a kind of *de facto*, and occasionally impromptu, editorial support team, helping me wrestle with questions that arose in the process of compiling this book. Although some are also contributing authors, I wish to again acknowledge their help in such matters. They are, in alphabetical order: Kent den Heyer, Joanne Kilgour Dowdy, Andrew Gilbert, Robert J. Helfenbein, Jr., Jennifer H. James, and Brian D. Schultz. Particular thanks goes to Janice Hutchison for her keen mechanical editing eye. I would also like to acknowledge all those whose thoughts and mentorship over the years has in many ways laid the groundwork that makes this work possible, Reba N. Page and William F. Pinar in particular.

On a more literal note, this book would not exist were it not for the help, guidance, and skill of Michel Lokhorst at Sense Publishing, all of which were provided not only with kind candor but also in an impressively timely fashion. Finally, and certainly by no means least (in fact, first and foremost), I would like to thank my wife and partner Dena J. Gershon whose wonderful artwork graces the cover of this book and our daughter Kate for their love, support, and patience throughout the process that has become this book.

JANICE KROEGER AND MARIE-FRANCE ORILLION

FOREWORD

In keeping with the spirit and theme of this book, Walter asked us to consider writing a collaborative foreword. The following is our response to his suggestion, a dialogic foreword in which we both write and respond to one another's thoughts about *The Collaborative Turn*, a process through which we also reflect on our process in putting this foreword together.

JANICE KROEGER: IS THIS A FOREWORD OR A FORWARD?

The foreword of any edited volume is like doorway to the space and time of understandings between the readers and writers of a text. In order to familiarize this work and consider what has been done here between researchers and their co-creators, I first attempt to capture a simplified holism of the chapters herein and then interpretively pull on ideas that stand out to me as a qualitative researcher, author, who most often employs critical ethnography, mixed methodology and discourse processes.

To capture the intricacy and intimacy of what this volume has to offer, I first provide an overview the book, then draw from several of Mikhail Bakhtin's translated concepts (Brandist, 2002; Holquist, 1981; Morson & Emerson, 1990) to further interpret those offerings. This strategy will come as no surprise to some readers as many of the contributors to the volume share similar theoretical groundings. My hope is that readers search as I have, finding solace and direction in that which is oft not practiced or spoken about—the chronicling of research collaborations that reveal the "joy and terror and sorrow…[and] desperation" as well as the uncertain "emotional and spiritual" compromises, burdens, successes and quandaries that such qualitative work brings (Smithies, in Gershon, Lather & Smithies, this volume, pp. 17, 28)

At first glance, through my lens as a qualitative methodologist and educator, I saw the book as offering a variety of curriculum and pedagogic threads including teaching and learning in urban settings, academic settings, and performative spaces (Coulombe; George & Meggitt; Gershon, Peel & Bilinovich; Schultz & Banks; Smith & Helfenbein; Steeves, et al. this volume). However, it also features prominent contemporary social problems and issues of the day such as women's rights in immigration, AIDS support networking and awareness, the social construction of homophobia, and performance as social commentary, activism, and development for communities and students (Conrad, McCaw, & Gusul; Gooden & Gastaldo; Gershon, Lather & Smithies; Sawyer & Norris, this volume).

The books' authors crest a wave of both contemporary social issues and complex qualitative methodologies that include but are not limited to: duo-ethnography; transformational narrative; critical transformational methods; video production and photo-action; collaborative discensus; and ethno-drama. At the same time, each author explains his or her own collaborative process as researcher, colleague, teacher and student, support group participant and psychologist, choreographer and dancer, and so on. While the simplified subject/object terminologies I use in this paragraph creates "binaries" that do not exemplify the intent of the work herein, it is in the following pages of each chapter that the reader will find how authors begin to deconstruct the ways in which such binaries are shattered in the between spaces of collaborative inquiry. Working together as co-equals to responsibly forge working lives, their projects are often discussed as being difficult to capture in writing or as "beyond words." As importantly, many write of research projects that are built upon moral commitments towards others in the interpretive act.

In this volume, the broad idea of what Gershon has called a "collaborative turn" in qualitative methodology is the genesis of a collection of works crossing disciplinary boundaries of the fine and performing arts and the social sciences, a framing that seems rarely if ever done in an academic text. Moreover, that this book represents one of the more unique collections of work on collaboration in and among qualitative researchers is also a testament to researchers' retrospective analyses of their projects. Here, the collective authors grapple with a set of relatively common yet also uniquely embedded and unwieldy issues indicative of the extraordinary contexts that each chapter portrays.

When considered as a collective whole, what stands out to me is the generative nature of dialogism (Bakhtin, 1935) in the collaborative research process. According to literary theorist Mikhail Bakhtin, dialogism is the multifaceted, layered social linguistic chain that is the starting place for all things including the self (Bakhtin, 1935; Morson & Emerson, 1990, pp. 52–55). Most co-equals (contributing authors/ research partners) in this volume speak of ways in which a constant redefinition of project and self shapes and coheres their collaborative work. While the context and content of conducting collaborative qualitative research is an individual and emergent task, it is also one rich in unknown possibilities, shaping intent, affordances, and products of work. Many authors in this text see the collaborative process of research as a polyphonic (cf. Bakhtin, 1935; Clifford, 1988) tool—an orchestration of meanings drawn between participants and collectively constructed from various individual and/or group processes.

Raising the dialogic the bar of conversation between readers and writers in this volume may well engender common considerations and post-modern quandaries of qualitative work—for example, at the onset of their collaborations authors in this volume pose their own value assumptions. Similarly, for many authors in this volume, simple-seeming intentions like bringing the least often "voiced" perspective to the fore is a central value-guiding practice. The ethical considerations of power and voice figure prominently in the collection with many authors striving to catapult the voices of youth, the disenfranchised, and those most vulnerable into the forefront of meaning making. Least-often heard voices placed to the fore in this book include survivors, outsiders, queers, artists, inmates, aboriginals, youth, scramblers, angels and the like.

Contributors to this book explicitly note the ethical tensions surrounding questions of voice in qualitative research collaborations, rendering transparent the roles and relationships between collaborators. Authors acknowledge and break hierarchical boundaries between self and other or claim that space more definitively by asking directly, Am I as a researcher an "I-for-myself," an "I-for-another," and who is "the-other-for-me" in this work (Brandist, 2002, p. 46)? It is in these acts that the transcendence and searching that occurs behind the scenes of collaborative project work is revealed.

Finally the collection causes me to question and break the bindings of the idea of consensus in community—that to collaborate one must agree with the others (see Gershon, Peel & Bilinovich, this volume). Commonly consensus is a form of implicit or explicit social contract between people of various oppositional perspectives with an appeal toward deliberate compromise. In this volume, researchers reveal how consensus is not necessarily the ultimate focus in collaboration. Alongside or in its stead, conflict and disagreement, as well as accidental and incidental previously unimagined happenings, are welcomed and utilized, leading to the transformation of researchers, problems, and projects alike.

Marie's Response

As I read your contribution, three aspects resonated with me: collaboration as generative, moral, and transformative. These are some of the most powerful aspects of the book.

These chapters document how knowledge is formed through dialogic processes that involve deeper, more demanding quests for understanding than ordinarily required by researcher-centered methods. To engage in these forms of collaboration, researchers, who are often accustomed to or socialized in the notion of researcher authority, must allow space for alternate perspectives.

It is a moral undertaking that often emerges from a deep commitment to social justice. This undertaking has a profound effect on the authors' perspectives of self, other, and the research project. It is an intense social experience that requires a substantial commitment to reflexivity.

As we mindfully collaborate, our selves and projects are transformed. While this transformation has the potential to threaten representations of self as expert, the commitment to reflexivity and to creating space for others to speak fully offers the reward of producing multilayered, multidimensional texts that illuminate the complexities of social relations and structures in ways that are not possible using traditional methods.

MARIE-FRANCE ORILLION: A PERSONAL RESPONSE TO *A COLLABORATIVE TURN*

I wish I had this book when I was a dissertator. It would have saved me a lot of grief, and perhaps infused more pleasure into the experience, by providing me with models for collaboration. I received excellent training in interpretive research and issues of power and representation. However, this did not prepare me for the complexities of collaborative research in practice. As Walter notes in his introduction, while there is collaborative research in print, there is little documentation of *how* others engage in such research. As a doctoral candidate, I knew I didn't want to engage in researcher-centered practice. Yet, my first effort to attend to power relations, a dissertation on general education at a research university, was a near-disaster. I was unprepared for the complexities of "studying-up"—studying faculty when I myself was a graduate student. For multiple reasons, including my naïveté and disciplinary politics, I never established rapport with the faculty. Problems that began the first year of the study shaped relations during the second year. A consequence was that understanding (Gershon, 2008; Wolcott, 1990) their perspectives became an ongoing challenge.

During the first year I observed in the classroom of a professor who claimed to use critical pedagogy in her instruction. I was undeniably starry-eyed and hoped to document best practices. However, a request made during our first meeting resulted in complications that had significant and negative effects on the study. She wanted to see and respond to my work. Her request wasn't surprising, and I intended to share and discuss my research with her. However, she also implied that I had been trained in "fly on the wall" ethnography and, as a condition of her participation, required that I assume the undergraduate student role. As a graduate student and learner of research studying a tenured professor and critical ethnographer, I felt vulnerable. While I observed her, I knew that she would also be observing me. Her request increased my feelings of vulnerability. I was now aware that my training was suspect and my new role, as a student in her course, increased the intensity of her gaze. A second complication emerged when her students related to me as a teaching assistant, and I responded in kind. Many were English learners, and some of the texts, such as Kondo's (1997) critique of orientalism, were beyond their abilities without additional scaffolding. While I worried about the effects of this involvement on my data, it felt wrong to refuse.

I began the study intending to engage in a collaborative relationship with the professor, and found myself instead collaborating with the students and in tension with the professor. To understand her perspective I had to rely on "expressions of culture" (Gershon, 2008, p. 48); attending to the intent documented in an article she wrote about her teaching practice and how this intent was expressed in classroom interactions (Orillion, 2009). My analysis, which was not submitted until the end of the year, while acknowledging the many strengths of the course, asked challenging questions about her teaching. The next year, while I was allowed to observe in other courses, the professors denied all requests for interviews. While it is the case that reporting ethnography to informants is a process that involves substantial risk to field relations (Page, Samson & Crockett, 2000), I wonder if engaging in that process earlier might have enabled us to move past barriers we both erected.

The importance of transparency is a theme that emerges in various forms throughout this book. However, the chapter that resonated with me is the one on collaborative discensus, by Gershon, Peel, and Bilinovich. It offers a theory and a framework, a highly usable tool for working through *and* representing tensions much like the ones I struggled with in my dissertation. Moreover, the text is performative. The theory, and their story of applying the theory, is organized according to a four-part framework that enables each participant to be equally represented. The performative nature of this chapter, and many other chapters in the book, elicited the pleasure that I referenced in the beginning of this essay.

Many chapters transcend description and analysis by performing the collaboration as the authors tell their stories, recalling Geertz's (1973) performance of thick description. And, as with Geertz's writings, it is a pleasure to read them. For example, Steeves, Pearce, Orr, Murphy, Huber, Huber, and Clandinin's critique and response to the dominant discourse of individualism begins on a playful note, with a word image, before shifting into a poetic and multivocal story of trust, respect, and improvisation. It also offers, through its structure, insights into how to manage multiple voices in a text.

Finally, the book offers a sense of community. Collaborative research violates tacit norms borrowed from quantitative research, e.g., objectivity. For example, the inevitable, and often passionate, conversations that I have with my current research participants/collaborator teachers often leave me uneasy because they violate the distance dictated by the classic participant-observer stance (Erickson, 2006). However, I can't not engage. Through these interactions we begin to understand (Gershon, 2008; Wolcott, 1990) each other. An important benefit of this book is the way it connects the reader to a community of practice. These connections offer validation for and exemplify what Janice refers to above as the "generative nature of dialogism in the collaborative research process."

Janice's Response

It seems to me that many qualitative researchers are confronted with decision making and unexpected surprises when establishing rapport and building trust with their participants as they seek to find the fine line between trust and truth. The general ethos of doing qualitative research is to respect participants. However, actually understanding what that means in practice is a difficult construct, especially for new researchers. I appreciate your candor about your struggles.

As I listened to your passages and we spoke about your experience it seemed to be about tensions of representation as well as transparency. On the one hand you shared what may have been threatening to the professor's image of self and thus lost ground within an alliance to her. On the other hand, clearly you had what seems to me to be a sense of moral obligation to students who were English Language Learners and with considerably less power and status. Indeed, as you point out, critical pedagogy in practice may not always live up to its rhetoric.

What do we do when our representations cause disruptions in the very images our constituents want to hold of themselves? How do we handle our sense of duty toward the least powerful in our work when the nature of the constructed images of self collide with our moral integrity? This seems a difficult but not uncommon dilemma.

Very similar dynamics also marked my early work. I shared transcripts with a man who was professionally educated, a late-comer convert to Judaism (from Christianity), and he was what I considered fairly "hegemonic" (classed and raced) in his thinking about poor kids. To me how he described children in his son's school was similar to most dominant constructions of social class and education—but for my very valuable informant I was being what he considered "racist and anti-Semitic."

I was crushed. I didn't understand what I had written incorrectly in my member checks from his view. Moreover, my portrayal of him was very similar to how other critical theorists had conceptualized social class among professionally educated parents who call themselves middle-class but are probably of the upper-middle class because of their high social capital, income, or both (Brantlinger, 2003; Lareau, 2003). As a result, I had to rebuild that very damaged relationship and it felt as if it could cost me other alliances I had made in the field. In its moment, this crisis was very real and felt dangerous to me. Like you, I learned.

I think what your writing reveals are the risks that researchers take when they attempt to be transparent in their member-checking and methodological processes. Vulnerability to losing valuable time and effort as well as resulting research opportunity or written products is real to us. Being successful as academics often interfaces with the very nature of who we think we are as people and what our work can help our professions accomplish. For most of us our successful work production is associated with economic, political, social, and emotional losses, particularly if our mistakes in the field close down opportunities for other opportunities in research.

I also see now why you turned to the chapter (Gershon, Peel, & Bilinovich, this volume) as you did. The process they describe could be a very important framework and template for practice at the foundation of collaborative inquiry.

CONCLUDING THOUGHTS

Marie

For me, collaborating with Janice was truly generative. Through our conversations, I came to a richer understanding of the meaning that I was trying to express in my early drafts of this foreword. I remain grateful to her, as I am grateful to Walter for including me in his project.

Janice

I agree with Marie that it was a productive writing experience. We used Walter's suggestions about the process of writing this non-traditional foreword and found that although we may have written from very different places, not only could we understand each other but we could also push each other's thinking forward/foreword. Walter was a skilled editor, helping me with expression and economy of words. I enjoyed reading the contributing chapters, finding insight and metaphors I hadn't considered. Writing with Walter and Marie allowed me to delve again into Bakhtin's work, which reminds me that language *is* formidable action, just as the contributors of the volume remind me that processes are actions that do not always have adequate words to describe them.

REFERENCES

Bakhtin, M. M. (1935/1981). Discourse in the novel. In M. Holquist (Ed.), *The dialogic imagination: Four essays by M. M. Bakhtin* (pp. 259–422). Austin, TX: The University of Texas Press.

Brandist, C. (2002). *The Bakhtin circle: Philosophy, culture, and politics*. London: Pluto Press.

Brantlinger, E. (2003). *Dividing classes: How the middle class negotiates and rationalizes school advantage*. New York: Routledge Falmer.

Clifford, J. (1988). *The predicament of culture: Twentieth-century ethnography, literature, and art*. Cambridge, MA: Harvard University Press.

Erickson, F. (2006). Studying side by side: Collaborative action ethnography in educational research. In G. Spindler & L. Hammond (Eds.), *Innovations in educational ethnography: Theory, methods, and results* (pp. 235–258). Mahwah, NJ: Lawrence Erlbaum.

Geertz, C. (1973). *The interpretation of cultures*. New York: Basic Books.

Gershon, W. S. (2008). Intent and expression: Complexity, ethnography, and lines of power in classrooms. *Journal of the Canadian Association for Curriculum Studies, 6*(1), 45–71.

Kondo, D. (1997). *About face: Performing race in fashion and theatre*. New York: Routledge.

Lareau, A. (2003). *Unequal childhoods: Class, race, and family life*. Berkeley, CA: University of California Press

Morson, G. S., & Emerson, C. (1990). *Mikhail Bakhtin: Creation of a prosaics*. Palo Alto, CA: Stanford University Press.

Orillion, M. (2009). *Negotiating authority over knowledge in a general education diversity course*. Manuscript submitted for publication.

Page, R. N., Samson, Y., & Crockett, M. (2000). Reporting ethnography to informants. In B. Brizuela, J. Stewart, R. Carillo, & J. Berger (Eds.), *Acts of inquiry in qualitative research* (pp. 321–352). Cambridge, MA: Harvard Educational Review.

Wolcott, H. F. (1990). On seeking–and rejecting–validity in qualitative research. In E. Eisner & A. Peshkin (Eds.), *Qualitative inquiry in education: The continuing debate* (pp. 121–152). New York: Teachers College Press.

WALTER S. GERSHON

INTRODUCTION: WORKING TOGETHER IN QUALITATIVE RESEARCH

The Many Faces of Collaboration

Collaboration in qualitative research is ubiquitous. Qualitative researchers have a deep history of working with one another in a multitude of configurations and on a wide variety of questions (cf. Bellack, Kliebard, Hyman & Smith, 1978; Denzin & Lincoln, 2005; Given, 2008; Lecompte, Millroy & Preissle, 1992; Spindler & Spindler, 1982; Weis & Fine, 2005). In addition, interpretive studies are in and of themselves forms of collaboration between those conducting the research and the local actors and contexts they study, a differentiation that is itself a source of debate (Clifford, 1988; Denzin & Lincoln; Wolcott, 1990). It is therefore somewhat surprising that with a few notable exceptions (cf. Erickson & Christman, 1996; Jipson & Wilson, 1997; Lather & Smithies, 1997), most qualitative studies have tended not to make explicit either a) the ways in which co-authors worked together or b) the implicit and explicit collaborations between "researcher" and "researched," the inherently collaborative nature of interpreting the meanings of other people's lives.

The decision by qualitative scholars to address their specific means of collaboration as a kind of explicit methodological footnote in order to turn their attention to the contexts, collection, presentation, and analysis of data is certainly understandable. However, such choices can mask important methodological questions that pertain to every step of research, from considering who "counts" as a researcher and what can be considered research, to what research partnerships mean and whose ideas remain when findings are presented for publication. This is important because compromise can be not only a mutually mitigated solution but also an implicit or explicit means of marginalization and omission (see Gershon, Peel, & Bilinovich, this volume). In short, while collaboration in interpretive research is not in and of itself news, attention to how it is conducted and the ways in which such choices impact all aspects of scholarship have been largely overlooked.

Furthermore, the previous decade or so in qualitative research can be seen as a kind of turning inwards (Page, 2000). This movement towards foregrounding the personal can be understood as a response to recognizing the impossibility of separating one's self from the research one conducts, the necessity of more transparently acknowledging and locating one's biases, and a growing recognition of the importance of people's personal knowledge.[1] Rather than avoiding the elephant in the room, such scholarship addressed the impossibility of separating self from research context to their advantage, melding and molding existing methodologies into methods that were specifically designed to explicitly collect, analyze, and present data through the lens of self.

This movement in qualitative research, one that Foley (2002) refers to as "the reflexive turn" in his description of its possibilities for his ethnographic processes, is represented by such methodologies as autobiographical studies, autoethnography, and the rise of action research as a means for teachers to examine and reflect upon their own teaching practices (Chamberlayne, Bornat & Wengraf, 2000; Moss, 2001; Okely & Callaway, 1992; Pinar, 1995). Variations of narrative inquiry similarly fit this category in the ways that narrative researchers rely upon the telling of one's own stories and/or the stories of others as a means to locate themselves within the contexts of their research (Clandinin & Connelly, 2000; Ellis & Bochner, 2000).

Contrasting such scholarship, authors in this book represent the crest of an emerging methodological trend in qualitative research. In ever-increasing numbers, interpretive scholars are reaching out across the methodological divide between research methodologies, the presidium to local actors in research contexts, and to the complex juxtapositions of multiple identities and possibilities that reside within individual researchers (cf. Clandinin et al., 2006; Erickson, 2006; Mehan, 2008; Springgay, Irwin, Leggo & Gouzouasis, 2007; Valli & Chambliss, 2007). Turning towards one another in order to provide more complex and rich pictures of the contexts we study—a movement that includes retaining a firm regard for the personal, individual, and other complex contexts that inform our work—adds to the depth and richness of the questions asked, the findings co-authors present, as well as the processes of data collection and analysis utilized to arrive at such findings.

Contributing authors' means of collaboration and their decisions to work with others have methodological, practical, and ethnical components. To work collaboratively in qualitative research, they argue, is much more than the inescapable necessity of engaging others in the collection and production of data. It is the process of explicitly wrestling with questions of representation and analysis. It is also the need to struggle with the paradox of interpreting complex contexts to non-participants in an organized, transparent, and clear fashion—the difficulty of representing the voices of those who work, live, and play in the contexts one studies in a nuanced and rich manner that is neither overly reductionist nor over-detailed in delivery. In sum, questioning and pushing at the boundaries of what collaborative research might mean and to whom such meanings matter are simultaneously an exploration of the meanings and purposes of qualitative research.

Thus, in light of this recent trend towards collaboration and a general absence of any collection of work about *how* participants collaborate across qualitative studies,[2] the purpose of this book is twofold. First, it fills a gap in the literature on qualitative methodologies. Despite a long tradition of collaboration in qualitative research, it is the rare occasion in which collaborators either share (Spindler & Spindler, 1982; Valli & Chambliss, 2007) or otherwise make explicit (Lather & Smithies, 1997; Marshall et al., 2006) the means through which they work with one another. In asking contributors from across the qualitative spectrum to write about their decisions to collaborate and how those collaborative processes were enacted, the chapters in this book provide newcomers to the field and current qualitative methodologists alike a largely unprecedented, concrete discussion of just how such relationships are fostered and function in practice.

INTRODUCTION: WORKING TOGETHER IN QUALITATIVE RESEARCH

Second, this volume is also designed to highlight the processes through which qualitative methodologists are collaborating with one another and, perhaps most importantly, with the local actors whose lives become the data utilized in their studies. Through collaboration, authors in this volume are challenging implicit yet widespread notions of what collaboration means as well as what such relationships can foster in both their scholarly work and in the communities in which their work is conducted. In these ways, authors in this work also performatively (Austin, 1961) demonstrate that a desire to extend the boundaries of current interpretive methodological possibilities, in addition to turning inwards towards our own experiences, also requires turning outwards towards one another in collaboration.

The work in this book is not intended to be exhaustive in its representations of methods of collaboration. Instead it has been compiled as a representation of the depth and breadth of possibilities for working together in qualitative research. Therefore, the purpose of this book is to exemplify some of the ways collaborations can function; demonstrate both the viability and the possibilities such cooperative work can foster; illustrate the growing tendency for qualitative methodologists to reach out to one another and across methodological lines; and document a few emerging collaborative methodologies.

Although there are many overlapping themes that resonate between chapters, I have divided this volume into two overarching sections. Part I addresses the ways in which contributing authors have expanded upon existing qualitative research methodologies through their collaborations. Part II presents emerging collaborative methodologies and the use of collaboration in the arts, both of which utilize forms of collaboration as qualitative research methodology.

PART I: EXPANDING QUALITATIVE METHODOLOGIES THROUGH COLLABORATION

This section begins with a chapter that revisits one of the more often-sited collaborative works in qualitative research in the past twenty years, Patti Lather and Chris Smithies' (1997) *Troubling the Angles: Women Living with HIV/AIDS*. What makes this book stand out is the combination of the transparency of its authors, the book's juxtaposed location as research and informational resource, and its muti-modal, intertextual layout. Although aspects of their collaborative process have been outlined not only in the work itself but also in Lather's (2001, 2007) subsequent books, this chapter represents the first time Lather and Smithies have addressed in depth how their own collaboration functioned, an emergent process that produced one of the more polyphonic texts (Clifford, 1988) in the field.

Lather and Smithies enunciate the importance of being open to and trusting the emergent, organizational nature of qualitative research. Their ability to improvise within, through, or around frameworks of process and expectations helped create strong collaborations between the authors and the women who participated in their study. Central to this process was their shared understanding of feminism as a verb, the need to act in ways that helped call attention to issues of women's health, safety, information and justice as the AIDS crisis crescendoed in the early to mid-1990s.

It is, in fact, this very trust in the emergent, improvisational nature of collaboration that turned what I had conceived as a transcribed interview of Patti and Chris into the polyphonic chapter here. They requested and entrusted me to organize our recorded conversation in a way that represented the tone, tenor and content of the conversation in a meaningful manner—a decision in which my outsider status (e.g. male, heterosexual, HIV negative) served only to underscore their beliefs in both collaboration and its potential in qualitative research methodology.

The result of that trust is a multi-vocal, split-panelled rendering of our conversation that often places similar processes or ideas in parallel. In keeping with the transparent nature of Lather and Smithies' work to date, this chapter also contains a running commentary in which I wrestle with my charge of the chapter. Additionally, as a final nod to *Troubling the Angels* and the continuing struggle of women with HIV/AIDS, this chapter also includes recent information about the effect of this ongoing pandemic on women's lives around the world, a list of online resources for women, and help numbers for women who have questions about their own health and safety or that of those whom they care.

As with Gershon, Lather, and Smithies, authors of the second and third chapters in this book reflect upon and trouble the collaborative processes they utilized to create previously published works. Schultz and Banks' chapter embody this task literally and figuratively. Citing *Troubling the Angels* and other work that make splits in narrative explicit through their literal embodiment as split-framed texts, the co-authors present "a hermeneutic commentary (Ricœur, 1981)" in which they "reflect on a previously published article that we co-wrote" (p. 35). Starting with the "devastating news that one of his [Paris'] closest friends had been shot and killed in broad daylight directly in front his house" (p. 36), Schultz and Banks provide running conversation along side their previously published work that contextualizes, complicates, and problematizes their collaborative effort. Unlike the previously published article, this chapter foregrounds Schultz's struggles with differences between himself and Banks (one of his former fifth grade students), presents how Banks' candid, insightful responses to adults' questions complicate how adults make meanings about youth, and concludes with the notion of the possibilities for collaboration that are manifest in collective memory.

In the third chapter, Steeves, Pearce, Orr, Murphy, Huber, Huber, and Clandinin seek to "interrupt the institutional narrative of individualism" through layered dialogs about the collaboration that provided the space for seven authors to write as one voice in their book *Composing Diverse Identities: Narrative Inquiries into the Interwoven Lives of Children and Teachers* (2007). Similar to Lather and Smithies and Schultz and Banks, this group of authors cites the importance of the improvisational nature of collaborative work and the need for respectful, transparent engagement in moments of seemingly inevitable tension. Citing Heilbrun (1999), Steeves et al. emphasize the possibility of liminal spaces as places for wonder and addressing tensions, the potential for the impermanent nature of liminality to serve as a springboard for movement rather than concretizing either inquiry or interpersonal agitation.

Ultimately, for Steeves et al., it is the strength and communal nature of their counterstories that are of greatest importance. Stories are composed in relation: "in relationships seeking to find hope in the midst of dominant narratives looking to keep people in place, dominated by, and submissive to, paths well worn or laid down, to narratives often taken for granted within institutions" (p. 67). Here, Steeves et al. have provided a counterstory to their own counterstory, a deconstruction of the singular voice of their book in their nuanced, multi-vocal rendering of their collaboration. In doing so, they interrupt not only the hegemonic narratives their book is designed to disrupt but also their own work with one another.

As with the first three chapters in this section, chapters four and five are also related. This pairing begins with Gooden and Gastaldo's explication and reflection of their "critical application" of Participatory Action Research (PAR) for their project *Revisiting Personal is Political: Immigrant Women's Health Promotion Project (RPP)*. Similar to Lather and Smithies, Gooden and Gastaldo's project is a collaboration that reaches across locations and methodological boundaries in documenting "how immigrant women in Toronto, Canada, collaborated with researchers from academic and practice settings" (p. 71). As "two immigrant women who are also academic researchers," (p. 71), this chapter complicates the literature on PAR in two significant ways. First, through their location as immigrant women and researchers, the co-authors' participation is doubly layered; in studying with their participants they are simultaneously studying themselves, a complication they explicitly address in narrative form in this chapter. Second, where reporting of findings in PAR often favors discussions of findings and the presentation of participants' perspectives over talk of how such collaborations functioned, Gooden and Gastaldo explicitly document both their collaborative processes and outline how they applied those "principles of collaboration."

The remaining chapter in this section has close ties to PAR. In it, Smith and Helfenbein seek to trouble "the role of universities in communities while simultaneously challenging researchers with the task of redefining our conception and practice of contemporary research efforts in schools of education" (p. 89). They are concerned by the linear nature of research practices that promote a lack of deep, sustained contact and collaboration between researchers and the people and contexts they study, often serving to reify lines between researcher and subject. Furthermore, Smith and Helfenbein argue that traditional research practices produce less meaningful research, missing important nuances central to understanding educational practices and possibilities that can serve to improve the daily lives of local actors.

In its stead, Smith and Helfenbein suggest translational research in practice (TRIP) as one possible framework for disrupting traditional research patterns. While the collaborative nature of the relationship between "researchers" and "subjects" shares some similarities with PAR, there are significant differences between the two collaborative research methodologies.

> For example, while there is an expectation that project directors, teachers, administrators, and grant writers are actively engaged during the conception and fleshing out of ideas and proposals, we typically do not train teachers and

community members to collect data but rather intentionally build in time to review data, both raw and analyzed. (p. 94)

Grounding their argument in their work as directors of the Center for Urban and Multicultural Education (CUME) at Indiana University, Purdue University at Indianapolis (IUPUI), the co-authors document how TRIP has lead to research practices that are more collaborative in nature and the ways in which these collaborations engender deeper, sustained relationships between research partners to the benefit of all collaborators, local actors and university researchers alike.

PART II: EMERGING METHODOLOGIES AND THE ARTS: COLLBORATION AS QUALITATIVE RESEARCH

The emergent collaborative research practices and the uses of collaboration in the arts presented in the latter section of the book share a central, salient feature: collaboration as a means for conducting qualitative research. Additionally, while aspects of the arts—uses of arts metaphors to describe qualitative research practices, or particular arts practices as qualitative research methodologies are well-documented—are often organized into research practices that utilize the arts such as "arts-based research," (McNiff, 2009), "arts research in education" (Cahmann-Taylor & Siegesmund, 2008) or "a/r/tography" (Irwin & de Cosson, 2004; Springgay et al., 2007). Although each of these research practices calls for the use of the arts in/as qualitative research practices, it is far less frequent that an art is considered to be a methodology unto itself (cf. Knowles & Cole, 2008; Leavy, 2009; Sullivan, 2005). Furthermore, discussions of the collaborative nature of the arts and the role of collaboration the arts-as-qualitative-research are generally even more absent from most discussions of qualitative research methodology. Because the arts-as-collaborative-research-practice and the particular arts (the processes of data-as-playwriting, dance, improvisational musics [Nettle, 2005]) presented in the last three chapters of this book remain largely undocumented, they represent another aspect of an emerging understanding of what collaboration in qualitative research might mean and present possible models for how it could function in practice. It is in light of such possible meanings that I have placed these final six chapters together.

The first three chapters in this section represent emerging collaborative methodologies in qualitative research. In the first chapter of this section, Willis and Siltanen continue to build upon and wrestle with their evolving construction of reflective team research. Similar to concerns raised by Lather and Smithies, Willis and Siltanen "developed and implemented" these research practices "in order to take seriously feminist and post-positivist orientations to social science knowledge production" (p. 105). This is the authors' "third (re)storying" of this process, following the initial collaborative research process and "a second story [presented] in a publication whose main agenda is to argue for the possibility and interpretive value of team-based reflexivity (Siltanen, Willis & Scobie, 2008)" (p. 105).

The co-authors describe the difference between their previous publication and this chapter in the following manner:

> Looking again at our previous paper "Separately Together: Working Reflexively as a Team," we realized that although we had intended to set out how reflexivity can be done in the context of team research, we did not quite reach this goal. The orientations and practices we outlined do not actually describe how to do reflexivity but rather suggest ways of providing opportunities for reflexivity. In re-examining our efforts from the perspective of narrative inquiry, we hope to move closer to identifying how reflexivity can be done in and by research teams. (p. 105)

Here Willis and Siltanen document how they moved from working reflexively *in* a team and working reflexively *as* a team in their creation of this qualitative research methodology. Through their process, the inclusion of their own stories with those they collected, wrestling with the layers of meanings within and between these narratives, lead to a rich, polyvocal, overarching collective storyline that was more than the sum of its parts. In so doing, they also do justice to the subjects of their study, "the ways in which inequalities affect peoples' capacity to cope with work change (Siltanen, Willis & Scobie, in press)" (p. 106).

In searching for a similar kind of reflexivity and complexity, Sawyer and Norris came to tell their own stories together, a process they have come to call "duoethnography." Drawing from ethnographic research practices, duoethnographic studies are stratified, nested autoethnographic accounts of a given research context or question. Each participant conducts her/his own authoethnographic account, situating her/himself fully within the research context. The research partners then place their separately analyzed findings together, creating dialogic inquiries in which the researchers themselves are firmly located within the scope of the gaze of their research.

> Examining personal artifacts, stories, memories, compositions, texts, and critical incidents, duoethnographers excavate the temporal, social, cultural, and geographical cartography of their lives, making explicit their assumptions and perspectives. Considering themselves the site rather than the topic of their research (Oberg, 1992), duoethnographers seek to discover and explore the overlapping grey zones in-between their perspectives as intertwined intersections that create "hybrid identities" (Asher, 2007, p. 68) instead of binary opposites. (p. 127)

Sawyer and Norris compare duoethnography in practice to the emergent, transformative aspects of jazz performance in which collaborators work separately together to create complex meanings from intertwining, simultaneous narratives. When exercised to its potential, Sawyer and Norris argue, duoethenography has the potential "to allow participants to engage in dialogic self-study and thus to empower and intellectually liberate its participants" (p. 138).

Similar to Willis and Siltanen's chapter, Gershon, Peel, and Bilinovich's chapter presents another iteration of their ongoing struggle to understand a difficult semester they shared together as professor and preservice teachers. Instead of sweeping their "semester-long" struggles over "the intersections of race, education, and social studies content" (p. 142) under the proverbial rug, the co-authors elected to examine their challenging semester together (Gershon, Peel & Bilinovich, 2008).

Different from their previous work on the topic, this chapter is performative in that a process of collaborative discensus serves as both the content of their chapter and the methodological process through which they examine that content. Where the purpose of duoethography is the empowerment and liberation of its participants, collaborative discensus is a four-part framework designed for collaborators to work together without the need to compromise their perspectives, language, or findings through consensus. Where processes of consensus can serve to marginalize participants' perspectives, discensus can serve as an ethical act, providing the space for all collaborators' voices, ideas and ideals.

Collaborative discensus is a process comprised of four key components: Participants frame their collaboration and inquiry, conduct research according to their own perspectives, present their findings without compromise, and respond to one another's presentations. In their use of collaborative discensus, Gershon, Peel, and Bilinovich illustrate the potential of collaborative methodology to mitigate possible inequities in research, provide space for collaborators to transparently negotiate difficult contexts or content, and provide complex, layered interpretations of meaning. Additionally, in their open framing of the process, there are several chapters in this volume that could possibly be considered forms of collaborative discensus including the next chapter in this section, Conrad, McCaw, and Gusul's dialogue about their collaboration in turning Conrad's data set into a script.

Conrad, McCaw, and Gusul's chapter on their work together in rendering Conrad's data set as a play is the first of the three chapters on collaboration in the arts as qualitative methodology. As Conrad describes their process in the introduction to the chapter,

> [T]his is a collaborative piece of writing. It is an intertwining of the personal journals of its three authors, engaged collaboratively in a process of ethno-dramatic playwriting—a collaboratively written piece about collaboration based on collaborative research. (p. 165)

This writing is based on a three-year project of conducting participatory drama with youth in the Native program of an Alberta jail. Reflecting "a symptom of systemic racism within the Canadian justice system," the "majority of incarcerated youth in Alberta are Aboriginal" (p. 165). Conrad's collaborators in this chapter are McCaw, the project's dramaturg and faculty member in the Drama Department at the University of Alberta, and Gusul, a graduate student who served as a research assistant on Conrad's project. Together, the three co-authors share their perspectives of the playwriting process through a chronological presentation of entries Conrad and McCaw's research journals and transcriptions of McCaw's oral responses to their entries.

The resulting chapter is a story about the possibilities and struggles of collaboration in the field and between participants, the use of qualitative data as theatre, and the birth of a play. As with the two other chapters in this section on collaboration in the arts as qualitative methodology, the questions Conrad, McCaw, and Gusul raise about the nature of collaboration in the arts—such as that between performer and audience, playwright and dramaturg—are also questions about the nature of qualitative

INTRODUCTION: WORKING TOGETHER IN QUALITATIVE RESEARCH

research methodology and collaboration in qualitative research.

Discussions of qualitative research methodologies rarely include conversations about dance as qualitative research (Blumenfeld-Jones, 2005; Leavy, 2009; Toncy, 2008); dialogues about the role of collaboration in dance and qualitative research are even more infrequent occurrences. As George and Meggitt state in the introduction to their chapter, examinations of dance are important because,

> Dance makes clear and expands that which cannot be otherwise articulated, be it through language, image, or sound. The creation and the watching of dance are powerful and intimate exchanges that inform participants in ways that are both immediate and vast. (p. 185)

George and Meggitt have divided their chapter in half in order to provide each author an opportunity to discuss how collaboration functions in their lives as dancers and choreographers. For George, collaboration is implicit yet embedded within every aspect of her work as a dance educator. Her approach to dance and dance education is through Laban Movement Analysis (LMA), a "system of observing, understanding, and notating movement...organized into four interrelated categories: body, effort, shape, and space" (p. 187). Strongly informed by LMA, George's approaches to dance and working with students' includes a focus on inquiry and problem solving and an expectation of transformation in her process—what she envisioned at the beginning of a work is not the work that emerges by its performance (pp. 187–188). These understandings parallel the steps of strong interpretive research both in education (cf. Erickson, 1986) and non-educational contexts (cf. Hammersley & Atkinson, 1995).

Unlike George's relationship to collaboration in dance and choreography, Meggitt approaches collaboration in her work explicitly, illustrating the central role collaboration plays in her work as choreographer and leader of Antaeus Dance. For Meggitt, collaboration is the vehicle through which she works with the dancers in her company and the other artists (composers, set designers, etc.) who contribute to the productions Antaeus Dance mounts. What George and Meggitt share in their stories of collaboration is attention to the ethical considerations of working with others; the collaborative nature of dance as a medium; improvisation as a means for exploring possible form and functions of collaboration in movement, thought, and otherwise; and the relationships between choreographer and dancers, performers and audience.

In the final chapter in this section and the book, Coulombe provides another rarely represented voice in discussions of qualitative methodology (cf. Gershon, 2006), the collaborative nature of improvised music as research methodology, a topic she addresses directly in the beginning of her chapter.

> The unique nature of improvisation, as spontaneous expression in the act of performance itself, has no "translation" from abstraction into metaphor and therefore no language, no syntax. Other than a few notable exceptions (cf. Bailey, 1993; Lewis, 2002), this abstract nature also explains the relative lack of theorization and documentation in comparison to other performance disciplines. This does not diminish, however, the vast community of improvisers

and improvisational genres in culture, or the burgeoning quantity and quality of scholarship in the area. (pp. 209–210)

What is needed, Coulombe argues, is more detailed examinations of how improvised music functions as qualitative research methodology, a research practice that is inseparable from its location in performance and collaboration.

To illustrate how freely improvised music can serve as a site for inquiry, similar to George and Meggitt's chapter on dance, Coulombe draws upon her work as a teacher of improvised music in a university context and as an improviser with other professional improvisers. In her conclusion, Coulombe posits that,

> Deploying collective improvisation as methodology beyond performance to research events allows *both* participants *and* audience members to themselves enter the symbolic order in real time, broadening the conscious rewriting of signifiers and narrations of the past and allowing new meanings to collectively emerge. This eliminates what has been a fundamental dissociation of artistic practice—the separation of process and product, in which the negotiation of meaning has traditionally occurred apart from the work itself, hidden from the audience and sometimes even from participants themselves. (p. 221)

She also enunciates recurring themes that resonate throughout this book: collaborative approaches to qualitative research provide the space for critical reflexivity in such a way that the possible meanings of research contexts are rendered in a complex fashion where a multiplicity of perspectives does not usurp the individual but instead engenders a deeper, more rich representation of local actors, their meanings, and the contexts that inform their actions.

A FINAL NOTE

The chapters in this book represent a relatively wide swath of qualitative methodologies (e.g. feminist research practices, participatory action research, narrative inquiry, theatre, transactional research) from a variety of perspectives and fields (e. g. anthropology, dance, education, music, nursing, Pan-African Studies, sociology, students, theatre, youth). However, despite an effort towards a broader inclusion of possible voices in this book, fields, perspectives, and qualitative methodologies that rely on collaboration are missing. There are three central reasons for this orientation. First, to paraphrase Denzin and Lincoln's (2005) preface to their most recent edition of the *Handbook of Qualitative Research*, there is, to some degree, an overreliance on perspectives with which I am familiar (p. xvii). However, this bias is strongly mitigated by the remaining two reasons.

The second reason this book contains these works is because, as in all edited volumes, potential authors and the fields and topics their work represents were unable to participate due to the usual culprits of previous commitments and timeline to completion. Third, and perhaps most significantly, much of the current collaborative turn in qualitative methodologies has been occurring more in fields such as education than in journals specific to fields such as anthropology or sociology. For example, the second half of Spindler and Hammond's (2006) book on ethnography in education is dedicated to questions of collaboration. Similarly, editors of a recent special issue in *Anthropology and Education Quarterly* (2008) on "activist educational anthropology" refer to the articles in that volume as being "very collaborative approaches to theorizing and writing ethnography" (Foley, Dworin, Foster, Urrieta, & Villenas, 2008, p. 1); the *International Journal of Qualitative Research in Education* has published several recent articles that focus on collaboration (cf. Gerstl-Pepin & Gunzenhauser, 2002; Krøjer & Hølge-Hazeltonk, 2008).

Finally, in the spirit of collaboration, I wish to again acknowledge the contributors whose work graces the pages of this book. I am much indebted to the hard work and strong contributions from all who gave of their time, thought, and effort to this project. I remain impressed by not only the richness of their chapters but also the respectful, timely manner in which they collaborated with one another and gave me the space to serve as their editor. Specific information about each contributing author and their research interests can be found in the contributors section at the end of this book.

REFERENCES

Agar, M. H. (1996). *The professional stranger: An informal introduction to ethnography* (2nd ed.). San Diego, CA: Academic Press.

Austin, J. (1961). *Philosophical papers*. Oxford, UK: Oxford University Press.

Bakhtin, M. (1981). *The dialogic imagination* (10th ed.). Austin, TX: University of Texas.

Behar, R. (1996). *The vulnerable observer: Anthropology that breaks your heart*. Boston: Beacon Press.

Bellack, A. A., Kliebard, H. E., Hyman, R. T., & Smith, F. L., Jr. (1978). *The language of the classroom*. New York: Teachers College.

Blumenfeld-Jones, D. (2005). Dance, choreography, and social science research. In G. Knolwes & A. L. Cole (Eds.), *The handbook of the arts in qualitative research* (pp. 175–184). Thousand Oaks, CA: Sage.

Cahnmann-Taylor, M., & Siegesmund, R. (2008). *Arts-based research in education: Foundations for practice*. New York: Routledge.

Carrick, R., Mitchell, A., & Lloyd, K. (2001). User involvement in research: Power and compromise. *Journal of Community & Applied Social Psychology*, 11, 217–225.

Chamberlayne, P., Bornat, J., & Wengraf, T. (2000). *The turn to biographical methods in social science: Comparative issues and examples*. New York: Routledge.

Clandinin, D. J., & Connelly, F. M. (2000). *Narrative inquiry: Experience and story in qualitative research*. San Francisco: Jossey-Bass.

Clandinnin, D. J., Huber, J., Huber, M., Murphy, M. S., Orr, A. M., Pearce, M., Steeves, P. (2006). *Composing diverse identities: Narrative inquiries into the interwoven lives of teachers and students*. New York: Routledge.

Clifford, J. (1988). *The predicament of culture: Twentieth-century ethnography, literature, and art*. Cambridge, MA: Harvard University Press.

Denzin, N., & Lincoln, Y. (2005). *The Sage handbook of qualitative research* (3rd ed.). Thousand Oaks, CA: Sage.

Eisner, E., & Peshkin, A. (Eds.). (1990). *Qualitative inquiry in education*. New York: Teachers College Press.

Ellis, C., & Bochner, A. (2000). Autoethnography, personal narrative, reflexivity: Researcher as subject. In N. Denzin & Y. Lincoln (Eds.), *The Sage handbook of qualitative research* (2nd ed., pp. 733–768). Newbury Park, CA: Sage.

Erickson, F. (1986). Qualitative methods in research on teaching. In M. Wittrock (Ed.), *Handbook of research on teaching* (3rd ed., pp. 119–161). New York: Macmillan.

Erickson, F. (2006). Studying side by side: Collaborative action ethnography in educational research. In G. Spindler & L. Hammond (Eds.), *Innovations in educational ethnography: Theory, methods and results* (pp. 235–258). Mahwah, NJ: Erlbaum.

Erickson, F., & Christman, J. B. (1996). Taking stock/making change: Stories of collaboration in local school reform. *Theory into Practice, 35*(3), 149–157.

Erickson, F., & Schultz, J. (1982). *The counselor as gatekeeper: Social interaction in interviews.* New York: Academic Press.

Erickson, K. C., & Stull, D. D. (1998). *Doing team ethnography: Warnings and advice.* Thousand Oaks, CA: Sage.

Foley, D. E. (2002). Critical ethnography: The reflexive turn. *International Journal of Qualitative Studies in Education, 15*(4), 469–490.

Foley, D. E., Dworin, J., Foster, K. M., Urrieta, L., Jr., & Villenas, S. (Eds.). An introductory note on "activist educational anthropology." *Anthropology & Education Quarterly, 39*(1), 1–2.

Gershon, W. S. (2006). Collective improvisation: A theoretical lens for classroom observation. *Journal of Curriculum and Pedagogy, 3*(1), 104–136.

Gershon, W. S., Peel, A., & Bilinovich, C. (2008, March 22). *Sorting through the pieces together: A teacher and two students' perspectives of a challenging social studies class.* Paper presented at the American Association for the Advancement of Curriculum Studies.

Gerstl-Pepin, C. I., & Gunzenhauser, M. G. (2002). Collaborative ethnography and the paradoxes of interpretation. *International Journal of Qualitative Studies in Education, 15*(2), 137–154.

Given, L. M. (2008). *The Sage encyclopedia of qualitative research.* Thousand Oaks, CA: SAGE.

Hammersley, M., & Atkinson, P. (1995). *Ethnography: Principles in practice* (2nd ed.). New York: Routledge.

Heilbrun, C. G. (1999). *Women's lives: The view from the threshold.* Toronto: University of Toronto Press.

Irwin, R. L., & de Cosson, A. (Eds.). (2004). *a/r/tography: Rendering self through arts-based living inquiry.* Vacouver, CA: Pacific Educational Press.

Jipson, J. A., & Wilson, B. (1997). That dialogue at night. In J. A. Jipson & N. Paley (Eds.), *Daredevil research: Re-creating analytic practice* (pp. 161–183). New York: Peter Lang.

Knowles, G., & Cole, A. L. (2008). *Handbook of the arts in qualitative research.* Thousand Oaks, CA: Sage Publications

Krøjer, J., & Hølge-Hazeltonk, B. (2008). Poethical: Breaking ground for reconstruction *International Journal of Qualitative Studies in Education, 21*(1), 27–33.

Lather, P. (2001). *Getting smart: Feminist research and pedagogy with/in the postmodern.* New York: Routledge.

Lather, P. (2007). *Getting lost: Feminist efforts toward a double(d) science.* Albany, NY: State University of New York Press.

Lather, P., & Smithies, C. (1997). *Troubling the angels: Women living with HIV/AIDS.* Boulder, CO: Westview Press.

LeCompte, M. D., Millroy, W. L., & Preissle, J. (Eds). (1992). *The handbook of qualitative research in education.* San Diego: Academic Press.

Leavy, P. (2009). *Method meets art: Arts-based research practice.* New York: Guilford Press.

Marshall, J. D., Sears, J. T., Allen, L. A., Roberts, P. A., & Schubert, W. H. (2006). *Turning points in curriculum: A contemporary American memoir* (2nd ed.). Upper Saddle, NJ: Prentice Hall.

McNiff, S. (2009/1998). *Arts-based research.* Philadelphia: Jessica Kingsley Publishers.

Mehan, H. (2008). Engaging the sociological imagination: My journey into design research and public education. *Anthropology and Education Quarterly, 39*(1), 77–91.

Minh-ha, T. T. (1989). *Woman, native, other.* Bloomington, IN: University of Indiana Press.

Moss, P. (Ed.). (2001). *Placing autobiography in geography.* Syracuse, NY: Syracuse University Press.

Nachi, M. (2004). The morality in/of compromise: Some theoretical reflections. *Social Science Information, 43*(2), 291–305.

Nettl, B. (2005). *The study of ethnomusicology: Thirty-one issues and concepts.* (2nd ed.). Champaign, IL: University of Illinois Press.

Norris, J. (2008). Duoethnography. In L. M. Given (Ed.), *The SAGE encyclopedia of qualitative research methods, Vol. 1* (pp. 233-236). Los Angeles: SAGE.

Norris, J., & Sawyer, R. D. (2004). *Hidden and null curriculums of sexual orientation: A dialogue on the curreres of the absent presence and the present absence*. Edited yearbook from the 4th Curriculum & Pedagogy Annual conference, Dectur, GA.

Okely, J., & Callaway, H. (Eds.). (1992). *Anthropology and autobiography*. New York: Routledge.

Page, R. N. (2000). The turn inward in qualitative research. *Harvard Educational Review, 70*(1), 23–38.

Pinar, W. F. (1995). *Autobiography, politics, and sexuality: Essays in curriculum theory 1972–1992*. New York: Peter Lang.

Pugh, A. J. (2005). Selling compromise: Toys, motherhood, and the cultural deal. *Gender & Society, 19*(6), 729–749.

Ricœur, P. (1981). What is text?: Explanation and understanding. In J. B. Thompson (Ed.), *Hermeneutics and the human sciences: Essays on language, action, and interpretation* (pp. 145–164). Paris: Cambridge University Press.

Rosaldo, R. (1993). *Culture and truth: The remaking of social analysis*. Boston: Beacon Press.

Shircliffe, B. J. (2000). Feminist reflections on university activism through women studies at a state university: Narratives of promise, compromise and powerlessness. *Frontiers: A Journal of Women Studies, 21*(3), 38–60.

Siltanen, J., Willis, A., & Scobie, W. (2008). Separately together: Working reflectively as a team. *International Journal of Social Research Methodology, 11*(1), 45–61.

Siltanen, J., Willis, A., & Scobie, W. (In press). Flows, eddies, swamps and whirlpools: Inequality and the experience of work change. *Canadian Journal of Sociology*.

Spindler, G. (Ed.). (1982). *Doing the ethnography of schooling: Educational anthropology in action*. New York: Holt, Rinehart, & Winston.

Spindler, G., & Hammond, L. (2006). *Innovations in educational ethnography: Theory, methods and results*. Mahwah, NJ: Lawrence Erlbaum.

Spindler, G., & Spindler, L. (1982). Roger Harker and Schoenhausen: From familiar to strange and back again. In G. Spinder (Ed.), *Doing the ethnography of schooling: Educational anthropology in action*. (pp. 20–47). New York: Holt, Rinehart, & Winston.

Spindler, G., & Spindler, L. (Eds.). (1987). *Interpretive ethnography of education: At home and abroad*. Mahwah, NJ: Erlbaum.

Springgay, S., Irwin, R., Leggo, C., & Gouzouasis, P. (Eds.). (2007). *Being with a/r/tography*. Rotterdam: Sense Publishers.

Sullivan, G. (2005). *Art practice as research: Inquiry in the visual arts*. Thousand Oaks, CA: Sage.

Toncy, N. (2008). Behind the veil: An in-depth exploration of Egyptian Muslim women's lives through dance. *International Journal of Qualitative Studies in Education, 21*(3), 269–280.

Valli, L., & Chambliss, M. (2007). Creating classroom cultures: One teacher, two lessons, and a high-stakes test. *Anthropology Education Quarterly, 38*(1), 57–75.

Weis, L., & Fine, M. (2005). *Beyond silenced voices: Class, race, and gender in United States schools* (3rd ed.). Albany, NY: State University of New York.

Wolcott, H. F. (1990). On seeking—and rejecting—validity in qualitative research. In E. W. Eisner & A. Peshkin (Eds.), *Qualitative inquiry in education: The continuing debate* (pp. 121–152). New York: Teachers College Press.

PART I: EXPANDING QUALITATIVE METHODOLOGIES THROUGH COLLABORATION

WALTER S. GERSHON, PATTI LATHER AND CHRIS SMITHIES

1. TROUBLING THE ANGELS REDUX

Tales of Collaboration Towards a Polyphonic Text

GETTING STARTED

Chris: Okay. Ready, set, go.

Walter: Good. Okay so I guess the first question I'm curious about is how did this come to fruition? What is the genesis of the project? How did the two of you meet and how did you decide that this might be a course you'd want to go on?

Patti: And, of course, part of my interest in being here is to hear what Chris has to say about that, our very memories and readings of things. So if you want to start on that one, Chris. Where did we get started here?

Chris: A Partner, a Collaborator, a Guide, a Feminist	*Patti: You would be a fool not to open this door and go in*
Chris: Well, I think we got started, and correct me because some of this is memory and it's filtered through at this point, because when did we start? 1992 or 3?	Walter: What were some of your trepidations, Patti, going into it? Chris was talking about some of hers in choosing you, and you said that even with the drive out for some space what was…?
Patti: Something like that. Two-ish.	Patti: Oh I'm a loner.
Chris: Yeah, so it's been 15, 16 years since we've actually started. But I was a psychologist and AIDS activist, a feminist, and had the opportunity through a position at the University of Cincinnati to work with one of the	Chris: That's just who she is. Walter: I know that you like the space in general.

This chapter is the end result of an over two-hour conversation with Patti Lather and Chris Smithies on their collaborative processes as they created the work that became *Troubling the Angels: Women Living with HIV/AIDS*. I originally conceived of this chapter as a relatively straightforward interview transcription. In my mind, I was going to drive down to Columbus, either interview Patti and Chris or have them interview each other, get the interview transcribed, check and edit the transcription, first women's HIV-positive/AIDS support groups. And found that work very intriguing, gratifying, and intense.

Patti: What was the year on that? When did you get started?

Chris: That must have been, it was January of 1989. Yeah, cause I had just got my Ph.D. and that was in December. So, I started the group.

Walter: You got a Ph.D. in?

Chris: In counseling, and was working with the Center for the Treatment of Eating Disorders at the University of Cincinnati. Then HIV of course at this time was brand new, terrifying, a huge mystery. And at the University of Cincinnati to this day has an excellent physician and researcher by the name of Dr. Peter Frame, who invited me to do the group for a small stipend, and I thought, "Oh I'm done with my Ph.D. I have room for something." And thank goodness I said yes because it certainly changed my life. This was a time of great crisis where women were infected and became ill very quickly. It was a time of urgency. They often had been infected by men that they didn't expect to be infected by; there were just remarkable stories and a coming together. I think one of the things I remember most of all is that this group of women, in many cases, had not really relied on other women frequently throughout their

Patti: I'm a loner, and I don't like getting sucked into zones of proximal development.

Chris: She was gonna be stuck with people all weekend.

Patti: Particularly retreats. I usually get physically ill if I'm captured in a space, especially with strangers…

Chris: It's the intensity, the emotional intensity of it.

Patti: …and, see here I am, I don't even have my own car now, and we're out in the middle of some cornfield in Indiana with bunch of old nuns and people I don't know, and I don't have a car. I was ready to get sick, but it didn't [happen]. I remember I took a lot of walks. I got outside.

Chris: You did. And we didn't feel like we had to be side-by-side the whole weekend.

Patti: I walked around that graveyard a lot. That was my space. But in a way it's my personality of claustrophobia and low tolerance for really the social in any sort of intense and long term. You know like family reunions for example. Like an afternoon I can take but…

Walter: A whole weekend is a little much.

---

and send it back to them for review. Given my outsider status in relation to *Troubling the Angels*–I'm male, HIV-negative, and straight for starters–I was leaning towards the option of setting up the necessary equipment and letting the authors have a recorded conversation that they then could edit as they saw fit after transcription. In spite of Patti's insistence that I participate more fully as interviewer, I was still envisioning a chapter with Patti and Chris as authors "interviewed by Walter S. Gershon." How, then, did I end up as lead author of this chapter and how did it take this particular shape?

lives for emotional support, for getting through the tough times and that emerged in this group. Very diverse group of women especially in terms of class, from very modest education or impoverished really all the way up to individuals with Master's degrees. And so as I did this work over a couple of years, two or three years, the women would talk about, "oh we should write a book," and I always thought that was great. We certainly had plenty of material. I moved back to Columbus and continued to go down to Cincinnati and started also a group in Columbus. It just became very clear to me, partly as the women's voices said we want our stories out there. We want the public, we want the community, we want other women, especially those who undoubtedly become HIV-positive, we want them aware that there are groups like this and other women who can support them. And I knew that because the women had grown from their support of each other, I knew, it was just crystal clear to me that any work that I would do would be in a collaboration with someone. That was just not ever even a question. And so I went looking through an HIV educational center here at Ohio State. There was a good guy named Jim. I don't remember his...

Patti: Pearsol.

Chris: Pearsol. And I said I'm looking for someone, I'm looking for a colleague.

Patti: A whole weekend starts making me, I mean, again, I get physically ill.

Walter: So then let me ask that a different way cause there's a bit that was an answer to the question I asked, but I don't think that was the question I had in mind once it came out of my mouth. The thing I'm wondering is, you speak to it a little bit in the book and Chris spoke a little bit on her concern about sort of "testing" you out. When you started thinking about HIV and AIDS and when you started thinking about participating with women and having connections to social justice you have and to methodology and most particularly to feminism. How did these pieces fit together in a way that you became involved and what were some of the questions you had as you started this process in the beginning that you can remember?

Patti: I remember thinking, I mean I was pretty, what would the word be, careerist isn't exactly the right word but I was a woman in search of a project in terms of the trajectory of my own career at that time. I finished *Getting Smart*. I'd given myself a little vacation after that, and I kind of had an empty plate and I was searching for a topic and I felt like this dropped on high from heaven. And I could see it from the get go that this was a project from heaven, in terms of timing, engagement, academic interest, in terms of there wasn't much out on women and HIV/AIDS and there was such rich praxis. I mean it was just like neon

---

After turning on the microphone, setting up a pad so anyone could take notes, and tucking into the tea and cheese Patti kindly offered, we began to set the parameters for our recorded conversation/interview. I began by stating that Patti and Chris would receive copies of the audio recording and transcripts, review the final version pre-submission to the publisher, and have full veto power of any aspect of the chapter they found problematic. Because I had not met Chris before and only met Patti a few months prior at a conference (although I was familiar with her work and we have mutual friends and colleagues)

Patti: And you knew to say qualitative researcher didn't you?

Chris: I knew I wanted it to be qualitative research. You know, the women actually wanted a K-mart book, and I knew we weren't gonna write that. But I knew enough about qualitative research from my own degree—I did not do qualitative research for my dissertation partly just I wanted to get done to be honest—but I knew enough to know that this was an incredible opportunity for qualitative research. But I knew I needed a partner, a collaborator, a guide, and Jim knew Patti. He literally got us together, and we had a blind date.

Patti: Mmm, hmm. It was awesome, I remember.

Chris: You take it from there because you probably...

Patti: Well, Jim taught for me. He was one of my adjunct professors in qualitative research. So when Chris went looking for a feminist, she knew she wanted a feminist.

Chris: There were a few criteria.

Walter: What were the criteria?

Chris: Well, a woman. It had to be a feminist. It had to be someone who would have an interest in women living with HIV/AIDS, and then it needed to be somebody who had a stronger research background than I

lights for everything I cared about. And I could see that Chris and I were gonna be able to figure things out and I've never done fundable research before. But remember we even talked to Jim about possibilities for getting funding. To me, it was like the first project I'd ever been involved with that actually might be fundable. Remember that time we had with him where he came and he had us meet with potential funders?

Chris: He did; you're right.

Patti: And they wanted such personal information about the women. All they cared about was their sex habits and their drug IV habits, and I said, you mean you're gonna ask us to go ask these women. I'd say hi my name is Patti and how many times have you had unprotected anal sex?

Walter: With random people you didn't know.

Patti: With random people I didn't know, yeah. And in the name of building trust and research empathy and relationships—I said I don't think so. So remember we had a talk after that and decided we just weren't gonna go with the funding route if that was the kind of data we were gonna have to collect in order to get funding. And you could say in a way that was part of our bonding, too, because we were so much on the same page with that.

Chris asked me several questions to which I responded at length about my research and this book in order to have a better sense of to whom she would be speaking and to further clarify the purpose of our conversation. About 15 minutes into the conversation, Patti stated, "Chris and I haven't talked about this but I'm very happy to have you be the author, like 'with' us." When I replied that I would prefer that they be lead authors "as interviewed by" me and that I had been "trying to wrestle out of this role" of a more full participant since the process began, Patti responded: "Yeah, well we want you to do all the work." Then she and Chris laughed. It quickly became clear that what Patti and Chris preferred was not had, and, I think, access to the world of publication because whatever this was going to be I wanted to see it published for the sake of the women. The publication certainly has brought riches into our lives, and probably Patti's in particular, but to me it was the women that needed to see something published. They did not have the means. I had more means than they did, but I didn't really think I had the qualifications or the expertise to do it solo and I didn't want to do it solo. So having someone with stronger academic credentials and certainly a passion, as I quickly discovered, with qualitative research. Those were my criteria and more criteria emerged as we got going. But that's what I presented to Jim, that's what I needed and wanted and did he know anybody. And I was checking it out. I was using all my contacts to try to find somebody, and Jim found Patti.

Walter: Can I ask one more follow-up question before we get to Patti?

Chris: Yes.

Walter: You said a few times now that you wanted a collaborator.

Chris: Absolutely

Walter: That seems to be really important to the [research] process and it also seems important to the process of the groups as we discuss it…

Chris: It was parallel process.

front I was ready to get engaged on. I remember saying to myself, you would be a fool to not open this door and go in.

---

a straightforward, lightly edited conversation but a tightly organized, edited version of what transpired that wintry afternoon in January. This chapter is the result of their request. Like the collaborative processes that became *Troubling the Angels*, the form of this chapter was emergent, organic, and member checked. As I checked, reworked, and began to organize the transcription, it became evident to me that using the book as a framework for the chapter would provide both the organizational structure and complexity needed to convey the warp and weft of the interwoven themes and meanings that

Walter: And I wanted to know a little bit about that.

Chris: Yeah. It was just very clear to me that they weren't doing anything alone. That, for these women, their survivorship, the quality of their life, had really become just dependent and interconnected with their relationships with each other, and those were very positive. Not that there weren't ever disagreements, but overall their lives they would have said, and I'm quoting them, the collaboration in their lives in many cases, well, not many, in several cases women said actually my life's better now that I have HIV because all of the relationships and connections and support I have for the first time in my life. So, I saw that again and again and again and again, and loved it, appreciated it. So, to me, it was just never a question that I would certainly collaborate with them but I needed someone else to collaborate with as well. And then I think in the purely personal piece, by this time was doing full-time private practice, which you do by yourself, and so in a very personal level, having the opportunity to collaborate, to maintain an academic connection. I'm not an academic, but I appreciate and value academia and I knew that academia could benefit from these women's stories and from what I had to offer, that academics didn't have access to this group typically. Just as I needed access to the world of publication, so, yeah.

---

surfaced over the course of our time together. In this spirit of transparently presenting the complex layers of talk, I have elected to: offer split pagination, use participants' words to form most of the titles to the sections, rearrange the conversation to fit these categories, add a final section of HIV/AIDS resources at the end of the piece, and provide a reflexive running participant's conversation, adding another layer to our interview. Finally, I opted for a middle ground in the case of authorship. As I did indeed end up doing the work of a lead author at the request of my now-co-authors, I have gone

First Steps: Defining and Testing Roles

Walter: And then Patti you were on, I think, your take on meeting in Jim's office before we left that off.

Patti: Yeah, we met at Jim's office and Chris and I had a pretty good connection as I remember and decided to probably have another meeting where we followed up on that, and I'm trying to think, maybe in Jim's office as well. I'm kind of remembering he was involved a bit at the front end. And for a while we actually talked about collaborating with him.

Chris: We did.

Patti: It was a little fuzzy at the front end in terms of his role. He actually got us together with the idea that maybe the three of us would write together. And I think we sort of kept it loose but "possibles" here and there. And then we got out in the field, and quickly could see that it was a woman thing, having a man in the room was not gonna work.

Chris: And fortunately Jim is the kind of gentleman who's not at all self-serving. He was very much a catalyst and was content with that.

Patti: I'm having some vague memory that at a certain point we went back to him and sort of said…

Chris: See, I don't remember that at all.

Patti: It's starting to be clear to us that it just needed to be the two of us and how did he feel about that.

Chris: And then I kind of put Patti to the test.

Patti: At the retreat.

Chris: Yes. I ran retreats for women who were HIV positive. And this particular retreat was held at a nunnery just over the line in Indiana, correct me if I'm remembering any of this wrong.

Patti: No, that's right

Chris: And women came from all over Ohio.

---

forward with Patti and Chris' kind offer to take the lead author spot for this chapter, an offer also extended with full recognition of my Assistant Professor status. However, rather than "with" Patti and Chris they remain co-authors, for without their years of hard work, dedication, vision, perseverance, and willingness to participate in a recorded interview for this volume, this chapter would not exist. I wish to again thank and publicly acknowledge Patti and Chris for their candor, kindness, and participation as well as for a wonderful conversation full of intelligence, wit, and laughter.

Patti: I don't remember a nunnery.

Chris: It was a former convent or a current convent.

Patti: Maybe actually an active convent.

Chris: It may have been an active convent.

Patti: It had a wing for retreats.

Chris: I think it was a convent that had a wing for retreats.

Patti: It was a retirement home for old nuns.

Chris: That's what it was. It was a retirement home for old nuns.

Patti: And it had one wing of these old girls and then a wing for retreats.

Chris: And here are these nuns welcoming our HIV positive group, and I had set up workshops and various support activities at a very low cost that women came in from all over Ohio. And of course this was still when most people were becoming ill and dying, so we had women at all stages of illness or wellness depending upon how you wanted to put it. And I had said to Patti come and see, come see what you think, come meet the women. I really needed to know, and I laugh at this now because I know where you're at now, but I really needed to know that the passion I had for these women would not get lost in working with Patti or working with anybody else. So as it turned out your car broke down and you and I had to ride there together. We had planned on going separately.

Patti: I had wanted the space, cause I always want my space.

Chris: Yes. It was too much too quickly. You wanted the space. So she was stuck riding with me, and we had a great time.

Patti: That was kind of our real bonding.

Chris: Yes.

Patti: I think it was the car trip both there and then particularly on the return where we...

Chris: Processed.

Patti: Where we fell into our process of Chris driving and us just talking a mile a minute and me taking notes while we're driving down the road. And then many of those notes ended up in the book. Those were my field notes.

Chris: Yes. At that point I didn't realize that I was gonna be data.

Patti: I don't know that I did. I didn't know either.

Chris: But I caught on pretty quickly. Maybe you didn't know either.

Patti: I mean, in my mind, I think I was taking my field notes towards getting better data from the women, but that was at a time when field notes, the whole kind of autobiography thing, didn't necessarily end up in the final product. So I certainly didn't write those notes with the idea that they'd end up in the book.

THE ORGANIC, EMERGENT NATURE OF COLLABORATION IN QUALITATIVE RESEARCH

The Format: Emergent and Evolving

Chris: And we didn't know what the book was gonna look like, right?

Patti: Correct. Very correct.

Chris: I mean it definitely was…

Patti: That was an emergent situation.

Chris: An emergent, yeah.

Patti: The form was so very emergent. And I think I've said this before but I don't think people pay enough attention to it. Much of the form of the book was a matter of convenience between you and me with our very busy lives, not being able to get together very much, figuring out how to keep things up.

Chris: I adopted a daughter

Patti: You take this hunk; I'll take that hunk. And at that time we weren't even emailing all that much,

Chris: No, that's right we weren't.

Patti: So it wasn't like you could just throw things back and forth to each

The Process: Emergent and Organic

Walter: And did that emerge as well? Or Patti did you as the "qualitative researcher" of the pair more sort of say hey do we try it this way or was it something that the two of you decided that it would be easier or it just sort of happened?

Chris: I think there were some things that happened first. I think aside from just Patti's phenomenal expertise you were always very transparent. I found that my conversations with Patti were intellectually engaging. I felt valued by Patti for what I could bring. I always felt valued for what I could bring to this, and we brought different things. Our feminism we each brought, and I think that was a profoundly common bond and yoke. We had a, help me with the word, we had a perspective, a grounding, a foundation, an ideology that was very shared despite her being in more of an academic world, and I of course with a Ph.D. am familiar with that academic world but living a very applied life. So I think there was a tremendous foundation that we shared in common, other. And so we sort of farmed out, we tried to figure out a way to put the book together that would let us work pretty independently, write independently and get together really as little as possible given our lives.

Chris: That's all true. Mmm, hmm. Oh when you were tested I do remember in our conversation we did ask what if Patti was positive? What would it do to our work? That was pretty interesting; I don't even remember what we said.

Patti: Well, that was a methodological issue, insider/outsider.

Chris: Yes, that was a methodological issue, yeah. So I remember we kind of tried that on for size.

Walter: Yes. And thinking about these ideas, can you talk to me a little bit about the form because the book has about four or five key components. It has the conversations; it has…

Patti: Factoids.

Walter: Factoids. It has also researcher text.

Patti: Researcher text, reflective text.

Walter: And also the…

Patti: Angel intertext.

Walter: the resources for women. How did this piece come to be? Was this, again, emergent? How did this evolve? How did you get to this multiply layered text?

Chris: We just had so…
Patti: I think it was so evolving.

but Patti was transparent. She sometimes used words or phrases that I had no idea. She still does, and I can just say I have no idea what you're talking about and please explain that to me.

Walter: Was that directness comfortable from the beginning?

Patti: We're both pretty…

Chris: Yes Patti: We were a pretty good personality [fit].

Chris: Right from the beginning.

Patti: Yeah but we were a pretty good personality mix. I mean it was a pretty easy connection. And I don't remember having…

Chris: We liked each other.

Patti: Having to negotiate much space. I mean we had our tensions but they were substantive.

Chris: They were substantive. I don't think there was ever a personal tension that I can recall, even around why haven't you gotten something done, absolutely none of that I recall.

Patti: Very in sync with one another's life issues. Cause you know this process it started in '92. That manuscript didn't go to the publisher til '96 so you've got about a four year…

Chris: We had a long relationship.

Patti: Four years of getting data, analyzing the data, trying different approaches to the writing. Many life changes in both your life and mine, that we were good enough friends about…

Chris: Yeah. It was so evolving, and we agreed on most. I mean the angel intertext, I think, required the most discussion between us. The opportunity to educate women, that's certainly our agenda, but it was the agenda of the women. See, we had guides. We had guides in terms of what these women envisioned and while what we ended up creating was far different than what any one of them envisioned, we had guides that kept us on track. Patti, for all of her academia think tank stuff, never questioned that the women who read this book, it's a chance to educate them. And you actually did most of the research on the educational pieces.

Patti: The factoid part.

Chris: The factoid parts those were mostly [Patti's doing].

Patti: I remember that really being the hardest because it kept changing.

Chris: It kept changing and we knew some of it would become dated, but as it turns out it's wonderful because the piece is a historical chronicle now as well because AIDS changed so much. So I think we needed to find ways to include all those components. We wanted the women's voices. I wanted a room of women talking. How do you actually capture that? And the women all along would say we want to get our voices out there, and we came back to that again and again and again. That was a shared [value] and so, like I said, I think we had guides and we wanted to educate. We wanted to encourage other support groups to start. So there were some very practical missions that we didn't lose sight of in part because of our commitments, because our guides

Chris: We made space for each other.

Patti: that we were pretty much in touch with those life issues and shifts and figuring out how to get our work done within that in a way that honored our lives.

Chris: And I think the other thing that happened is that we had, you know, Patti passed all the tests and was clearly moved personally by these women. I think that's what I was looking for, is whatever research we did, I wanted to know that I would be working with someone who could let them in and who would be moved by them, and that weekend kind of really moved you. She was definitely affected by it and it was deep and significant, and that was very, very important to me. So I think as we went through our process over the next four or five years, there continued to be, in addition to our feminism, it always came back to the women, and it came back in different ways at different times. But I always felt that Patti was on board. That whatever individually we were living, whatever individually we were accomplishing, that there was a continuing commitment to the women and to those women feeling that they counted on us as a team to get their voices out there. And we brought different things to the team, but we had this higher goal to get their voices out there and in a way that they would respect and feel good about. And, yes, we did have some differences about what that would look like, but it became very clear to us, and I think to the women, that what we did would work in a way that they would feel very proud of. So, yeah, I think that were going to hold us accountable.

Patti: And I think the factoid, the little boxes emerged, I want to say, out of some of the models I looked at.

Chris: Yeah, I don't know how they emerged.

Patti: I was gonna say when Nancy and I sat down to lay that out, but I clearly had that laid out in rough form before she [began]. And I had such limited skills with the computer, so when she put it into PageMaker she could make it much prettier. But I know I'd already found how to draw those little boxes. I had to draw them all the way across because I didn't know how to do anything else, but I'd already figured that out. And the only way I would have figured that out would have been through some of the models I was looking at cause I knew I wanted multiple things going on the page. And the decision to do the underwriting, I think as we talked we couldn't figure [it] out. We didn't want to put ourselves first or frame things. We wanted the women to be the first thing people saw and we didn't want to put ourselves at that back where we would say what things really meant. So [our voices] first didn't work. The end with the women's voices didn't work so then, once we sort of experimented with [it] on the same page, it just clicked. And then that was perfect. And then we divvied up the data and looked for themes, and then you'd write like you did the support group. You'd take that group and I took the families or, I don't know how we divided it up, but we sort of looked for themes together and then divided the themes up and took the first crack at writing the data stories as we called them. Then [we] would exchange

we kind of had a third colleague, a higher cause, and Patti maintained sight of that even with her more academic bent and brain. She maintained sight of that, and I could always bring it back to that, and I tried not to get too bogged down with that. Because there were times that I had to say, "I don't think the women like this but we should do it anyway "or "You're right." But I think that we had a higher purpose to what we were doing.

Patti: And that was certainly a blessing and a motivation, but it was also the main source of anxiety.

Chris: Yes.

Patti: and the sense of responsibility and whatever the depths of despair were in the project wherever they came in. It was always about feeling like maybe we wouldn't pull this off.

Chris: Yes, and we would disappoint the women.

Patti: And that between your life and my life we wouldn't be able to figure this out or…

Chris: They would die before they got to see it.

Patti: …they would die before we get it out. I mean, there was a certain sense of press that was in quite a bit of tension with [our process]; it's almost like the project needed its time. You know, if we would have been forced to write that book in two years instead of four or five it would have been a very different book and I think not as good. I think whatever chance it has of standing up for X amount of years it is because it had its time. It needed a and plug in bottom writing. Like you wrote most of the bottom for the support groups and I would go back through all my notes and see what fit where and run it by you, and then you'd fill in.

Chris: And often you would come and say Chris could you write something on this, okay.

Walter: So Patti would watch the overall scope?

Chris: I would say she did. She had the bigger overview.

Patti: Particularly once it started happening, once there was a template then it sort of took care of itself. But at the front end where we were trying this and we were trying that and see what works, and then, like I'm thinking of the decision to have that up front part where each of the women wrote her own self description. That was very much a conversation we had: How will we introduce the women?

Chris: Well, let's let them introduce themselves.

Patti: And I told you of a few models that were not unusual in ethnographic work, and I think it was your idea. You said, "Well why don't you just have them write their own?"

Chris: And that spoke volumes to them. It was like, wow, you guys are really gonna do this and I'm really gonna get my words out there and represent my own name.

Patti: And again, I have to keep saying this that was before email.

fullness of time, including that touch with their lives, the evolution of their lives, and the evolution of our lives, and in some ways the evolution of the field. You know, the sort of methodological literature I was reading and feeding my head with, and it had to be what it was even though there were, maybe this was me particularly, the tension between my intellectual and academic desires. You know I could speak very specifically about the angels. You know, did the angels cost us a year or two because I had to do that? Could I have gotten the book or could we have gotten the book out a year or two earlier if we wouldn't have had all that in there? But it had to be in there. I mean there's no way I could make it happen without that being in there so.... But if there was anything that was about losing sleep it was about that.

Chris: I think whenever we disagreed about something one of the things I liked about collaborating with Patti and I hope I did the same thing neither one of us quickly positioned ourselves. There were times that we said I couldn't give that up or that couldn't change entirely. But I learned very quickly with Patti and we didn't have a lot of impasses. The ones that we had I think we talked about.

Patti: Yeah.

Chris: Yeah. But I always felt like if we had an impasse or a disagreement, and we were very selective; we didn't have lots, that discussing it, bringing it forth it brought something better out. And I came to trust that in Patti. That if I'm feeling uncomfortable with something she's gonna go off and do

Chris: Yes.

Patti: Nobody had email so whatever we did it had to be done I remember it got done by mail.

Chris: Yeah. A lot of that was done by mail.

Walter: Sure.

Chris: Yeah.

Patti: So it was a stumbly, bumbly, back and forth and then we would show some parts to some of the women. Like I remember going to Dayton and the decision to do the desktop publishing came out of the Dayton group where I was showing them [the work to date]. I'd just print stuff off of my computer and take it over to them and they'd look at it. They didn't even want to read it. They would say well where's the book? We want a book, and so I could see that getting them to do member checks was not gonna be easy with just computer paper. So then we started talking about this possibly and I started poking around seeing what it would cost and who might fund it [a desktop published version]. So in a way that would be a good example actually of a sort of field based, emergent decision. We did not go into this saying, "Oh we're going to do a desktop published version."

Chris: No, that emerged.

Patti: That absolutely emerged out of interaction with the women. It felt [like a] kind of organic interaction with the women.

Walter: Right. And so I'd like if you wouldn't mind momentarily talking about that tension sort of between the her little think tank thing and very likely come forth with something that both of us feel good about. And I never felt like I had to give anything up, that maybe I had to change.

Patti: But it didn't even feel so much like compromise.

Chris: No, I did not feel like we had to compromise. I feel like we collaborated until there was something that worked, but we weren't saying, "Okay we've got to stick this out until we find something." There was just a sense that when we had a difference of opinion it was a really useful pause sign. I think you in particular would go off and come back with something that you were excited about that also took my concerns into account.

Patti: That I wouldn't have come up with if you wouldn't have raised the concern.

Chris: If I hadn't said I'm not feeling real comfortable with this or I don't understand this. She would go away with that. She'd just go oh. And then you would come back with something.

Patti: Instead of fighting or sticking our heels in the sand.

Chris: Yeah.

Patti: I don't remember much defense of certain positions. I mean you made me articulate the angels more than once and continued, if my memory serves me right, to the bitter end saying you still didn't really understand it. But if I felt like I had to have that in there in order to do the project.

deeply spiritual and the deeply meaningful and also the terribly tragic, which they seem to be kissing each other throughout the book.

Patti: Well, that was again one of the gifts of the project was that was part of the glorious complication of it that could not be tidy. I guess I've read some AIDS stuff that avoids all that, but it's pretty hard to be in that territory and do superficial work. I mean the territory itself is just so complicated and layered, and it is about joy and terror and sorrow just all implicated with each other. You just can't take one thread out and not have the others in there. And I would say part of our work together was to make sure we kept all that in there.

Chris: The emotional, the spiritual.

Patti: That we helped each other negotiate that territory so that we were honoring all of that, and we weren't just telling the happy stories and we weren't just mired in the tragic stories; and we did pay attention to the trials and tribulations of daily life; and who's gonna feed the damn kids as well as some of the more dramatic. I mean it's also a territory where it's pretty easy to get high drama and in a cheap sort of way and end up doing a disservice to the women because of how easily it lends itself to soap opera sorts of stories.

Chris: I think that [was part of] our decision to include the data about the support group that was having a very hard discussion about race. You know we didn't want to, I mean, at a very practical level I wanted this book to inspire more support groups. So we didn't want to idealize it or imply that there weren't also these tensions and

Chris: And what I was most concerned about is that the women wouldn't understand.

Patti: Yes. And of course some did and some didn't as we found out in the member checks.

Chris: Some loved it, some understood it, and some didn't understand it, but it didn't matter. They skipped chapters [they didn't like] and others didn't like [the angels]. And that was the other great thing about Patti is if someone didn't like something, that wasn't a reason not to do it.

Patti: Right, articulate your arguments or whatever and then, if they still don't like it, maybe try one more time and then if they still don't like it; I'm trying to think how that would have worked with you and me. Well, what I think with the angels that you had some insistences, like you insisted that they be short. They were at one time those angel inter-chapters were two and three times longer. And Chris says, well, if you just have to have them in there then cut them down and make them as understandable as possible.

Chris: Well, and I was concerned. Like I didn't want it to become alienating to the nonacademic population. But Patti got that. I mean that we were writing to a diverse audience. She had probably a little more investment in one audience, and I had more investment in another audience but we wanted a book that would speak to both.

Walter: So if I heard that correctly the moments where there was just sort of very firm and a finite sense of jeez challenges that these women had had in group with each other. There was a woman who came to the group who was very vocal in our data collection who was faking that she had HIV. Yeah, so there it was important to keep that real. We wanted these women to continue to be real to themselves—that was the best thing like when you read this you recognize yourself and that will help make the book a success. And that's where the member check [came in]. I think some of the process themes that were, really this is with hindsight, but I don't know if this was done other places. I've never asked you this before, but the big print at the top and our smaller print voices at the bottom…

Patti: I had a few models for that.

Chris: That just clicked. That just worked for me. That was like, wow, it keeps them most important.

that's not gonna work for me were so few and far between that when they actually happened each of you listened to the other and thought, "Oh, this is one of the few times. Okay. I have a difference of opinion about this, but I'm gonna let this ride and see what comes of it rather than pushing at it." So it was almost simpatico in the way that let these differences emerged in a deferential, respectful way.

Patti: I think that's very right and I was thinking, one of my big really life lessons was that if you're up against the wall with somebody, and it feels like you're in a stuck place, take a vacation. Engage with one another as well. You can [engage] at that point in time around it and then back off and let some time happen. And you call it my think tank, and one certainly does, hopefully not obsessively, but, you know, let it cook a little bit. Let it move around over X amount of time and then something will emerge. Some unstuckness will happen and, like you said, it will be better than what I would have done on my own or that if we would have [had we] just let it out [at each other rather than waiting]. Like one of the things was the title. Well, it was about the angels, too.

Trust that Process: Enjoy the Collaborative Nature of Qualitative Research

Walter: Are there any ideas or frameworks or things that you would like to keep in mind or that you would suggest others keep in mind were they to do this? Because the process itself sounds very emergent, that word has come up over and again.

Patti: I say be comfortable with the emergent nature of things. Don't feel like you have to have a lot of things set in stone. I mean, like when I was trying to get the book published, in a way that was a pulling together too, of format. You have to get a proposal together so you've got to have something, so you have to make some kind of a template. So that would be an example of the kind of forcing of the process. But there's like organic steps where you have to pull some things together.

Walter: And by organic steps you mean not something preplanned but things that come out and emerge?

Patti: Well, like the pulling a proposal together to submit to a publisher is an organic step in the process. But we had no idea at the front end what the format would look like. We didn't feel the need to.

Chris: No.

Patti: And we got a little research design together when you and I were talking because that was part of my passing inspection was you wanted me to submit a research proposal. It was probably like only two pages.

Chris: Right.

Patti: Two or three pages of a research design, but you wanted to see what I had in mind. So that forced me to put [my thoughts] down on paper. We certainly changed a lot of it, but it got the ball rolling and then the logic of the field, like the decision to do support group interviews, was emergent. We were gonna do one-on-one interviews. We didn't even think about support group interviews until we met with the Cincinnati group to come up with some questions that we were gonna ask in the one-on-ones.

Chris: I remember on the way back I said let's do group interviews.

Patti: It went so well we decided why would we break this frame.

Chris: Yeah, yeah. We were gonna do that, I forgot.

Patti: Yeah. So we did support group interviews and supplemented them with the one-on-ones, but we didn't do very many one-on-one interviews.

Chris: Which, again, I think just lined up with everything else.

Patti: Oh it was perfect. But we didn't know that at the front end.

Chris: Yeah.

Patti: So I would say that in a way the big thing would be to enjoy the emergent nature of qualitative research. Trust that process to steer you in good directions. And I want to say enjoy. I want to say be comfortable and curious and awake to it, and not anxious about not having a lot of it up front, cause if we would have a felt need to be real firm at the front end and then a felt need to stick to it, it would have been a very different project.

NEGOTIATING STUCK PLACES

We were set up to be Quite Complementary

Walter: Stuck places. The title and the angels are the two stuck places that you write about and they're the two stuck places that have come up [here]. What were some other stuck places that you remember if there were any? Or were those just two sort of places where that was just difficult to get around?

Chris: I think there were; I think they were so well resolved for a lack of better word that they're almost erased from memory.

Patti: I mean, I'm just trying to think where our decision trees were. We had decision trees around who would go to what group sort of scheduling because we did very few of the interviews together.
Well, we did the ones here in town together.

Chris: And we did Cincinnati together.

Patti: And we did Cincinnati together mostly. Although you did a couple by yourself.

Chris: I may have done some extra.

Patti: And I went to Dayton pretty much by myself.

Chris: That's right.

Patti: And I went to Cleveland.
Chris: I think we went to Cleveland together.

Patti: We went to Cleveland at least once together.

We Couldn't get the Goddamn Book Published

Patti: Oh, can I talk about another stuck place? We couldn't get the goddamn book published. I couldn't find a goddamn publisher. That was terrible.

Walter: Was it the form or was it the topic?

Patti: It was the form. The topic was hot, but I sent to 13, was it 13 different publishers?

Chris: It was a lot.

Patti: And by then we had this [desktop published version] which usually when you can send them a mockup like that they just fall at your feet. So I sent to 13 publishers, and I sent them this and a little proposal and all that stuff, and they come back: oh if you just change your format and do this and do that kind of thing they might be interested. But they wouldn't take the book and it was Joe Kincheloe and Shirley Steinberg that took me by the hand, and Joe just died at 57 of a heart attack.

Walter: Oh, it is so shocking.

Patti: Took me by the hand at AERA and took me over to a handful of publishers and gave that personal talk with the publisher, you know did the bridge, and got me the contract at Westview.

Chris: And it had to be camera ready, remember?

Patti: Yes. Yeah, they made us pay. We paid big time for that book. Well, we

Chris: So we did maybe half by ourselves, probably half.

Patti: Yeah. That's about right. It sort of took care of itself because it just made sense whose life lent itself to what. Like going up there to see what's her name in the hospital, I wanted us together. I didn't want to do that by myself. Chris had been at many a hospital scene and I had not and there was no way, I don't know that I would have done that by myself. But going in there to interview her in the hospital with her family around her, I needed you to be able to do that. And I remember I was very quiet, in that interview; I did not say much. Chris definitely took the lead and that was another part of the collaboration. There were things that I didn't have the, I would almost say the strength for, that you were at great ease with. And then there were other times, I don't know, maybe some of our conference presentations or whatever, where I could take the lead, although you never seemed very nervous about that. Were you nervous?

Chris: No. No, I mean you've had many more opportunities to speak and be out and about, but no I've never felt nervous or second chair. I mean there was no question from the beginning who first author was gonna be so that was never [an issue].

Walter: Why is that out of curiosity?

Chris: I think for me it was, I don't even really remember there even being a discussion but…

Patti: Oh no, we did have a discussion.

paid for that one, but we got a grant for that one [the desktop version]. The Westview one just came out of our pockets.

Walter: Unreal.

Patti: So the publishers were not our friends in many ways, but by the time we got to here I was so desperate that our contract wasn't a very good contract. They acted like it was a big favor they were doing us to publish this book, and by that time we were willing to take it on those terms. So we just, I mean I knew that I wasn't gonna have any other offers, so we just signed. We signed pretty quick.

Walter: Have you thought about putting an updated version out?

Patti: Well, no one has approached me on that. And in terms of what it would mean to bring that group of women back together again. You know some of course are dead, but not as many as you might think because the new treatments kicked in.

Chris: Just as our book was finished the pervasiveness of crisis diminished significantly. We didn't realize this when we wrote the book, but our book really chronicles the first phase of the AIDS crisis in this country. Pre-antiretrovirals. I haven't said that word for awhile. So are you familiar with *Getting Lost?* There is a chapter that I write about some of the follow up, and I think there's things you write about, too.

Patti: Well, Linda B., one of the women has one of the little inter-texts in there.

Walter: That's right.

Chris: Did we have? Okay, you say what you remember then.

Patti: Well, I remember that we talked about it rather early on because as an academic…

Chris: No, we did talk about it. Absolutely.

Patti: And that's probably about as much follow up as we're prepared to do.

Chris: Yeah. And it's interesting it's not as grabbing because the intensity is not there at this point.

WOMEN AND HIV: SNAPSHOT BY REIGIONS

Sub-Saharan Africa — Sub-Saharan Africa is the hardest-hit region in the world. In 2007, there were 22.5 million people in sub-Saharan Africa living with HIV. Globally, 68 percent of all people living with HIV live in sub-Saharan Africa. Around 61 percent of all adults living with HIV in sub-Saharan Africa are women. Most women with HIV here have been infected by their husbands or sexual partners. Nearly 12 million children under the age of 18 living in sub-Saharan Africa have lost one or both parents to AIDS. Many grandparents, who have lost all of their adult children to the disease, are left raising their grandchildren, many of whom also are HIV-positive. Fortunately, in most sub-Saharan African countries, HIV rates are stable or showing signs of decline. Prevention efforts appear to be having an impact in some countries. Coinfection with tuberculosis (TB), which is a major cause of illness and death in people with HIV, also is a big problem in this region. Here, roughly 50 percent to 80 percent of people with tuberculosis (TB) also are HIV-positive. Addressing both infections is an urgent need.

Asia — About 4.9 million people were living with HIV in Asia in 2007. Trends vary by region and country. Southeast Asia is the most effected, with the epidemic growing at especially high rates in Indonesia. New HIV infections had climbed by almost 20 percent since 2001 in East Asia. In China, roughly 700,000 people are living with HIV. About 2.5 million people in India are living with HIV. In many parts of Asia, HIV is found mainly in high-risk groups, such as sex workers and injection drug users. But in India, HIV has spread to the wider population, including women thought to be at low risk of infection.

Caribbean — The Caribbean is the second most affected region in the world. There were 230,000 people living with HIV in the Caribbean at the end of 2007. Nearly three-quarters of people with HIV in the Caribbean live in Haiti or Dominican Republic. Unprotected sex between sex workers and clients is a main cause of HIV spread in the region. Especially at risk are young girls, who commonly have relationships with older men, who because of their age are more likely to have HIV.

Eastern Europe/Central Asia — The number of people with HIV in this region rose in 2007 to about 1.6 million, 40 percent of whom were women. Nearly 90 percent of new HIV cases were in the Russian Federation and Ukraine. Injection drug use has fueled the spread of HIV in this region, followed by unprotected sex between men and women.

Latin America — In 2007, about 1.6 million people were living with HIV in this region, where HIV rates are stable. Unprotected sex between men is a main cause of HIV spread in many Latin American countries. HIV transmission between female sex workers and their clients is another major factor in the spread of HIV in this region. Widespread stigma, discrimination, and cultural issues keep prevention and treatment efforts from reaching at-risk populations in this region.

North America, Western/Central Europe — About 2.1 million people in North America and Western and Central Europe were living with HIV in 2007. Access to life-prolonging treatment has helped the numbers of AIDS-related deaths in this region to stay low compared to other parts of the world. Still, the United States has one of the largest HIV epidemics in the world, and certain populations are more affected. AIDS is the leading cause of death among African American women aged 25 to 34 living in the United States. Canada's epidemic is much smaller, with an estimated 58,000 people living with HIV in 2005. In Western and Central Europe the number of new HIV diagnoses has climbed since 2002.

> Middle East and North Africa — In 2007, there were an estimated 380,000 people living with HIV in the Middle East and North Africa. Limited data here makes it hard to see patterns and trends related to the HIV epidemic. We do know that unprotected paid sex is the main way HIV is passed in some counties, while injection drug use is the way HIV is passed in other counties. Most HIV cases are found in men. But in some countries, more and more women are getting HIV as it is passed to them from men who pay for sex or use injection drugs.
>
> Oceania — In Oceania there were about 75,000 people living with HIV in 2007. Papua New Guinea's cases account for more than 70 percent of HIV infections in the region, and the epidemic is growing at an alarming rate. Women are heavily discriminated against in Papua
>
> New Guinea and high levels of sexual violence against women have been reported. Both paid and casual sex encounters are the norm, and there is generally no condom use. Unsafe sex between men is the main way HIV is spread in New Zealand and Australia.
>
> Retrieved from http://www.4woman.gov/hiv/worldwide/#d April 20, 2009

We were set up to be Quite Complementary (Con't)

Patti: Just like I did with Walter here. I mean you want to see where does it go on the vitae and whose name comes first is always a big concern.

Chris: No, it was very upfront.

Patti: If I remember right, I suggested I be first because I was gonna end up writing. I wrote some proposals for funding. We were writing a grant; we got a little grant from Women's Studies. I was gonna write that. I knew I was gonna write the proposal for the book to the publishers, negotiate that territory. I knew that I would probably take the lead at least at the front end in terms of data analysis cause I knew how to do that and I was taking the lead in terms of I did all the transcriptions.

Chris: Yes.

Patti: At first we tried to hire transcriptions out, but that didn't work.

Chris: You got the transcriptions done and then I organized them for the book.

Patti: Jim gave us money to hire a transcriber but it didn't work. It just didn't work.

Chris: Yeah, a graduate student that just didn't work out.

Patti: So then I had to do all the transcriptions so then just as we sort of laid out, if I remember right, my argument was here's this sort of labor involved in the project and in my mind it makes most sense for me to be first author, and Chris said sure.

Chris: Yeah, and Patti has an academic career. I do not, and that may have been part of what worked in the whole thing. We were never ever competitors. We were never one ego over the other. We functioned in very different worlds with great respect for each other's world, but there was not a…

Patti: That is interesting. If we both would have been academics, would it have been different, a little more competitive?

Chris: It might have been a different.

Walter: Or if you had both been practitioners?

Patti: Or that.

Chris: Yeah, yeah.

Walter: Because then the questions about the sort of drive and things that we have [as academics to get things published] because you can let these things pass, but the second you go to work or you go to a conference you hear someone else is working on something. And it's not necessarily competitive, but there's a sort of [a feeling] like, oh nuts. There's this thing I really wanted and you get sort of inspired and you're constantly being reminded of that, and not being reminded of that it might have taken longer too.

Patti: And I do think because we had somewhat different worlds, that let us more easily [work together]. Like I remember that conference of doctors that we spoke at. What was clear to me was that that was your bailiwick. I mean, I was out of my element there. So whatever it meant for one of us to take the lead or the other one to take the lead there was not much debate about it.

Chris: It was like, please.

Patti: It was just so clear.

Chris: Yeah. So that might have been part of it.

Patti: Materially, we were set up to not be competitive. In fact, we were set up to be quite complementary

ON COLLABORATION: WORKING WITH RESEARCHERS AND RESEARCH PARTICIPANTS

Collaboration between Researchers: Ripeness, Timing and Friendship

Patti: And remember we were taking that walk and you were hating that title and those angels and what were we gonna do about it and then we came up with the "The."

Chris: Mmm, hmm.

Collaboration between Researchers and Researched: Romance, Layers, and Negotiation

Walter: So it's clear that this is driven by the members of the support groups. On the other hand, in the introduction to the book, in its conclusion, and now a few times each of you has said that this is different from what the women

Patti: "The." "The." It was so simple.

Chris: I remember out walking and it came to me and I called you up and I said could you accept "Troubling *the* Angels?" And she said, YES! That's exactly how it went. YES!

Patti: Yeah, yeah. But I often think of that walk as that could have been a break that might have not killed the project or anything; we were too far into it by then but create a little bad blood that would have simmered there, but it just didn't.

Chris: It didn't, no. I never felt . . .

Patti: And I wouldn't say we learned to fight. I wouldn't say we learned to compromise. It was something else that was very good. Like I said, it was life [changing]. I mean, I do this with my girlfriend all the time now. When we run up against that brick wall, then we do that back away thing.

Chris: And our lives built some of that in. You know, there were times that I think we had the wisdom to back off. And other times it just kind of happened. And those pauses were probably good opportunities for more to emerge.

Walter: What I would like to know is a little bit more about the ways in which you were able to support each other in the complexities.

Patti: Hot tubs.

Walter: I heard about that; I read that.

Chris: Naked methodology.

envisioned. And it may not be the book that they envisioned so it seems like, on the one hand, there's this deep honoring of the women and their space and their words, and on the other hand its putting together is removed. I don't know if removed is the right word but somehow different from, with no connotation attached, that experience. And I'd like if you wouldn't mind talking about . . .

Patti: No, not at all. I think that's a really important one. I think that's the realities of doing the work is that at a certain point the researchers are making decisions if for no other reason than in terms of pulling things together to have somebody do a member check. You've got to do that first template or whatever you want to call it. We were not co-writing with them. We invited them in and there's as you know some poetry and a few essays and speeches and things, and we issued sort of broad invitations around more collaborative co-writing at the front end. But the message by and large was, "We're pretty busy dealing with our lives and don't have the time or the inclination to like analyze data and look for emerging themes and patterns and write up first drafts and experiment with textual format."

Chris: And it was a foreign language to most of the women.

Patti: Yes.

Chris: And their need to take care of their lives and their health I think would have precluded co-writing even if the group was populated by doctoral students.

Walter: Yeah and I thought naked methodology and I thought how clever.

Chris: Well, most people probably don't get naked in a hot tub with their clients either.

Walter: Probably not...

Patti: I don't know. Yeah, but part of me thinks that's feminists. That's not unusual.

Chris: That's true. Women colleagues will strip down and go into the hot tub together, that's for sure. But there was, yeah, there was a friendship developed and a friendship that I think will persist. A friendship that's supported our individual lives and changes that were occurring. When we got together we didn't just talk about the research, we talked about our personal lives. I was adopting a baby during this time and becoming a mother, and that was not something Patti was interested in doing, but she was wonderfully excited and supportive and never once said but you know what about our book. And so I think that the friendship and the support and the personal sharing we did what the women in the group did. It happened I think relatively easily.

Patti: That's actually a great example of the rhythm of the book. You could say that your adopting Elena cost us a year in that book, but it was so clear that you needed that to feed your soul and your life at the time that would then feed the book.

Chris: It did feed the book.

Patti: That the book was better for getting slowed down so that you could have that baby.

Patti: And there was one.

Chris: There was one.

Patti: And I remember going to her particularly thinking maybe she'd want to do something more collaborative. She said, "I'm doing my damn dissertation. I'm busy."

Chris: Another one was pre-med.

Patti: Yeah. Even the ones who might have had more background, they didn't want to. They were busy. So it became, I think, actually a very important statement about the romance of collaboration that often exists, you think you're issuing this invitation and it falls on busy lives.

Chris: And I think the women's trust in us had grown. One of the reasons this project worked is, from the outset at least, some of the women already knew and trusted me. There were other women that I met just as strangers in this process. But I think through the process of collecting our data, we did that very informally just like we're doing it today. And I can't think of any counter examples to this, but they came to trust that we were going to have integrity around the project. I think bringing them a box of books where their stories were evident helped. That this is taking longer than you [the women] thought; it's not looking like what you thought. I think, too, at some other level what happened in support groups is bigger and more than any one woman or participant, and the end product was certainly different than any one support group or bigger and broader than any one woman. But yeah, I think they felt they had personal relationships with Patti and I.

Chris: Yeah.

Patti: In the fruit is the ripeness of its own time. The project had the ripeness of its own time, in a way, even though we were under urgent pressure from the women. You know the decision to do the desktop published book was part of that urgency.

Chris: Yes. Oh that's good.

Patti: And I remember my immense sense of relief when we handed those mothers [the desktop published versions] out at Christmas two years into the project, like in '94, whenever it was. I could sleep again.

Chris: Yes.

Patti: And I thought, now I can slow down. Now if we're having babies and new affairs and whatever all of that can have its time because we've met really what the women [wanted]. The women had a book in their hands and that was what they really cared about. The later book, the orange book [the book published by Westview Press] they were happy enough with, but it was that first book, that white book [the desktop published version] that really mattered to them.

Chris: Yeah, yeah. No, that was a turning point where we had in a sense delivered to them.

Walter: On your promise.

Chris: Yeah. On our promise. In all honesty, I think timing, and this is something I'm learning from our conversation today, just how much timing And I think they did to a degree.

Patti: Much more with you.

Chris: Yeah, much more with me, and Patti could kind of ride on my coattails in terms of entrée into the support groups but then established her own good reputation.

Patti: Well, I didn't screw up the opportunity that you offered.

Chris: You didn't screw up. And I rode on her coattails into the publishing world so we definitely brought different strengths to the project, but I think with the women it was, you know, I think they were guides. I think we couldn't honor that 100%, but we honored it enough that it kept working.

Patti: Well, and there was a rough spot or two that negotiating that with some sensitivity worked to create more possibilities. I'm thinking of, remember at the retreat where I didn't announce myself as a researcher that first night?

Chris: Oh yeah.

Walter: At the first retreat?

Chris: Yeah.

Patti: And I got called to account at lunch when what's her name stood up and said, I'll never forget that, she said I want all the helpers to identify themselves so she knew who was HIV positive and who was a helper.

Walter: Oh, right.

Patti: She said, "I want all the helpers to identify themselves."

was on our side in so many ways. And I think for me, and I do write about this, fortunately, I mean my time of being so fully invested emotionally, in hindsight, it needed to wind down. You burn out. And the fact that our project wound down and the AIDS crisis wound down and the need for me as a psychologist in this arena it changed and then diminished. That was good timing too because I couldn't still be doing the work I was doing then.

Patti: It was a young woman's gig.

Chris: And I think young but also just the intensity of it and the desperation of it and even the joy of it. I don't know that I could have continued and been a good mother. And that's certainly became the top priority as I became a parent, things shifted. But timing-wise it worked out fine because I was able to wind it down gracefully. I didn't have to quit. I didn't have to face quitting. It just wound down because the need diminished.

Patti: Organic.

Chris: Yeah, it was. It was so.

Patti: Yeah, I would use that word with my experience. It was all organic at a time when I had an enormous amount of energy for it, there it was. And by the time it was done I was starting to, well, I maintained my energy. Each phase was its own thrill. I remember when this [desktop published version] came out, that was about half way through and that was thrilling. And when this [published version] came out I was just beside myself.

Chris: And when I think about Peter Frame the physician at Cincinnati, I

Chris: That's right. She did.

Patti: So I stood up cause I was clearly one of the helpers.
Chris: Yeah.

Patti: And she was not overly happy about it.

Chris: She wasn't quite sure how you fit in.

Patti: No.

Chris: And I remember we had debated whether to announce you. We didn't know even for sure that we were gonna proceed together. I mean, it was looking good, but we didn't know because the retreat was the test and so we probably weren't as prepared. I remember we talked about it.

Patti: How should we announce ourselves?

Chris: Yeah, how should we announce ourselves? How should I announce you? How should we announce my role changing?

Patti: People just went around and said their names. So it got to my place and I just said, "Hi I'm Patti from Columbus," or whatever it was.

Chris: Yeah, yeah.

Patti: I didn't say, "I'm Patti and I'm here to maybe do some research if Chris decides I'm worthy."

Chris: And now we'll vote.

Patti: Yeah. So that would be one example and there was a handful of mean, if he hadn't asked me to do this. [It] was innovative on his part that, okay, we're starting to see some women who are HIV positive, and could you do a support group? I mean, if he hadn't asked that, if he hadn't been caring and far thinking, then who knows, this probably wouldn't have happened. So there was a lot of good timing. For all that was awful about HIV/AIDS there was a lot of good timing.

Patti: For this project.

Chris: For us to do our work.

Patti: For this project and relationship to it, yeah.

Chris: It gave me opportunity to reflect on it far more than I think I would have been able to by myself or...

Patti: And you think in a way that sustained your work then in counseling?

Chris: Yes. I think it sustained my work.

Patti: You were able to maybe sustain yourself longer in that work.

Chris: Yeah. Well, and because while we occasionally helped each other with a personal problem, you know Patti was always, I mean you're solid. You're mentally healthy and I am too. So there was the opportunity, I think, to talk and share, whether we were there at the same moment or not, in a way that I didn't have to worry I would burden you because you were interested, too. And you were okay. You were fundamentally okay so I didn't have to be in a helper role ever with you. So that was probably a good thing.

others where it was a little confused. There was a woman at Dayton who, when we did the member check with her, she wanted to pull out, and the way that got negotiated kept her in.

Walter: How was it negotiated?

Patti: Oh, I said, "I'll come over, we'll go word by word through everything that I've used of yours. You can take anything out you want."

Chris: Was it Amber?

Patti: No, it was, God I'm forgetting her name, and I can't remember what we called her. She was the one that had two little girls and she was worried about those two little girls growing up, and she'd been around the block several times and she didn't want them to see. She'd gone through drug and alcohol counseling, and she'd sort of changed her life. But some of the stories that we originally had in the book were pretty rough and she didn't want her girls to read that.

Chris: When she was dead to be reading about that aspect of her life. And then Amber, she was a false positive.

Patti: Yeah, but she was thrilled to be. She was kind of a Bette Midler type.

Chris: She was. She wanted to stay in the book.

Patti: Even though she was HIV negative.

Chris: "Will you keep me now that I'm HIV negative?"

Patti: Yeah, but this other woman I just sat with her, and we crossed out

Patti: That might be a good point too in terms of we're both pretty strong, pretty psychically stable, so that you could go into that intensity, that sort of long term intensity, and, not that we didn't spell one another now and then, but we never worried that you'd fall apart or wouldn't be able to hold your end up in things, or that you'd be a burden on my life or whatever. There was never a minute of that.

Walter: So in a way you were able to go through the process because you were each other's support person implicitly or explicitly?

Patti: Well, and also we knew that each other were their own support system. I mean, the idea that you could lean on each a little bit because you knew it wasn't gonna be too much. I had other people leaning on me, and Chris had other people leaning on her. The last thing in the world either one of us needed was another person who was gonna be leaning on us that we were gonna have to carry through. And it felt more like a shoulder-to-shoulder going through it.

Walter: And were there moments so when the moments came where it was particularly difficult for each of you, did you have a tendency to reflect on that yourself? Each of you write about different moments where you had particularly difficult transcripts to go through or particularly difficult sections of things to go through.

Patti: Oh. I remember that time when you called me and, I'm trying to think. See, I was taking notes all the time so whenever Chris would call me I'd grab my notepad, and I'd start taking notes anything she [didn't want in]. I just said, "I want to work with you in such a way that we can keep as much of what you're comfortable with as possible." So we went line by line, and she actually ended up letting me keep in more than I thought she would. We got rid of, I don't know, maybe a fourth of it, but three quarters of it she okay'd to go forward. And then of course I taped our conversation so then that became another conversation in the subtext was her and me negotiating what to keep in here. So it added another really rich layer.

Walter: That was one of the questions I wanted to ask you. You looked at groups in if I remember correctly Cincinnati, Columbus, Toledo…

Patti: No, not Toledo. Cleveland and Dayton.

Walter: Oh, I'm sorry, Cleveland and Dayton. Were there differences regionally between how people thought and talked about HIV even within the state?

Patti: It's hard for me to relate to the question regionally because the cultural makeup of the groups was different and that mattered more than regionality. The Cleveland bunch was mostly Latina. The Dayton bunch was mostly White. The Cincinnati bunch was quite a mix of White and Black, and the Columbus bunch was mostly White.

Chris: Mostly White, yeah.

Patti: So that mattered more.

Chris: I think we saw more similarities, and part of what we liked was that this was Ohio women. It wasn't California or Boston or even Portland. It was

on whatever we were talking about. But where something had been difficult...
Chris: I think it was when the baby died.
Patti: The baby, the mom with the baby.

Chris: The mom with the baby.

Walter: Which?

Patti: The one chapter in there, and actually, that was an add-in.

Chris: The Hispanic one.

Walter: Is her name "Lisa" in it?

Chris: Yeah.

Walter: Whose son is "Alex? "

Chris: Yeah, and it says they took him to Disneyland.

Walter: Honestly these are hard things for me. I was reading this; I'm on the plane crying. Both of the sections with children, are just, I'm so glad you included them, but I'm welling up just thinking about it.

Chris: It is hard.

Walter: Were those things that you wrestled with yourself and then share with each other? Or were these things that sort of you kept in your own world so you didn't burden one another?

Patti: I don't think we ever thought about, "Oh, I don't want to say anything, I don't want to burden Chris." That was never a minute's thought for me partly because I knew she was tough. She's a tough girl. And I did. Again maybe that's a very good example of actually not having to worry about taking care

Ohio. It was breadbasket women, and while they certainly were diverse in terms of their experiences and background they were all Ohioans, right?

Patti: And they knew each other. Many of them knew each other through the retreats.

Chris: Because we did these conferences together where they met each other.

Patti: Some of the Cincinnati women knew some of the Dayton women.

Chris: Yeah, so we encouraged them to know each other. And that wasn't because of the book necessarily. That was just my work was to get women from across the state together. So in the course of just the work I was doing and then the work we were doing they did know each other, or would ask about each other, or follow each other. But you know? You get these women together at a retreat and it was a damn good time.

of her. And if I needed to talk to somebody she'd be the first one I'd do it with because I knew she'd understand. And I knew that my burden was not gonna burden her somehow.

Chris: Like when you were testing.

Patti: Yes, that's another good example.

Chris: That's a good example that had various levels.

Patti: I was worried.

Chris: While it was unlikely, blah blah blah, you were worried. And I remember when we went to get the results.

Patti: We walked around the park.

Chris: We walked around the park when you got your results, and it was just that was personal then, oh you know you're okay. But there was a certain sharing of what women who are wondering about their status or men, but women in this case, what they go through. I mean, we couldn't distance entirely from this, one, because we need to know she was okay. And I had been tested earlier than that so I had experienced it, but you were tested during the course of the research, you don't mind that I say that?

Patti: Oh, no, no. It's in the book for God's sake.

Chris: Okay, I thought so. I just wanted to make sure.

Patti: But that actually would be a good one. I mean I look back at that and I just think of, that's what friends do. That felt more like just that's what friends do for each other.

Don't Do it by Yourself: Suggestions for Doing Richly Complex, Reflective Work

Walter: What would you say to other folk who wish to try and do richly complex, respectful, and reflective work like this?

Patti: I almost want to say don't do it by yourself.

Chris: Oh, I would definitely say you can't do it by yourself.

Patti: Find a buddy.

Chris: Yeah.

Patti: Well, you could. I mean I know people who have. But I think it actually results in a much better product.

Walter: When you have others?

Patti: When you have at least one other person involved.

Walter: As a researcher not just having the members be the other voice?

Patti: I want to say as a researcher, a co-equal. A strong co-equal. It's hard for me to think of doing it by myself.

Chris: I can't imagine doing it by myself.

Patti: And I could add especially with this intense of a topic, but part of me wants to think any topic can be intense when you start poking around in it.

Chris: Well, and I think there was, this is my orientation as a psychologist, but I think people grow from relationships and interaction more than from anything else. And the growth we did, you know we did some growth at so many levels, but certainly some of it was personal as well, and I wouldn't have wanted to have missed that part.

Patti: Without those conversations.

Chris: Yeah. I just can't imagine having done it by myself even if I had all the skills, I cannot imagine having engaged in that process by myself. But of course I felt that way from the very beginning.

Patti: And I would just ditto that. It would have been a much poorer project including the product. The product is such a production of our, and I don't want to use the word negotiation, but our partnership. It's like this is a little bit of an overstatement, but it's like a child that a couple raises. And that that child is so much the product of that joint effort that you can't imagine what that kid would be if it would have been just this one or that one...Well Walter, this has been fun.

Chris: It has been fun. I feel like it's been a walk down memory lane.

Need help now? Call now!

CDC National Information Hotline
800-232-4636 (English/Español)
TTY/TDD: 800-232-6348
email: cdcinfo@cdc.gov

National Sexually Transmitted Infections Hotline:
800-227-8922
En Español: 800-344-7432 (8a-2am, EST)
TTY/TDD: 800-243-7889

Teen AIDS Hotline:
800-440-TEEN (8336) Fri & Sat 6pm-12m (EST)

Retrieved 3/19/09 from http://www.aidsquilt.org/hivaidsresources.htm

---

ONLINE HIV/AIDS RESOURCES FOR WOMEN

The Global Coalition on Women and AIDS
- http://womenandaids.unaids.org/about/default.html

Health Information for Women with HIV and AIDS from the Well Project
- http://www.thewellproject.org/

HIVWoman.com
- www.hivwoman.com/default.htm

Women's AIDS Network
- www.womens-AIDS-network.com

AIDS Memorial Quilt/The NAMES Project Foundation
- http://www.aidsquilt.org/hivaidsresources.htm
- Has a very large database of phone numbers/contact information on a wide variety of AIDS/HIV-related topics on the front page of their website.

The Body: The Complete HIV/AIDS Resource
- http://www.thebody.com/

US Government HIV/AIDS Information
- http://www.aids.gov/

US Dept of Health and Human Services
- http://www.aidsinfo.nih.gov/

AIDS Education Global Information System
- http://www.aegis.com/

AIDS.org
- http://www.aids.org/

BRIAN D. SCHULTZ AND PARIS BANKS

2. CO-OPTATION, ETHICAL DILEMMAS AND COLLECTIVE MEMORY

A Writing Story

In this chapter, we explore the collaborative and complicated nature of what it means to write together. Writing as hermeneutic commentary (Ricœur, 1981), we reflect on a previously published article that we co-wrote[3]. The current interpretation found in this chapter exemplifies our ongoing collaboration regarding efforts to make sense of our experiences, as well as to better understand our views (and relationships) about teaching, learning, and working together. The purpose of this interpretation-upon-interpretation is to present the complexity inherent in our collaborating to conceptualize co-written texts between two authors—Brian, a former elementary classroom teacher who is now a university professor and his former fifth-grade student, Paris, a high school sophomore—whose social locations and positionalities are notably different in multiple dimensions (Bahktin, 1981).

When we constructed the original published piece, we collaborated through dialogue as writers, as theorizers to develop a cohesive narrative split text (Blumenfeld-Jones & Barone, 1997; Lather & Smithies, 1997; Oyler, 2001; Schultz & Oyler, 2006). In the original piece, we worked to keep Paris' voice prominent as we depicted his perspective and our shared understandings of how and what teachers and teacher educators could learn from their students. In this chapter, we present an additional dimension of split text analysis to the original essay. In so doing, we further make meaning, present tensions and ethical dilemmas, and write into the collaborative process of the previous text.

We see this chapter as an opportunity to become readers of our own written text as we continue to collaborate together. We believe that we are working towards thinking into the disruption about *What is text?* presented by Ricœur (1981):

> Dialogue is an exchange of questions and answers; there is no exchange of this sort between the writer and the reader. The writer does not respond to the reader. Rather, the book divides the act of writing and the act of reading into two sides, between which there is no communication. The reader is absent from the act of writing; the writer is absent from the act of reading. The text thus produces a double eclipse of the reader and the writer. It thereby replaces the relation of dialogue, which directly connects the voice of one to the hearing of the other. (pp. 146–147)

Through a doubled split text re-reading/re-writing, a "writing-story," or the story of how the text was constructed, emerges (Richardson, 1995, p. 189). The authors' writing-story—through hermeneutic commentary arranged in bold font in an *in situ*-side bar to the right of the original published essay—becomes a method of discovery (Richardson, 2001). This side bar commentary explains not only how parts of the original text were constructed, but also exposes complexities of the process and product of such writing endeavors.

As a result of our re-reading and re-writing, we interrogate spaces of collaboration addressing Ricœur's dilemma of absence in the reading/writing of text as we try to explain, examine, problematize, and reconcile our previous work. With attention to literature on postcolonial knowledges and research (Coulter, 2006; Denzin, 2005: Hoagland, in press), dual/multiple relationships (Blevins-Knabe, 1992; Moleski & Kiselica, 2005; Rubert & Holmes, 1997), and collective memory (Assman, 1988; Halbwachs, 1980), we wrestle with what it means to collaborate. Through our commentary, we honor the narrative sociologist Laurel Richardson's (1995) challenge to "valorize writing-stories" in order to "extend reflexivity into our writing practices, demystify writing…and deepen and expand our writing/reading strategies" (p. 189).

A SHORTY TEACHING TEACHERS: ONE KID'S PERSPECTIVE ABOUT "KEEPIN' IT REAL" IN THE CLASSROOM

Brian D. Schultz, Northeastern Illinois University
Paris Banks, Chicago Public Schools

In Pedro Noguera's (2008) critically acclaimed book, *The Trouble with Black Boys…And Other Reflections on Race, Equity, and the Future of Public Education*, readers are challenged to boldly look to students for perspective on how to improve schools, teaching, and learning (pp. 61–71). Noguera contends that possible solutions to issues related to achievement gaps, school safety and discipline, as well as student motivation might be remedied by looking to actual children in classrooms. There is deep potential to transform education since, as he argues, "students may very well have ideas and insights adults are not privy to [which] could prove to be very helpful to improving schools if adults were willing to listen" (p. 69). Whereas Noguera makes a convincing argument, much of the current literature in

AGAINST COLLABORATIVE CO-OPTATION

Earlier in the week, Paris' mother left me a voicemail urging me to get in touch with her son. Although, I had a wonderful relationship with Paris' family and spoke with both his parents fairly regularly over the past five years since Paris was a student in my fifth-grade classroom, Paris' mother never initiated a call. Something was wrong.

Just days later, Paris and I were sharing a plate of French fries at a local diner. We had several tasks at hand: putting finishing touches on the *Shorty* article as well as preparing for a talk to future school counselors we were giving together at a local university. Before getting started on our work, however, Paris detailed devastating news that one of his closest friends had been shot and killed in broad daylight directly in front his house. Paris told me that he was "dealing with it," that his "momma was looking for a new teacher education and practice in schools falls short of his thesis. If his contention were something new, radical, or even controversial it might be understandable, but the premise of looking to students for what is worthwhile has a rich, yet often ignored, history in American public education.

Why is it that such theoretical guidance over the century in curriculum history (Kliebard, 2004) and the history of public education in the United States we cannot find it in ourselves to leverage the insight, imaginations, and creativity of our students? Certainly one can easily look to John Dewey's (1897, 1916, 1938) detailed notions of involving learners in designing curricula and overall schooling experiences. Likewise, L. Thomas Hopkins (1954) questioning of what makes the curriculum, where he purports that classroom content was always developed by adults outside the classroom to (their own) unsatisfactory results, could be a starting point not only to rhetorically value student input in curriculum making, but also to embrace the possibilities. A rereading of Joseph Schwab's (1971) argument about curricular commonplaces could shed light on the value and necessity of students' interplay on teaching and learning. And, certainly looking to Freire's (1970) insistence on people's critical reading of their worlds could be paralleled to this plea for not only listening to students but also learning from, with, and alongside them as well.

Using the constructs from the rich history of curriculum studies outlined by the theorists noted above, it becomes evident that involving youth and tapping into their perspectives in teaching and learning has great potential for improving education and increasing young people's participation in school. Unfortunately, given current educational policy, top-down mandates, and prescriptive education, place to live," and that "even though the police know who done it, nothing will happen cause them boys must of already left out of town."

"Even though it ain't right, this is just what happens between kids in this neighborhood," Paris explained, but assured me that he was staying out of the trouble and laying low at his auntie's house far from where the incident occurred.

This incident was so removed from my experiences. I tried to relate to it, but really struggled. Out of awkwardness and not knowing what to say, I suggested that we review our article and organize our talk for the future school counselors.

My feelings of awkwardness did not subside with the change of topics. If anything they became more apparent, as I read aloud the introduction to our article and Noguera's book title—*The Trouble with Black Boys*... I looked to Paris for a reaction, quickly offering an explanation of who this "Noguera" person was and why I had decided to frame our piece in such a way. Wondering if I was off-base in how I conceptualized *our* co-written text, I explained (somewhat convincingly) to Paris why I thought this worked for the article.

The irony swirled about us—caught up with/in Noguera's book title and the news that Paris had just shared. After a short silence, I began reading further, and then interrupted myself to ask Paris: *Why do you want to write with me?* His response was quick and succinct.

"This is something that I like to do," he said. "I especially like student participation in curriculum development is seldom practiced or even seen as a possibility (Au, 2009; Schultz, 2008). Students typically have very little control over how they learn, what they learn, and are largely left out of discussions about what is considered to be worthwhile within teaching and learning (Schubert, 1997). This disregard for students' insights or perspectives regarding content taught and approaches to classroom dynamics are closely related to how many students are viewed in urban schools—merely as empty vessels for (someone else's) knowledge to be deposited (Freire, 1970). As Lipman (2003) and others argue, the structures associated with schools further this disconnect, and often as a result, either silence or push children—especially historically marginalized groups from urban areas—further away from the classroom (Au, 2009; Fine & Weis, 2003; Noguera, 2008). With the common belief that urban students are nothing more than deficits and pathologies (Ayers, 2004), and the (inaccurate) inclinations that the majority of this particular group of students does not value their learning, schooling reinforces the notions of cultural reproducetion (Apple, 1995). Challenging these beliefs are youth that have a stake in their learning and a tremendous will not only to think about, but also to act on the challenges of (inequitable) expectations they face in schools (Schultz, 2008b). Looking to students for insight about what it takes to motivate and engage them has tremendous possibilities in transforming our schools. It rejects commonly held assumptions about urban youth, while it also has the potential of leveraging students' insights in "constructing a rigorous, practical, culturally and socio-economically sensitive, just, and engaging urban education" (Kincheloe in Kincheloe & hayes, 2006, p. 3).

telling stories—you know getting people to think and all. You know I've got a lot to say. And, I don't get to do much in school."

I accepted Paris' answer, but wanted to continue the discussion. On one hand, what Paris articulated reflected not only Noguera's message about listening to students, but also connected with the curriculum theories about starting with the students that were highlighted in the remainder of the introductory section. Yet, on the other hand, I was hung up on my positionality and the ethical dilemmas of writing with a former student. Perhaps this act was not serving Paris' interests. I wanted to avoid what Cathy Coulter (2006) insightfully refers to as "the colonialist trap of co-opting the study, the story, and the outcome for my own personal gain" (para. 3). Our writing needed to be what Paris wanted and what he believed. In this collaborative writing project, Paris needed to "own the research process" (Denzin, 2005, p. 944) in order to resist the potential oppressive nature inherent to our (former and ongoing) teacher/student relationship and our differing social locations. Working through my own "ethical sensibilities" (Coulter, 2006, para. 9), I wanted to answer broad questions with Paris related to: Who was benefitting from our collaboration? Whose interests were served in and through our writing? Who was our co-writing ultimately accountable to? And, who had authority over the text (Bishop, 2005)?

Paris and I discussed these questions and others not to necessarily come up with answers or conclusions but to think through

This essay is an attempt to capture one student's perspective and insight about teaching and learning in the hopes that others can begin to learn from and listen to youth's perspectives about teaching and teacher education. In this article, a former classroom teacher and his student from five years earlier reflect on what is meaningful, striking, and pertinent about the student's learning experiences—then and now. Together, the co-authors are embracing the idea that students not only have perspectives about what good teaching is and what good teaching looks like, but also have the capacity to affect change for how both future and practicing educators perceive, connect, and engage with their students. Inherent to the insight and emergent storytelling should be a challenge to the common assumptions and stereotypes about city kids. Through this discussion, the authors believe they are beginning to heed Noguera's (2008) call to listen to students for help with solving the dire problems our urban schools face.

NARRATIVE INQUIRY AND PERSPECTIVES OF STUDENTING

The following narrative inquiry emerges as co-written text, storytelling, and reflection (Easter & Schultz, 2008). Although a singular essay is told through the narrative construction (Barone, 2007), the reflections are based on the two authors synthesis of ideas, telling, and "retelling and reliving of stories" (Clandinin, Pushor, & Orr, 2007, p. 33). Together the authors worked to keep the student's (second author) voice (and that of his peers) prominent and authentic, while also working to be accurate to language and form. For the purpose of this article, the accuracy referred to is meant to be reflective of the narrator's point of view, perspective, and language usage in an effort to capture the essence of his student voice as narrator, student, and teacher. His authentic voice, uncertainty and complexity. As I asked Paris about the coloniality of knowledge, querying him with questions like "is this something you said or I putting words in your mouth?" and "do you want to change how that sounds so it is more real—more you," it became clearer to both of us that I was not co-opting his ideas, but rather was working to *think and act with* him (Hoagland, in press). He made remarks like "I'm feelin' it," and "I'm diggin' working this paper together." I suspect, perhaps, beyond these sentiments, the collaboration and working together was of value to Paris in other ways, too. I think our collaboration filled a void he describes of his schooling and the ongoing relationship with me—a former teacher that has been consistent in his life for years—is something we both hold in high regard.

Maybe the complicated nature of collaboration—where each of us gets what we need depending on circumstances—is where this commentary and writing-story is headed? Yet, despite attempts to co-author postcolonial research and accomplish hermeneutic commentary, I cannot deny issues of power and authority in general or as they pertained to our specific work. As Richardson (1995) reminds us, when developing a writing-story, especially a co-authored one, the question of "who has the power to have their will prevail" (p. 200) becomes especially important. I have to recognize that based on language, style, and the mere fact that this re-reading is written in my first-person singular voice, that I am dominating the which isn't in conventional, standard written English captures more "truth" and wisdom because of his particular forms of expression that name ideas and concepts precisely.

The construction focuses on *studenting* (Fenstermacher, 1986; Gershon, 2008; Hughes & Wiggins, 2008; Schultz, Baricovich, & McSurley, in press). According to Hughes and Wiggins, studenting "involves a struggle to gain new and difficult concepts," with specific insight to "learning for the sake of learning," and where "an intrinsic motivation…to reaching one's highest potential are inherent and unquestioned" (p. 58). In the process of being and doing in school, studenting perspectives take on the analysis and introspection of teacher and student lore. Lore is a form of educational inquiry that is an interpretive, artistic practice both teachers and students engage in as they actively seek to learn from their own experiences in classrooms (Schubert, 1992; Schubert & Ayers, 1999). Constructing and analyzing lore affords readers an opportunity to gain insight through the "practical research and inquiry" that the students conducted "through daily practice" (Schubert, 1989, p. 282) within both formal schooling and informal learning experiences. Related to Connelly and Clandinin's (1988) ideas of "personal practical knowledge," the co-written text becomes the "nexus of the theoretical, the practical, the objective, and the subjective" (Clandinin, 1985, p. 361), helping to seek meaning about a particular phenomenon.

A multiplicity of data were used to inform the storytelling including: informal conversations in out-of-school learning contexts (Schubert, 1981); semi-structured, emergent interviews; dialogue between the authors; presentations scripts from the American Educational Research Association (2008) annual meeting and the Center for Civic Education (2004); as well as classroom dialogue drawn from a previous inquiry in which both authors were involved (Schultz, collaboration with/ from my (academic and privileged) perspective.

CO-CONSTRUCTION AND ETHICAL DILEMMAS

We had been fielding questions from the university class for some time. As I began to answer the next question, Paris gently interrupted, "I got this one." But, rather than simply answering the query, he posed a question back to the entire room. It was clear Paris was getting more comfortable explaining his perspectives about how classrooms could and should be in the course of participating in presentations to university-based groups such as this one.

Wondering aloud, Paris responded with a somewhat raised voice, "If you asking us 'bout that, what do you think about us writing or presenting together?" His reply echoed our earlier conversation at the diner concerning ethical dimensions of our collaborative work. Although I may have been more curious about it earlier especially in terms of co-opting his story, Paris showed his willingness and his interest in engaging in such a conversation.

Paris' approach was much different than mine would have been. The space, however, was his to respond as he wished. Our voices that night were in constant complement and contrast with one another; there were multiple perspectives at play within our answers to the provocative questions. Yet, it was clear to me, as Barone (2001) states,

> [Polyphonic] exchanges serve as constant reminders of *otherness* in speech, as they celebrate a diversity of voices

2008). We present the data in the form of a narrative split text (Blumenfeld-Jones & Barone, 1997; Lather & Smithies, 1997; Oyler, 2001; Schultz & Oyler, 2006). The stories, in italics and captured from primary documentation, are followed by co-written analysis in the form of speculative essay (Schubert, 1991). This joint analysis maintains the student's voice as prominent so as to keep language and form in as authentic a construction as possible, leveraging the words and thoughts of the second author while the first author assembled the text for presentation here.

"KEEPIN' IT REAL": AN INTRODUCTION

Teachers have got to make school exciting for students; they need to "keep it real" in the classroom. Keepin' it real means that school connects with the students. It also means that school is related to the students' lives. When school connects and relates to the kids, it reflects what is on the students' minds in every way. When this happens, kids want to be in school and are motivated by what happens in the classroom. Unfortunately, too often school is not the place that kids want to be because there is a big disconnect with what goes on in school with students' lives. It is no wonder that kids drop out, skip, or sleep through school. There are many reasons school does not seem right for city kids. Some of the reasons that kids check out of school is because of how their teachers approach what they are teaching, the content teachers actually teach their students, how teachers relate to the kids' parents and neighborhoods, and how they view the kids themselves. Based on my experiences, teachers can do things differently in their classrooms. There are ways teachers can make school a place that gets students excited or as we call it, "geeked up." Now

offering varied interpretations of phenomena (Bakhtin, 1975/1981). Often conflicting, the voices heard in the textual conversation may raise important questions about topics under discussion, challenging the reader to rethink the values that undergird certain social practices. (p. 157)

Looking back on this moment, Paris and I were co-constructing our verbal texts for the audience just as we had earlier in the article.

The heart of Paris' response or problem-posing back at the questioner is a part of that very important notion of our relationship of doing scholarly work together. Paris' response was complex. I suppose we were fortunate to have been engaging with a school counseling classroom as the adult students and their professor counterparts related our collaboration to ideas they had been studying—dual and multiple relationships between practitioners and clients. They encouraged us to think how our working with one another paralleled some of this conceptualization, especially in regard to the ethical dimensions of our shared inquiry.

In school counseling, "a dual or multiple relationship exists whenever a counselor has other connections to a client in addition or in succession to the counselor-client relationship" (Moleski & Kiselica, 2005, p. 3). Further, these kinds of relationships "occur when the professional tries to simultaneously fill two or more different roles.... [and] there are conflicts between the demands of the two roles" this is where you, the reader of my writing, probably ask, "How can a teacher create this sort of interest for students in school?" Well it is not something that is simple, but it starts with some things that are simple. Let me explain.

Problem-Posing, Letting the Kids Ask the Questions, and Just Doing Things

I was more than excited. I was on my first-ever airplane ride. Me and my old classmates headed to St. Louis with our old teacher to present to a bunch of adults about the last school year when my classroom fought for a new school building for our neighborhood. At the time I was in the sixth grade and at a different school, but the Center for Civic Education people wanted us to tell a whole slew of grown-ups about our experiences the year before in identifying a problem in our neighborhood of Cabrini Green and coming up with a solution. Before we got to St. Louis, believe it or not, I was just plain old excited, not nervous at all. I presented so many times about this stuff for over a year by then that I figured it would be the same old-same old...

What was nice about the trip was that it was not all planned out for us in advance by some old folks. We got to do the planning, just like we had done all the time the previous year. It really felt like a reward for all the work we were doing to help ourselves and it reminded me about all the activities we had done during our fight for a better school. This is important because we DID things during that year. We petitioned, surveyed, produced documentaries, and all sorts of other things during that year of school instead of just hearing about others doing it or reading about it in books....

After we got to explore the city and get some good eats, we headed to the big presentation. We got a proper-style intro by the head person from the Center for Civic Education while we were on center stage in

(Rupert & Holmes, 1997, p. 661). Although this topic is mostly unexplored between teachers and students (Blevins-Knabe, 1992), thinking through our split text narrative account of Paris engaged in critical storytelling (Barone, 2000) is an important exercise to think about concerning the ethical boundaries of doing such work. Citing the American Psychological Association's ethical principles, Blevins-Knabe (1992) provides areas to examine when engaged in an activity that might push ethical boundaries emphasizing: "conflict of interests, impaired objectivity, impaired professional judgment, and increased risk of exploitation" (p. 152). No doubt our collaborative efforts touch on all of these aspects; I wrestle with these issues in terms of what our ongoing relationship entails.

Yet, when pushed about these ethical dimensions, Paris gives short responses that indicate he does not see a problem. "Don't matter none," "I enjoy it so what's it matter," or "it's fun to talk about these things" are all common assertions. At the same time, it is clear to me that he is readily in touch with the fact that some might think it is problematic or questionable, especially in light of the above anecdote in the classroom where he demonstrated his desire to interrogate such spaces. This same contemplation is be exemplified when Paris told me that he "likes the way that our working together makes me think in different ways or think about things I am not used to thinking about."

front of over 600 people. Me and my old classmates dusted off some speeches about our fight for what was right and our push in the 'hood of trying to get a better place to learn. Even though I thought it was going to be the same old talk, it was different. I had never been in front of so many people—and all them adults seemed to be paying such close attention to us—with them beady eyes watching us closely. Good thing we had practiced with the technology and our speeches because we could've really messed it up. As we told them our story, we showed them some video documentaries, movies, a PowerPoint presentation and took them to our website...

While the last one of my classmates showed off that website, I stayed busy taking some notes. I knew that once we finished our bang-up presenting job there were going to be some important folk that wanted to question us all about our project. Not only did I need to be prepared, I had some things on my own mind that I figured I would ask the audience—only fair, right? As the MC got up to the microphone to thank us and start allowing all them questions, I shortstopped her and got her to listen to what I had in mind. I whispered in her ear and convinced her to let me take the mike before all them questions were fired at us from the audience. After she heard what I had to say, she did get back up to podium but I think her message was a little different. She said, "instead of having questions from the legislators and all of you, Paris would like to address you all again."

As I watched how this went down on the video of this presentation, I laughed at myself. I was all pimped out—pinstripes and fancy shoes—not sure I would ever dress that way again! I was a real shorty back then, too, barely able to see above the podium. I cleared my throat before I began speaking to the crowd again and said,

Paris' ideas resonate with what Ellis (2004) describes in discussing co-constructed narratives in that "relationships between people are jointly authored, incomplete, and historically situated. Connections hinge on contingencies of conversation and negotiation that often produce unexpected outcomes" (p. 71). I think these unexpected outcomes of our thinking together helps push us beyond "the ethical risk of the relationship" (Blevins-Knabe, 1992, p. 154) and help us to contemplate ethical risk questions related to learning, power, choice, objectivity, and consequences (Blevins-Knabe, 1992).

Given all of this contemplation in thinking through our approaches to collaboration, I am not sure where we are to go from here given our experimentation with voice in our writing (Creamer, 2005). The point is certainly not to arrive at a conclusion of any sort, but to muddle through our relationship(s) heeding attention to how Paris and I feel about the work that we are doing together. This collaboration can viewed as "text(s)...used... to decenter authority by acknowledging the co-constructed nature of most scientific inquiry, creativity, thought, or insight, regardless of the attribution in a list of authors" (Creamer, 2005, p. 531). At the same time, it is important to recognize that we may very well be pushing boundaries in our work together as former student and teacher. Some may be skeptical. But, together (although I acknowledge that I may be the initiator of such theorizing that Paris and I do together), we believe/think

"Before you ask us any questions, I have a few questions for all of you!"

The audience snickered and laughed at what I was saying. But, y'know I think that kids should be able to ask the questions that are important to them. So, I repeated the same thing again and then started to read off some of my notes that I took while my classmates were presenting minutes before. The audience responded with some props when I asked if they liked what we had done. But to be honest, I don't think that crowd understood what we was all about. As they continued their hoorahs and fast claps, I talked over them. This quieted them down real fast. I wanted them to get our point. I said,

"It is fine and good that y'all think we did good work, cause I agree, we did. Thank you. But, how you gonna help us? You know it costs a lot of money to get a new school, and kids can't go to schools like our bootleg, old one. I am not saying we want your money now, but when you leave out of here, I bet there are schools just like ours in y'all cities. What are you going to do to make a difference for them kids and them schools? You can't just think we did good, clap a lot—which I like by the way—and then not do something in your communities. Think about it."

-Paris Banks, Keynote Address, Center for Civic Education National Conference on Project Citizen, St. Louis, Missouri, 2004

First off, how teachers teach is real important. The best experiences I have had in school were when the classroom was based on doing activities. When I got to actually do things rather than just hear the teach talk about them, the learning was much more interesting to me. In classrooms where kids got to experiment, I was always involved. But, if I had to sit still, with my hands folded on my desk, and (supposedly) listen, that honoring and paying attention to a youth's perspective about teaching can have profound possibilities in not only thinking about collaboration, but also in their capacity to influence teaching and learning in schools.

COLLABORATING VIA COLLECTIVE MEMORY

Paris named several possibilities: "How 'bout the time we were all at O'Hare airport practicing our speeches;" "We could write about being on the street in NYC before we went live for the national radio show;" "Or, what do you say 'bout them long car rides in traffic?"

We were attempting to come up with a "perfect" story that would illustrate how our storytelling—the narratives that we constructed for the *Shorty* article—could be understood in context. As we brainstormed potential ideas, we also talked about complicated questions we thought others might wonder about: How was it that we recalled and remembered the same things? How could we present a unified voice when we were hyper aware that for every shared experience over the past five years, we responded and reflected in markedly different ways? It made us ponder other complex issues: Were we remembering the past correctly? Or, better yet, how were we helping each other in our remembering?

Through our brainstorming, we came to understand that our attempts provoked many ideas and recollections in and of themselves. We were, in fact, engaged in the process of building what the French sociologist, Maurice Halbwachs (1980),

I did not pay any attention to that teacher. This should be of no surprise to teachers, but some still need to hear it out loud because I have come to realize that most of my teachers talk at kids rather than with them. And, most don't listen to them neither. Everyone knows it is boring and makes you sleepy to have someone lecture to you for hours on end.

To build on this idea, I think one of the biggest problems is that so many teachers think that kids don't know what they are talking about and don't know anything. This is the farthest from reality. My friends and I know a lot, but almost all my teachers treat me as if I am an idiot. I know that many of my teachers judge me before I even have the chance to speak in the classroom. They draw conclusions by how I dress, or the friends that I hang out with in the halls—I can hear them muttering under their breaths that I must be some drug dealing, gangbanger. It amazes me about what they do not know. This is bogus 'cause I know I am smart but you would never know it from the way the teacher approaches learning or treats me in the classroom. This is one of the worst things about schools. It seems like most teachers are always jumping to conclusions about their students. And, when a teacher makes a mistake and the kids try and correct it, they don't want to hear about it.

Since I have been a little kid, I have wondered why school is like this. It seems that school is all about memorizing stuff rather than really trying to learn things. Just cause someone can recite something does not mean they know it—you know I can remember stuff, just ask me that same old question us kids always be hearing: How is it that you can learn all them hip hop lyrics but not learn my history facts or math equations?

My idea is to make the school all about the kids. Asking the students in your calls collective memory.

This idea generation was very similar to the way we had developed previous narratives together. We had helped each other think about prior events and detailed the perspectives about what we individually experienced. Even though we might have had differences in our viewpoints or disagreements about how something transpired, we shared specific thoughts about what had happened. In spite of such possible differences in perspective, we were able to "agree on the essentials that permit us to reconstruct a body of remembrances that we recognize" (Halbwachs, 1980, p. 22). As we further teased out various anecdotes, our "confidence in the accuracy of our impression increase[d]" since it could be "supported by others' remembrances" (p. 22). It was in the chronicling of our lore and looking to documentation of past events that we "conceive[d] their unity and peculiarity through a common image" (Assman, 1988, p. 127).

Rather than picking an "essential" story, we decided it was more appropriate to describe our dialogue—this very discussion—as it helps us to better understand our collaboration and, thus, may shed light on these collaborative ways for others. Our co-constructed stories, including this writing-story, were created because "a great many of our remembrances reappear because other persons recall them to us" (Halbwachs, 1980, p. 32). It is in these actions of sharing, of working and thinking together, that we find the potency in our collaboration. These co-created classroom what they think is important can make it fun for everyone. Let the kids do things. Let them make things. Let them build and even break things. Kids will pick challenging ideas and concepts if they are given opportunities because they know that they will never get better by just picking something easy. Kids got a lot of great ideas but it always feels like no one wants to hear about them. When kids get to choose what they want to learn about, they can be as creative as they can be. If they are focused on something that is important to them, they want to represent well. This means that not only will they put in a lot of effort, they will work hard at it make sure they understand it from all directions. They will make it look cool with technology and art because they know that it will help them in understanding what they are studying.

Bottom line: school is usually all about what the teacher wants to teach, or at least, what they are supposed to teach. But what if this little thing was different? Kids have lots of questions that are important to them, just like I was ready with questions after our presentation. What if teachers let the kids ask the questions in school instead of always being the ones asking the questions? What if they did activities that were relevant to the kids' lives instead of just reading or hearing about them? While I have been in schools for what seems like forever—actually shuffled around from various high schools and alternative schools recently—I have had some experiences particularly in elementary school where kids were asking questions that changed the way I think about learning and school.

Community, Parents, and Getting to Know the Students

Ann was straight up about kids and education and...demonstrat(ed) that classrooms do not have to be only in school but can be perspectives have power to affect others' views on who has the capacity to be a teacher and what we can learn from students (including our own). Through our narratives, we "transformed the text into a site where two separate approaches—styles, voices, personae—were co-existing" (Richardson, 1995, p. 199). We transcended boundaries of audience, approach, and method through our collaboration in interpretive inquiries.

REFERENCES

Assman, J. (1988). Collective memory and cultural identity. In J. Assman & T. Holscher (Eds.), *Kultur und gedachtnis* (pp. 9–19). Frankfurt: Suhrkamp.

Bakhtin, M. M. (1981). *The dialogic imagination: Four essays.* Austin, TX: University of Texas Press.

Barone, T. E. (2000). *Aesthetics, politics, and educational inquiry: Essays and examples.* New York: Peter Lang.

Barone, T. E. (2001). *Touching eternity.* New York: Teachers College Press.

Bishop, R. (2005). Freeing ourselves from neocolonial domination in research: A Kaupapa Māori approach to creating knowledge. In N. Denzin & Y. Lincoln (Eds.), *The Sage handbook of qualitative research* (3rd ed., pp. 109–138). Thousand Oaks, CA: SAGE.

Blevins-Knabe, B. (1992). The ethics of dual relationships in higher education. *Ethics & Behavior, 2*(3), 151–163.

Blumenfeld-Jones, D. S., & Barone, T. E. (1997). Interrupting the sign: The aesthetics of research texts. In J. A. Jipson & N. Paley (Eds.), *Daredevil research: Re-creating analytic practice* (pp. 83–107). New York: Peter Lang.

Coulter, C. (2006). *Whose story is it?: A retrospective study of ownership in narrative analysis.* Paper presented at the American Educational Research Association.

Creamer, E. G. (2005). Experimenting with voice and reflexivity in social science *part of the community just as the community should be part of them....*

Growing up in a place like Cabrini Green there weren't many people that cared about us kids other than family. The Greens, as we called our housing project, was a rough ghetto neighborhood where you really got to be careful in every part you go. When I met Ann, I came to realize that there were people outside in the world besides family that care about kids. She did not care about where we were from, how bad our neighborhood was, or anything else, she just cared about what we were doing to get a better place to learn. Our classroom ended up being not just our teacher and us, but we got other people involved. These other people, like Ann, gave us some wonderful ideas that we would never have thought of doing. For me this made school different than ever because people with fresh ideas and experiences showed them to us fifth graders. This made our subjects in school much more exciting because it was not just using books and dictionaries, but getting other people's thoughts. To further describe, Ann's involvement in our classroom showed me that there are different ways everyday folks can get involved in schools without even having to come to them.

-Tywon Easter, Journal of Curriculum & Pedagogy (Easter & Schultz, 2008, pp. 70–73); Interactive Symposium, American Educational Research Association Annual Meeting, 2008

Just like Tywon said how it is really important to get the community involved in urban classrooms and to get classrooms involved in the community, I am here to tell you about how important it is to get parents involved in the classrooms. Getting our parents involved in school is so important. My teacher used to call my house every week! At the time, I thought it was too much—Mr. Schultz is calling again—but he

texts. In C. Conrad & R. C. Serlin (Eds.), *The SAGE handbook for research in education: Engaging ideas and enriching inquiry* (pp. 529–541). Thousand Oaks, CA: SAGE.

Denzin, N. (2005) Emancipatory discourses and the ethics and politics of interpretation. In N. Denzin & Y. Lincoln (Eds.) *The Sage handbook of qualitative research* (3rd ed., pp. 933–958). Thousand Oaks, CA: SAGE.

Ellis, C. (2004). *The ethnographic I.* Walnut Creek, CA: AltaMira.

Halbwachs, M. (1950/1980). *The collective memory.* New York: Harper and Row.

Hoagland, S. L. (in press). Epistemic shifts: Feminist advocacy research and the coloniality of knowledge. In *Feminist epistemology and philosophy of science: Power in knowledge.* London: Springer.

Lather, P., & Smithies, C. (1997). *Troubling the angels: Women living with HIV/AIDS.* Boulder, CO: Westview Press.

Moleski, S. M., & Kiselica, M. S. (2005). Dual relationships: A continuum ranging from the desctructive to the therapeutic. *Journal of Counseling & Development, 83,* 3–11.

Noguera, P. (2008). *The trouble with black boys....and other reflections on race, equity, and the future of public education.* San Francisco: Jossey-Bass.

Oyler, C. (2001). Extending narrative inquiry. *Curriculum Inquiry, 31*(1), 77–88.

Richardson, L. (1995). Writing-stories: Co-authoring "The Sea Monster," a writing-story. *Qualitative Inquiry, 1*(2), 189–203.

Richardson, L. (2001). Getting personal: writing-stories. *Qualitative Studies in Education, 14*(1), 33–38.

Ricœur, P. (1981). What is text?: Explanation and understanding. In J. B. Thompson (Ed.), *Hermeneutics and the human sciences: Essays on language, action, and interpretation* (pp. 145–164). Paris: Cambridge University Press.

Rubert, P. A., & Holmes, D. L. (1997). Dual relationships in higher education: Professional and institutional guidelines. *Journal of Higher Education, 68*(6), 660–678.

was not calling to tell bad news and it was really a good thing.

I think most teachers only call kids mommas when their kids are in trouble. This is not good. If teachers call parents regularly and tell what is happening in the classroom the parents can support the teacher. They want to support the teacher. Parents should be involved all the time and in our case it was good because most of the parents really got involved in our cause. I think too many teachers think that city kids' parents don't care about their kids' education. This is just plain wrong.

My momma really cares about what I am learning, why I am learning it, and what she can do to support help me. Without my teacher inviting to get her involved she could not help out. An example of this was when my mom took off work to travel with us to present a conference out of town.... And now here in New York, is another one of our mommas...So the bottom line—make sure you find ways to get the parents involved. They do care! They can help!

-Kaprice Pruitt, Interactive Symposium, American Educational Research Association Annual Meeting. 2008

Schultz, B. D., & Oyler, C. (2006). We make this road as we walk together: sharing teacher authority in a social action curriculum project. *Curriculum Inquiry, 36*(4), 423–451.

Getting to know the kids in your classroom is extremely important. Really, it is all about respect and seeing the kids as having something to offer. In all the years that I have been in school, the teachers seemed never to care about learning what the kids are all about or what interests them. Teachers never understood my friends or me, they only talked to my parents when there was trouble, and they certainly did not want to come into my neighborhood. They even thought my parents were trouble! There are a lot of different ways that a teacher can do better by the kids in front of them.

If teachers got to know the kids' interests and learned about them, I think school could be a better a place. Most of my teachers really never knew me. Most don't have a clue and did not try to find out what was important to us kids. To them, I was just another Black face in the class. To them, we all blended together. No distinctions by attitude or behavior or smarts. This makes for a bad situation. A teacher ought to want to know about his or her students. Teachers and students need to have a connection, but this won't happen if they don't even try to know each other. Stated differently, if the teacher gets to learning about the students in their classrooms, they can make the kids want to be in school much easier. For instance, when I get to know my teacher and have a personal relationship with him or her, believe it or not, I actually want to be in school. Just check my attendance record; it shows clearly which teacher made that effort and which teachers did not. With a connection, I actually want to be around in school. Unfortunately, most of the time I really don't care to stay in school cause my teachers have no idea what I am all about.

I think part of it is that teachers see themselves as different than the kids in their classrooms. This is especially true in terms of the teachers working with the students' parents. It always seemed weird to me that the teachers might be the same age as the kids' parents. They don't want to build relationships with the parents. And, what I see almost every single day is that teachers are always putting it on the parents when some kid gives them a problem in they classroom. I just gotta ask all the teachers: What are you doing to make the parents feel welcome, like they can be a part of the conversation in the school or the classroom?

Learning about the neighborhoods that the kids come from is something that might help teachers in getting to know kids in their classrooms. So many of my teachers think that the kids are bad because they come from a bad neighborhood—or should I say, a supposedly bad neighborhood. Most of my teachers did not grow up in the ghetto. Not only that, most had never set foot in one before. For this reason, I think that teachers see themselves as different or even better than us kids. They think the ghetto is so terrible. They see it as dangerous. They are scared of it. All this makes some of them believe that us kids are terrible, dangerous, and scary. I am not saying everything is fine in the hood, cause its not, but there is distance between many teachers and me cause they see me as different. It just goes to show that most teachers no so little about what the projects and the kids in their classrooms from the projects are all about.

Teachers need to understand that because bad things are happening in a neighborhood does not mean that everything in that neighborhood is bad. To tell you the truth, everybody that is from the projects where I grew up in is like a big family. We all have each others' backs and really do care about each other a lot. My advice is that teachers should sometimes go into our hood with their students so they can begin to learn about us through our neighborhood. I am not saying that they should come in all the time, but if they even visited a little, they would get to see what our lives are really like—not just what the inner city is like on TV. If teachers got this kind of first hand experience, I think they would see us as people just like them, people that have to put up with a lot. From this sort of experience, they may begin to understand their students and the neighborhoods where they teach better.

To be honest, I believe that kids really can teach their teachers—a lot. My hope is that if you have gotten this far in reading what I have to say, is that maybe, just maybe, you will try some of the things I've been thinking about here. I bet school could be a better place for everyone—students, teachers, parents—if kids got to ask the questions; if kids got to have real life experiences in schools; if kids were not immediately looked down upon because of their skin color or how they dressed or what crew they hung with. I cannot encourage you enough to listen to the young folk in your classrooms. Let them ask questions. Go to their all communities. Spend some time with they parents. Not only will you learn something, maybe you will make that connection to them by letting them teach you. Maybe you could keep it real.

[1] This extended quote comes from the Perspectives section of an issue of *Journal of Curriculum & Pedagogy* (2008) titled: Collective Memory, Curriculum Studies, and a Scoffing Dragon: Celebrating the Life, Love, and Legacy of Ann Lynn Lopez Schubert. Tywon refers to the ongoing relationship he and his class had with the outside community and in particular, Ann Lopez Schubert during a previous school year.

REFERENCES

Apple, M. W. (1995). *Education and power*. New York: Routledge.

Au, W. (2009). *Unequal by design: High-stakes testing and the standardization of inequality*. New York: Routledge.

Blumenfeld-Jones, D. S., & Barone, T. E. (1997). Interrupting the sign: The aesthetics of research texts. In J. A. Jipson & N. Paley (Eds.), *Daredevil research: Re-creating analytic practice* (pp. 83–107). New York: Peter Lang.

Clandinin, D. J. (1985). Personal practical knowledge: A study of teachers' classroom images. *Curriculum Inquiry*, 15(4), 361–385.

Clandinin, D. J., Pushor, D., & Orr, A. M. (2007). Navigating sites for narrative inquiry. *Journal of Teacher Education*, 58(1), 21–35.

Connelly, F. M., & Clandinin, D. J. (1988). *Teachers as curriculum planners: Narratives of experience*. New York: Teachers College Press.

Dewey, J. (1897). My pedagogic creed. In L. Fiedler & J. Vinocur (Eds.), *The continuing debate: Essays on education*. New York: St. Martin's Press.

Dewey, J. (1916). *Democracy and education*. New York: Free Press.

Dewey, J. (1938). *Experience and education*. New York: Macmillan.

Easter, T., & Schultz, B. D. (2008). There are all sorts of possibilities—and take notes. *Journal of Curriculum and Pedagogy*, 5(1), 70–74. Note: First authorship is shared.

Fenstermacher, G. D. (1986). Philosophy of research on teaching. In M. O. Wittrock (Ed.), *Handbook of research on teaching* (3rd ed., pp. 37–49). New York: Macmillan.

Fine, M., & Weis, L. (2003). *Silenced voices and extraordinary conversations: Re-imagining schools*. New York: Teachers College Press.

Freire, P. (1970). *Pedagogy of the oppressed*. New York: Seabury.

Gershon, W. (2008). Intent and expression: Complexity, ethnography and lines of power in classrooms. *Journal of the Canadian Association for Curriculum Studies*, 6(1), 45–71.

Hopkins, L. T. (1954). *The emerging self in school and home*. New York: Harper and Brothers.

Hughes, S., & Wiggins, A. (2008) Learning to reframe academic inequity: Revisiting the "structuralist" vs. "culturalist" dichotomy in educational research. *The Sophist's Bane*, 4(1/2), 51–62.

Kincheloe, J. (2006). Introducing metropedagogy: Sorry, no short cuts in urban education. In J. Kincheloe & k. hayes (Eds.), *Metropedagogy: Power, justice and the urban classroom*. Rotterdam: Sense Publishers.

Kliebard, H. (2004). *The Struggle for the American Curriculum, 1893–1958* (3rd ed.). New York: Routledge.

Lather, P., & Smithies, C. (1997). *Troubling the angels: Women living with HIV/AIDS*. Boulder, CO: Westview Press.

Lipman, P. (2003). *High stakes education: Inequality, globalization, and urban school reform*. New York: Routledge Falmer.

Noguera, P. (2008). *The trouble with black boys....and other reflections on race, equity, and the future of public education*. San Francisco: Jossey-Bass.

Oyler, C. (2001). Extending narrative inquiry. *Curriculum Inquiry*, 31(1), 77–88.

Schubert, W. H. (1981). Knowledge about out-of-school curriculum. *Educational Forum*, 45(2), 185–199.

Schubert, W. H. (1989). On the practical value of practical inquiry for teachers and students. *Journal of Thought, 24*(1), 41–74.

Schubert, W. H., & Ayers, W. (Eds.). (1999). *Teacher lore: Learning from our own experience.* Troy, NY: Educator's International Press.

Schultz, B. D. (2008). *Spectacular things happen along the way: Lessons from an urban classroom.* New York: Teachers College Press.

Schultz, B. D. (2008). Challenging expectations: Counter-narrating an urban classroom. *Thresholds in Education, 34*(1/2), 13–25.

Schultz, B. D., & Oyler, C. (2006). We make this road as we walk together: Sharing teacher authority in a social action curriculum project. *Curriculum Inquiry, 36*(4), 423–451.

Schwab, J. J. (1971). The practical: Arts of eclectic. *School Review, 79*, 493–542.

ACKNOWLEDGEMENTS

Many thanks to Debra Freedman, Cathy Coulter, Jake Burdick, Jenny Sandlin, and Erin Mason for their insight and feedback on earlier drafts of this chapter.

PAM STEEVES, MARNI PEARCE, ANNE MURRAY ORR,
SHAUN M. MURPHY, MARILYN HUBER, JANICE HUBER
AND D. JEAN CLANDININ

3. WHAT WE KNOW FIRST

Interrupting the Institutional Narrative of Individualism

INTRODUCTION

When we were approached with the opportunity to write a chapter about our experiences of collaboration, a message was sent to the whole group asking about the possibilities for such a project. There was no talk of "lead author." The idea of leaders and followers is not part of our shared story of collaborative writing. It was only after we all agreed to the initial request that plans for imagining how this chapter might look began to take shape. Because each of us decided it mattered that we write this chapter, there was an understanding that together we would share the responsibility for the work. Our joint responsibility lies in the very nature of our overlapping lives, of our feelings of responsibility to, and with, one another. It is this responsibility that deepens our understanding of collaboration, of learning with and alongside one another.

As our chapter unfolds we write about how the overlapping of our lives was first shaped by an academic homeplace[4], a relational space, an educative space where we first came to know each other. Although this academic homeplace was the initial space that brought us together, it is the stories of relationship and responsibility we learned to live there that continue to hold us together.

We begin with a wordweb on the following page…

Beginnings in the Form of a Word Image

```
Lead author                  world travel                   filled with hope
                             draws me toward
    Fulfilling a role                    co-composing       counterstories
Write alone                  stories of collaboration                co-composing our
         Work       alone                                                    life
         spaces,           imagination                      deepens our understanding

         places
                          think out loud                             changing the world
On our own                                                  learning with, alongside
                          continued conversation                   one another
Ownership                             interrupted          in relation
                                                                        the only
No talk                                                                 way now
                            thinking about                              that
                            possibilities                               makes
Being responsible                    playfulness,                       sense
         independently               improvisation
                          unfolding                         share responsibility
Solitary                                      recursive
                                   reflexive                Change the taken for
Doing a job                        convergent                        grantedness
         fulfilling a role    layered                       necessary and healthy
         maintain    status                                           Sustaining place...
         quo                                  messy                   a   place
    dominant story         collectively weaving                       that
                                                                      keeps me
                                       making    my                   going
                                       life  visible,
                                       vulnerable
Covering over my stories,    attending to particular        narrative reverberations
    other's stories
         to fit dominant     tensions not                            able to see
         story               smoothed out or over                    more deeply

Erasure of others' voices
Stand at distance,           who i⁵ am becoming             our collaborative writing
                   judge     stretching    malleable        becomes us,
*one size fits all*                                                  continuing    to
singular right answer                                                become me
fixed in place               diverse places                 writing my way
                                 diverse people             into being
         Isolation           responding                     all of you shape me
Isolating                        alternative
                    Alone        perspectives               in relationship
                                                                     draw   courage
                                                            hopefulness

    Competition
Independently                                                        collaborative
owned                                                       writing - end point of
research                                                    collaborative living
                                                            deeply embedded
                                                                     relational roots
         Individual voice/signature
              hidden,                                       see big while positioned
              secreted from view                            in place(s) that typically
                                                                 sees small
```

Note: "who i⁵ am becoming" — the 5 is a footnote reference: who i[5] am becoming

As a way to visually and textually represent aspects of our collaborative research and writing, we chose to begin our chapter with the above word image. Following our agreement to write this chapter, in the busy-ness of September 2008, we engaged in a conference call connecting us in a cross-Canada conversation. During this conversation we decided to begin our chapter over the fall by composing a written conversation shaped by each of our memories and thoughts in relation with our collaborative book, *Composing Diverse Identities: Narrative Inquiries into the Interwoven Lives of Children and Teachers* (2006). As fall lengthened and, at least in some of our contexts, as snow arrived, our written conversation traveled via email across the country, from one coauthor to another coauthor and so on until we had each participated in the written conversation. In late November we engaged in a second conference call. At that time we collectively imagined composing word images from our written conversation, an interim research text process we had used in our book. In earlier and subsequent writing, composing interim research texts was a process we felt allowed us to show some of the ways ongoing negotiation shapes and reshapes our collaborative living as well as our collaborative writing.

The opening word image, a result of that work, can be read horizontally or vertically. Through our word image we attempt to show two differing, although not completely separated, institutional narratives. On the left side of the page we show an institutional narrative that is, still, in many institutions, dominant; it is a narrative composed around a plotline of individualism, a plotline that rewards single-authored publications even as we live on a landscape that calls for inter-disciplinary, collaborative research. The institutional narrative appears, for example, in tenure and promotion cases and scholarship applications, and is shown in our word image through words such as "ownership," "isolation," and "competition." On the right side of the page we show another possible institutional narrative inspired by resistance to the dominant narrative. This narrative is a counterstory[6] composed around a plotline of collaboration, a narrative intended to push back against the dominant narrative. The space in the middle of the right and left columns, a space between the dominant institutional narrative and a possible counterstory composed around a plotline of collaboration, is a space to imagine interruptions that seek to create change, that seek to shape spaces within institutions in which collaboration, relationships, responsibility and lives matter.

As we first talked about our word image, we each felt the middle space was a space where we wanted to spend time, to linger. This was a conscious, intentional choice shaped by an embodied story known well from years of trying to stay at the co-composition of remaking dominant institutional narratives composed around plotlines of individualism (Clandinin, Davies, Hogan, & Kennard, 1993; Hamre & Oyler, 2004; Hollingsworth, 1994). Lingering in this space, we talked and thought again about an idea that had emerged in our written conversation over the fall:

> ... our collaborative writing, particularly in our book, does not show our dialogues, in the Bakhtinian (1986) sense. We have covered over the dialogue in the sense that we have composed a text that speaks for us all. It is, at least for the moment when we wrote it, the text that we can each claim as speaking

for us, the us that co-composed it. What we make visible is not the improvisatory process that we co-create in the telling and retelling process of inquiry that lives in our writing but the representational result of our inquiry process. (Written Conversation, Fall 2008, p. 4)

Attending to this idea, that is, that in our collaborative writing we had not made visible the processes we had lived as coauthors, we realized a form for our chapter was gradually emerging. It was in this way, then, that we decided to compose three dialogues drawing upon the feelings, insights and ideas expressed in the middle space of our word image. The language in the middle space is the language of living, with terms such as "improvisation," "imagination," "messy," and "tensions not smoothed out or over." This is the language that resonated with our thinking about living and writing collaboratively.

In our three middle space dialogues, then, we do two things. Firstly, we start to move into the creation of interim texts, draft writing from which we move toward written chapters and papers. Inquiring into the field texts of our conference calls and written email conversations, we identified three threads that resonated through our collaborative writing. We tentatively titled the threads: relationship, improvisation and tensions, and liminal spaces. The interim texts are our way of ensuring there is coauthoring, authoring that allows for the multiplicity and fluidity of voices. Secondly, we find strength, possibilities, ways to move toward counterstories of co-composition of our written pieces, counterstories that move us away from the dominant work-alone institutional narrative in which there is a "lead author." This chapter then, like our book, comes out of dialogues about our research, our writing and our lives, over time and across places and spaces.

It is important to name these dialogues as *ours* because collaboration takes many forms and emerges from the relationships in which we live. It is significant that our collaborative relationship has been threaded through our lives and sustained over time. Within this larger relationship many of us write and research in smaller groups. However, one of the sustaining qualities of the smaller working groups is our life within the larger community. Dialogue creates educative spaces, middle spaces, and, for us, our earlier word image represents our understanding of these spaces even as it shapes a recursive movement that created further dialogue.

Our three dialogues may be considered fictionalized[7] because we co-composed them from our field texts. In constructing these research texts, then, we changed the order of the conversation, placed different pieces of text in new juxtapositions, assigned speakers' names and composed what we hope is a telling research text. Included in each dialogue is our theorizing about the writing as well as our memories of events and processes we lived during and through our writing.

We begin with the dialogue thread of writing as relational process.

DIALOGUE ONE: COLLABORATIVE WRITING AS RELATIONAL PROCESS

Pam: Our collaborative writing is the end point of collaborative living, a way of engaging in relational inquiry that shifts who we are as researchers in relation with others with whom we engage in research. We see this as a way of composing a counterstory of what matters in research, a counterstory threaded not around funding, publications and ownership, but around the possibility of creating educative spaces with teachers, parents, children, administrators and ourselves; spaces that support each of us to move forward with possibility, to imagine and live out what seems impossible on our own but becomes possible within these relational spaces.

Jan: I think we all appreciate the notion of creating educative spaces with people whom we are in collaborative relationships. I think we learned to think and live in this way as we gathered at the Tuesday Research Issues Table in the Centre for Research for Teacher Education and Development at the University of Alberta. As each of us came to know what it felt like to be really listened to in a safe gathering place, we learned to turn toward, and attend to, one another with our whole lives. As we learned to engage in this way with others, and had others engage with us in this way, we began to see that collaborative work, including collaborative writing, is about ourselves and how we each live in the world as well as about how we can live alongside others. Working with, not against, one another was what we came to know first in this place.

Pam: You remind me that these relationships, these spaces in which we learn with each other, are educative spaces. Giving voice to our own thoughts, stories and ideas and having them given back by others creates spaces of imagination and possibility. Such dialogic relationships (Buber, 1947) give each of us multiple possible ways to think about our lives and writing, illuminating resonance, gaps and contradictions between our own and others' ideas.

Anne: Listening to you talk, I remember a moment I was working for most of a day with Shaun on one chapter of the book while we were both at the American Educational Research Association (AERA) conference in Montreal. We took turns doing the typing on the laptop perched on a tiny table in a hotel room as we tried to make our ideas somewhat coherent. I felt I was able to see more deeply into the meaning we were trying to make clear because of the conversation that threaded through the day punctuating the silences as one of us typed, the small disagreements and the flashes of insight, the attempts to say out loud what seemed so clear in our minds, the laughter, the negotiating and re-negotiating of language when this proved not so easy. This memory represents for me a number of such moments when I realized the power of the process of writing together, of that dialogue we cover over, as Jean so often says, in our representations.

Marni: As our imaginations are ignited in relationship we feel a sense of playfulness. And it's a responsive kind of playfulness growing naturally out of deeply embedded relational roots. As we make our work together, the possibilities expand. We come to see what's not yet there, to come to live what's not yet dreamed about ~ to imagine the impossible. And that is so much of what becomes possible if we learn to really listen to the other and to give back the other's stories with added possibility. There is a kind of courage to imagine the impossible in that. And there is also so much respect.

Jean: Who would have imagined a seven-author book? We imagined it up together. There was no recipe, except the care and respect for the narrative authority, as Margaret Olson (1995) reminds us, of one another. There was no agenda to follow but rather protocols, ways of living alongside, to draw from. This idea of protocols has also become very powerful through the work of Mary Young (2005) who has helped us so much to think about what it means to live protocols that reverberate backward and forward across intergenerational cultural narratives.

Maril: We have the privilege of sharing stories that shaped our lives in relation to, and with, one another and our becoming as narrative inquirers. Many layers of relationships lived over different times and places, with different people and events in different relationships, shaped *Composing Diverse Identities*. These multiple layers help us see that relationship is central in collaborative writing, in composing identities and in understanding what is happening when teachers, children and their families negotiate a curriculum of lives.

Shaun: The idea of a seven-author book came out of those shared imaginings and a program of research that had become a shared program of research. It had become a collaborative program of research and we all named ourselves as part of it. The research projects that were shaped by, and shaped, the eventual collaborative writing had begun years before in the works of John Dewey, Joseph Schwab, Michael Connelly and others. The projects emerged and were shaped by those people who came to work in the various projects as they engaged in their masters, doctoral and post-doctoral work in the contexts of the larger projects. All of us, in one way or another, did our doctoral work in the context of the larger research projects.

Jean: The two unique projects that were the central projects in *Composing Diverse Identities*, and the people who worked on those projects, were vital to the imagining up of a book. I remember how we gathered around phones in different places early on as we began to believe a book was possible. I think we tape recorded the conversations so that we could remember how in our improvised planning we came up with what seemed like a possible table of contents.

Pam: As I think about those tape recorded telephone calls, my mind slips forward to remember how we moved from those calls to our beginning time at Jean's house in Whistler when we began to actually write drafts of the chapters of the book. Winding our way up the Sea to Sky highway it was castles in the clouds, laughter and catching up as we squashed together on slippery seats in the trusty oversized van. Driving from Vancouver to Whistler there was such an air of anticipation of what was possible.

Jean: But I remember some anxiety, some nervousness too. Could we really do this together?

Jan: Remember how each day started? After coming together over coffee each morning we began to disperse in groups of two and three, with transcripts, books, papers and laptops in hand. We were spread out over bedrooms, living and eating areas and some of us even opted for the sunny back deck with a mountain view. It was a familiar feeling of being together to talk through our ideas aloud, a bit like story response groups nurtured in our experiences of becoming teacher educators and researchers in curriculum classes or shared writing spaces in our interconnected office spaces at the Centre.

Anne: Oh yes, and then in the afternoons, we sat on the living room carpet, or perched on and among the furniture to create a circle place where everyone could see one another while we shared the morning writing and listened to one another's responses. It seemed natural to create a coming together space, like gathering together at the Research Issues Table on Tuesdays at the Centre. The Centre table experience lives in all of us as the heart of our academic knowing in relationship. As well we'd experienced Works in Progress groups on an ad hoc basis to energize our work. The felt memories of these spaces were something to latch onto and ground us as we improvised ways to move forward with the writing of the book.

Shaun: Yes and after we were back in our own homes spread across the county, the memories we created at Whistler were powerful in helping to sustain us as we continued the writing of chapters over email. Often one of us would mention a moment from Whistler and add it to the email greeting accompanying the chapter—moments like, "Remember Mary's full moon above the forest at the pizza restaurant on the last night?"

Maril: I remember, too, how we sometimes also shared fears about not being quite adequate to send along the chapter to the next one of us through thoughts like, "I'm thinking it's not finished yet but here it is...." Shared memories and feelings helped keep us connected and safe in relationship as we wrote the chapters week by week from our various home places.

Marni: As we reflect on what it means for us to write collaboratively, we recognize it is through our working collaboratively that we are able to move together, traveling to other worlds, to see with our hearts, those things we had not seen before. Yet, we have so often felt the lack of a language and way of showing this process. We want to say so much more. Trying to shine a light on the co-composing processes we've been part of, to begin to try to find a language as we are doing here as one possible way to offer a counterstory to the work-alone spaces, seems to me to be one of the most hopeful projects in which we could engage.

DIALOGUE TWO: IMPROVISING WAYS OF WRITING TOGETHER

Jan: What happens when people are able to get together, to be together across time and space? Relationships invite improvisation. In collaboration the quality of improvisation becomes nested; it is dialogic and responsible, simultaneously shaped by, and attentive to, the hearts and imagination, the stories to live by, of all of us. There is a particular quality of daring to think outside the boundaries, and a hopefulness that arises from this willingness to improvise, that makes collaborative writing an experience unlike any other.

Jean: Yes, and I see the messiness and improvisatory ways of narrative inquiry growing naturally out of deeply embedded relational roots. Thinking about the writing of our book and some of the other ways we have collaborated in re-imagining teacher education, works in progress, and writing articles, I see how we imagine ways to work together that are responsive to our lives even as we are situated in storied landscapes concerned with maintaining status quo, managing down expectations or striving for, and rewarding, singular right answers.

Pam: We make things up, we engage in a sort of wondering out loud ... until things begin to make sense. I know how much I figure out when I talk. I just need to say things out loud and get some response to figure things out. There is no one way but a sense of something unfolding, something that begins with an appreciation of hearts, laughter, tears and "author"ity of other(s) in our midst. In making sense together we expand the possibilities, imagine the impossible. And, picking up on Jan's point, then we dare to believe.

Shaun: I agree, Pam, that improvisation has the most potential when it is situated in relationship. We expand the space of our knowing the possible and the impossible. However, it can be risky to improvise, to adventure alone. It is the trusting relationship in collaboration that keeps us safe yet allows us to be daring...to try out, to join in, to go on. When I did improvisation work with a theatre group it had a rhythm to it when we all trusted each other and could count on the other people to understand and play along with the themes we were exploring. I have the same kind of sense about us and the writing of the book. I trust all of you, I trust you with our book, my ideas, and mostly I trust you with me. That was big during the writing, knowing that I had a safe community in which to work. That did not mean I didn't feel anxiety on Sunday nights when I sent the latest chapter I had worked on to the next person, but knowing my thinking would be part of the work allowed me the courage to press the "send" icon. The relationships in the group also gave me an opportunity to play with ideas and to move within the ideas of everyone else. I do not think I could have done this if we had set a rigid structure.

Maril: When you talk about the possibilities, this makes me think about what collaborative writing enables us to inquire into. As we compose our lives in the telling and writing of our stories, what happens when we compose our lives in the collaborative relational telling and writing of our stories? What are the dangers and possibilities of erasing our own stories in order to fit into others' stories? In silencing ourselves? What are the dangers of speaking over another's stories, what might be seen by the cynical as an erasure of others' voices? As I reflect on our collaborative writing, I think more about how writing together has opened up more possibilities, more ways that I might live my life through laying my stories alongside others' stories, making my life visible and vulnerable and open to others' inquiries and responses and, through that process, allowing me to recompose my stories and my life possibilities. There is education and growth for both who I am becoming and who we are becoming. If my writing becomes me, then our collaborative writing becomes us, becomes our retold and relived stories, through this improvisatory process.

Marni: I think what you are saying is important, Maril, for you are making me think of our collaborative book writing as a life writing process. You are helping me see this connection so much more clearly here.

Anne: I know that having been able to live alongside each of you during my doctoral student years, through the writing of the book, and in a variety of ways since then, has been a gift, one that shapes the ways I try to live as a narrative inquirer. One example of how I have been deeply influenced by the improvisatory nature of narrative inquiry happened in my second year of doctoral studies. I was living in Edmonton with my then 9-year-old daughter, Erin. I had childcare problems one Tuesday and brought Erin to the research issues table. I did not want to miss the conversation because I had been at school the day before and had some things I hoped to bring to the table that day. I worried that others might be annoyed that I had brought her along. Instead, Erin was invited to sit at the table, right next to Mary, to take a turn to talk, and to be a valued part of the conversation. Mary gave Erin a little stone with a turtle on it. I remember how that research issues gathering made me feel, how Erin talked about it long afterward, and I think about how it illustrates for me what Jean says about "the messiness and improvisatory ways of narrative inquiry growing naturally out of deeply embedded relational roots." Maybe it is harder to have a multi-generational research issues conversation happening, but it is this willingness to be improvisatory and relational that makes narrative inquiry what it is.

Jan: Yes, and with this kind of experience, this willingness to improvise our way, we improvised the living and writing of our seven-author book. We did not know ahead of time how so many of us would work together on the book; each new stage of writing brought new challenges for us to figure out. But we each believed that working together it could be done. We did not turn back when the way was not clear. As Bateson (1994) reminds us, people "are strengthened to meet uncertainty if they can claim a history of improvisation and a habit of reflection" (p. 6). Our shared knowing of narrative inquiry as emergent and ongoing gave us the confidence to carry on. It's like Maril says, improvisation, opens up possibilities by creating a space where we attend to the stories we tell alongside each other and co-compose in that space. It makes me think of the afternoon times at Jean's house in Whistler, when we shared our work for the day and our response and ideas shaped the work of the next day. I remember when we were leaving Whistler how uncertain I was about how we could continue to write collaboratively when we were not all together in one place. I cannot quite remember who suggested that we work on a chapter for two weeks and then on Sunday night we would send the chapter to the next person on the list. I remember we decided not to do track changes but only to continue to add, edit, and revise before we sent it off. And then, of course, as soon as you sent it off you could count on a little ding and know that "you've got mail" as the next chapter arrived in your in-box.

Marni: I do remember that little ding! I also remember how, after we had worked on the first eight chapters in Whistler and over email, we had the opportunity to gather together at a conference in Victoria. Even now, all this time later, I recall how good it felt being there but also how intensely we worked— sometimes talking until late into the night. I also remember that we each read the eight chapters before we arrived and that even though Jan could not be with us as she was welcoming her new daughter, Ellee, at that time she still sent heaps of response to each chapter. As we sat on the bed and talked about our responses to each chapter, someone would say, "What did Jan write about it?" Each time someone read her words it invoked her presence in the room. As we read and talked and talked and read I recall our making plans for how we were going to continue to work on those first eight chapters.

Maril: I think about how we discussed the last chapter and how it would contribute to shaping the book. We talked about whether the focus would be teacher education, curriculum or policy. Our conversation still stays with me—I had some real "aha" moments.

Shaun: Those face-to-face moments in Victoria were important, not only for the writing, but for the living. So much of the writing had been online, the every-two-week work with one of the chapters and the various telephone conversations, that the chance to reconnect in person was important for me. It was good to see everyone who was there and to have Jan's voice present with us and to be together to figure out the next step in this improvisatory process. We left the hotel room with more to do and ideas for the final chapter. I remember feeling we were ready to move forward.

DIALOGUE THREE: TENSIONS AND LIMINAL SPACES

Maril: As you said earlier, Jean, as we engaged in our collaborative writing we relied on protocols and relationships we learned to live with each other through years of gathering at the Centre table. When we were writing our book we had also all written, or were writing, dissertations, dissertations that centred on wonders about the experiences of children and teachers as their lives intersected on the complex storied landscape of schools. In this way we each had skills as researchers, as narrative inquirers. While some of us were more confident about naming our knowing as narrative inquirers, because of the protocols nurtured at the Centre table, and gradually within each of us, we each knew the value of respecting our own and others' differing ways of knowing.

Marni: Yet, even as we embodied our knowing in this imagined book writing, we didn't know how to coauthor with six other people. No one of us had previously engaged in such multi-layered collaborative writing. So while it was exciting to be stepping into this new territory, this liminal space, to coauthor a book among seven people, it was a somewhat unknown experience. Especially in the beginning, but also throughout the process, the layers of our collaborative writing often felt daunting.

Shaun: This is where the relational nature of our work was, again, so important. Our relationships, created and re-created as they have been across multiple landscapes, many years and numerous life changes shaped a grounding that supported our living, thinking, inquiring, imagining with one another. By the time we came to our collaborative writing, we knew multiple stories of the lives we had each composed as teachers, stories we had gradually learned to inquire into at the Centre table and through doctoral study. Learning to inquire into our stories was significant because it was through inquiry that our sense of our own vulnerabilities and uncertainties were nurtured. As we increasingly came to understand in a deep lived way what Maxine Greene (1995) and Janet Miller (1998) say about no person or idea ever being fixed or finished, we also continued to work to shape openings that allowed us to inquire into, to self-face, the tension-filled experiences we had lived as teachers.

Anne: I'm smiling because I'm just remembering so much. I think that by the time we were coauthoring the book, tension and staying with tension were accepted by all of us as a central part of our work as narrative inquirers. We knew, for example, that tensions may arise in relation with the particular focus of our research, tensions may arise within relationships between co-researchers and ourselves or tensions may arise in relation with ideas emerging from within the inquiry that demand attention to the importance of our relationships.

Pam: We all entered into our collaborative writing then, expecting to learn, to be stretched, to be changed, through the process. I think we recognized, in some moments with more ease or comfort than in other moments, that there were always alternative ways to understand a situation in a field note or the lives of children, families, teachers, administrators or ourselves as we lived alongside each other in classrooms, schools and, in some cases, in the children's and families' homes or community spaces.

Jean: Hmmm. I wonder though, if you recall that, as we began to write, at first we did not openly discuss the possibilities of tension emerging in our collaborative writing. It seemed as if we were all trying to think about noticing, naming and inquiring into tensions in our inquiries with teachers, families and children as co-researchers. We seemed to expect tensions in those relationships somehow and were not overly surprised when they did emerge.

Jan: We were, perhaps, not quite as ready to name the tensions in our living of our collaborative writing. I remember that sometimes tensions emerged as one of us tried to describe experiences we had lived alongside a child, family member, teacher or administrator and others seemed unable to grasp the meanings expressed or felt that the experience described showed something else.

Jean: This seemed to be more common as our chapter drafts circulated to each of us over email but similar tensions emerged at times when we were in conversation, gathered together as a whole group, or in conference calls. Sometimes, too, I remember how we questioned one another about how we positioned ourselves in relation with co-researchers.

Pam: It seemed that, in time, as we continuously negotiated and re-negotiated our collaborative writing, we were gradually awakening to how we were working within, and actually composing, liminal spaces.

Jean: I think I began to have a sense of how we were composing liminal spaces for ourselves, Pam, but I had not really named it. I remember thinking at one point how difficult it is to live in those liminal spaces that Heilbrun (1999) has written about.

Maril: Yes, Jean. Heilbrun was important in our thinking. She reminds us liminal comes from the root limen, or doorway. While she described these spaces as uncertain, ambiguous and never completely comfortable, she also highlighted the capacity they hold for imagining alternatives that break with dominant narratives. I think our histories, as we have been positioned on and off school and university landscapes, have shown us that while it is rare to find or create spaces to name and to try to understand tensions, it is equally as rare to find or create spaces for entering into and dwelling within liminality.

Anne: And Heilbrun (1999) wrote that liminal spaces are not "designed for permanent occupation" (pp. 101–102) but she also explored their need if we are to understand in new ways, if we are to live in new ways.

Shaun: Um, hum. And, I think that as we began to see that we were, through attending to and inquiring into tensions, creating liminal spaces, it seemed that we gradually became more willing to inquire into liminality. I think part of our wakefulness to creating, inhabiting and inquiring into liminal spaces was shaped through our evolving understandings of our need to pay close and particular attention to tensions. Living tensions sometimes creates liminal spaces, liminal spaces defined by ideas and wonders, spaces in relation to the worlds in which we travel.

Marni: I think we saw in new ways the importance of relationships where we could inquire into, and not smooth out or over, tensions. And, increasingly, we saw our responsibilities with participants and one another, to value, to inquire into tensions and liminality and liminal spaces shaped by living within, and inquiring into, tensions. And, of course, this all came to, and shaped, our book writing. We were, as Maril pointed out, collaboratively authoring our lives and our book. And so we were all learning to inquire into those tensions.

Jan: Yes, I remember how we frequently noted the centrality of our relationships as we negotiated and inquired into tensions and liminality. And, yet, our relationships could not and did not stay static or unchanged as we lived through these processes. They, too, were transformed, as were each one of us. So, too, was our trust in one another and in liminality transformed.

Jean: We realized that we needed to care and respect each other enough to say our tensions, our differing thoughts and perspectives. We saw, too, that in our beginnings as narrative inquirers we had sometimes believed in the ease of just keeping quiet when we felt tensions or understood something differently from those around us. In this group our hearts did, and sometimes still do, pound when we are about to express a tension or differing opinion but we have grown to know that at least some one, if not more than one of us, as friends, colleagues and coauthors, will hear our tensions and respond.

Marni: And we learned that it was not very respectful of each other if we silenced our own tensions and tried to smooth over the bumping moments when they became visible in the writing.

Pam: Of course there were times when we became pragmatic, dwelling less within inquiry into tensions and liminality. I remember as the week at Whistler was drawing to a close, we felt more pressure to just get something into place for each chapter. We felt the pressure to have something on the page, something that was at least a start, for we knew how difficult it would be to leave with only liminality.

Anne: And so that last day, don't you think it seemed as if we all pushed just a bit harder? I remember we were going out to supper and the hour we were leaving kept being pushed back as we rushed to get ideas down. Were we fearful that when we were not together we would not be able to find words or ideas or stories to hold the writing together? Was it that we had learned to welcome the improvisation that was needed to help us compose stories that would help us enter and live for a time within those liminal spaces?

Shaun: Throughout our time in Whistler, and the writing that followed, we learned to live through moments of thinking out loud, of writing and thinking and talking alongside one another, people who have, and continue, to support one another to *write our way into being* ... even when we hesitate, our bodies call us to remember that it is in these places of hesitation, places that cause us tensions, where we have the most to learn.

WHAT WE ARE CONTINUING TO COME TO KNOW: REVERBERATING NARRATIVES OF COLLABORATION

Looking backward and forward, we find ourselves returning to the word image that opened our chapter. As earlier described, our dialogues in the previous section were shaped as we lingered in the middle space of our word image. We now move toward the right-hand column of our word image, a space showing something of our experiences and thinking in relation with the importance of staying at the work of co-composing stories that counter dominant institutional narratives with plotlines of individualism.

As mentioned already, we first came to recognize and name the power of counterstories through the work of Hilde Lindemann Nelson (1995). She wrote that counterstories are shaped "to resist the authoritarian notion of the 'sure interpreter'" (p. 38) and cautions that:

> A counterstory that merely inverts existing orders of dominance and submission, seeking to overthrow a reigning interpreter only to put another in his [or her] place, is not as good as a counterstory that forbears. And as a most pernicious consequence of authoritarianism is to flatten out or exaggerate differences among people and so to marginalize them, a counterstory that understand, celebrates, and sometimes argues with those differences is a morally better—as well as a more accurate—story than one that does not. (p. 38)

As we showed in our word image, staying at the hard work of co-composing counterstories is not easy work, nor can counterstories be composed alone. Counterstories are composed in relation in what Nelson (1995) calls "communities of choice." Counterstories that, as Nelson says, "forbear," are composed in relation, in relationships seeking to find hope in the midst of dominant narratives looking to keep people in place, dominated by, and submissive to, paths well worn or laid down, to narratives often taken for granted within institutions. Across our individual and collective multiplicity, including our living out of stories as teachers, researchers, sons, administrators, mothers, community advocates, sisters, teacher educators, daughters, and so on, we have felt, and at times lived, the miseducative reverberations of sure interpreters. For many of us, as we first came to the Centre, these experiences sometimes kept us quiet and watchful, not quite sure, and sometimes fearful to speak, sometimes distrustful of entering into relationships.

Yet, as we learned, narrative inquiry requires relationships, relationships with the people with whom we engage in inquiry, and relationships within a broader response community. The Tuesday Research Issues table offered, and shaped, these kinds of relationships, relationships in which we, and others who have gathered and continue to gather, learned new narratives of shared responsibility for, and with, one another. Part of this responsibility meant valuing difference, meant trying to understand the spaces, the new possibilities shaped in the meeting of our and others' difference. As we learned to tentatively story and restory our experiences and our lives, in and outside of schools, in and outside of research relationships, around this table, trust, relationships and responsibility grew. So, too, did our vulnerability, and our humility. What we might, at first, not have imagined saying or sharing, soon became necessary to say, to inquire into. Ever so gradually in this process, nascent counterstories began to be shaped, counterstories filled with our longings to change the institutions we had experienced or were currently experiencing. And as authors of, and participants in, these nascent counterstories we, as tellers and livers of counterstories, have continued to compose counterstories that forbear. These counterstories continue to forbear as we stay at finding relational ways to resist comments made by sure interpreters we met during our graduate experiences who warned us against, or shamed us, for staying with collaborative work, for staying with our desires for living more relationally with participants. These counterstories continue to forbear as we now find ourselves living in differing contexts and engaged in differing kinds of work across Canada, still focused on collaboration, on relationships.

When we find ourselves asking, as often happens when we seven have opportunities to reconnect, if our nascent counterstories of collaboration will ever completely undo the dominant narrative of individualism, we are reminded that much has happened in our lives, in our teaching, in our research, in our community work, in our parenting and so on because we keep seeking collaborative, relational ways to compose our narratives of experience. It is our relational knowing, what we came to know first[8] as graduate students in our academic homeplace that stays with us. And we stay hopeful as we, in differing contexts and ways, stay at this work, with new generations of teachers, with new generations of young people in schools, with new generations of graduate students and so on. It is our shared knowing and these reverberations that sustain us, that leave us hopeful about the future of collaboration in the institutions where we live and work and in the communities and families in which we live.

REFERENCES

Bakhtin, M. M. (1986). *Speech genres and other late essays* (V. W. McGee, Trans.). Austin, TX: University of Texas Press.
Bateson, M. C. (1994) *Peripheral visions: Learning along the way.* New York: Harper Collins.
Buber, M. (1947). *Between man and man* (R. G. Smith, Trans.). London: Collins.

Clandinin, D. J., Huber, J., Huber, M., Murphy, M. S., Murray Orr, A., Pearce, M., & Steeves, P. (2006). *Composing diverse identities: Narrative inquiries into the interwoven lives of children and teachers.* Toronto: Routledge.

Clandinin, D. J., Davies, A., Hogan, P., & Kennard, B. (1993). *Learning to teach, teaching to learn: Stories of collaboration in teacher education.* New York: Teachers College Press.

Greene, M. (1995). *Releasing the imagination: Essays on education, the arts, and social change.* San Francisco: Jossey-Bass Inc.

Hamre, B., & Oyler, C. (2004). Preparing teachers for inclusive classrooms: Learning from a collaborative inquiry group. *Journal of Teacher Education, 55*(2), 154–163.

Heilbrun, C. G. (1999). *Women's lives: The view from the threshold.* Toronto: University of Toronto Press.

Hollingsworth, S. (1994). *Teacher research and urban literacy education: Lessons and conversations in a feminist key.* New York: Teachers College Press.

Huber, J. in relation with Keats Whelan, K. (2000). *Stories within and between selves: Identities in relation on the professional knowledge landscape.* Paper-formatted Dissertation, University of Alberta, Edmonton, AB.

Lindemann Nelson, H. (1995). Resistance and insubordination. *Hypatia, 10*(2), 23–40.

MacLachlan, P. (1995). *What you know first.* Joanna Cotler Books. Harper Collins.

Miller, J. L. (1998). Autobiography and the necessary incompleteness of teachers' stories. In W. Ayers & J. L. Miller (Eds.), *A light in dark times: Maxine Greene and the unfinished conversation.* New York: Teachers College Press.

Murphy, M. S. (2004). *Understanding children's knowledge: A narrative inquiry into school experiences.* Unpublished Dissertation, University of Alberta, Edmonton, AB.

Olson, M. (1995). Conceptualizing narrative authority: Implications for teacher education. *Teaching and Teacher Education, 11*(2), 119–135.

Trinh, T. Minh-Ha. (1989). *Woman, native, other: Writing postcoloniality and feminism.* Bloomington, IN: Indiana University Press.

Young, M. (2005). *Pimatisiwin walking in a good way: A narrative inquiry into language as identity.* winnipeg: pemmican publications inc.

AMOABA GOODEN AND DENISE GASTALDO

4. PARTNERSHIPS FOR PARTICIPATORY ACTION RESEARCH

The Case of Recent Immigrant Women in Toronto, Canada

INTRODUCTION

This chapter examines how to apply the principles of Participatory Action Research (PAR) from the vantage point of immigrant women's perspectives—a methodology that, if applied critically, can have implications for promoting social change within a particular socio-political space. We begin with a description by two immigrant women who are also academic researchers on how immigrant women in Toronto, Canada, collaborated with researchers from academic and practice settings on the project, *Revisiting Personal is Political: Immigrant Women's Health Promotion Project (RPP)*. The chapter then details how RPP members used collaborative principles embedded in PAR to ensure a high level of participation and leadership by the community partners and participants involved in this project researching health promotion among immigrant women.

The need to give varying voice to the experiences of immigrant women who have participated in health studies before but, unlike the women described here, had not often been in a primary collaborative position was important for both academic and community collaborators in this study. Furthermore, as immigrant women and women of color working within our communities, we wanted to use an approach that reflected our social and political values of inclusion and socially-relevant knowledge production rather than other methodologies that tend to reify hierarchies and divisions between those who think, those who do, and those who live the problem. As such, there was the recognition that the principles of PAR and health promotion share theoretical foundations; empowerment is the goal of both as they are each essentially collective processes designed to increase one's control of living circumstances (Freire, 1992). PAR was also used because we recognized that enablement happens when people change and that, epistemologically, the search for real social change reveals a privileged opportunity to understand the social and economic forces that reproduce the existing *status quo* (Freire). Ultimately what we wanted was a methodology that would acknowledge our positionality as well as privilege the experiences of immigrant women by putting them at the center of the research and treating them as experts on migration and women's issues.

As immigrant women and/or women of color ourselves, we used our positionality as a point of departure to search for the political in everyday life. We recognized that our understanding of health and well being within the Canadian context

W.S. Gershon (ed.), The Collaborative Turn: Working Together in Qualitative Research, 71–87.
© *2009 Sense Publishers. All rights reserved.*

allowed us to acknowledge that new and current policies and programs that hoped to tackle health, employment, family welfare as well as other sectors that also directly address the economic, social and political realities faced by recent immigrant women (Health Canada, 1997).

PROJECT BACKGROUND

In the late fall of 2000, two immigrant members of the Faculty of Nursing, University of Toronto came together to figure how they might address a number of issues that were increasingly concerning local and national Canadian health promotion advocates. At the forefront of these concerns was recent data (Dunn and Dyck, 2000), which indicated that although immigrants were more educated and in better health than the average Canadian on arrival, they had a poorer than average health status after approximately 10 years. In a seemingly contrary motion, increased national and policy driven attention was being paid to the recruitment of professionals from abroad by Canadian immigration officials in order to bolster the Canadian labour market (OECD, 1999). Although citizenship and Immigration Canada had been actively recruiting highly skilled professionals to come to Canada, they were not providing enough information about the myriad barriers immigrants would most likely face as they began to take steps towards socio-economic integration.

Then and now, global migration has been a defining phenomenon of the twenty-first century with millions of people participating in border crossings annually. Included in these numbers is the increased migration of highly skilled women. The pattern of Canadian immigration history has moved from male and white immigrants towards non-European workers of both sexes. In a nutshell, the pattern has been:

— The encouragement of immigrants from Northern and Eastern Europe to populate and open up Canadian west in the late 1800s to the earlier 1960s
— The recruitment of African American men by the railway to serve as porters (even when their families were not allowed into Canada)
— The encouragement of British and other whites males to fill the professional areas of the labour market; the continual recruitment of immigrant women and other women of color by the Canadian government to serve as domestics, a practice starting in 1911 and continuing presently in order to support middle and upper class Canadian families in light of the lack of a national childcare program
— The creation of a migrant worker program through which men of color are brought in as farm labourers on temporary work visas, which is of great importance for Ontario farming
— The opening up of the Canadian borders in the late 1960s with the creation of the universal point system aiming at supporting human capital accumulation (Mbaye, Gooden & Wilson-Fall, 2008; Papademetriou, 2007)

In sum, Canada's immigration policy directs demographic growth to meet the economic needs of the labor market.

Based on the rigorous health selection process that newcomers had to pass before they were allowed to cross Canada's borders, many expected that there would be better health policies and programs in place to assure immigrants' well being after they landed in Canada. However, by working and living among immigrants, the researchers were aware that this was not the case. Canada, preceded only by Australia, has the second highest percentage of foreign-born residents; 19.8% of the Canadian population is made of immigrants (Hawthorne, 2008). Yet, for these new migrants to Canada, both wage and health outcomes were dismal. It may, for example, take 20 to 30 years for the principal immigration applicant to achieve economic parity (if they ever do) with a comparably qualified Canadian-born individual. Numerous Canadian studies indicated that migration was increasingly associated with the entrenched disadvantage of being under-employed, unemployed, and poor (Hawthorne; United Way, 2004). Further, the decline in the health status of immigrants has major implications. Barriers faced by new immigrants limited access to the health care system often leads to a worsening of health status in general and over time in particular. Because the majority of people who migrated to Canada did so to seek better economic and life chances, this is particularly alarming.

As immigrant women themselves, the investigators were additionally concerned for the health and well being of recent immigrant women, particularly given the under utilization of gender as a variable in health research and the increased health disparities of immigrant women and the feminization of poverty in Canada (United Way, 2004). There was also the recognition that access to health services in the Greater Toronto Area may be particularly limiting for immigrant women whose "immigrant lives" as family health promoters and transnational caregivers had negative bearing on their health and well-being (Gastaldo, Gooden, & Massaquoi, 2005).

In light of these complications and tensions, between 2000 and 2004 Faculty of Nursing members at the University of Toronto and health promotion advocates from Women's Health in Women's Hands (WHIWH), a women's community health centre that worked primarily with immigrant women and women of color, came together to research and write a proposal to fund the project *Revisiting Personal is Political: Immigrant Women's Health Promotion*. The project was funded the Canadian Institutes of Health Research in 2002.

PROJECT PARTNERS: DEVELOPMENT OF THE PARTNERSHIP

Initially, the coordinating group included four women, the principle investigator (second author) and 3 co-investigators. To complete the research team, a research coordinator (ABD in Black Studies) was hired in the Fall 2002 once the project was funded (first author Amoaba Gooden). The principle investigator and one co-investigator, both academics, had been in Canada for approximately 7 and 20 years, respectively. The other two investigators were agency staff members at WHIHW. One was a social worker who had been in Canada for approximately 25 years and was in the process of conducting her PhD and the other was a mental health counsellor and a child of immigrants who would begin her PhD before the project ended.

From the beginning, the research was set up as collaboration with a stated participatory intent. PAR was used in this project because it is an "alternative" model of research due to the ways it expands democratic practices within social institutions and questions traditional approaches to knowledge production. Affiliated with critical theory and to the Latin American movement of community development (Freire, 1992; Kemmis & McTaggart, 2005), participatory action research is commonly defined through its "shared ownership of research projects, community-based analysis of social problems, and an orientation towards community action" (Kemmis & McTaggart, p. 560).

Following principles of practice-relevant research (Butler-Jones, 2009), the community agency and academics identified practice needs, academic expectations for career development in academia, and areas of study that would be innovative in the field. Benefits for both sides were discussed—for example, the community agency researchers would be trained in PAR as a research methodology while the academic researchers would have recruitment for the project facilitated by the community health centre and have contacts to other centers for knowledge translation. This process was informed by a multi-disciplinary approach, mutual respect, trust, anti-racist and feminist understandings, and respect for diversity and differing points of view (Kemmis & McTaggart, 2005). All these values were made explicit from the beginning of the partnership, at the time of the project planning.

The proposal-writing phase lasted one year, during which monthly meetings were held alternating between the university and the community health center. The principal investigator (PI) took the lead in writing the proposal, but all members of the collaborative team had input in the process. A common language emerged among the four investigators to define the project. Academic and agency partners were formally identified as researchers with two representatives from each source type (university and agency). It was also determined that a research coordinator with experience in both the academic and community realm needed to be hired. An agreement document stating the roles of the researchers and institutions was also drafted at this time and a letter of support from the community health centre was also submitted with the research proposal. One of the most important features of this research partnership was that it was built on a collegial relationship that evolved over a number of years through personal contacts, shared educational activities, and joint publication efforts, the combination of which facilitated and ensured the building of trust and mutual respect of members.

Because the identification of the research problem was done in partnership between the professionals working with immigrant women in the community health centre and the academics studying the subject, the project was identified by the researchers as a participatory action research rather than a community-based research project—it was not a research problem identified by the "immigrant community," a defining aspect of community-based research. Given the social isolation that most immigrants face during their first years in Canada and our interest in working with immigrants of several nationalities, we identified the project's problem and conducted three focus groups to discuss the adequacy of such a topic from the participants' perspective. However, it is important to note that this is not the same as to say the community members identified the issues themselves.

METHODOLOGY AND FOCUS

We now turn to the focus and methodology of our work, both of which are important in understanding how collaborative methodologies function in practice. This study explored settlement experiences of recent immigrant women who had lived in Canada for up to five years. The main goal of the study was to analyze social determinants of health in the context of recent immigration in order to understand which strategies would promote health and empower immigrant women. In addition, the project explored how being an immigrant (detailed as place issues in RPP) and a woman (gender issues) shaped the power relations in which these women were engaged in their everyday lives.

Participants and Preliminary Meetings

The first phase of the project was exploratory in which researchers met with immigrant and refugee women from various cultural backgrounds to examine their perception of their health in the context of displacement and gender relations as well as the strategies and resources they employed to promote their own health. Thirty-three women, recently arrived to Canada (most had been in the nation under three years and a few under five) participated in this phase, which held three focus groups (11 participants in each). The research team facilitated discussions that focused on how place, displacement and gender relations informed the women's experiences of health and well-being. Food, transportation cost, and childcare cost were provided. To facilitate communication in this first phase, a hired interpreter as well as the PI provided interpretation for those whose first language was not English.

Participants were recruited from health centers, language instruction classes, and community centers. The age range of the women varied from those in their early 20s to 60s with younger people comprising the majority of participants. Women with children were also in the majority, but married women with no children, grandmothers, and single women with no children were also part of the study. Participants were from a variety of countries: Eastern Europe, Latin America, Asia, Middle East, and Africa. Reasons for migration varied among participants. They included, but were not limited to, educational goals for self and family, personal safety, and a better quality of life. In reality, a number of women in this study immigrated to have a better quality of life. Many were willing to sacrifice their high standard of living in their country of origin for a better quality of life for themselves and their families in Canada, a place they considered to be a safer and peaceful country.

Although many of the participants are considered women of color in Canada, their lived experience in various parts of the world dispelled or called into question notions of "first" and "third" world experiences. Women from either place had shared experiences, regardless if they originated from "post-industrial nations." Both groups of immigrant participants had access to facilities and services we label in North America as "first world." Both were used to consumption levels relative to middle or upper class standards of affluence. The majority of participants had post-secondary education or a university degree and over half had professional careers in their home countries. A few women, however, had little educational experience and/or no employment experience. Yet in Canada, these attainments were irrelevant because all women faced similar hardships—most had not found a job at the time of the study and their personal or family income was low compared to the Canadian standard.

From this group of 33 participants, 13 women were invited to become members of the PAR phase of the study. Selection criteria included availability to meet, country of origin, language (some ability to converse in English), educational level, ethnicity, civil status, age and landed immigrants who came through the skilled worker program (point system) or family reunification program. We were searching for a diverse group that would have as its main feature the fact of being a recent immigrant woman to Canada. The participatory action phase described below lasted 18 months.

PARTICIPATORY-ACTION PHASE

In order to enable the women to voice their views and become participants in their own health promotion and empowerment, the research team adopted an interdisciplinary, participatory, action research approach. In this process, the intention was to address the following research objectives: (1) illustrate the resources and strategies the women employed in order to promote their own mental health; (2) explore how being an immigrant woman (being displaced) shaped the power relations in which they were engaged in their everyday lives; (3) describe how gender roles and relations influenced the degree of control they have over their lives; (4) examine the concepts of individual and collective empowerment as simultaneously key elements for health promotion and as a discourse for self-care and the care of others. The three main strategies for data collection during the PAR phase of the project included focus groups, photovoice (still shots and video) and diaries; they are described below.

Focus Group

During this participatory-action phase, the principles of PAR were applied with the 13 participants. Participants met bi-weekly with the PI, at least one co-investigator and the research coordinator to discuss their experiences with particular attention paid to place and gender as analytical categories. Most of the women came to all the meetings and only two had dropped off by the end of the project. The choice of working in English with most participants permitted the integration of the participants and allowed the researchers to also collect data about how recent immigrants relate to their "new" language as individuals and as a group. Two participants had translators and occasionally the PI assisted the Spanish-speaking participants. Those who spoke the same language also helped each other. Each researcher agreed to keep field notes as well as take turns keeping focus group observation notes during the bi-weekly sessions. This allowed for critical reflection which is a necessary and an important part of action research.

During each bi-weekly focus group meeting, snacks/breakfast was provided. Facilitated warm-ups and ice-breakers (stretching, jokes, and information sharing about self) also began each session. The researchers initially developed and facilitated the bi-weekly warm ups, but as the women became more comfortable with each other and with the researchers, they were encouraged and welcomed the chance to take charge of the ice breakers. Participants led the group (including researchers) in such warm ups as cultural dance and physical exercise. Eventually the women took charge of the entire sessions, particularly in the action phase of the project.

Working collaboratively, the investigators determined focus group discussion guidelines based on the project themes (gender, displacement and power). These thematic guidelines initially framed each discussion. However, after the second session, the women were also encouraged to determine what they wanted to know, and to share with the researchers what would assist them in having a positive migratory experience in Canada. There were opportunities to interview each other, to do individual presentations for the group, to work in small groups and to work as a single group. At this point in the project traditional roles of participants and researchers were disrupted because both the researcher and the participants had the same roles in all these activities (e.g. being both interviewer and interviewee). The women recognized the legitimate knowledge each brought, which fostered the sharing of experience, discussion and possible solutions. After discussion and if needed, the women identified problems they hoped the researchers (as resources) could address. They also requested sessions with health promotion professionals within the health centre that they felt could alert them to activities/resources that might assist with such issues, for example, as settlement, dealing with stress, and violence against women. In such group meetings, the community health centre provided written and verbal information in various languages. In addition, on the request of the participants, a two-day workshop was offered on job finding skills and resume writing. Here community experts (immigrants) were paid and hired to provide assistance in job search, Canadian nuances and resume writing. The participants were also provided with Canadian certificates of participation to help them to build references with "Canadian Experience."

The group work done during this time helped the women and researchers develop a sense of group identity and unity. In addition, an element of psychological empowerment experienced by the participants was evident when the women formed networks of social support with each other. Through these networks, some women found jobs, learned about resources available to immigrants, obtained career advice and socialized together. It also provided the researchers the time and opportunity to build trustful relationships with the women and each other. The researchers were also able to help clarify roles and secure understanding of the study. Perhaps the most important outcome of this part of the project's group work was giving the women an opportunity to create a Canadian network of friends and acquaintances who supported each other and shared ideas and new knowledge on how to promote personal and family well-being.

Photovoice

Photovoice uses the "immediacy of the visual image to furnish evidence and to promote an effective, participatory means of sharing expertise and knowledge" (Wang & Burris 1997, p. 369), Consisting of two major stages: 1) individual photographs taken by the participants, and 2) discussions about the photographs, photovoice draws attention to the individual's observations and stories. This method was used to encourage participants to become aware of their living environment and their use of public and private space. Entrusted with digital cameras, the women became our research partners. They photographed their living environment, friends and family as well as aspects of their daily lives. (Consent forms were provided for them to get permission from any person shown in the pictures.) They showed places they frequented, liked, visited or hoped to visit. They then shared their stories about the places they photographed and discussed how they used these spaces.

From the photographs we learned that despite their knowledge of street names, public places, and the Toronto Transit Commission system (TTC), most participants had a very limited use of the city. Immigrant women were limited in how they made use of space by barriers associated with economics, language, time and knowledge of the city. English was needed, for example, to access social facilities and to understand how to follow directions. There were a few malls, squares, food stores, second-hand stores, and particular roads that framed the women's everyday lives. Most, however, did not know "wealthy" neighbourhoods by their names, for example, nor did they recognize most cultural centers that were paid spaces in the city. Many had never visited the city's attractions (CN Tower, the ZOO and Ontario Place), nor had they been invited into the home of a Canadian (someone who was not an immigrant). Through their photos, by Canadian measures, we saw very modest and low standards of living: four people living in a one-bedroom apartment, very basic furnishing and homes situated in average to poor neighbourhoods are examples of living standards. In reality, the photographs revealed that recent immigrant women were primarily limited by economics in how they accessed and utilized the space of the city. Remarkable, and to their credit, although most did not have access to paid cultural events/spaces, many had a good knowledge of free services such as the library, swimming pools, community centres, religious centres and museums. With this limitation and given their need to study, work, and take care of the family, some referred to Toronto as "a place full of worries to immigrants."

Diary

Participants were given the option of using diaries to document their weekly lives in relation to the weekly project theme. To address issues of literacy both voice mail as well as written diaries were offered as options. All the participants preferred written diaries to record and explore their experiences. None of the women wanted to participate in a phone diary because it would mean talking into a voice recorder weekly. In explaining why she preferred writing one participant indicated that "I want to call but I don't you know, I feel I need somebody to speak with (her)." Diaries and pens (colourful and beautiful items according to the PI's judgement) were then provided after a number of sessions for each participant. Participants were instructed that they could write in whatever language they chose as they explored displacement, gender and power as themes in their pre and post-migratory experiences.

When this activity was initially proposed to the participants it was called "journal writing," but the women had a hard time understanding what "journal writing" meant, until one participant said: "if I understand it right, you are suggesting we write diaries!" Clearly, writing in a diary was familiar with the women. From that point on, "diaries" was the term used to describe the activity. A brief set of questions based on the project's themes was offered to guide the women in describing their experiences. Most participants exceeded expectations by writing very detailed accounts. We believe this can be explained in part by the high educational level of most participants within the project.

Diary writing was a successful and valuable reflective tool for the participants. By examining their experiences and noticing that all participants shared similar circumstances, the women partially moved beyond self-doubt to exercising power in Canadian society. They were able to identify some dominant discourses that limit the social inclusion of immigrants in Canada and which produce immigrant women's underprivileged positions. Also, by reflecting on a daily or weekly basis on their lives, the women came to the meetings (focus groups) prepared to participate, share stories, and give examples. We believe the diary writing strategy not only enriched the data generation but also supported and enhanced the content of the focus groups' discussions. In addition, the women valued the exercises as they provided practice in reading and writing English. One participant indicated that "For me is good for practice writing is very good, lovely and things and I find many new word in the dictionary (laughter)." The energy and effort the women placed on journaling was a direct reflection of their desire for adjustment as they saw that reading and writing English was a way of being equipped with the tools to effectively interact in Canadian society.

The diaries were copied at three different times in the project. The women had consented to have them copied and read by the research team at the beginning of the study and this is how we proceeded. After the diaries were copied, they were returned to the participants and the researchers worked with the copies. At no point in the focus group meeting were participants asked to discuss the content of their diary. When they shared some of what they wrote, they did so of their own volition and without prompting.

ACTION PHASE

This participatory phase was developed over a year, with and by the participants of the study, producing an intense, reflexive process. From the focus groups, photovoice and diaries the researchers understood that participants were busy attending school, working inside and outside the home and caring for family members locally and internationally (Gastaldo, Gooden & Massoquoi, 2005). But perhaps the most challenging part of the study was to move from the participatory approach, characterized mainly by discussions and individual and collective reflections on the life of recent immigrant women (focus groups, diary, and photovoice), into the action phase. As Freire (1992) explains, it is when people seek social transformation through action that we have the opportunity to get an in-depth understanding of the forces that make the status quo possible. In the case of this study, when the researchers reminded the group that it was time to plan a few concrete actions to address the issues identified as relevant for recent immigrant women's health promotion, we came to see in a much clearer way how much these recent immigrants had internalized discourses of inferiority and inadequacy of their skills in relation to what was "valued" and "needed" in Canada.

This call for action was initially received with a prolonged silence. The research team stressed the freedom the women had in designing this phase according to their own needs. To support the transition into this phase, the research team asked the women to identify their skills. The women described themselves as patient, good listeners and people with limited English. They acknowledged that they were also very good people who liked to help others, but they associated their skills, including their language, with other places and found it difficult to recognize value in the skills they possessed. This, of course, was directly related to the deprofessionalization and deskilling of professional women migrants brought on by the Canadian employers who do not consider the skills of immigrant professionals as valuable and equivalent to those of Canadian born workers.

In an attempt to qualify the skills that immigrant women bring to Canada, the researchers decided to center the conversation about language and language skill. All the women were asked to identify their language skills. In total, 18 languages were identified around the table. Paradoxically, given the fact that Canada, and Toronto in particular, was and still is highly multi-lingual, language did not at first appear to be an important and valuable skill that the women recognized or valued. This personal devaluing of their skill can be understood partially in relation to the Canadian labour market, which uses English speaking proficiency to justify why immigrants have not integrated into the Canadian labour force.

Through such conversations like the above and the answering of questions about their individual skills, the group came to value the focus groups meetings as a valuable source of information for other immigrants who, like them, also speak other languages and were in need of information before and after migrating to Canada. During this phase, some participants began requesting for friends/colleagues to join the group.

Stimulated by this reflective inquiry, gradually the women developed a plan. Through collaborative discussion the group decided on a plan of action to address issues they felt were important. The following products were created through collective practice: a poetry booklet, a website for newcomers and those planning to immigrate to Canada, a video, and a self-help group. These women wanted to create multiple ways of supporting prospective and new immigrants. By engaging with action, in four meetings the group worked in sub-groups for each action. The women divided themselves based on interest into an action group. Each group then selected one woman as facilitator and recorder. Acting as a resource person, each researcher assigned themselves to a group. This process turned out to be very effective for the participants and was an excellent action strategy. Below we have chosen to describe the production of the poetry booklet (The RPP project's poems comprise the second half of the booklet) and of the development of the online guidelines for immigrants by the women of this PAR project.

Poetry Book
(http://www.immigrationguide.nursing.utoronto.ca/30_Poems_by_Recent_Immigrant_Women.pdf)

The poetry was created in two ways. The group collectively identified key emotional moments in the focus groups and important themes that should be reflected in the poems. To create some poems, the PI worked on selected sections of the focus group verbatim, keeping the text very close to the participants' oral exchanges and presented them as poems for group consideration, who then approved them. The other strategy was to have the participant who volunteered to work on the poetry write poems about the topics she selected as most important, using the group's focus group exchanges as inspiration. The topics she selected were discussed and approved by the women.

To illustrate how the poems capture the participants' emotions, below we present a poem that speaks about post-migration stress and hardship. A participant contextualized her experience as well as provided a social critique of the Canadian immigration process. The group members really appreciated her use of a bridge as metaphor to express her feelings. Her comment about immigration, entitled in the poetry booklet as "The Bridge," reads:

Immigration is like entering a bridge
When you get onto a bridge, you know there are an entrance and an exit
My problem is that I got onto the bridge,
However I don't know whether I am at
The beginning, the middle
Or the end of the bridge
I also don't know where the bridge will take me
I feel anxious; I don't know how much longer I have to keep going
I can't tell if I am just at the beginning or if I am almost out of the bridge
My only hope is to reach the end; this is what keeps me moving
But this is such a hard process
I never thought the bridge was this long

Website
(http://www.immigrationguide.nursing.utoronto.ca)

Through the self-reflection that the women had engaged in, they realized that their post-migratory experience was directly related to their pre-migratory image of Canada. The information provided to the women about Canada, either in their home country or in Canada, by either immigration officials or immigration specialists, led the women to expect that their settlement and adjustment would have been significantly better in terms of terms of employment, language and culture. Thus, during the action phase, the participants identified information and resources that they felt were important for newcomers to know so that they would have some knowledge of what to expect before or on migrating to Canada. The women stressed that they wanted to provide experiential knowledge and "know how" for prospective immigrants so that they would be prepared before they arrived. The majority of the issues the women felt were valuable are commonly known by those living in Canada for some years, but new immigrants and those planning to immigrate, the women felt, needed to be aware of them as soon as possible. They acknowledged that to understand a country, one would first have to be a part of it. However, they also felt that recent migrants should think of a country's culture, of the opportunities and challenges it will present, as well as of their personal contribution, because they too can help by building a "better" self through their migration process.

Working in subgroups in the four sessions, the women used the information articulated and identified in the focus groups, photovoice and diary to create an informational website that would educate women intending to migrate or recent migrants about the economic, cultural and social life in Canada. A website, the women articulated, would allow access to this crucial information anywhere in the world. The women engaged each other in critical self-reflection to finalize their work that challenged the Federal government advertising on migrating to Canada. They provided information on standard of living, and what to expect on numerous things including employment, language proficiency, culture and health care. At the end of the fourth session, one participant volunteered to put it all together. She took the product home and returned to the next meeting with the document fully integrated. She then read the document to the group who affirmed or added points to make the document richer. The women then agreed that the document needed to be available in as many languages as possible. The document was translated into nine different languages. Many of the participants volunteered to translate the document, either alone or working with someone, although not all the women were comfortable completing the translation. The women who volunteered to translate the document were compensated at the same rate of pay as regular translators. The languages the women translated the document into included Russian, Ukrainian, Gujarati and Hindi. Additional research funds were used to provide translations in the other languages (Chinese, Farsi, French, Portuguese and Spanish).

THE RESEARCHERS' INDIVIDUAL PERSPECTIVES ON COLLOBORATION

Conducting research with immigrant women can be charged due to talk that centers around issues such as class, race, gender, sexuality, culture, language, and the like. At times all the researchers felt that situating self and reflexivity work was important especially when working in diverse settings and using participatory action research

Denise

At varying times in this project I had different concerns regarding my role as principal investigator and how I could impact the collaboration in positive or negative ways. At the beginning of the project, I was anxious to make the participants feel welcomed and to convey how much I appreciated their involvement in the project. At this time, promoting a friendly atmosphere and getting to know everybody was my main goal. Amoaba's sociable demeanour and excellent recruitment strategies facilitated this process.

Throughout the project, I was attentive to how participants would interpret my success in securing a job in my field of studies in Canada, while all of them were either unemployed or doing "survival jobs." I clearly addressed this issue by explaining to the group that I first got a job in Canada and then applied for permanent residence, doing the opposite itinerary that the majority of immigrants undertake.

Perhaps the most challenging moment in the study for me was realizing that the participants came to internalise the oppressive discourse of not being "good enough" to work in Canada. At that point, I feared for the action phase of the study. So I asked Amoaba to explain her skills to inspire the participants to identify their own talents. Several things Amoaba mentioned were picked up by the participants, as a result they started to mention how they could contribute to promote collective action. In this process, I felt it was necessary for me to speak last because I feared that my position as a professor would reinforce stereotypical views on settlement. Working with other researchers and being aware of the impact of my positionality helped me to collaborate with the participants.

Amoaba

As an immigrant women raised in Canada I was aware of my privilege daily working on this project: As a black Canadian woman, I had the "Canadian Experience" that the women yearned for: I spoke the language(s) of the land and I was employed in a relatively good paying position. This project reinforces for me the fluidity and intertextuality of my multiple identities (researcher, immigrant, women, straight, Black, English-speaking, etc.), as well as my social relation to others. It also reinforced for me the fact that I had not adequately interrogated what it meant to be a black middle–class person working with primarily poor white women (although most had come from a middle-class background in their country of origin). Working with the other researchers as well as with staff from WHIWH helped me to situate and understand how my experience and the experience of the participants intersect. In addition it allowed me to see the importance of the collaborative process, which allows both the researcher and the participants to be active in the world they want to change.

Whereas I had always privileged race or anti-racism in my conversations/work with immigrant and diverse women, in this project, class and age were my broader crossings as the majority of the participants were white women who were older than I and who held "survival jobs" or no job at all. The issue of racism as experienced by women of colour in Canada came up only once in the discussion (raised by an African Caribbean participant who had to leave the group). In relaying her experience of being denied a job because of the color of her skin, many participants expressed surprise to the participant on hearing that racism existed in Canada. What I reflected on from that one discussion was that that we (researchers and participants) did not have a common language with which to discuss and have an understanding of the issue of racism as constructed by the Canadian nation state. Indeed, to develop a common understanding of language would take time. One question that I asked myself as the research coordinator was "What is my role in this collaborative process in teaching about Canadian racism?" and "Is there a place in this project for that?" Although the issue of racism was never raised again, the women (and researchers) did spend time discussing other forms of discrimination based on gender, class and language and their construction within Canada, which could be extrapolated when discussing racism.

APPLYING PRINICPLES OF COLLABORATION

What follows are four basic principles of collaboration and a brief discussion on how the project applied them.

Community partners should have real influence on project direction

As the community partner, WHIWH, represented by two staff members, was involved at the earliest stage of the project. Along with the two researchers from the Faculty of Nursing, University of Toronto, WHIWH collaboratively defined the research objectives and had input into the project's methodology, goals, data analysis and dissemination. This shared leadership was put in writing and served as part of the proposal. In essence, community partners had enough leverage to ensure that the original goals, mission, and methods of the project were adhered to. During each bi-weekly focus group, the sessions were organized with the understanding that each researcher as well as participants brought valuable (and necessary) knowledge and history to the research table. This was also demonstrated during the action phase of the project as the participants facilitated the organizing. As well, the researchers acted as resource persons who provided knowledge about the participatory process.

Research processes and outcomes should benefit the community

The project partners ensured that community members benefited from the project in a number of ways. First, community (men and women) members and professionals were hired and trained whenever possible and appropriate. The hiring of the research coordinator (herself an immigrant) serves as an example. The research coordinator became trained in the principles of PAR and was able to obtain another job as a community researcher applying similar principles. The project also hired a recent migrant woman to design the project logo and other recent immigrant professionals to facilitate workshops and sessions on topics identified by the women. In addition, participants were hired as paid translators for focus groups as well as for the web-based immigration guide. This was an important element for the women since volunteer and paid work are central elements in becoming Canadian. For immigrants, Canadian experience along with English proficiency equated to employment. The hiring of these individuals benefited the migrant community and assisted with the building and enhancing of community assets. In addition to economic benefits, many participants identified focus group sessions in English as an important benefit as it offered another avenue for them to enhance their skills.

Community members should be part of the analysis and interpretation of data and should have input into how the results are distributed

All research team members participated in the analysis of the data to account for health promotion strategies among recent immigrant women. Each team member took at least one focus group verbatim and coded the notes using conceptual understanding from her discipline. She then generated a list of codes to be discussed by the team. The team then gathered to discuss the codes and the process and to determine a common understanding and language that would guide the analysis. The analysis of all data collected led into the three main analytical categories: experiences of displacement, becoming an immigrant, and limits to empowerment. Team members also conducted a secondary analysis, focusing on participants who referred to activities they undertake in a transnational social space. An article (Gastaldo, Gooden & Massoquoi, 2005) was then produced for publication from this secondary analysis. The community agency collaborated equally in this analysis, as well as the interpretation and dissemination of information from this project. Additionally, project participants also participated in the analysis phase. They identified key issues that they cared about, they became actively involved in the analysis of the issues they identified as important to them, and they took action to address some of their most pressing concerns as noted in the project outcomes above.

Furthermore, in addition to the joint publication by team members on Transnational care noted above, the community partner, WHIWH, took the lead and organized a one-day community conference (April 2005) for project dissemination. With over 100 people in attendance, research team members and participants presented on the project methodology, outcomes, and on some preliminary analysis. Community organizations, health centers, students, community members, academics and project participants also participated in this conference. Included in the conference was also a panel that addressed particular issues that immigrant women face such as underemployment, unemployment and increased health issues due to lack of access.

Productive partnerships between researchers and community members should be encouraged to last beyond the life of the project

Since participatory action research is a process of education as well as empowerment, for sustainability, creative alliances need to be established between researchers and community members. These alliances should be supported and encouraged to last beyond the life of the project. RPP supported the action outcome of a self-help group, which would go beyond the life of the project. The self-help group selected WHIWH as the community organization that they wanted to work with in educating recent immigrant women about migration. The agency identified a health promotion counsellor who would be the group's resource person. Before the end of the data collection phase of the project, the women had identified a meeting time and place to gather, as well as a structure for the group.

CONCLUSION

This chapter demonstrates the value of collaborative research between community and academic researchers. Our research emphasis was to involve community members in all phases of the research process, and as noted above, the project partner was involved in all phases of the study. Additionally, given the nature of the subject matter, the distance between "researchers" and participants" was partially bridged for a number of reasons including the fact that all but one of the investigators had personally experienced migration from their home country and were familiar with various settlement issues that migrants might face to varying degrees. This "benefit" of experience allowed the researchers to act as resource persons who had gone through similar, yet different experiences and helped put participants at ease.

Furthermore, the leadership success the women exhibited in the action phase of the study may be attributed to their involvement in a PAR study because of the empowerment philosophy of this approach to research. The participants engaged in direct advocacy. As such, their participation cannot be understood apart from the context of the participatory action research (PAR) study that facilitated their actions. Within this context of immigrants' health and health promotion both the researchers and the participants recognized that health and well-being policies must recognize and support women's health promotion activities by addressing issues of empowerment and self-advocacy within a migration context.

AUTHORS' NOTE

This study, Revisiting *Personal is Political*: Immigrant Women's Health Promotion, was a collaborative project between the Faculty of Nursing, University of Toronto and Women's Health in Women's Hands Community Health Centre (WHIWH). The Canadian Institutes of Health Research (CIHR) funded it. The opinions expressed here are the authors and not necessarily those of CHIR or WHIWH. The authors would like to acknowledge the support of WHIWH co-investigators during the period of study, Notisha Massaquoi and Deone Curling, whose support was instrumental in the execution of the study. In addition, we want to acknowledge the other co-investigator, Nazilla Khanlou, whose knowledge of the mental health issues faced by immigrant women assisted with the kinds of support provided to women. We also appreciate the collaboration of the many immigrant women who participated in the study and meetings described.

REFERENCES

Butler-Jones, O. (2009). Public health science and practice: From fragmentation to alignment. *Canadian Journal of Public Health, 100*(1), 11–12.

Dunn, J. R., & Dyck, I. (2000). Social determinants of health in Canada's immigrant population: Results from the national population health survey. *Social Science & Medicine, 51*, 1573–1593.

Freire, P. (1992). *Pedagogy of hope*. Sao Paulo: Paz e Terra Editora.

Gastaldo, D., Gooden, A. & Massaquoi, N. (2005). Transnational health promotion: Social well-being across borders and immigrant women's subjectivities. *Wagadu: A Journal of Transnational Women's and Gender Studies, 2*, 1–16.

Hawthorne, L. (2008, May). The impact of economic selection policy on labour market outcomes for degree-qualified migrants in Canada and Australia. *IRPP Choices, 14*(5). Retrieved January 26, 2009, from www.irpp.org

Health Canada. *Canada health action: Building on the legacy—Volume II: Synthesis reports and issues papers, What makes women healthy or unhealthy*. Retrieved April 15, 2009, from http://www.hc-sc.gc.ca/hcs-sss/pubs/renewal-renouv/1997-nfoh-fnss-v2/legacy_heritage8-eng.php#a3

Kemmis, S., & McTaggart, R. (2005). Participatory action research: Communicative action and the public sphere. In N. Denzin & Y. Lincoln (Eds.), *The Sage handbook of qualitative research* (3rd ed., pp. 559–604). Beverley Hills, CA: Sage.

Mbaye, B., Gooden, A., & Wilson-Fall, W. (2009). A history of black immigration in the United States and Canada with culture and policy implications. In Z. Williams, (Ed.). *Africana cultures and public policy: Scholarship and the transformation of public policy* (pp. 219–246). New York: Palgrave McMillan.

OECD. (2004). *Developing highly skilled workers: Review of Canada*. Retrieved March 30, 2009, from www.oecd.org/dataoecd/4/18/2727370.pdf

Ornstein, M. (2000). *Ethno-Racial inequality in the City of Toronto: An analysis of the 1996 census*. Access and Equity Unit Strategic and Corporate Policy Division Chief Administrator's Office, Public Health Services, Social Development of the Community and Neighbourhood Services Department and the Centre of Excellence for Research on Immigration and Settlement, Toronto.

Papademetriou, D. G. (2007, May). *Selecting economic stream immigrants through points systems*. Migration Policy Institute. Retrieved March 30, 2009, http://www.migrationinformation.org/feature/display.cfm?ID=602

United Way's Report. (2004, April). *Poverty by postal code: The Geography of neighbourhood poverty, 1981–1982.*

Wang, C., & Burris M. A. (1997). Photovoice: concept, methodology, and use for participatory needs assessment. *Health Education & Behavior, 24*(3), 369–387..

JOSHUA S. SMITH AND ROBERT J. HELFENBEIN, JR.

5. TRANSLATIONAL RESEARCH IN EDUCATION

Collaboration & Commitment in Urban Contexts

...to take responsibility for transforming our own practices so that our empirical and pedagogical work can be less toward positioning ourselves as masters of truth and justice and more toward creating a space where those directly involved can act and speak on their own behalf. (Lather, 1991, p. 164)

INTRODUCTION

The intention of this chapter is nothing short of troubling the role of universities in communities while simultaneously challenging researchers with the task of redefining our conception and practice of contemporary research efforts in schools of education. This chapter first questions time-honored assumptions about what constitutes research. This is followed by a brief review of Translating Research in Practice (TRIP), an alternative approach within the current scholarship frameworks in higher education. Next, we posit a role for translational research in education and describe specifically how we approach translational research in the Center for Urban and Multicultural Education (CUME). Central to this effort is a set of core commitments around which our work revolves from beginning to end—the commitment to learn, the commitment to teach, the commitment to work, and the commitment to people. The chapter concludes with two examples of CUME projects that reflect aspects of translational research and the four core commitments.

TROUBLING EDUCATIONAL RESEARCH

For the purposes of this chapter, we begin with a sense of what we have found in most academic research settings. The intention here is not to over-state; however, for the sake of troubling the current state of research in education, we refer to such work as "traditional research" as it is often talked about in inquiry classes, in the field, and among faculty in various venues. Traditional research, particularly as it emerges from university faculty and research centers, tends to be linear in design (See Figure 1). That is, researchers respond to requests for proposals (RFP's) as well as develop, research, or evaluate some idea, pedagogy, or intervention that has the potential for new knowledge. The direction of such inquiry is typically uni-dimensional and, in the case of education research, usually looks at students/ teachers as *subjects* and schools as *settings*. The greatest challenge for research participants in local settings lies in the fact that the work is often generated and disseminated to audiences outside of the schools and communities where the inquiry was conducted, leaving many teachers and administrators to wonder: what do we get out of it?

Figure 1. Linear nature of traditional research

This is a legitimate question in light of the increasing pressure by the Institute of Education Science and state departments of education for researchers to conduct randomized clinical trials in schools. This narrowing of educational inquiry models into a social science laboratory framework may be inconsistent with the complex nature of schooling and the types of questions of interest to teachers and administrators in our schools. The constructs and phenomena of interest in educational research are steeped in contexts within and outside of particular schools that, one could argue, are beyond what statistics can "control" for.

The third component in the linear nature of educational research figure above reflects the current character of the university promotion and tenure system. There is increasing pressure within research universities for faculty to publish in top-tier journals. The dissemination of findings into the public sphere is often limited to sharing results with other faculty or students enrolled in graduate programs. Journals in the teachers' lounge and on administrator bookshelves are less likely to be from AERA sponsored journals than from practitioner-friendly outlets. As if that were not enough, there is also a growing expectation that junior faculty secure external funding, an expectation that was heretofore seen as taking away precious time from writing articles for these top journals. We return to this notion later in the "What is at Stake" section, but it is important to point out that graduate programs (including those of the authors) do not adequately prepare students for the intense and increasing pressure to secure external funding for research projects. The lack and diminishing levels of state support for higher education have created intense pressure towards the pursuit of alumni donors and external grant funding—this is important to put on the table whenever possible.

While it is tempting to chalk up the prevalence of traditional faculty-driven research to the overplayed figure of the "ivory tower," this reduction is counterproductive to advancing multiple approaches to scholarship. Scholars such as Boyer (1990), Shulman (2000), and Issacson (2000) challenge a limited view of research—one that only values research that starts with a big "R." Research universities with a rather narrow charge to "discover" new knowledge and innovations in science, liberal arts, and professional schools have begun to expand and grow in other areas. In 1990, Boyer challenged higher education to think about integration, application, teaching and learning, and now, the 5th scholarship—the Scholarship of Engagement. *The Journal of the Scholarship of Teaching and*

Learning began in 2000 and continues vigorously as we near the end of this decade.

Issacson (2000) suggested that in order for inquiry into teaching and learning to be considered the Scholarship of Teaching and Learning (SOTL), it must be open to the public, peer reviewed, and disseminated to other fields. SOTL has the potential to positively affect students in a timely manner and to help faculty improve their pedagogical decision-making, and can be extended to others within the field and beyond who transfer a method or idea into their respective educative spaces. Furthermore, the assertion that it takes too long for the findings of university-based research to funnel down to practicing educators also holds merit and is cause for concern (Coleman, 2007; Shulman, 2000). One approach to inquiry that can address these very real concerns is translational research or Translating Research into Practice.

Translating Research into Practice

Translational research differs from other forms of educational research in that the latter is predicated on the idea of the external "fly on the wall." Conversely, translational research creates a space for collaborative, co-constructed inquiry that values and utilizes the expertise of all stakeholders involved. Translating Research into Practice (TRIP) is a research framework gaining a foothold in professional schools such as Medicine and Nursing and within the Liberal Arts in areas such as Communication Studies. TRIP values the timely application of new knowledge discovered throughout the research process. Its goals include the desire to move innovation into the marketplace at a faster pace, to facilitate evidenced-based practice in professions such as nursing, and, ultimately, to bring to bear university resources and research to pressing issues facing our citizens and communities (Petronio, 2007).

The Indiana University School of Medicine received a $25 million grant from the National Institutes of Health (NIH) to develop a research center that translates research into practice. According to the press release,

> The NIH created the Clinical and Translational Institute (CSTI) awards as a high priority effort to improve the process by which basic science laboratory discoveries are transformed into new medical treatments and products – a process called translational research. The CTSI will implement the NIH initiative in Indiana with new programs to accelerate translational research, train new translational researchers, interact with community health-care professionals and the public, build research resources and technologies, and leverage Hoosier resources with health care, business, government and foundation partnerships. (Indiana University School of Medicine, 2008)

Reihl (2006) contrasted educational research with medical research, particularly in his challenge to the dissemination and use of evidenced-based practice, noting that "non-use of research findings can be as worrisome as too-quick use" (p. 26).

Translational research in education. Translating Research into Practice situates inquiry around notions of collaboration and partnership (Petronio, 1999). Teachers and administrators have the expertise, know which questions are salient and meaningful to probe, and can assume participant, researcher, or participant-observer roles in scholarly inquiry. Directionality of inquiry matters in TRIP. Therefore, hot topics and/or burning inquiry questions must come from teachers and advising administrators rather than researchers from university contexts. This approach follows from what Lagemann (2008) refers to as "problem-finding research" that produces, or at least provides insight into, "usable knowledge" (p. 425).

The challenge of transferring the TRIP model into education and the role of educational researchers was discussed in detail in the recent issue of *Educational Researcher*. To this end, Bulterman-Bos (2008) took a bold step, calling for the creation of clinical researchers similar to those seen in Schools of Medicine. In a piece entitled "Will a clinical approach make education research more relevant for practice?" she makes the case that "sufficient experience as a teacher is required for becoming a researcher and in which researchers remain active as teachers during their research careers" (p. 418). The not-so-subtle implication here is that faculty, particularly in Curriculum and Instruction, are disconnected from the "real world" of teaching. The situation is exacerbated for the majority of faculty in fields such as Educational Psychology (including the first author) who rarely have K-12 teaching experience. In their criticism of Bulterman-Bos, where Labaree's (2008) is particularly poignant, calling the reader's attention to the differing roles and expectations of practitioners and researchers, Lagemann's (2008) critique is more balanced, citing the need for both Problem-Finding Research and Translational Research.

Lagemann's was the first American Educational Research Association (AERA) sponsored publication to use the term "translational research." His work brings up questions that include: What does it mean to say that as teachers and university faculty we have different roles and expectations?; Does effective teaching or research on teaching and learning differ widely in the two contexts?; How far (time and place) is the divide between knowledge generated/discovered by university-based researchers and the application of those ideas in real classrooms and schools that are in the neighborhoods adjacent to a research university?

Translational research addresses such questions by actively including a diverse group of possible stakeholders (researchers, teachers, students, administrators, parents, etc.) in the generation of ideas, knowledge, and inquiry questioning. This collaborative process has the potential to make the findings of educational inquiry more meaningful because it explicitly documents the process, uses formative findings for the modification of practice, and creates an impetus for immediate change in the lives of the same students and community members engaged in the program or intervention.

This model is juxtaposed against one of the primary goals of traditional research—generalizing findings to other contexts. While translational research in education does not preclude inquiry designs that culminate in findings that generalize or transfer to other similar schools and communities, the first order of business is to collectively review findings in order to improve conditions and practices where the inquiry takes place. Figure 2 displays the recursive nature of translational research in education.

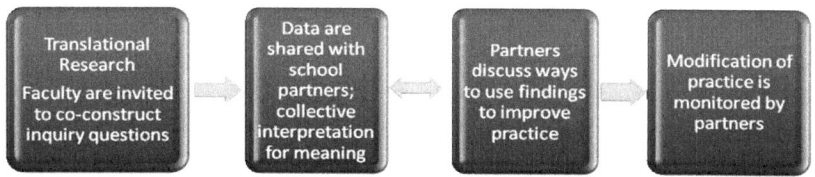

Figure 2. Translational research in education

Therefore, in order to effectively engage in translational research in education, researchers must truly understand the organization that is the subject of a given research agenda, not only the project/program in question or the teachers/staff involved. It requires that understanding grow with the project from its inception to conclusion and that researchers be formative parts of the project team. From a theoretical perspective, we argue that there are two key concepts that must be developed in order for a model of translational research to emerge: *collaboration*, which involves a level of trust not often associated with university-school partnerships, and a term we are calling *shared decision-making/generating inquiry questions*, which involves a pushback against objectivity or self-proclaimed independence.

Collaborative inquiry. According to D'Amour, et al. (2005), "The term collaboration conveys the idea of sharing and implies collective action oriented toward a common goal, in a spirit of harmony and trust..." (p. 116). Additionally, they describe collaboration as a dynamic process that necessitates a collegial relationship and some degree of reciprocity. The authors describe all collaboration as a relationship that, "...demands open and honest communication" (Stichler, 1995, p. 53) "and mutual trust and respect" (Alpert, Goldman, Kilroy & Pike, 1992; Siegler & Whitney, 1994, p. 119). This is no small feat considering the cultural distrust that often exists between schools and university researchers.

Because translational research in education requires an understanding of the inner workings of an organization's mission and its people, it is necessary to be invited into a position where all research participants are able to describe (or retell) events as well as the rationale for decisions from the organization's point of view. Fostering such a collaborative requires that both the schools/community-based organizations and university faculty simultaneously *give up something* and *take on something new* in terms of their roles and responsibilities.

This definition of partnership begins with "walking in someone's shoes" if even for a day as administrator or faculty training teachers to collect data instead of relying on researchers to conduct that component. These role changes need to be negotiated in the best interest of the individuals involved and of the project, and ultimately point to "collaborative theorizing" (Lather, 1994). The next step beyond this requires the wearing of two different shoes—one in which the fit is comfortable and one that makes you feel you can run fast or conversely, hurts your foot for some time. Only then can you understand the roles and expectations of another's responsibilities and perspectives on the issues.

Directionality matters. The second key concept in translational research is a belief that people in schools and community-based organizations are experts and know the context and history of their past efforts at reform, programming, shared commitments, and the like. Instead of bringing faculty research questions to schools and communities, translational researchers build relationships with individuals that may or may not result in a collaborative project.

In doing so, this relationship pushes back against scholarly independence and the false promises of objectivity. Shared ownership of the research process presents conditions for empowerment and can serve to create a dynamic exchange of ideas about how to best implement and study an intervention/program. This perspective also produces highly credible research because the investigations have been conducted based on the needs of the schools according to a clear cultural understanding of the standpoint held by the administrators, students, and teachers. The process increases capacity for sustaining interventions, initiatives, or reform efforts. Without shared ownership, the process can be seen as another passing fancy that "will soon pass" or become another *thing* on an overflowing plate of the growing responsibilities for classroom teachers.

The burden of considering issues of power and hierarchy tends to rest with researchers, but they never lie far from the surface. When dialogue—both collaborative and generative—happens within these relationships for the first, second, and tenth time, the nature of the power relations changes (hopefully, lessen) but never disappear. Indeed, we take up these two concepts to protect our projects from ourselves, or, as Lather (1991) notes, "Research designs can be more or less participatory, but some amount of dialogic encounter is required if we are to invoke the reflexivity needed to protect research from the researcher's own enthusiasms" (p. 64).

An argument might be made that translational research as described above is just another form of participatory action research (PAR). Although the translational work at CUME has elements of PAR (as described in the next section of the chapter), the transactional research we conduct does not contain some of the necessary elements of PAR. For example, while there is an expectation that project directors, teachers, administrators, and grant writers are actively engaged during the conception and fleshing out of ideas and proposals, we typically do not train teachers and community members to collect data, but rather intentionally build-in time to review data, both raw and analyzed.

About half of the projects associated with CUME begin with co-writing proposals; the other half are in response to an invitation to conduct an independent evaluation of a program or intervention. Seen through the lens of Schafft and Greenwood's (2003) characteristics of conventional and participatory community planning, our work generally leans toward the participatory, but, as they note, these characteristics are not absolute. For example, outcomes tend to be fixed in our state and federal projects.

However, our research teams spend considerable time, energy, and money conducting formative assessments and implementation fidelity studies to help feed information back into ongoing projects that call for improvement. Data are shared with teachers, and the interviews are equally construed as professional development (reflective practice) and data for synthesis at a later date. Finally, there are timelines and finality to many of the projects, and therefore, the emergent properties of PAR are sometimes limited in our projects.

CUME IN CONTEXT

The Center for Urban and Multicultural Education (CUME) is the research arm of the Indiana University School of Education at Indiana University-Purdue University Indianapolis (IUPUI). CUME's mission is to create connections between research, theory, and practice with the ultimate aim of improving the quality of education throughout the P-20 continuum—from early childhood through graduate school levels—including formal, alternative, and community-based education. This mission is furthered through sustainable partnerships with schools and other educational organizations in communities around Indiana. Our work seeks to support inquiry, facilitate public discussion, and critically challenge stereotypes about diverse students, families, and schools.

Together with our community partners and faculty affiliates, CUME continues to engage in research and evaluation leading to improved practices, assessment, leadership, and policy within and across diverse educational settings. The first level of collaboration CUME established has been internal to the university, building partnerships with other schools and units within IUPUI including the Urban Center for the Advancement of STEM Education (UCASE), the School of Medicine, School of Science, and University College. These important campus partners accounted for approximately twenty percent of research dollars generated by CUME in the 2007–2008 academic year. The second level of collaboration is with our community partners who represent the bulk of funding generated for CUME—the Center has experienced a steady increase of funding over the last five years.

CUME uses a team approach to all projects. We have a faculty team leader, a Ph.D. or advanced MA student team leader, and one or more undergraduate/graduate hourly or independent study students working together on each project. The term "leader" simply connotes that a faculty member and advanced graduate student are ultimately accountable for the completion of the project from the university side. In order to facilitate this process, the Associate Director for Research and CUME Project Manager have created and continue to offer training modules for all CUME staff. These trainings range from Endnote software use, interviewing skills, observation protocols, data entry and descriptive analysis using SPSS, coding and generating reports using NVIVO, and research ethics.

In addition to the formal leadership guiding the Center, eight faculty members from a variety of areas of expertise comprise the CUME Advisory Board. The board meets periodically without the Director to review the status of the Center and its projects, to generate questions, and to review the financial status and projections of the Center. Additionally, approximately six faculty—some on the board and some not—lead active research grants through CUME that were generated either by the individual researcher or invited by CUME to take the lead on a project secured by the Center. Furthermore, there is an annual research fellowship that CUME sponsors, providing summer salary and an opportunity to write on a project conducted during the academic year.

CUME employs between five and eight full-time funded graduate assistants, five to ten hourly employees (undergraduate students, graduate students, and individuals with terminal BA's), and students taking independent research study courses throughout the year or during summer terms. As part of a campus commitment to increasing undergraduate research, we also work closely with the Ronald McNair Scholars program and Undergraduate Research Opportunity Program (UROP) every summer.

During the first few years of developing CUME, internal and community partners contacted us to collaborate on exciting and innovative inquiry projects. We jumped at the opportunity to form partnerships that would grow the Center. As a result, we found ourselves working at a pace that prevented serious consideration of a guiding framework for our work or careful examination of the extent to which our work met our definition of translational research. While we reject the notion that we were chasing funds or taking on projects that fell well outside of the Center's mission, it was clear that were responding, more often than intentionally planning, the direction of the work. The remainder of the chapter provides space for us to articulate the framework, present two examples of our research, and put forth a note of cautious optimism for expanding this type of work to other educational researchers and centers.

Core Commitments in Translational Research

A useful framework for collaborative inquiry revolves around terms of commitment. Borrowing from George Noblit (1999) and his reflection on ethnographic study (as noted in the introduction), we name four core commitments that exemplify translational research in education—the commitment to learning, the commitment to people, the commitment to teaching, and the commitment to work. We remind ourselves that as we embark on new research projects, our first commitment is to learn. The way in which educational inquiry is taken up is rooted in the pursuit of deep understanding—understanding in the communicative sense; in the sense of more listening than talking, at least in the beginning of projects. Commitments to people and social advocacy are tied together, driving both the *why* of taking up a research project and *who* of the decisions to collaborate. Teaching, in the sense of communicating our core values and collaborative approach, remains a way of thinking through our work with graduate students and staff that may have been trained in a more traditional research model. This, we have learned, cannot be taken lightly and must be a key component of our ongoing professional development. Finally, there is the explicit commitment to work itself, or rather, a commitment to work *through*. As one can see, these commitments are all wrapped together; but this last one is prominent because in taking seriously all of the commitments, the process of working through becomes complex and rich, necessitating a fluid and emergent approach to research.

Holding up the Mirror to the Work

We would now like to hold our work up to the mirror of research practices described above. While we are first to say that not all of our projects reflect the abstract or tangible components of translational research, the two projects we outline below reflect some, but not all, of the essential elements of translational research. This said, the projects and all of our work at CUME, stand up to the core commitments outlined in the previous sections of this chapter.

Pathways Initiative. The Dean in the Indiana University School of Education signed Memorandums of Understanding with three high-needs school districts in Indiana but found that few faculty were responding to the long drive to Gary, Indiana, or that this initiative did not fit with faculty members' research agendas. In response to this lack of action on the part of faculty, the Dean made research funding available for those who might consider participating in/with the three schools. Several faculty teams responded to the two-step Request for Proposals developed by the Research and Development Committee in the School of Education to compete for research funding.

The first step ensured that faculty communicated with teachers in the schools to generate a letter of intent describing the major elements of a partnership and a commitment to complete the longer proposal collaboratively. Both authors were part of teams that included several other faculty and teachers in two of these high schools. Faculty participated in professional learning community time at the schools and sponsored two working meetings at the university. The letter of intent was approved and the second proposal was funded.

The teams received two years of funding to move the project forward. Teachers requested that the day-long meetings be held outside of their school so they could focus on the task at hand without interruption. They articulated the strengths, needs, and challenges at their school. It took considerable time for teachers to believe that we, as university faculty and researchers, were serious about collaboration. They indicated that they were used to the district or university coming in to provide professional development or to conduct research on teachers and students. Conversely, we indicated that we wanted to hear their perspective on the challenges presented and for them to take the lead on articulating the direction they expected in a university-school partnership.

The first author worked with a team that consisted of four School of Education faculty, the Academic Dean of the high school, and six teachers at the high school to design, implement, and assess the impact of a parallel to addressing student engagement. The first component of the project provided dual credit courses for high achieving eleventh and twelve grade students, and the second involved actively engaging ninth grade students in literacy and numeracy during their math and English labs. The over-arching goal was to actively engage students early in their careers in order to increase the number of students who were prepared to take college level courses while in high school.

We were feeling very positive about the progress and momentum of the project; however, over the summer the Academic Dean of the school was reassigned and on the third day of school, the lead English teacher left to take a lecture position at a local college. After speaking with the new Academic Dean, who was supportive but cautiously so, the involved faculty made the decision to give him some time to establish himself as the instructional leader. This lull turned out to be a mistake. In approaching the problem from our perspective as university researchers, we forgot that it was the teachers who generated this project. Our lack of presence at the school led teachers to question what happened to us.

After a time, we reconnected with the Academic Dean and discovered that he was struggling with moving forward. Thus, he welcomed our engagement and, at this point, we began to advance our project in the following manner. A CUME researcher was assigned to support four students enrolled in a dual credit English class and eight undergraduates tutored students in the AVID program (Advancement via Individual Determination) as part of their service learning credits in their first undergraduate education course. One of the faculty colleagues conducted professsional development around the Critical Web Reader (CWR) as a response to teachers' request for support in content literacy.

The teachers generated the content ideas, and graduate students worked to identify respective websites to load into the CWR. Ninth grade students signed up for individual accounts and have recently begun to explore the tool. For most of the following semester, the project was back on track. However, periodically, communication difficulties and changing expectations at the district level for teachers' classroom work presented barriers to moving forward as the teachers planned.

Despite these efforts to move forward the new program, the small school where the Pathways Initiative began has dissolved (as we write this chapter), and the teachers have been reassigned to other magnet programs within the larger, comprehensive high school. We are currently discussing ways to keep momentum and to continue exploring areas of inquiry with the teachers who co-created the program of study.

The Peace Learning Project. The Peace Learning Project represents a long-standing collaboration between the Peace Learning Center (PLC) of Indianapolis and CUME. As the PLC evaluates and expands its programs in peace education, conflict resolution, and violence prevention in Indianapolis and abroad, detailed inquiry into the various components and objectives of the multi-faceted organization provide an essential first step in supporting this work. Sustained at various times through funding from the PLC, CUME, and the School of Education, multiple research efforts have been utilized to evaluate this program including qualitative research methods, literature reviews, document analyses, and collaborative work with program directors in correlation with Indiana State Curriculum Standards.

Beginning with in-depth conversations with PLC leadership on program goals and historical impact in the city, research and evaluation goals were collaboratively generated. Where initial efforts focused on work with incarcerated juvenile girls, a more recently formed project between PLC and CUME is an effort at fostering interfaith dialogue that seeks to bolster civil society in Indianapolis. Continuing research and evaluation with the PLC involves school-based programs and the recent expansion to international work in creating peace-building curricula with teachers and counselors in Negril, Jamaica. An initial finding of this research project maintains that the programs of the PLC represent their goals of community-based efforts in peace-building, conflict resolution, and peer mediation. Research literature on effectiveness supports an understanding that characteristics of the PLC, such as the fluidity of programs, mediation role of program directors, conflict identification, and the impact of self-regulation training are effective practices that positively impact research participants in Negril (Helfenbein, 2008). Additionally, member-checks with participants and presentations to the PLC Board found this work to be both well received and useful in pursuing further funding for local school actors. Furthermore, our research concluded that the PLC is uniquely situated as a site for further and wide-reaching research and evaluation efforts, potentially serving as a national model for similar programs and the replication of local efforts.

In exploring the possibilities for future research initiatives with PLC programs, a finding of this project revolved around the need for a shared language across programs in terms of formative evaluation efforts and research projects. A strength of the PLC remains its fluidity and responsiveness to different community partners and contexts; however, this fluidity often creates differing understandings and stages of readiness for programmatic evaluation—the deep understanding provided by our collaborative approach enabled this nuanced critique. Our report to the PLC suggests that moving toward shared understandings and commitments to research and evaluation efforts would only strengthen PLC programs and the potential for continued funding.

Finally, considerable dialogue with program directors on varying PLC curricular components revealed certain patterns in enacted programs across the various initiatives. This finding suggested to the program directors and PLC administration that consideration be given to program components and the curricular commitments in various contexts in the hopes of a more consistent intentionality in program design and enactment.

Struggles along the way included an initial resistance to research on PLC programs due largely to experiences with university researchers in the past that were reported as less than useful. In fact, some members of the leadership of PLC reported being "burned" by other research project evaluators—a research situation where a lot of time and energy was given by PLC for very little return. Arguing that the CUME model of translational research was possible despite its differences took time as trust needed to be built, benefit for PLC members needed to be clarified, and initial efforts needed to feel useful to the partners from PLC. Further, a strenuous process of member-checks throughout each step of the research and evaluation components in this process, in the spirit of "did we get it right," required that the core commitments of our translational approach be explicitly noted and followed. Time, dialogue, and humility when we "got it wrong" were all necessarily part of this process.

WHAT IS AT STAKE?

The rewards of Translational Research are many. We have had the pleasure of creating and maintaining partnerships in ways that Professional Development Sites in teacher education have rarely achieved. CUME faculty are consistently called upon to participate in new and evolving research and evaluation projects and we actively invite/involve community partners in for School of Education events, advisory boards, and the like. Being out in schools and the community provides a broader, more inclusive lens to consider the myriad of issues surrounding contemporary urban education. CUME faculty speak about the ways in which this work has helped to improve their teaching; infusing method, approach, and connection to the lives of teachers, students, and families.

Our campus is poised to be a leader in TRIP, and CUME has positioned itself as a leader in this regard. Throughout the campus, the question is asked: What is the role of the urban university? Our answer is straightforward: Is it not to serve as an engine of knowledge within and around the schools and communities in proximity to the campus? A place that is part of, not separate from, the community that surrounds it? A place that fosters new ideas, challenges old ways of thinking, and ultimately sets the conditions for meaningful change in students training to be teachers and researchers who then enter the community as agents of change informed with a deep understanding of local contexts? Perhaps most saliently for our lives in the acadmy, the best reward for those of us who work at CUME is the fact that this type of work is exactly what we wanted to do but thought would not be possible when we entered the tenure-track world of educational research.

We now turn briefly to the risks, or rather, the question of what is at stake in holding to these commitments. CUME researchers in general and the authors of this chapter in particular have been cautioned against conducting the work documented in here by colleagues and strangers alike. For example, at a faculty retreat a few years ago, a presentation on the Scholarship of Engagement prompted two full professors to state in response, "I would never let a junior faculty mentee of mine do that kind of research," and "It would be stupid." Their reasoning made sense in light of the possible hurdles they listed: (a) the time it takes to build meaningful partnerships, (b) many top-tier journals do not publish this type of work, and (c) there are too many variables and the inquiry could all fall apart, leaving the researcher with nothing for all their time and effort. These are valid concerns—challenges that have been deeply felt by those affiliated with CUME.

Another potential barrier for junior faculty involves the assumption that this type of collaborative research is appropriate for some but not for others. For example, the Council of Great City Schools is releasing its second round of funding for the Senior Urban Education Research Fellowships. A recent *Ed Week* article on the program stated,

> With funding of more than $2.5 million from the US Department of Education, the fellows work on research projects they have pitched to a panel of district officials from the Council of Great City Schools…If a project is approved, the researcher works directly with district officials to conduct the study. (Cech, 2008, p. 1)

Two major problems reside in such a seemingly innocuous news article. First, restricting applicants to *senior* researchers says something about who is capable or eligible to do this work. For example, Catherine Snow is quoted in the piece as stating,

> Studying problems of direct relevance to K-12 educators is not what the academy rewards, so it's hard for junior faculty members to do. They (meaning junior faculty) have to do what the arts and science faculty do, and rules are rules. You publish in the best journals, and to do that, you mine the research in those journals to find gaps in research. (2008, p. 4)

Other scholars represented in this article agreed with the seeming inevitability of such conclusions.

Secondly, the approach being proposed does not seem to trouble at all the tensions around the issue of *who* gets to generate such questions. Returning to the description of the faculty panel described above, the process outlined in the article sounds like senior faculty experts applying for a job—and they get to write the job description. Thus, the directionality of inquiry questions and perceived challenges facing the school appears to be coming from the researcher and not from the educators at the school level.

Our intention here is not to suggest that other researchers have not struggled with the same issues of power, purpose, directionality, and impact as we have here. Rather, our hope is that the CUME model may be one in which further dialogue is sparked in the hopes of learning from other like-minded researchers. The core commitments that we have chosen—to learning, people, teaching, and the work—provide us with a framework from which to proceed. Certainly, our dedication to a collaborative and generative research model has had varying levels of success; we have lived up to our ideals only partially and we learn by doing, working together with our community partners in the hopes of generating knowledge together that is useful in a variety of arenas. This is most evident in our last commitment—the commitment to work. The relationships that form the foundation for the research work of CUME do not end at the conclusion of studies or funding cycles, indeed they are often merely the beginning. Our translational approach necessitates a deep understanding of contexts and is necessarily dialogic, reciprocal, collaborative and, in all good hope, generative.

REFERENCES

Alpert, H., Goldman, L., Kilroy, C., & Pike, A. (1992). 7 Gryzmish: Toward an understanding of collaboration. *Nursing Clinics of North America, 27,* 47–59.

Boyer, E. L. (1990). *Scholarship reconsidered: Priorities of the professorate.* Princeton, NJ: Carnegie Foundation for the Advancement of Teaching.

Bulterman-Bos, J. A. (2008). Will a clinical approach make education research more relevant for practice? *Educational Researcher, 37*(7), 412–420.

Cech, S. J. (2008, November). Program lets urban districts call shots on research. *Education Week,* 1–5.

Coleman, A. (2007). Leaders as researchers: Supporting practitioner enquiry through the NCSL Research Associate Programme. *Educational Management Administration & Leadership, 35,* 479–497.

D'Amour, D., Ferrada-Videla, M., Rodriguez, L. S. M., & Beaulieu, M. D. (2005). The conceptual basis for interprofessional collaboration: Core concepts and theoretical frameworks. *Journal of Interprofessional Care, 19*(S1), 116–131.

Helfenbein, R. J., Jr. (2008). *Jamaican peace education programme* (Res. Rep. No. 13). Indianapolis, IN: Indiana University-Purdue University Indianapolis, Center for Urban and Multicultural Education.

Indiana University School of Medicine. (2008). *NIH awards $25 million clinical research grant to IU for statewide initiative.* Retrieved June 4, 2008, from http://www.medicine.indiana.edu/news_releases/viewRelease.php4?art=876

Labaree, D. F. (2008). Comments on Bulterman-Bos: The dysfunctional pursuit of relevance in education research. *Educational Researcher, 37*(7), 421–423.

Lagemann, E. C. (2008). Educational research as a distributed activity across universities. *Educational Researcher, 37*(7), 424–428.

Lather, P. (1991). *Getting smart: Feminist research and pedagogy with/in the postmodern.* New York: Routledge.

Lather, P. (1994). Staying dumb? Feminist research and pedagogy with/in the postmodern. In H. W. Simons & M. Billig (Eds.), *After postmodernism.* London: Sage Publishers.

Noblit, G. W. (1999). *Particularities: Collected essays on ethnography and education.* New York: Peter Lang.

Petronio, S. (1999). "Translating scholarship into practice": An alternative metaphor. *Journal of Applied Communication Research, 27,* 87–91.

Petronio, S. (2007). *JACR* commentaries on translating research into practice: Introduction. *Journal of Applied Communication Research, 35*(3), 215–217.

Reihl, C. (2006). Feeling better: A comparison of medical research and education research. *Educational Researcher, 35*(5), 24–29.

Schafft, K. A., & Greenwood, D. J. (2003). Promises and dilemmas of participation: Action research, search conference methodology, and community development. *Journal of the Community Development Society, 34.*

Shulman, L. (2000). From Minsk to Pinsk: Why a scholarship of teaching and learning? *Journal of Scholarship of Teaching and Learning, 1*(1), 48–53.

Siegler, E. L., & Whitney, F. W. (1994). What is collaboration? In E. L. Siegler & F. W. Whitney (Eds.), *Nurse-Physician Collaboration.* New York: Springer Publishing Company.

Stichler, J. F. (1995). Professional interdependence: The art of collaboration. *Advanced Practice Nursing Quarterly, 1*(1), 53–61.

**PART II: EMERGING QUALITATIVE METHODOLOGIES AND
THE ARTS: COLLABORATION AS QUALITATIVE METHODOLOGY**

ALETTE WILLIS AND JANET SILTANEN

6. RESTORYING WORK INSIDE AND OUTSIDE THE ACADEMY

Practices of Reflexive Team Research

In this chapter, we outline the practices of team-based research that we developed and implemented in order to take seriously feminist and post-positivist orientations to social science knowledge production. Reflexive practices became central to our endeavours both to create collegial working conditions for ourselves as academic researchers, and to create our collective interpretation of the substance of our research—neo-liberal transformations of work.[9]

This chapter represents the third (re)storying of our experience of working reflexively in a research team. The first story is embedded in the questions and answers that we posed to each other during the day-to-day conduct of our research. It exists in our memories of our conversations, and in more material form in the transcripts that we made of team meetings over the course of the research project. The second story is in a publication, the main agenda of which is to argue for the possibility and interpretive value of team-based reflexivity (Siltanen, Willis & Scobie, 2008). A central aspect of the second attempt to make sense of our team-based experience was a shift in our understanding of reflexivity—from abstracted reflection on how the researcher's self affects and is affected by the research to an understanding of reflexivity as a continuous interpretive resource embedded in the research process.

We present our next iteration in this chapter. We have drawn on slightly different social theories and theorists so that we might thicken our understanding of what it is to practice reflexivity as a non-hierarchical, collaborative research team. In our current story, we develop an understanding of reflexive research practices as involving particular forms of everyday conversational storytelling. In doing so, we draw inspiration from recent work that points to the close conceptual and practical connections between the activity of everyday storytelling and the collaborative dialogic analytic work of research teams. Looking again at our previous paper "Separately Together: Working Reflexively as a Team," we realized that although we had intended to set out how reflexivity can be done in the context of team research, we did not quite reach this goal. The orientations and practices we outlined do not actually describe how to do reflexivity but rather suggest ways of providing opportunities for reflexivity. In re-examining our efforts from the perspective of narrative inquiry, we hope to move closer to identifying how reflexivity can be done in and by research teams.

The chapter is organized into three main parts. In part one, we provide some background to the configuration of our research team and particularly to those practices and understandings that facilitated our ability to work as a reflexive team. In parts two and three, we explore in detail the ways in which everyday storytelling becomes a means of doing reflexive work in research teams. In part two, we distinguish between working reflexively *in* a team and working reflexively *as* a team. In this discussion we show the limitations of regarding team members as fixed voices of positioned experience. Rather, we argue that researchers working reflexively as a team engage in a continual flow of storying and restorying of selves, and that these efforts of everyday storytelling form the interpretive groundwork for constructing the overarching narratives of academic explanations. In part three, we turn explicitly to the construction of such overarching narratives. We argue that working reflexively as a team can be understood as a form of collective storytelling that moves beyond polyvocality to produce a common understanding as well as a thicker and richer account of how lives are lived.

CONFIGURING OUR REFLEXIVE RESEARCH TEAM

For purposes of the current discussion, we introduce three issues that were central to how we functioned as a reflexive research team. While our understandings and practices evolved over the course of the research project, we present here those that represent our most recent views. The three issues are: the ethos of team work and organization, the understanding of reflexivity, and the use of polyvocality within the research team.

The Ethos of Team Work and Organization

In this chapter we re-tell the story of our experiences working together on a research project entitled "Social Citizenship and the Transformation of Work." This project aimed to intervene in contemporary discussions about the "new economy" by excavating alternative knowledges of work. The public narratives that currently dominate are those that reduce work to paid employment relations, treat labor as a mobile, flexible production resource, represent productive activities as amenable to hierarchical and horizontal division, and represent workers as self-investing entrepreneurs with sets of skills to be plugged in and discarded as required (Beck, 2000; Purcell, 2008; Shalla & Clement 2007). These stories are part of broader discourses about neo-liberal transformations of work in the "new economy."

Our project explored the ways in which inequalities affect peoples' capacity to cope with work change (Siltanen, Willis & Scobie, in press). As contemporary commentators have noted, the narratives about work that dominate contemporary western societies also impact upon understandings of work in the academy. Team-based work in the social sciences has tended to be based on an "academic division of labor" that assumes research, including qualitative research, can be divided into discrete tasks and, further, that people ought to be assigned to tasks based on the sets of skills they have accumulated (Mauthner & Doucet, 2003). Through these assumptions, the dominant stories of the "new economy" echo. Had we engaged in team-based research in this way, our practices would have served only to reify the very narratives we set out to challenge.

Care had to be taken to avoid reproducing those same constellations of power/knowledge in our academic workplace. Therefore, both for the strategic reasons of wishing to challenge dominant discourses of work in Western societies and theoretical reasons to do with our post-positivist understandings of the construction of knowledge, we set out to share academic labor rather than divide it. To do so required a commitment from all involved to collaborate in non-hierarchical and supportive ways. It also required everyone on the core research team to be involved in all aspects of the research process.

A specific aspect of this team approach included ensuring everyone participated on as equal footing as possible in every part of the fieldwork. In particular, all of the core research team (including the principal investigator) shared equally in the interviewing process. We interviewed in pairs with one team member acting as interviewer and the second team member handling the recording equipment and taking occasional notes. After each interview, both team members were responsible for writing up joint fieldnotes on their impressions of the interview. This shared fieldwork experience, and the decision to interview in pairs, proved to be a vital component of our ability to work as a reflexive team.

The Understanding of Reflexivity

As we stated above, we were committed, for theoretical and strategic reasons, to practicing reflexively. Unfortunately, the methodological literature is not particularly helpful for those wishing to work reflexively in a team setting. Typically, it assumes a solitary researcher, and gives very little practical direction for contests in which there is more than one person involved in the research process. However, an important, recent shift in the literature on reflexivity does offer greater scope for its role in both individual and team research. Reflexivity initially tended to be viewed as a form of meta-analysis, a time-out from everyday research practice to examine the researcher's relationship to the research process and the participants. The act of reflexivity was utilized to consider how the researcher's position in society, embodiment, life experiences, etc. was implicated in the generation, analysis and presentation of data, as well as how undertaking the research impacted on the researcher's own state of being. Lately, there has been a noticeable shift away from conceiving of reflexivity as meta-analysis towards conceiving of it as an integral part of the process of making sense of the data and of all selves involved in the research.[10]

As we set out in Siltanen, Willis and Scobie (2008), our own understandings of working reflexively in a team changed over the course of our project–essentially following the trend in the literature. Initially we required that all team members commit to reflecting individually on how they were impacting and being affected by the research process. Team members were also expected to share their personal experiences and reflections with the group. These two requirements were situated in the conception of reflexivity as meta-analysis. We understood our research texts (the interview transcripts and notes) as constructed through the research process and our selves and our experiences as influencing and influenced by that process. Each of us took time to reflect on how our experiences, responses and perceptions were involved in the conduct of the interviews, the subsequent production of notes and transcripts, and interpretation of those texts. Similarly to Barry et al. (2003), we organized a special reflexivity team meeting in which to share our individual experiences of reflecting on our selves and the construction of research texts. This meeting was facilitated by a colleague from outside the team and was held while we were still in the midst of conducting our interviews.

We had thought that qualitative research in a team would involve a group of reflexive researchers working together separately. However, it became apparent that our commitment to working collaboratively and non-hierarchically was creating conditions for daily, on-going, reflexive dialogue between team members. Rather than doing reflexivity in quiet, private moments with a pen and journal, we were entering into reflexive dialogues in cars as we drove to and from interviews, as we struggled to articulate reflections in our shared interview notes, or as we ate our brown bag lunches at the table in the middle of our office. This embedded form of reflexivity was a conversational process in which we were engaged not only in trying to make sense of our interviews in relation to our research questions, we were also trying to make sense of our own lives. It also involved a shift in our understanding of working reflexively from something we did individually in a team, to something we did together as a team. This distinction also became central to our orientation to the team's polyvocality.

The Use of Polyvocality

Our realization of the embedded role of reflexivity in research processes strengthened as we came together to forge a collective interpretation of our interview material. We quickly came to see that reflecting together as a team meant reflecting on one's self in relation to a research process that not only involved participants but also involved other researchers. To borrow a phrase from Erickson and Stull's (1998) discussion, this "sets team members up for a double whammy" (p. 25). We found that in the face of this double whammy it was impossible to avoid being reflexive, as we were constantly being reminded of the partiality of our own perspectives. Sometimes team members had similar interpretations of what had happened and what had been said, but frequently they differed. In our previous paper (Siltanen, Willis & Scobie, 2008) we wrote that "we were routinely reminded of the specificity of our own interpretations, and needed routinely to negotiate the specificity of interpretations made by our team members" (p. 47). In team-based research contexts—at least in non-hierarchically-organized ones—we found that the reflexive nature of interpretation becomes unavoidable.

Once this became clear to us, we knew we needed to work with a different understanding of how our partially situated knowledges contributed to the interpretive work of the research project. In terms of "good" research practice, many researchers have written about the inevitability of bringing one's own personal biography to the generation and interpretation of data and of the importance of accounting for this (cf. See, for example, Breuer & Roth, 2003; Doucet, 1998; Fawcett & Hearn, 2004; Findlay & Gough, 2003; Mauthner & Doucet, 2003; McCorkel & Myers, 2003; Russell & Kelly, 2002) and still others have argued for the importance of polyvocality in post-positivist social science (Calhoun, 1992; Flyvbjerg, 2001; Haraway, 1991). These insights brought us to a commitment to consider the diversity of situated knowledges within the team as an interpretive resource.

However, diverse situated knowledges cannot be usefully employed as interpretive resources unless they are brought into conversation around a common goal. As Erickson and Stull (1998) remark, teams that remain polyphonic do not stay teams for long (p. 49). In our experience we had to begin, not end with, polyvocality. We tried to use polyvocality, and the diversity of situated knowledges within the research team, to work toward the construction of what Taylor (1995, p. 39) terms a "common understanding" of the research subject/object. As Taylor explains, "Understandings are undecomposable. That is…it is essential to their being what they are that they be not just for me and for you, but for us. That we have a common understanding presupposes that we have formed a unit, a 'we' who understands together" (p. 139).

Our goal, therefore, was not to preserve polyvocality, but to make use of it in forging a collective narrative. In our reflexive collaborative work, which was based on a sharing of research roles, our multiple and constantly shifting "voices" provided an essential interpretive resource, enabling us to develop a thick and common understanding of the subject/object of research. Rather than reflecting the subject/object of research through the multiple stories told by the individual voices of researchers working in a team, we sought to develop a common story, one that was thickened through being told and retold through our processes of working as a team.

The Link to Everyday Storytelling

These insights into the ways reflexivity and polyvocality were figuring in how we were working together as a collaborative, non-hierarchical research team have led us to appreciate the close relationship between everyday efforts to narrate experience and academic efforts to narrate experience. Conceiving our team's reflexive process as involving instances of everyday storytelling implies not only a conceptual link, but also an affinity of practice between academic research and everyday living.

Ochs and Capps (2001) argue that "the activity of narrating" in conversation "serves as a prosaic social arena for developing frameworks for understanding events. Narrative activity becomes a tool for collaboratively reflecting upon specific situations and their place in the general scheme of life" (p. 2). In what follows, we use this idea to explore practices of reflexive team work. Specifically, we build on the following three insights: 1) narrative conversation is part of "scientific" processes; 2) narrative conversation can be creative and move beyond particular stories toward what might be considered theory-building knowledge; 3) narratives, including academic narratives, are constructed within a tension between coherence and authenticity.

Reflexivity assumes that people are already "self-interpreting subjects" (Alcoff, 1996). As self-interpreting subjects, we constantly reflect on our own lives in light of the stories we are told by others or that we read in books or watch on television. Some narrative researchers would argue that the self arises out of such acts of reflection (Bruner, 1996; Holstein and Gubrium, 2000; Nelson, 2001). We agree with Pillow (2003) that much of what passes as reflexivity in academia does not go much beyond such an uncritical "recognition of the self"—albeit the self is recognized in this context in relation to research processes and research participants. We also agree that there can be a slippage in solitary reflexivity towards reproducing modernist assertions about subjectivity and representation. In contrast to this tendency, we begin from the perspective of the relational and de-centered narrative-self in order to examine reflexivity as a dialogical process in the particular context of collaborative, non-hierarchical qualitative research.

Early in our fieldwork, we scheduled and recorded a meeting for the explicit purpose of doing reflexivity. This meeting was subsequently transcribed. In our previous analysis (Siltanen, Willis, & Scobie 2008), we used this transcript to show the interpersonal dynamic of reflexivity in a team context. We were concerned to make the point that teams in reflexive dialogue bring a more complex range of interpretive resources to the table. To make this point, we extracted parts of this meeting to show team members making statements that involved three reflexive relationships—to the self, to the interviewees and to other team members. We have since revisited that transcript and now have additional stories to tell about it.

We can now see a contrast between how team members speak when they offer the results of their independent self-reflection, and when they reflect on themselves and others as an aspect of the on-going team discussion. We set out this contrast in terms of practicing reflexivity in a team and practicing reflexivity as a team. In addition, we highlight acts of everyday storytelling in our discussions and identify these as the beginnings of the interpretive narratives that eventually formed the core of our analysis. Previously, while we were aware of how much reflexivity was involved in our analysis meetings, we had underestimated how much analysis was involved in our reflexivity meeting. We see now that the two processes are even closer than we had originally thought.

We engage in this re-examination of how we talked about ourselves and others, as well as how we talked with others, in order to demonstrate two issues. First, working reflexively as a team can thicken understandings of research subjects as well as the selves of researchers in ways that are useful both analytically and in terms of practicing qualitative research in post-positivist ways. Second, working reflexively as a team with a commitment to creating a common understanding of the research subject/object involves moments of collaborative dialogue that concern both the co-construction of individual selves and the co-construction of the narratives connecting the many selves in our research process. We explore these two issues in parts two and three of the chapter, respectively.

RESTORYING OTHERS, RESTORYING OUR SELVES

From Working Reflexively in a Team...

Our reflexivity meeting was set up with our initial conception of reflexivity as meta-analysis in mind.[11] This conception is visible in our decision to have this session as a time-out from our normal research routines. It is also reflected in our decision to have an outsider facilitate our meeting, in our commitment as team members to prepare in advance through solitary reflection, and in the questions we identified to guide us. These questions were:

How did *your* own experiences of work affect *your* thoughts and perceptions of the interviews?

How did the interviews affect *you* and *your* thoughts on work, change and planning?

These questions invite monologues from team members about themselves and the partial knowledges from which they speak. As we demonstrate over the next few pages, it is only after the possibilities of solitary reflection have been exhausted that the discussion moves from being one of reflecting *in* a group to one of reflecting *as* a group.

AW starts the meeting with a summary of the solitary reflecting she has been doing concerning her location within the group as the sole contract researcher.

> AW—It's been interesting for me because I'm a contract employee ... I'm not doing any research for myself in this field and I don't work in the university so much as working for this project, there's a distinction ...It's been an interesting process to just step back... But it's not a common institutional context for doing research. ...The key is the institutional location but not having a lot of the background in terms of the theory, the literature.

In this interjection, AW reflects on her self in relation to her teammates. In so doing she creates both a narrative about her self as well as a story about who her teammates are. She defines her self as someone who speaks from a position of "contract employee" and who does not have a lot of background in the literature. Her teammates are storied in contrast to this self, but no details are provided about their individual stories.

Rather than engage with these stories, which include stories about her self, WS instead presents a report on her own self-reflexive experience. In this excerpt, we can see that WS positions her self in relation to the research topic as someone who is in the midst of change, and stories her self in relation to the interviews in a dynamic way.

> WS–I'm going to take a totally different tack on this because while we were doing the interviews from April until the end of July absolutely everything in my life changed on a very personal level. And I think that while I was

listening to people talk about their lives ...I was taking that home and thinking about it and then bringing back my own questions to the interviews...So I could see an exchange happening.

The narrative-self comes into being through asking the question: How ought I to live? (Frank, 2002; see also Nelson, 2001; Zoloth & Charon, 2002). We would suggest that WS is actively exploring this question through her participation in the research process. She brings new questions to subsequent interviews in part to figure out how to story her own as yet unresolved life decisions. Rather than being a self clearly situated in some sort of positionality in relation to the interviews, her self is being co-constructed through consideration of the interviews. However, while the "voice" she brings to the discussion is one that emerged out of dialogue with the interviews, in her initial contribution to the meeting she does not relate her experiences to AW. Similar to AW, she resorts to talking about other selves in a generalized way, with no room for "exceptions." Her interjection continues,

> WS— ...Just so interesting to have so many conversations with people where they start off talking about how important their families are then go on to describe their lives where their work time is the bulk of how they spend their time. And I can't think of any exceptions to that.

Once WS has finished speaking, the third researcher steps in. Like WS, she makes passing reference to the previous speaker but engages only sketchily with that speaker's view. Instead, she launches a report concerning how her understandings of her self and her experiences have been impacted by the interviews.

> JS–Those things also affected me a lot... In trying to think about things for today I think one of the things that affected me about it was that there was a sense of... "Oh I wish I could do that" you know...when people had a strong sense... of what was important to them, what their skills were, how they could put them together to create this perfect–well it wasn't a perfect life, a good life. When I look back at my own work change and strategies, it's been mostly opportunistic... one of the things that I was struck by was how knowledgeable they were about themselves ...And like WS that sense of–I don't know if it's going against the flow but actually opting for a happy life... They really thought about what was going to make them happy and that was so compelling.

There is a sense of rehearsal in these three interjections. At one point JS even says as much ("In trying to think about things for today..."). In anticipation of the reflexivity meeting each researcher had gone away to reflect on their own, they had decided how to story the interpretations of their self-reflections in relation to their perceptions of the context of the meeting and their audience of co-researchers. They then came to the group and made their reports. In the transcript excerpts above, each team member recites their own experiences and reflections with very little reference to what others have said during the meeting. Each speaker presents a position from which to speak but not in relation to each other. There is a sense that while these interjections report on reflections that emerged to differing extents through dialogue—WS's perhaps more clearly than the other two—in the context of the reflexive meeting, these interjections read like a series of monologues.

In these monologues, each researcher has taken a stand, a position in relation to the work and/or the interviews from which to speak. However, while reference is made to team members (AW) or interviewees (WS and JS) in the above excerpts, these "others" are talked about only in general terms, no details are provided about individual stories. This is important to note because as qualitative social researchers we are not only concerned with the construction of our own narratives but also with the construction of an overarching story about the subject/object of our research (more about this in the following section). Frank (2004) argues that monologues are problematic because they speak *about* other people, rather than *with* them. In speaking about people, particularly through disciplining practices of diagnosing or sociological practices of categorizing, monologues can foreclose on people's possibilities for being in the world. Even while the selves of the researchers are presented as being in flux, the three monologues presented above generalize about others in a way that risks foreclosing on *their* possibilities.

The monological nature of these interjections is highlighted both by the contradictions between the stories that WS and JS tell about the interviewees and by the fact that during the meeting neither of them pick up on these contradictions. WS reports that the interviewees claimed their families took priority, but then went on to story work as absorbing much more of their time and energy. JS says the interviewees not only knew their priorities but also strategically acted on them. Had WS or JS been working on this project alone, these may have been the seeds for two very different analyses.

Working reflexively but separately in a group makes obvious that different people, speaking from their different positionalities, interpret interviews differently. However, while engaging in reflexivity separately may enable unique voices to speak about a research subject/object from different positions, these voices tend to speak past each other. As with solitary researchers (Pillow, 2003), reflexivity in this situation risks being about the researcher's self and about making claims to authority over the research subject/object. We would identify these contributions as examples of reflexivity *in a team*. Team members working in this way do not interact with each others' stories or challenge or even discuss each others' experiences, rather they tell separate stories in parallel.

...to Working Reflexively as a Team

However, collaborative team research does not have to be conducted in this way. As a team we were committed not only to practicing reflexivity but also to developing a shared understanding of the subject/object of research. Following WS and JS, the first speaker, AW, re-enters the conversation. This time AW does not talk in a self-contained monologue. Instead, she begins to restory her self and her research experiences anew, this time in relation not only to the other two researchers but also to specific details within specific interviews. Her intervention turns the attention of the group to the details of one particular interview, to her connection with this interview, and to her similarities and differences to the two other team members in terms of the overall theme of this interview. AW's intervention begins to turn how the group talks, from a session of independent monologues (reflexivity in a team) to a dialogic interaction where the co-construction of all selves is in play (reflexivity as a team). With this intervention, the discussion moves from a presentation of parallel stories to the beginnings of collaborative storytelling. Her intervention is greeted with a strong vote of recognition by WS.

> AW–Just fixing the notes for one particular interviewee and … she said change has been good for her because she's always been in control of it. She's always planned for the next stage but at the same time this is someone who isn't 30 yet and already feels like she's achieved the level in her career she wanted to achieve and … I think she's in a bit of a life crisis right now in part because of that. … I'm like JS, I've never planned my job changes at all, I've been very opportunistic. And actually in contrast to JS through some of the interviews … I felt kind of validated in my approach … because a lot of people have planned things and then they haven't been happy with where they've gotten. I picked out from the interviews–and this is different—that it's not necessary to achieving happiness to actually go forth and plan your steps, because you still don't know what it will mean once you reach that step and you might not end up where you want to be. …So I internalize these interviews to validate my own approach.

> WS—Yeah, I can really relate to that, there's some things you're really looking for in those interviews to validate decisions you're mulling over.

The rest of the reflexivity meeting proceeds more or less in this vein, with the researchers storying and restorying their experiences and their selves in relation to each other and the interviews. The stories told and re-told about researcher selves and interviewees are detailed, and researchers engage with and sometimes challenge each others' interpretations. In reflecting *as a team* in this way, the selves of the researchers and the interviewees become destabilized and opened up for new possibilities of interpretation.

In our previous paper we argued that reflexivity is an interpretive resource. In the above transcript excerpts we have shown that processes of interpretation are irretrievably caught up in acts of reflexivity. One cannot reflect on one's self in relation to others without at the same time co-constructing the self and the other. Solitary acts of reflexivity may provide researchers with the opportunity to develop positions from which to speak about their selves and the research subject/object. However, academic practices that emphasize research as the product of creative individuals working alone risk reifying not only the positionality that the researcher has adopted but also the interpretation of the research subject/object. The benefit of practicing reflexivity as a team is that these positionalities and stories are continuously de-stabilized through dialogue. As we discuss further in Part 3, this has the effect of opening up possibilities for a common understanding of the subject/object of research.

INTERPRETING THE SUBJECT/OBJECT OF RESEARCH AS COLLECTIVE STORYTELLING

While telling stories about ourselves may be more easily grasped as an aspect of reflexive research practices, we maintain that it is also an aspect of the analytical practices that produce social science understandings and explanations. Maines (1993) argues that all social science data, even quantitative and behavioural data, draws on people's self-stories and should therefore be understood at least partially as being constructed narratively. This is consistent with Einagel's (2002) observation "that social research is very often about the telling of stories and (re)making of selves" (p. 234). Analysis in the social sciences can be conceived of as the creation of coherent collective stories out of the disparate and often contradictory self-stories told by research participants and, as we have seen above, out of researchers' own storied experiences.

Our objective in this part of the paper is to establish and illustrate this point – again by exploring transcripts from our team discussions. We examine what can be learned about the contribution of reflexivity to the creation of a "common understanding" of the research subject/object by looking at our team dialogues as examples of collective storytelling. A significant aim of this discussion is to illustrate how the polyvocalilty inherent in team research can be used as a reflexive resource to construct an overarching storyline.

As we have already mentioned, our research concerned experiences of work in the "new economy" and drew from resistant discourses of expanded feminist understandings of work and the household as well as post-positivist conceptions of a relational self. We were concerned with challenging dominant stories about the new economy, particularly stories about flexibility and about workers as un-embedded individuals. To this end, we sought to develop alternative stories about work, change, and the "new economy" which were grounded in lived experience. In doing so, we moved from individual narratives to collective narratives and from lived experience to public narratives.

Our efforts to develop alternative stories must be understood as running through the entirety of our research process, not just the analysis and write-up phases. Holstein and Gubrium (2000) explore local interactions in which people employ public narratives to give meaning to their experiences. They argue that for a public narrative to take on a life within society it must be taken up and enacted through the stories people tell about themselves. And yet it is in these highly local dialogues that public narratives are most vulnerable to being reinterpreted and changed. The interviews, the informal discussions we had with one another, as well as the formal reflexivity meeting and subsequent analytic meetings all provided opportunities for such potentially transformative local interactions.

During the reflexivity meeting, we discussed similarities in the ways in which interviewees presented their selves to us in interviews. Despite explicitly asking them to discuss work in the home, unpaid community work and the like, as well as how their household functioned as a whole, interviewees often resorted to dominant public narratives in storying their lives during interviews. These narratives downplayed the role of social networks and emphasized individualized capacities to be flexible. During the reflexivity meeting we came to call this "the script."

One of the team members, a male graduate student (MG) who was not able to attend the reflexivity meeting, transcribed it for us and added his comments and perspectives as a means to participate in our reflexive activities. With regards to our discussion of "the script" he wrote:

> MG: …I was happy when I had a sense of our interviews shaking people up and making them reflect on the conditions of their own lives and relationships. Particularly as it related to the household, I felt that the interviews had an important social function in making people think about their households and how it fit into their choices and opportunities. I think it is appropriate as critical researchers to create this effect, and consistent with the aims of this project. One person that I was in contact with after the interviews commented on how our questions really made him think for the first time about the connections between his household relationship and his life choices, and it sparked a new and fruitful conversation with his partner. So, if interviewees seemed particularly unaware of these relationships, I think I probably did make more of a point of asking questions about it. I suppose this is another example of how the interviews had a momentum, and I began to understand them within an exploration of the tensions/interconnections between the household and career choices, which also reflected things going on in my own life.

In other words, we saw the interviews as local dialogues in which we were actively engaged in co-constructing the interviewees' selves and the subject/object of research through providing alternative narrative resources. In discussing "the script" and the alternative story about embedded people, households and work, we were restorying them.

The following excerpt from our reflexive meeting shows the interplay between reflections on selves and reflections on a developing storyline about the subject/object of research.[12] Narratives at many different scales are evoked in this collaborative effort. To start, AW1.1 introduces a narrative about one of the interviewees and uses it to challenge her idea that a flexible attitude to work is associated with contemporary labor markets and younger workers, an idea that she associates with publicly circulating narratives ("everybody's always talking…"). JS1.1 responds to these thoughts by offering the observation that in the interviews she saw a gender pattern in thoughts on flexibility. AW1.2 responds by introducing the type of employer and employment sector as possible sources of difference in attitudes to flexibility. In these contributions, the focus is on identifying interpretive parameters for the collective storyline about flexibility.

> AW1.1–We interviewed one woman who was late sixties. I realized I have preconceived notions of what work was like, and everybody's always talking about how this is an era where people are expected to change jobs and that older generations stuck with one company and had this sort of straight career trajectory. This woman did not have this notion at all. Her husband hadn't

really taken that trajectory either. When she was talking about the good life she had this idea of changing jobs and trying different things...So I thought that was quite inspiring and interesting because I had these stereotypes that older people are not comfortable with change. I think women have often had part-time jobs and experience changing jobs and the man has more usually had the one career. I mean, with my parents my father had one job and my mother kept changing jobs. But this woman—her husband also had been into change and as a child her parents had changed jobs and moved around a lot. Everybody has the idea that their era is unique ... and her experience really combated a lot of that.

JS1.1–And it relates to the question we asked everyone about flexibility. I found it very interesting who went for that and said "oh yes, that's what we've got to be" and who challenged that idea...More often than not I found it was women who challenged the premise of that question. They challenged the notion that it's always individuals who have to be making change, and said that the system or the structure has to be willing to be flexible or adaptable and make change. Thinking about which people were a bit less individualistic in their sense of their circumstances, I found that question started to distinguish those people a little bit.

AW1.2–It was interesting too, there were some people who brought up their company, and they assumed that the company will be flexible. It was mostly high tech people saying that they can come in at 10 if they want or weekends or not work at all. ...but it was totally not done in a critical fashion. ...and I'm not sure what that says about these people.

As an act of everyday storytelling, AW and JS are struggling in this interaction with the same irreconcilable desires proposed by Ochs and Capps (2001) as ubiquitous: "All narrative exhibits tension between the desire to construct an overarching storyline that ties events into a seamless explanatory framework and the desire to capture the complexities of the events experienced, including haphazard details, uncertainties, and conflicting sensibilities" (p. 4). They argue that it is in raising alternatives and doubts that storytellers attempt to "regain the authenticity of the experience" (p. 6). The above transcribed comments move from a public overarching narrative that AW uncritically adopted, to the messiness of an interviewee's life, and again to proposals for alternative overarching plotlines about flexibility. JS and AW attempt to understand themselves and to articulate their own experiences in order to further their understanding of both particular interviewees and to develop an emerging collective storyline—the contrast between flexibility and stability.

After this exchange, both speakers move into a more self-reflexive mode positioning themselves in relation to what they have been talking about.

JS2–I don't know whether it's...again I'm trying to reflect on our own experience and how prepared we are to be flexible. There's this double message because there's the message that we have to be flexible to be okay under certain circumstances but...

AW2–I wonder if it's work and lifestyle as well. I enjoy flexibility but that's personality ...I worked 9 to 5 for a while and I hated it, I found it so stifling and I couldn't stand it and I'm actively seeking to avoid ever again doing that. But that's my personality and the way I like to work.

The two speakers then leave their self-reflexive attention, and return to the task of developing the overarching storyline. The contrasting dynamic of flexibility and stability is re-introduced by JS3 and further developed and modified by AW3.

JS3–Thinking about this meta-narrative that we're developing, there is the thing about flexibility but there is also the thing about security—invest in your pension fund, have your house paid off, etc. So we have this real conflict or tension. There are these messages about move, change and yet also messages about stay, invest.

AW3–Yeah but that's two different things. It's the money that stays, it's you that moves. And actually one interview I did with you, I thought it was very interesting how it was the money that, although very conservative, allowed her to do the change. So in some ways that ... can work together and in other circumstances that can be a tension.

In what follows, JS4 expresses some doubts about the developing storyline, again testing it against her own narrated experiences. After her interjection, the dialogue moves on to other topics, leaving unresolved the tension between the desire for an authentic expression of lived experience and the desire for an overall understanding.

JS4–I guess maybe I'm reflecting on my own experience with the cost of flexibility. My partner and I have two jobs and we went where the jobs were. I went where my job was and he went where his job was and that was very costly for us, in all sorts of ways financially and health-wise and all sorts of ways. And then making the decision to come here we lost pension entitlements. .... So I need to think about that. My experience of flexibility has been pretty negative in relation to this other part of the equation, in terms of security.

In the short interaction presented above, a number of different narratives were invoked and brought into dialogue with one another in complex ways as the researchers struggled to come to some knowledge of themselves and the research subject/object. Although we came together in this meeting to do reflexivity (as we originally understood it), interpretation of the subject/object of research was unavoidable. As all the above excerpts show, during this meeting we were collectively engaging in the co-construction of alternative storylines about work in the "new economy."

This restorying process had started with the interviews we did in pairs and the informal discussions we had with each other during our fieldwork. These initial forays drew on the diversity of our life experiences, our own narrative-selves, and our partially shared experiences of interviewing. They opened up a range of possible ways of understanding how people coped with work change. In the formal reflexivity meeting our initial understandings of our selves and the subject/object of research were brought into dialogue with each other. As Wasser and Bresler (1996, p. 11) describe so well, analytical processes within a group setting are highly recursive. The recognition of partiality and diversity fostered by polyvocality helped to create conditions for the creation of a collective storyline. However, this process involved not only many dialogic layers, but also many iterations of dialogic engagement The various storylines proposed, tested, reconstituted, and thickened during the reflexivity meeting went on to be subjected to many more discussions as we completed our fieldwork and moved into the analysis phase.

Converging on a Collective Storyline

Given that the most common genre for sociological storytelling is the journal article, our desire to provide as much of the messy details of lives lived through change as possible had to be tempered by the need to be concise. Our analysis meetings were held with the intention of working towards such a concise storyline.

In this section, we present an important moment in the development of our collective storyline – the moment when we converge on a common understanding of the different ways in which our interviewees were experiencing work change. This occurred fairly far into our analytical phase, after many formal meetings and many informal conversations. As we approached a common understanding, our individual interjections grew shorter and shorter (as can be seen below) and we spoke in a sort of short-hand, making reference to concepts and storylines that we had already agreed upon. This makes our transcript excerpts a little hard to follow, but we hope with some additional background information on the substantive issues in our discussion, readers will be able to appreciate how this extract illustrates convergence on a central theme of the collective storyline.

We initially planned to use a life course approach to help us understand differences in capacities for and orientations to work change. However, as we talked about our selves and the selves of our interviewees, it became apparent that this approach sacrificed too many of the messy details of people's lives for our purposes. By the time we had the meeting excerpted below, we had a rough sketch of an alternative story. We had decided to call the beginning of a work life the "launching" period. Those who had successfully launched then entered into a period of "solidifying." Many of the people we interviewed had made significant changes to their work profiles (indeed it was such people that we were most interested in). We categorised these experiences as processes of "relaunching."

Once we had established these preliminary categories, we each read all of the interview notes and tried to determine where interviewees were in relation to our emerging story. Not only did we find interviews that would not comfortably fit anywhere, some of us could not find our selves in the model. In the interaction excerpted below,[13] through retelling the stories of our interviewees and ourselves, we dialogue our way to the establishment of another category of work experience: scrambling.

JS—We were talking about whether we liked using the launching, solidifying and relaunching categories.

WS—I found that some of the people in my cluster of interviews didn't fit into any of these categories. The closest one was solidifying—but they were scrambling more then solidifying—just struggling to survive.

MG—I found it necessary to add another category as well. I guess everyone seems to be needing to re-launch, but not everyone's doing it really successfully. So, they're not really solidifying, and they're not managing to re-launch, they're just … scrambling.

WS—But one thing that I'll just put out there is that I thought about where I would be and I don't know. I mean, am I solidifying or am I still launching, because I'm still in school, the sense of permanence that I have is very temporary. I was just trying to think about that.

With one of the team members still unable to find herself in the developing storyline, we turn our attention to her circumstances, reflecting on them through one of the interviewee's stories. We begin by trying out our existing categories but conclude that we can only include the details of the researcher and the interviewee by creating another category: extended launching.

JS—I'd categorize you as launching.

WS—Which is kind of depressing (group laughter), I don't have it together yet.

AW—But you're not scrambling. This couple—Gary and Jane—they're scrambling.

MG—See, it's hard for me to tell. At the time that interview was taken, he's working part-time, he's writing. It's a picture of calm. The snapshot that the interview allowed was solid.

JS—Well, they have no money. They are trying to solidify, but …

AW—The money had run out at the time of the interview. I would almost say for them, it's an extended launching period. In part because of the field he's in. It takes a long time to develop a solid writing career.

JS—That's …

WS—Extended launching? There are a few people in our study who are in extended launching.

AW—Like perhaps WS and myself.

WS—Which is not such a bad thing.

We engaged in these interpretive discussions as our central practice of working collaboratively, non-hierarchically and reflexively through to a common understanding of the subject/object of our research. From the beginning we were seeking a coherent, overarching but dynamic understanding of people's experiences of, and strategies to deal with change. We hoped to produce a narrative or set of narratives that provided some overarching sense of people's experiences of the "new economy." As we engaged with the interview notes and with each other, we came to see a fluid and varied pattern of how people experienced work change. While lives have beginnings and ends, in the interviews and in our reflections on our own lives we saw many setbacks, many forks, loops and unforeseen circumstances challenging the more linear metaphor common in the life course approach. A little later in our analysis meeting, these understandings start to coalesce, forming the central idea of the story (circling) that we would eventually flesh out and write up in our publications:

JS—So, everybody launches, you could get an extended launch, and then you get to solidifying, or scrambling. I was wondering about who relaunches? Is it only people who have solidified that move to relaunching?

AW—No, I think that people who scramble can relaunch, try to relaunch.

MG—There's waves, like within the launch or extended launch, there's waves of solidification that either coalesce or it falls apart. People don't get into one track and stay there. That's the value of the idea of circling.

...

JS—And from scrambling there could be a circling back here to relaunching or a circling back to solidifying

...

AW—You see, what we've done here is that we've made it complicated—instead of the normal life course thing where you just go in a straight line from the beginning to the end.

JS—So you go from launch, maybe from an extended launch, you go either this way to solidifying or that way to scrambling. If you go this way, to solidifying, you can either hold on or deteriorate into scrambling. And from either situation you could go to relaunching.

WS—And this is the circling pattern.

AW—Yeah and we have that captured because the scrambling, solidifying, relaunching is really making a circular movement.

Our previous story about reflexive qualitative research in a team characterizes this dialogue as the moment in which "the interpretive insight about the non-linear flow of work/household experience really took hold and [was] adopted as a 'common understanding' within the team" (Siltanen, Willis & Scobie, 2008, p. 55). In the context of what we have been discussing in this chapter, we would argue that this was also the moment in which we achieved a compromise between the twin desires to develop an overarching storyline and to bring in some of the messy "complicated" authenticity of lived experience in a way that we all found satisfying. The resulting storyline is published in Siltanen, Scobie and Willis (2007) and Siltanen, Willis and Scobie (in press).

PARTING WORDS

We have argued here, and elsewhere (Siltanen, Willis & Scobie, 2008), that reflexivity and analysis cannot be cleanly separated. It was our experience that just as our reflexive meeting required us to begin to interpret the interviews, our analysis meetings continued to draw on reflexive relationships to the self, to interviewees and to other team members. Throughout this process we continued in dialogue to story and restory our selves, as well as the selves of the interviewees, as we struggled to find an overarching storyline about experiences of change in the "new economy." In examining the transcripts of our reflexivity and analysis meetings, we can see that everyday storytelling was at the heart of our reflexive interpretive process.

If dialogue enables the opening up and restorying of the selves involved in research and of interpretive possibilities, then collective approaches to research ought to be valued highly. After all, it is in such contexts that selves can be brought into dialogue around shared projects of collective story-making. However, to truly bring out a diversity of voices in relation to a sociological project, we believe that certain commitments have to be made. To allow for dialogue, rather than monologue, teams must be enabled to function non-hierarchically. Some degree of shared experience in relation to the research is also important in facilitating collective storytelling. For example, our commitment to an inclusive and equal division of labor in fieldwork and analysis was crucial to our own process.

While research teams offer the possibility of working with multiple voices, they must also be prepared to move beyond polyvocality in order to provide more comprehensive and coherent academic understandings. While solitary self-reflection may provide a useful starting point for reflexive collaborative research, it is important that dialogue between team-members be encouraged and enabled through and in regular team meetings. To work reflexively as a team, members must be prepared not only to reflect on how their experiences and interpretations relate to those of other team members and those of the research participants, but also to share, examine and challenge those reflections. To both use and move beyond polyvocality, teams must commit to working towards an overarching storyline that satisfactorily encompasses the messiness of both their own individual experiences and the experiences of their research participants.

In everyday, collaborative, academic storytelling, the tension between the desire to develop an overarching and yet concise storyline and the desire to represent the authentic messiness of lived experience can never be resolved once and for all. We see this as a good thing, for to finalize the subject/object of research would be to reduce its options for being and acting in the world (Frank, 2004).

Richardson (1995) is an advocate of storied forms of social research. She writes of the importance of providing new "collective stories" to individuals so that new lives can be lived. We submit that this is just as applicable inside the academy as it is outside:

> At the individual level, people make sense of their lives through the stories that are available to them, and they attempt to fit their lives into the available stories. People live by stories. If the available narrative is limiting, destructive, or at odds with the actual life, peoples' lives end up being limited and textually disenfranchised. Collective stories that deviate from standard cultural plots provide new narratives; hearing them legitimates a replotting of one's own life. New narratives offer the patterns for new lives. (p. 213)

In a context where the "religion of academic individualism is expressed in custom and is rooted in structure" (Erickson & Stull, 1998, p. 54), our experience of doing qualitative research collaboratively offers an alternative story to social researchers wishing to work in post-positivist ways.

How we do our work as academics is just as important as the content of that research. Dominant public narratives about work and the "new economy" have permeated academia. Research aimed at taking a critical orientation to such dominating discourses must also take a critical stance towards research practices themselves. Reflexive non-hierarchical collaborative research in which all aspects of academic labor are shared not only challenges neoliberal discourses about how work should be done and who workers are, it also produces thicker, richer descriptions of the social world.

REFERENCES

Alcoff, L. M. (1996). Feminist theory and social science: New knowledges, new epistemologies. In N. Duncan (Ed.), Bodyspace (pp. 13–27). London: Routledge.

Alvesson, M., & Sköldberg, K. (2000). *Reflexive methodology—New vistas for qualitative research*. London: Sage.

Barry, C. A., Britten, N., Barber, N., Bradley, C., & Stevenson, F. (1999). Using reflexivity to optimize teamwork in qualitative research. *Qualitative Health Research, 9*(1), 26–44.

Beck, U. (2000). *The Brave New World of Work*. Cambridge, MA: Polity Press.

Breuer, F., &. Roth, W.-M. (2003). Subjectivity and reflexivity in the social sciences: Epistemic windows and methodological consequences. *Forum Qualitative Sozialforschung/Forum: Qualitative Social Research, 4*(2), 1–8.

Bruner, J. (1996). *The culture of education*. Cambridge, MA: Harvard University Press.

Calhoun, C. (1992). Culture, history and the problem of specificity in social theory. In S. Seidmand & D. G. Wagner (Eds.), *Postmodernism and social theory* (pp. 244–288). Oxford: Basil Blackwell.

Doucet, A. (1998). Interpreting mother-work: Linking methodology, ontology, theory and personal biography. *Canadian Women's Studies, 18*, 52–58.

Einagel, V. (2002). Telling stories, making selves. In L. Bondi, et al. (Eds.), *Subjectivities, knowledges and feminist geographies: The subjects and ethics of social research* (pp. 223–235). Boulder, CO: Rowman and Littlefield.

Erickson, K., & Stull, D. (1998). *Doing team ethnography: Warnings and advice*. Thousand Oaks, CA: Sage.

Fawcett, B., & Hearn, J. (2004). Researching others: Epistemology, experience, standpoints and participation. *International Journal of Social Research Methodology, 7*, 201–218.

Findlay, L. (2003). The reflexive journey: Mapping multiple routes. In L. Finlay & B. Gough (Eds.), *Reflexivity. A practical guide for researchers in health and social sciences* (pp. 3–20). Oxford: Blackwell.

Findlay, L., & Gough, B. (2003). *Reflexivity: A practical guide for researchers in health and social science.* Oxford: Blackwell.

Flyvbjerg, B. (2001). *Making social science matter: Why social inquiry fails and how it can succeed again.* Cambridge, UK: Cambridge University Press.

Frank, A. W. (2002). Why study people's stories? The dialogical ethics of narrative analysis. *The International Journal of Qualitative Methods, 1*(1).

Frank, A. W. (2004). *The renewal of generosity: Illness, medicine and how to live.* Chicago: University of Chicago Press.

Gibson-Graham, J.-K. (1994). "Stuffed if I know!" Reflections on post-modern feminist social research. *Gender, Place and Culture, 1*, 205–224.

Haraway, D. (1991). *Simians, cyborgs and women: The reinvention of nature.* London: Free Association Books.

Holstein, J. A., & Gubrium, J. F. (2000). *The self we live by: Narrative identity in a postmodern world.* Oxford: Oxford University Press.

Maines, D. R. (1993). Narrative's moment and sociology's phenomena: Toward a narrative sociology. *Sociological Quarterly, 34*(1), 17–37.

Marcus, G. E. (1998). What comes (just) after 'post'?: The case of ethnography. In N. K. Denizen & Y. S. Lincoln (Eds.), *The landscape of qualitative research: Theories and issues* (pp. 383–406). Thousand Oaks, CA: Sage Press.

Mauthner, N. S., & Doucet, A. (2003). Reflexive accounts and accounts of reflexivity. *Sociology, 37*, 413–431.

Mauthner, N. S., & Doucet, A. (2008). "Knowledge once divided can be hard to put together again": An epistemological critique of collaborative and team-based research practices. *Sociology, 42*(5), 971–985.

McCorkel, J. A., & Myers, K. (2003). What difference does difference make? Position and privilege in the field. *Qualitative Sociology, 26*, 199–228.

Nelson, H. L. (2001). *Damaged identities, narrative repair.* Ithaca, NY: Cornell University Press.

Ochs, E., & Capps, L. (2001). *Living narrative: Creating lives in everyday storytelling.* Cambridge, MA: Harvard University Press.

Pillow, W. (2003). Confession, catharsis, or cure? Rethinking the uses of reflexivity as methodological power in qualitative research. *Qualitative Studies in Education, 16*(2), 175–196.

Purcell, M. (2008). *Recapturing democracy: Neoliberalization, and the struggle for alternative urban futures.* New York and London: Routledge.

Richardson, L. (1995). Narrative and sociology. In J. Van Maanen (Ed.), *Representation in ethnography* (pp. 198–221). Thousand Oaks, CA: Sage Publications.

Russell, G. M., & Kelly, N. H. (2002). Research as interacting dialogic processes: Implications for reflexivity. *Forum Qualitative Sozialforschung/Forum: Qualitative Social Research, 3*(3).

Shalla, V., & Clement, W. (Eds.). (2007). *Work in tumultuous times: Critical perspectives.* Montreal and Kingston: McGill-Queen's Press.

Siltanen, J., Scobie, W., & Willis, A. (2007). Flexible, branché et dans un cul-de sac!: Les inégalités stratégiques sans la négociation du changement au travail. In J.-L. Klein & D. Harrisson (Eds.), *L'innovation sociale* (pp. 193–206). Montreal: Presses de l'Université du Québec.

Siltanen, J., Willis, A., & Scobie, W. (2008). Separately together: Working reflexively as a team. *International Journal of Social Research Methodology, 11*(1), 45–61.

Siltanen, J., Willis, A., & Scobie, W. (In press). Flows, eddies, swamps and whirlpools: Inequality and the Experience of Work Change. *Canadian Journal of Sociology.*

Taylor, C. (1995). *Philosophical Arguments*. Cambridge, MA: Harvard University Press.
Wasser, J. D., & Bresler, L. (1996). Working in the interpretive zone: Conceptualising collaboration in qualitative research teams. *Educational Researcher*, *25*(5), 5–15.
Zoloth, L., & Charon, R. (2002). Like an open book: Reliability, intersubjectivity, and textuality in bioethics. In R. Charon & M. Montello (Eds.), *Storopies matter: The role of narrative in medical ethics* (pp. 21–36). New York: Routledge.

RICHARD D. SAWYER AND JOE NORRIS

7. DUOETHNOGRAPHY

Articulations/(Re)Creation of Meaning in the Making

In duoethnography, two or more researchers work in tandem to dialogically critique and question the meanings they give to issues and constructs. Examining personal artifacts, stories, memories, compositions, texts, and critical incidents, duoethnographers excavate the temporal, social, cultural, and geographical cartography of their lives, making explicit their assumptions and perspectives. Considering themselves the site rather than the topic of their research (Oberg, 1992), duoethnographers seek to discover and explore the overlapping grey zones in-between their perspectives as intertwined intersections that create "hybrid identities" (Asher, 2007, p. 68) instead of binary opposites. Through the juxtaposition of their stories, they examine their narratives of interpretation—how they have come to understand an incident or theme in and through their lives as well as the ways in which they have situated (and have been situated by) this understanding temporally, socially, and culturally. Further, they seek to explore the overall duoethnographic process itself as a way to (re)story their narrative perception of the particular topic or theme. (Re)creating as it archives, duoethnography thus acts as a form of praxis for its participants.

Duoethnography assumes, like most qualitative research, that human action is meaningful and that research "evince[s] an ethical commitment in the form of respect for and fidelity to the life world" (Schwandt, 2000, p. 193). Loosely based on Maurice Merleau-Ponty's (1962) belief that consciousness and culture influence experience and that experiences are always mediated by individual and cultural meanings given to past experiences, duoethnography is an examination of the process through which individuals make meaning out of a particular phenomenon. It is premised on the concept that as members of society we are suspended in "webs of belief" (Geertz, 1983) and are engaged in processes of enculturation (if not hegemony), even when we are attempting a reflexive stance.

Duoethnography, like autoethnography, focuses on "intersubjectivity thereby avoiding false claims to objectivity and failure-prone inner (hyper) subjectivity" (Roth, 2005, p. 3). By critically juxtaposing their stories, duoethnographers engage in a "radical suspension of judgment and submission to a systematic method of dealing with one's own prejudices and prejudgments" (Roth, p. 9). Duoethnography questions whether others, including researchers, can interpret the interpretations and meanings of others. Instead, in duoethnography two (or more) individuals create dialogic transactions (between and within themselves), as they seek critical tension, insights, and new perspectives. What distinguishes duoethnography from autoethnography is that rather than eschewing an emphasis on an individual's perspectives it provides multiple perspectives on a phenomenon, questioning the universality of meaning.

METHODOLOGICAL CONSIDERATIONS

To date, ethnographers have used three broad methodological approaches with their research (Norris, 2008). First, in duoethnography, as with many forms of qualitative methodology "The storytelling (collection) and discussion (analysis) are part of the writing process, not discrete phases" (Norris, p. 235). Data collection and analysis are integrated in creative, fluid ways. For example, Morna McDermott and Nancy Shelton write in their duoethnography of beauty,

> Layered within our individual histories and within our friendship as adults we struggle between the desire to resist dominant narratives taught to us by family, media, and society and yet we cannot completely untangle ourselves from it, and wonder if complete rejection of this grand narrative curriculum of Beauty is even possible. (McDermott & Shelton, 2008, p. 1)

As they present a collection of stories about beauty, they engage simultaneously in a process of collection, analysis, and writing. Their juxtaposition of once familiar stories leads to personal critique, as they "wonder if complete rejection of this grand narrative curriculum of Beauty is even possible." And as they do so, they find themselves in a new, "in-between location."

The second methodological consideration is that dialogic transaction is central to duoethnography and that this transaction is made explicit. Unlike the writing style of this chapter, duoethnographies are written like a play script through which the readers witness the writers in conversation. Because the text may be written as a conversation and like a play script, the reader can clearly distinguish each collaborator's writing. In this process, readers witness the two or more individuals in quest for understanding self and others as they compare and contrast their experiences.

The aim of this methodology is not to reduce a concept to universal statements gleaned from the conversation. Rather the conversations present both thesis and antithesis, enabling the readers to form their own synthesis. These readers included not only a potential audience, but also the ethnographers themselves. The format of distinguishing individual voices makes this work possible and is designed to lead to an ongoing meta-analysis of the actual act of articulation. Dialogue, underscored by a dialectical process, begets insight. By actively listening to the explicit voices during the process of articulation, researchers can seek a dynamic (and fluid) synthesis.

Consequently, duoethnographies generate multi-voiced texts, promoting a process of heteroglossia (Bakhtin, 1981)—of meaning generation found within dynamic texts. Bakhtin discusses the novel as the most flexible and open genre in writing. Novels incorporate every form of written language, from prose, to poetry, to dream sequences. Everything that people write about in their lives eventually finds its way to a novel. Furthermore, as a reader reads a text, she adds her own interpretation—her own poetry—to a particular reading, transacting with the text and creating a new text (Rosenblatt, 1994/1978). The heteroglossic dynamic found within a novel is similar to that found within curriculum, and especially the curriculum of duoethnography. Unlike literature, though, duoethnographies are lived and reported collectively and are open to the unexpected and unimagined.

In duoethnographies, the dialogue moves not only from person to person, but also from artifacts of our lived cultural media, which we include in our studies. For example, Sawyer and Norris (2004) included pictures of friends, schools, work and historical sites in their telling of a curriculum of sexual orientation. Along similar lines, Liggett and Sawyer (2008) created a multi-voiced text by juxtaposing high school yearbook photos from two different time periods and parts of the country (the 1970s Northwest contrasting with the 1980s Midwest) in their duoethnography of post-colonial education. Examining images and memories from a critical trip to Africa she took shortly after high school, Tonda writes,

> Even in high school, while there were many clubs and organizations, there was no rallying around anything political and notions of diversity at my school meant the French and Spanish language clubs. I can only think that this provided fertile ground for shaking me to my very core as I stepped out of the Nairobi airport and realized that it was nothing like Kansas. Little did I know that my dominant white, middle-class orientation was about to be deconstructed. (in Liggett & Sawyer, 2008, p. 7)

Scrapbooks, photo albums, report-cards, saved letters or other memorabilia can be "vocal" participants in a duoethnography. Norris and Greenlaw (2008) examined their archived personal writings from their public school and university experience. Such an activity evoked personal memories of what inspired them as they wrote, enabling them to (re)trace their experiences uncovering dimensions of their curriculum/currere of writing. While they found both similarities and differences with their motivation to write, a sense of a "muse" was common for the co-authors. In this way, duoethnographers are encouraged to reexamine their entire life histories as evoked by such artifacts.

Third, duoethnography is framed as a lived-curriculum. Pinar's (1975) concept of "currere," a critical form of autobiography and curriculum studies, examines the curriculum of everyday life—it is the process of examining the various dialectical relationships in one's life. In *currere*, this critical examination process unfolds as a regressive, progressive, analytic and synthetic endeavor, premised on the recognition that conceptualization is transtemporal and changes over time (Norris, 2008; Sawyer, in press). This form of self-study, then, can be regarded as a looking back to make new meanings of previous experiences and conceptions. The process of awareness in tracking of how one comes to believe something leads to a change in those beliefs, a reconceptualization of self and world.

The notion of *currere* informs duoethnography in two key ways. First, as can be seen from this definition, the dialectical process ("regressive/progressive, analytical/synthetical") is central. The goal of a dialectical interaction is not a greater understanding of existing meanings and interpretations. Rather, it is the actual reconceptualization of those meanings. The engagement in the process leads to reconceptualized understandings. Secondly, duoethnography draws from *currere's* emphasis on learning to read self as text—as fluid/fixed, linear/recursive, lingular/multi-layered within a given cultural context. The act of recalling events and reading beliefs within a playful yet disciplined dialogic frame itself becomes part of the *currere*.

We (Sawyer & Norris, 2004), for example, examined the concept of *currere* in their duoethnography on "the hidden and null curriculum of sexual orientation." As we have continued to examine this duoethnography over the past few years, the sense of meaning for both of us related to these events has been transformed. Initially, Rick focused on specific events in this research. As he went to high school in Seattle in the early 1970s, he examined how the null curriculum found in school and society around sexual orientation—specifically a usually unstated hostility towards gay and lesbian issues projected in a null curriculum—did not lead him to internalize the relatively hostile heteronormative culture. Instead, he initially considered how it led to his development of a dual lens focused on a dialectic between heteronormativity and gay agency a private curriculum of liberation expressed in a shared code with friends. In this duoethnography, Rick explored this theme through an analysis of his and two friends' artwork from an earlier time in their lives. Here is a passage from four years ago about two deceased friends, one who was a photographer and the other a writer:

Behind the jarring angles and sharp shadows in Steve's photography, for example, are passionate people. Even the very objects in his pictures seem animated and infused with beauty. And the characters in Jean's stories are sometimes damaged and often eccentric, but their pain is self-contained as they act with compassion towards others. (p. 157)

As I (Rick) wrote the above words and initially considered their meaning, I recognized my and my friends' agency and wit in complex situations. But my meanings have continued to change. I now am struck by how many of our public acts of communication transcended our own situations to encompass a profound respect and hope for humanity. My and my friends' art and acts of rebellion sought tolerance for all.

In this early duoethnography, Joe wrote:

Fast-forward from the mid-seventies to the early nineties to a time when my daughters were six and nine. By this time I had acted with gay men, some had taught me and others were colleagues. But I found that I too practiced the null curriculum at home. I did not want to make a big deal over gay rights as I wished that my daughters would consider the life style as a natural and legitimate lifestyle. I thought then that making it a big deal would reinforce the difference, possibly in a negative way. But my silence was problematic. (Sawyer & Norris, 2004, p. 148)

As can be seen, in this study on the null curriculum of sexual orientation, we traced and redrew our emergent and changing meanings on this topic. By juxtaposing our stories which expressed very different meanings while we lived in similar cultures at the exact same time, we looked back to look forward, were regressive to become progressive, and transformed our meanings related to this complex topic through our *currere*.

THE TENETS

Duoethnographies are emergent and their methodology remains open to avoid becoming prescriptive. As a project unfolds, it begins to define itself with spontaneity promoting change. This process is aligned with Dewey's (1934) discussion of an artist's role: "If the artist does not perfect a new vision in his process of doing, he acts mechanically and repeats some old model fixed like a blue print in his mind." (p. 54). As such, each group of researchers is free to adapt the method to their unique circumstances. In this process, creativity and playfulness can help researchers both develop and sustain multiple dialogues, including those between researcher/researcher, researcher(s)/artifacts, past/present, text/text, and different unfolding combinations. Thus, core tenets of duoethnography revolve around themes of a) communal and dialogic conversations, b) the transformation of meaning, c) a focus on the phenomenon or construct, not the person, d) the importance of difference, e) the need to recognize power differentials and f) noting the placed-situatedness of meaning. Although we discuss these tenets as discrete themes for the purposes of clarification here, in reality, they overlap and rely on mutual definitions.

Focus is on a Communal Conversation [dialogue]

Levinas (1984) claims that we need the Other in order to understand self. Open dialogue is central to this methodology and those who read the research witness the changes in the individuals as they converse with one another. Rather than being fixed with the predetermined conclusions provided, the readers witness the organic progression of the individuals in conversation—the meanings to which the parties subscribe change as a result of the conversation. This notion of a communal conversation is consistent with Bakhtin's (1981) notion of dialogue, the idea that dialogue can lead to a shattering, and reformation, of meaning. As opposed to authoritative discourse, in true dialogue the act of utterance creates a context in which a word "becomes relativized, de-privileged, aware of competing definitions for the same things" (Holquist, 1981, p. 427). In reviewing Bakhtin, Holquist, states that "dialogue may be external (between two different people) or internal (between an earlier and a later self), as well as spatial (A to B) or temporal (A to A) (1981, p. 427)."

Holquist's (1981) definition of heteroglossia, another construct central to Bakhtin's constructions of talk, delineates how a dialogic situation can lead to change

> Heteroglossia is...[t]he base condition governing the operation of meaning in any utterance. It is that which insures the primacy of context over text. At any given time, in any given place, there will be a set of conditions—social,

historical, meteorological, physiological—that will insure that a word uttered in that place and at that time will have a meaning different than it would have under any other conditions; all utterances are heteroglot in that they are functions of a matrix of forces practically impossible to recoup, and therefore impossible to resolve. Heteroglossia is as close a conceptualization as is possible of that locus where centripetal and centrifugal forces collide.... (Holquist, 1981, p. 428)

In duoethnography, the dialectical situation, the heteroglossia, is fluid and dynamic, created by our reading/transacting with a variety of media. We encourage the use of artifacts and pictures to stimulate recall and provide other media representations. The act of this methodology also transforms previous meanings held by adding multi-voices to the text, as archived photos are reconceptualized (given new meanings) through the processes of reflection and conversation. Furthermore, this dialogue involves the reader or hearer of a duoethnographic text as well, as duoethnography is generated for an audience (readers, hearers). As Roth (2005) states, referring to Derrida (1985), "biography (ethnography)...comes to life only through the countersignsature of the reader or hearer" (p. 11). When one writes with the awareness of a reader's response (Rosenblatt, 1978 and Barone, 1990), one attempts to create a dialogic space, in which the reader's voice is recognized, inviting a "countersignature."

The following photo was an artifact in a duoethnography that Rick wrote with Joe.

Rick's artifact-evoked story. I was with my friend when he took this photo, which I have used as an artifact in a duoethnography. Over time, this photo has become increasingly abstract, with its images—disconnected legs, shadowy bodies, scraggly grass, amorphous background landmasses now triggering a deeper meaning of the actual events of that day: A friend and I made a rare excursion to a beach. We took off our shirts and felt self-conscious. We saw beautiful people sharing a very concrete, sensual moment. We felt disconnected, abstract, hopeful, ironic. When I see the photo now I love the sculptural quality of the bodies as well as the sense of disruption of a "normal" beach scene. I also now appreciate the photo not for its abstract quality or its "clever" framing, but rather for its sense of humanity. This reading of the photo follows a dialectical process, of creating a thesis (original meaning of the photo), antithesis (new reading of photo), and synthesis (meta-articulation of the process). Throughout, I am trying to create a hermeneutic circle in which I move from the specific to the general, from the detail to the context, from the reflection to the insight and then back to the reflection. Through this process I am changed as I "transact" with this photo.

Joe's photo-shoot story. To accompany Rick's photos, I (Joe) revisited my former elementary and secondary schools as well as a local historical site to photograph them. The once fond memories were now etched with the scars of homophobia. I felt embarrassed taking the pictures as I was making explicit the null and hidden curriculums of my schooling. I wondered what the Sisters of Charity would say about my exposure. In choosing one photo, I decided to use the blurred image of my elementary/junior high school, rather that the clear one, to visually demonstrate the heteroglosia of the image.

After the publication of Rick's and my article of sexual orientation, my high school, St. Patrick's High School, was to be merged with our rival non-Catholic high school, Queen Elizabeth High School. A new site was chosen at the foot of Citadel Hill, an historical landmark, for the new construction. The name "Citadel High" was chosen and I voiced to the deputy minister of education and the incoming principal that I thought "Queen Patrick" would be more appropriate to make some amends for previous history. The act of taking photographs heightened my perspective of my schools' legacies bringing in the shied away from conversations.

Duoethongraphy in action: Blending our stories together. To generate new thoughts, the use of artifacts and pictures to stimulate recall and provide other media representations is encouraged. The act of this methodology also transforms previous meanings held. When we examine the above photographs, each time that we look at it we will form a transaction with it. Our understanding and appreciation of it will not be contingent on our finding its "essential" meaning, but rather our understanding of it at that moment. This process, similar to Rosenblatt's transactional theory (1994/1978), implies a transaction between the reader of a text and the text. Reader and text enter into dialogue, with the meaning of this dialogue residing exclusively in either, but rather from the relationship unfolding between the reader and the text. This relationship creates a new poem of meaning. Similarly, as we tell or retell our stories to others, our relationship to that story is always different in time, space, and dialogic framing. We are not seeking the inherent meaning of that story, but rather our transaction with it at that moment—a transaction that may be expressed or represented through a variety of media.

Focus is on phenomenon, construct, or issue, not the person. Antoinette Oberg (1992) encourages those who write autobiographies to be the sites of the research but not the topic. Duoethnography's approach is not biography or autobiography with the emphasis on a person. Nor is it autoethnographic with an emphasis on an individual. Rather it is, at minimum, duo-directional and dialogic as two or more individuals' stories intertwine and inform one another with those that read their juxtaposition adding yet another layer to the discussion. As researchers engage in duoethnography, they explore the particular topic with self as a very human context of exploration. This process of exploration can create a dynamic between our subjective theories and histories and the complex cultural contexts in which we find ourselves. The goal of duoethnography is not for the researcher to get to know herself or himself better but rather to begin to reform the dynamic between personal meanings and their sociocultural inscriptions.

Focus is not on uncovering meanings but creating and transforming meanings. One's life history and analytical frame toward any particular event or theme is inextricably interwoven with that theme, making it impossible to assume a distant or objective stance toward any inquiry. Instead of being able to study a topic—e.g., gender, illness, ethnicity—independent of self, one instead can study the situated nature of self within that theme or topic. Duoethnographers, then, do not research themselves, but a construct made manifest in themselves.

Nor does duoethnography attempt to access the meaning that is or has been held on a given topic/issue. If duoethnographers enter into the research and writing with fixed ideas, the result will not be dialogical. The emphasis is on the "quest," the questioning, as the conversation with the OTHER should change one's personal stories in some way. The researchers must be open to (re)storying their own lives and existing meanings that they give to their experiences may change as a result of the conversation. Consequently, duoethnography is an explicit meaning making process. Once trust is established between the researchers/writers, they become willing to provide their insights on each other's meanings. This provides a necessary rigor to the research, similar to that of a second reader. Furthermore, duoethnographers try not to situate themselves as either the hero or victim. Such a stance places the researcher, rather than the topic, at the center. Placing self as a pilgrim on a journey toward meaning recognizes that present understanding is incomplete. This is what keeps the conversation moving forward and the final writing open.

This process of transforming personal meaning was cyclical for Maryam Nabavi in her duoethnography with Darren Lund, involving and discussing earlier experiences.

> I work to reclaim my multiple identities and become more aware of both the challenges and advantages that I carry. Finding a middle place to the extremes, as constructed by dominant rhetoric, is an ongoing process that I embrace through transformative approaches to social change and always being counter- hegemonic. (Lund & Nabavi, 2008, p. 27)

Nabavi continues provocatively,

> I really think this was the most poignant experience in learning about how we can carelessly take advantage of our social locations and perpetuate power imbalances in our communities. I find that this understanding has created a tension that, at times, I do not know what to do with, from within my standing in the Eurocentric milieu of Canada. (Lund & Nabavi, 2008, p. 29)

Thus, in a duoethnography we view our stories and histories (discourse and practice) not as indicators of essential themes, but rather "as the media around which socially and historically positioned persons construct their subjectivities in practice" (Holland, et al, 1998, p. 32). Through this dialogue, we constructed our emergent subjectivity in practice in relation to phenomena under investigation. Often the dialogue itself between the writing pair is included in the study and becomes part of its data collection and the analysis.

Difference is a strength. In duoethnography, differences among the researchers/ writers' points of view are considered strengths. Since duoethnography does not seek universals but examines how different individuals give both similar and different meanings to a shared phenomenon, it looks to the margins to create a range of meanings. The gaps that lie between the different perspectives and different voices create a space for the exploration of the fluidity of identity, the layered, recursive, often inconsistent, and buried and implicit layers of who we are. Instead of finding the mythology of our lives, we search to unpack the hybrid nature of our identity. This multiplicity may be found in the "in-between" spaces. For example, the gay/straight difference between Sawyer and Norris, the class difference between Shelton and McDermott and the different attitudes of reading and writing between Norris and Greenlaw increased the range of perspectives experienced by the researchers and forced them to begin to articulate implicitly experienced but uncharted territories. In these pieces, the researchers focused their quests on both their similarities and differences, on the specific and the general.

The Importance of Trust and Recognition of Power Differentials

As can be seen from the above examples, the creation of a safe space for researchers is central to duoethnography. While traditional ethnography attempts at uncovering the meanings that participants hold, duoethnography promotes the interrogation of meanings. Those involved in duoethnography can expect that the Other partners will generate counter-narratives. Joe and Rick began as respected colleagues who were accustomed to discussing contentious issues. The addition of articulating personal stories was a natural progression. McDermott and Shelton (2008) were long time friends and colleagues who often shared stories of a personal nature. Making these a formal research process that would become public was a welcome extension. In these cases and others, the research grew from established partnerships. However, it is anticipated that as the methodology grows, trust may not be a prerequisite, but an openness to be questioned and to question would be.

Trust, respect, and collegial relations become more complicated when power differentials that are all too real in society are present. The inequitable conditions that exist in the "real world" can be easily (re)inscribed by researchers as they conduct a duoethnography. Lund, who created a duoethnography with a former high school student (Lund & Nabavi, 2008), first discussed the nature of the work with her, entering into the research with her as an equal collaborator. In order to help work towards a lessening of the possible reification of the kinds of power inequities this methodology has been designed to deconstruct, we recommend that before beginning a duoethnography, researchers take the time to talk about how they want to work together, covering everything from their roles as they collect data to their participation in the analysis and reporting of their findings.

The Articulation of Place-Situated Meanings

As members of still relatively place-based cultures, we are all deeply implicated in ongoing projects of colonialism, social and environmental injustice, and health and education inequities. These injustices certainly take place within countries but they also occur across countries and continents as the divisions increase, and with them so do possibilities for more deeply engrained preconceived views of others. Such perceptions can and do frame international and multi-cultural research, especially research where there are more explicit power differentials not unlike the relationship between researcher and researched. Recognizing that consciousness and culture influence experience and that experiences are always mediated by the meanings given to past experiences, duoethnography asks researchers to examine how they are situated in relation to other forms of inquiry and make this explicit to themselves and their readers.

THE PROCESS: JAZZ PERFORMANCE AS METAPHOR

Often an audience will experience a jazz performance as a seamless and nearly self-generating expression of innate genius. As an audience member, I have often gotten lost in seemingly spontaneous, creative, and effortless sounds. The music almost appears to be self-generating, a new composition springing forth from the players and their instruments. For jazz musicians, however, the process is quite different. Playing together, they draw from years of training both in music as well as other more theatrically located aspects of performance (cf. Berliner, 1994; Fischlin & Heble, 2004; Zorn, 2000). They listen closely to each other and respond to the emerging improvisation between them. The know how to ground their contribution in something larger and more theoretical than themselves. And, what and how they play are closely tied to who they are and the contexts that inform those understandings. In a successful performance, personal and musical identities as well as musical theory and history interact dialogically.

Of course, the creation of a duoethnography is very different from a jazz performance on many levels such as the medium of expression and the immediacy of interactions with one's audience. However, there are similarities. Both jazz performance and duoethnography are premised on participants' creating a process of relatively deep personal engagement, one tied to their identity. They both promote a goal of participants' and listeners' (re)storying their narrative meanings (see Baily, 1993; Berliner, 1994; Fischlin & Heble, 2004; and Zorn, 2000 for discussions of the narrative nature of both jazz improvisation and improvisation in general). In both, the process is emergent and its performance the product. Duoethnography shares a goal of transformation with great art and music. And, duoethnography is framed by theory and intellectual history. Unlike improvisational music, however, duoethnography's emergent methodology focuses on both form and "content." They use a medium that potentially will change previously held meanings.

When Tonda and Rick wrote their duoethnography on post-colonial education, they worked together in a number of ways which were more recursive than linear, more collaborative than individualistic. Well before starting to write, they talked at length about their project and how they wanted to work together. They first wrote an initial draft that they considered a rehearsal, if you will, for the next draft. From the first draft they identified three emergent themes that they chose to explore in the next draft, their early socialization in their respective public schools, their familial contexts, and their subsequent teaching. As they began to work together, they slowly decided to explore these themes through the use of very specific artifacts from their lives: old photos, high school yearbooks, and personal lesson plans from their own history as public school teachers.

After this initial discussion, they separated and began to write sections of the paper, corresponding to the themes, in parallel. This was not a parallel process in the Piagetian sense, as in "parallel play," which is characterized by an egocentric disconnection between infants. Rather it was more Vygotskian (Vygotsky, 1986), as they intentionally explored and internalized aspects of their previous dialogues. The co-authors wrote a number of drafts and, almost without planning, ended up meeting together and discussing each successive draft. As part of this process, they made formal presentations to themselves, and, using a theoretical lens related to post-colonialism (i.e., Pennycook, 1998; Shuck, 2001; Shuck, 2006), asked questions and made connections, associations, and disconnections between their respective findings. Their comments to each other were focused not on each other as individuals, but rather on their understandings and meanings. For example, by applying postcolonial theory in this particular conversation to his emerging ethnography, Rick began to see how societal structures framed his perceptions. A key insight was that if these societal frames were present in one form at one point in his narrative, they may still exist, albeit in a more insidious form, at another point (which they did). Then, they went back and revised and repeated the process. While this revision process was informed by an intentional theoretical framework (e.g., postcolonialism theory), it was organic in that it was grounded in their particular and unique dialogue. It was a transaction created by the dialogue of these various perspectives.

How Tonda and Rick worked together illustrates a few key considerations of duoethnography. While the process is dialogic, each participant, while challenging the Other's assumptions, is non-judgmental about the work of the other as the goal, through dialogue, is to transform one's own narrative meanings, not the other person's. The two of them listened to each other and responded respectfully by recognizing each other's ideas and ways they are situated historically and socially. The theoretical framework they used in post-colonial theory gave them a lens that transcended themselves and further promoted new ways of thinking.

Because duoethnography does not take place "in a vacuum" it can easily reflect taken-for-granted patterns of interaction and normality that reinforce (often but not always subtly) inequities in society. For example, by not listening and responding to each other participants can reinforce inequities. Issues may arise at different points in the process as duoethnographers work together and present their work in public. A worst-case scenario might be where there is a major power differential, one that is historically and socially situated and masked by normativity, between the duoethnographic partners. In such a case, the more "powerful" one might choose (perhaps unintentionally) to appropriate and redefine his or her partner's story and in doing so, despite the dialogic nature of the project, ultimately reify hegemonic traditions, ideas, or ideals.

However, as a method, duoethnography holds considerable potential to surface, expose, and rectify such patterns. As a research methodology, part of its strength lies in the way its participants can explicitly use it to move beyond a "broken record" scenario and establish new ways of interacting with self and others. For example, Diedre LeFavre, an educational researcher in New Zealand, has been engaged in a collaborative research project with a colleague in a different discipline. She thought that duoethnography would allow her to explore "dangerous conversations" with her partner as preparation for their study (actually on the dangerous conversations that their adolescent participants have with one another). As with this example, the goal of duoethnography is to allow participants to engage in dialogic self-study and thus to empower and intellectually liberate its participants.

CONCLUSION

Underpinning duoethnography is the belief that, given each individual's geographically and culturally situated history, socially constructed meaning is transient with multiple perspectives on a construct. With the recognition that there is meaning embedded in the medium (McLuhan, 1967), the writing style is coherent with its epistemological belief as each writer's voice made explicit, showing the diversity of meaning and its making. Such a style breaks the metanarrative of a solitary writer, inviting readers into the space created by dialogue between the duoethnographers. Duoethnography's writing style is also organic as readers witness progressions in meaning making as the researchers converse. Consequently, it is a pedagogic (Denzin, 2003) methodology as the researchers come to better understand themselves and the world around them as a result of the study. By sharing this pedagogic journey others may conspire with the researchers (Barone, 1990) as they juxtapose their stories with the written text. Finally, duoethnography makes little claim to a fixed style or approach as it encourages each team of duoethnographers to create their own emergent styles as the content and the personalities dictate. In so doing, the dialogue also continues…

REFERENCES

Asher, N. (2007). Made in the (multicultural) U.S.A.: Unpacking tensions of race, culture, gender, and sexuality in education. *Educational Researcher*, *36*(2), 65–74.

Bakhtin, M. M. (1981). *The dialogic imagination*. Austin, TX: The University of Texas Press.

Bailey, D. (1993). *Improvisation: Its nature and practice in music*. New York: De Capo Press.

Barone, T. E. (1990). Using the narrative text as an occasion for conspiracy. In E. W. Eisner & A. Peshkin (Eds.), *Qualitative inquiry in education* (pp. 305–326). New York: Teachers College Press.

Berliner, P. F. (1994). *Thinking in jazz: The infinite art of improvisation*. Chicago: University of Chicago Press.

Denzin, N. (2003). Performing [auto] ethnography politically. *The Review of Education, Pedagogy, and Cultural Studies*, *25*, 257–278.

Derrida, J. (1985). *The ear of the other*. Lincoln, NE: University of Nebraska Press.

Dewey, J. (1934). *Art as experience*. New York: Minton, Balch.

Fischlin, D., & Heble, A. (2004). *The other side of nowhere: Jazz, improvisation, and communities in dialogue*. Middletown, CT: Wesleyan University.

Geertz, C. (1983). *Local knowledge*. New York: Basic Books.

Holland, D., Lachicotte, W., Jr., Skinner, D., Cain, C. (1998). *Identity and agency in cultural worlds*. Cambridge, MA: Harvard University Press.

Holquist, M. (1981). *Introduction to the dialogic imagination*. Austin, TX: The University of Texas Press.

Levinas, E. (1984). Emmanuel Levinas. In R. Kearney (Ed.), *Dialogues with contemporary continental thinkers* (pp. 47–70). Manchester: Manchester University Press.

Liggett, T., & Sawyer, R. D. (2008, March). *Towards the dialogic and critical engagement of duoethnography in search of a post-colonial curriculum*. Paper presented at the 2008 annual meeting of the American Educational Research Association, New York.

Lund, D. E., & Nabavi, M. (2008). A Duo-ethnographic conversation on social justice activism: Exploring issues of identity, racism, and activism with young people. *Multicultural Education*, *15*(4), 27–32.

McDermott, R., & Shelton, N. (2008). *A curriculum of beauty*. Paper presented at the annual meeting of the American Education Research Association, New York.

McLuhan, M. (1967). *The medium is the massage*. New York: Random House.

Merleau-Ponty, M. (1962). *Phenomenology of perception* (C. Smith, Trans.). New York: Humanities Press.

Norris, J. (2008). Duoethnography. In L. M. Given (Ed.), *The SAGE encyclopedia of qualitative research methods* (Vol. 1, pp. 233–236). Los Angeles: SAGE.

Norris, J., & Greenlaw, J. (2008). *The curriculum of writing*. Paper presented at the 9th Annual Advances in Qualitative Methods conference, Banff, Alberta.

Oberg, A. (1992). Side by side: Being in research autobiographically. Published as Part of Wilson, T. & Oberg, A. Side by side: Being in research autobiographically. *Educational Insights*, 7(2).

Pennycook, A. (1998). *English and the discourses of colonialism*. New York: Routledge.

Pinar, W. (1975). Curerre: Toward reconceptualization. In W. Pinar (Ed.), *Curriculum Theorizing*. Berkeley, CA: McCutchan Publishing Corporation.

Rosenblatt, L. (1994/1978). *The reader, the text, the poem: The transactional theory of the literary work*. Carbondale, IL: Southern Illinois Press.

Roth, W. M. (2005). *Auto/biography and auto/ethnography: Praxis of research method*. Rotterdam: Sense Publishers.

Sawyer, R. D. (In Press). Curriculum and international democracy: A Vital source of synergy and change. *Journal of Curriculum Theorizing*.

Sawyer, R., & Norris, J. (2004). Null and hidden curricula of sexual orientation: A dialogue on the curreres of the absent presence and the present absence. In L. Coia, M. Birch, N. J. Brooks, E. Heilman, S. Mayer, A. Mountain et al. (Eds.), *Democratic responses in an era of standardization* (pp. 139–159). Troy, NY.

Schwandt, T. A. (2000). Three epistemological stances for qualitative inquiry: Interpretivism, hermeneutics, and social constructionism. In N. K. Denzin & Y. S. Lincoln. (Eds.), *Handbook of qualitative research* (2nd ed.). Thousand Oaks, CA: Sage Publications, Inc.

Shuck, G. (2001). *Imagining the native speaker: The poetics of complaint in university student discourse*. Unpublished Doctoral Dissertation, University of Arizona.

Shuck, G. (2006). Racializing the nonnative English speaker. In T. Ricento & T. G. Wiley (Eds.), *Journal of language, identity, and education*. Mahwah, NJ: Lawrence Erlbaum Associates, Publishers.

Vygotsky, L. (1986). *Thought and language*. Cambridge, MA: MIT Press.

Zorn, J. (Ed.). (2000). *Arcana: Musicians on music*. New York: Granary Books.

WALTER S. GERSHON, AMANDA PEEL AND CARRIE BILINOVICH

8. COLLABORATION WITHOUT COMPROMISE

Reflecting on Collaborative Discensus in Action

FRAMING (WALTER GERSHON)

Context: A Challenging Semester

In the spring of 2007 I agreed to take on a course for a colleague who had too many classes in that semester's teaching load. This class was the final course for future Social Studies teachers and the only class taught concurrently with student teaching. I was excited to work with preservice teachers as they went through their semester of student teaching and conceived of the class as a way to have meaningful conversations about the connections between teaching, learning, and academic content. I thought that the possibility of having day-to-day experiences in classrooms would serve to bolster the work we did in class, deepening conversations and providing recent examples to which students could relate.

Rather than closed, "known answer questions" (Mehan, 1979; Wills, 2006), I sought to foster more open-ended explorations into the relationships between theory and practice as well as those between academic content and its expression in classroom lessons. To facilitate such discussions, I utilized an inquiry-based approach through which questions were intended to lead to further questions and talk about what happened as students taught was informed by broader educational contexts, particularly as they pertained to sociocultural precepts such as race, class, and gender.

To my mind, this was a strong and natural fit for future Social Studies educators. Not only did such an orientation reflect the goals of the National Council for Social Studies (National Council for the Social Studies/Creating Effective Citizens), the Ohio Standards for the Teaching Profession (ODE-Ohio's Educator Standards), and the Ohio Social Studies Academic Content Standards, (ODE-Social Studies Academic Standards), but it also matched the kinds of understandings my colleagues sought to foster.

Unfortunately for both the preservice teachers in this section and me, this was not the case. As a result, our experience in practice was markedly different from my imaginary. Students were displeased with the workload they received. I, too, felt constrained by a course of study based on decisions that I did not make, were programmatically quite difficult to vary from, and I felt obligated to maintain in my colleague's absence.

W.S. Gershon (ed.), *The Collaborative Turn: Working Together in Qualitative Research*, 141–164.
© 2009 Sense Publishers. All rights reserved.

Were that not difficult enough for all involved, students were even more displeased with the way I elected to approach both course content and its delivery. As we document below, where I wished to pose questions and consider possibilities, they pushed for static, infallible answers that could be applied in any situation regardless of content or context; when I presented concrete suggestions for approaches to situations in the daily life of classrooms, they often asked to know which one worked best and could be most universally applied. Perhaps the most explicit manifestation of their resistance to complicated, contextualized conversations was our semester-long struggle to talk about the intersections of race, education, and social studies content.

However, our first couple of sessions that spring went generally well. Students talked about their time in the classrooms where they were student teaching, shared the kinds of Social Studies ideas that they found exciting and/or interesting, and thought aloud about their concerns as they took over more teaching duties in the incremental fashion our program advocates. Because students' initial discussions presented an understanding of historical events as socially constructed and bolstered by my colleagues' perspectives that they had utilized a similar approach throughout students' time in our program, I moved quickly to broader questions about the implications of conceptualizing history in this manner.

The beginning for our misunderstandings and tensions was just such a question: Could someone please talk a bit about the relationship between race and education? I waited, students resisted. I wondered aloud about some possible connections as a means to open the conversation to the class, students resisted further, a palpable, tense fog of silence filling the classroom.

In response to students' resistance to the topic, I planned a jigsaw activity for the following week's lesson. Dividing the class into groups of three of four, each group was to devise a situation in which the relationship between race and education was integral to a classroom context. Each group would then pass that situation and context to a different group for a response to be shared with the class as a whole.

No group in this overwhelmingly majority Anglo class (there was a single non-White person in the group, an African American woman) arrived at a positively connoted hypothetical situation. In each situation and context, race was an "issue" or "problem" that required a teacher's intervention to "fix" the situation. When it was Carrie's group's turn to share their answer, unfamiliar with language to talk about race and framing questions of race as issues or concerns, Carrie spoke for the group, responding with an answer that was laden with implicit biases about teaching, students, and race. Asking clarifying questions only made matters worse and Carrie became quite upset. Instead of seeing the relatively leading questions I thought would provide her both some language for her to speak about race and a means for her to quickly extricate herself from what was an obviously uncomfortable situation, Carrie felt exponentially put upon and put out by each question I asked.

This event served as a catalyst to our difficult semester together, a distance that students and I were largely unable to surmount despite attempts to do so from both sides of the metaphorical desk—even my decision to sit with them in desks in a circle as I facilitated discussions rather than lecture them on facts and procedures was something that several students claimed made them uncomfortable. My struggles with this class did not end with the semester's completion. Deciding to give voice to this experience and my difficulties, I began to write what soon felt like yet another article by a teacher educator outlining his pedagogical struggles with preservice teachers. Instead, I thought it would be better to engage students in a written dialogue about our time together.

Amanda came immediately to mind as a potential co-author. Over the course of the semester, she spent much time talking to me during office hours about her difficulties with what she perceived to be her peers' inability to meaningfully engage in social studies-related ideas. However, this also quickly seemed to feel like a cop-out of sorts—while engaging one of the few students who agreed with the professor's opinion would certainly add student voice to the piece, it would not convey the majority perspective(s) of those who resisted or otherwise disengaged from classroom discussions.

When I asked Amanda if she knew of anyone from the class who might represent the majority perspective, she replied that she knew Carrie from their work together in a volunteer activity outside of class and would be willing to ask Carrie if she would like to think and write with us. To my surprise and pleasure, Carrie agreed. Rather than sweeping our difficult semester under the proverbial rug, our work together enabled us to engage one another in a meaningful, longer discussion about academic content, pedagogy, and students. This process gave us all the space to grow and learn from one another, an ironic twist given that these were the very kinds of dialogues I had hoped to foster during our semester in class together.

Process: Collaborative Discensus

What was needed was a way for each of us to write and think together so that no one's voice went unheard or one person's perspective was privileged over the others'. Given my relationship to these women, these were particularly important questions. For example, I was their former professor, the only one of the three of us with an advanced degree, and the only male. The process that I have come to call collaborative discensus (Gershon, 2008, 2009) emerged from our working together and in conjunction with a few other collaborations in which I was simultaneously engaged that had similar questions about voice, process, and form.

Grounded in an understanding of discensus as an ethical act (Ziarek, 2001) and in the possibilities of collaboration in communities of discensus (Miller, 1998; Page, 2001), collaborative discensus is a framework designed as a means for multiple partners who hold different and perhaps disparate perspectives to engage one another so that all voices are heard and space is created for collaborators to publicly think and respond together. It is a process designed to produce emergent commonalities, a complex map of findings that cannot be easily reduced to relatively monolithic answers and makes the inner workings of collaboration more transparent.

Such a framework is important for at least the following two reasons. First, although consensus is certainly of paramount necessity when two or more groups are at points of physical, intellectual, or emotional violence, the compromises consensus engenders can simultaneously serve to marginalize one perspective in favor of another (Carrick, Mitchell & Lloyd, 2001; Nachi, 2004; Pugh, 2005; Shircliffe, 2000). For example, dominant sociocultural norms and values are often perpetuated through a kind of implicit consensus, a process that can silence and devalue non-mainstream perspectives and voices (Apple, 1999; Kumashiro, 2002, 2008; Varenne & McDermott, 1998; Weis & Fine, 2005). Second, in situations where a) collaborators share a common perspective or goal yet lack either a common language or b) in which compromise on a single point of disagreement means yielding a central element to a partner's identity, consensus can serve as a stumbling block rather than a enabling force (Lakoff, 2004; Mitchell, 1998).

Similar to other qualitative research methodologies, collaborative discensus is simultaneously a framework and a process, a way of both collecting and analyzing data (Agar, 1996; Denzin & Lincoln, 2005; Given, 2009). Although it is expressly designed to be open to the participants' interpretation and practical needs, to date, processes of collaborative discensus have followed a similar four-part framework.

The first component of collaborative discensus is its *framing*. This sense of framing is three-fold in that it speaks to the ways in which (1) a collaborative group is established due to mutual interest in a given question, context, issue, or concern that serves as the site for their research (2) how that group frames their particular inquiry and (3) any additional, particular points of ideas, ideals, or process collaborators agree upon to facilitate their working together.

Collaborators then approach the site of their inquiry from their own perspectives and research paradigms, collecting and analyzing data utilizing their preferred research methodology, regardless of its process or location as qualitative or quantitative. In cases such as this chapter, rather than approach the same context from different research perspectives, we utilized collaborative discensus as a means to mitigate concerns about status, power, and perspective to engage one another in a candid, respectful dialogue about the difficult semester we shared together. As such, our methodology reflects many aspects of narrative inquiry (Clandinin, 2007; Clandinin & Connelly, 2000); Lincoln and Guba's (1985) suggestions for data analysis[14]; Gooden and Gastaldo's explication of participatory action research (Chapter 4); and the duoethographic processes Sawyer and Norris outline in this book (Chapter 8). Because this step involves all stages of the research process and what research methodology means is up to each participant to decide for her/himself, this second step falls under the broad category of conducting *research*.

Third, collaborators *present* their findings in written, round-robin form. In this stage, each collaborator is free to contribute her findings according to her own methodology and analysis and without concern for her fellow collaborators' findings. There is no need for any of the accounts to agree in any aspect of the data collection, its analysis, or how/what is reported. Finally, each collaborator has an opportunity to *respond* to one another's findings and re-examine her own in light of her colleague's(s'). A brief conclusion serves as an opportunity for collaborators to enunciate aspects of the study they found to be particularly salient as well as possible future directions in light of the data presented. Thus, the four components of collaborative discensus can be understood as framing, conducting, presenting, and responding or as an FRPR process. However, it is important to note that while processes of collaborative discensus should have all four aspects, they need not follow this exact pattern. For example, collaborators could elect to weave their responses and the presentation of their findings together rather than present them as separate sections.

In all aspects of this process, dissonances in collaborators' perspectives are not reconciled, just as points of congruence are not expressly sought but instead emerge throughout the process. The net result of this process is collaborations in which emergent commonalities buttress one another in rich, nuanced ways and where points of dissonance and tension serve to form complex perspectives of sites of inquiry that cannot be readily reduced to static, monolithic possibilities. Because each collaborator has an opportunity to present her findings and respond to her collaborators in an uninterrupted fashion without the need to sublimate any aspect of her work in the name of compromise or consensus, collaborative discensus can be understood as an ethical act of meaning-making. It is a process that provides multiple iterations and spaces for all involved to voice their perspectives in a way that simultaneously interprets the meaning of the data set, is meaningful to each collaborator, and contributes to the complex set of meanings that are the end result of their combined work together.

Such representations of voice are of particular importance in contexts such as this chapter in which there is a clear difference between participants' sociocultural capital and where the topic of inquiry is contentious and potentially unsettling to all parties. In these ways, collaborative discensus also responds to Erickson's (2006) concerns that more explicit collaborations between those more commonly categorized as "researcher" and "subject" have the possibility of causing the university-based researcher to become less critical (p. 254). As we document here, it is precisely because of the space to directly address one another in an unfettered fashion and respond to one another's perspectives that enabled us to have the kind of respectful, candid, critical, and catalytic dialogue we present in this chapter.

Thus, the purpose of this chapter is twofold. First, in keeping with the purpose of this volume, it is an opportunity for Carrie, Amanda, and me to discuss what it meant for us to engage one another through an emerging process collaborative discensus. Second, in utilizing the FRPR framework of collaborative discensus to present how we worked with one another, this chapter is performative (Austin, 1961) in nature, an act that simultaneously describes and illustrates its possibility through its enactment. In the case of this chapter, our combined narrative about working together utilizing collaborative discensus also demonstrates one way that such processes can be enacted in written form. Because Carrie's perspective represented the majority view, we begin with her thoughts, followed by Amanda's, then to my own.

REFLECTING ON OUR PROCESS: DIFFICULTIES, QUESTIONS, AND UNDERSTANDINGS

Carrie Bilinovich

Working collaboratively with others can be a struggle; add working with a former professor and the difficulty level rises. These were my first thoughts and feelings when I was asked to participate in writing an article about race with a former classmate and professor. The article was to focus on the experiences we had during student teaching and what occurred in our class with Professor Gershon. I was a little apprehensive at first to commit to the project. I did not have the greatest relationship with Professor Gershon during the semester I was enrolled in his course and was not sure how this discomfort was going to play a role in my participation in the project. A large part of our poor relationship had to do with the very subject that he wanted me to write about and I was unsure of whether I could honestly compose a piece of writing given the experiences I had in his class—it was less than a year since I had graduated and completed his course. Additionally, I did not know what I truly thought and felt about the experiences I had during that semester; I had kind of just put them off, thinking I would never really have to deal with those concerns again. Little did I know I was going to be given the opportunity to deal with my experiences head on and finally come to some resolution about our uncomfortable time together.

All this was going through my mind in the initial conversation I had with Dr. Gershon; I felt it was a very important decision I was going to be making. After all, how many students get to write with one of their former professors just after receiving their undergraduate degree? In talking to Dr. Gershon, discussing briefly what had occurred in his class and how I felt now that some time has passed, I decided this was a project in which I wanted to participate. Even though we may have had differing views in the past, I believed it was the time for Amanda, Dr. Gershon, and me to put our thoughts and impressions of those events into words together to create a single piece of writing with three versions of similar incidents that may or may not have a common outcome.

In my first, brief conversation with Professor Gershon we outlined the expectations for the paper and the role that each of us was going to play in the writing. From the very beginning, it was made quite clear that the three of us were going to equally participate and there would be no division between professor and student. It was even requested that Amanda and I call Professor Gershon by his first name, a suggestion he made during class that I didn't feel comfortable with at the time. While this seems like something small, it really made a difference for me, making it easier for me to look at Walter as a co-writer on the article instead of a former professor. It also helped to ease the apprehension of working with someone who has more credentials and who, I felt, was qualified to write about the subject.

Little did I know, Amanda and I, too, were qualified to write about our topic of choice. While Amanda's and my formal credentials did not compare to Walter's, we had experiences in talking about race both in Walters's class as well as during our student teaching experiences. Amanda and I were also assured that what we wrote was to be *our* opinions and perspectives on the topic and that at no point would Walter alter any of our pieces. The only help he would give would be for grammar and spelling, as well as giving us suggestions should we ask; he was quite clear that it was by no means mandatory we adhere to his suggestions.

The first step in beginning my portion of the article was to have conversations with both Walter and Amanda separately. Although a lot of the content I wanted to add into the article was fresh in my mind, I had no clue where to start or even begin to decide what the focus of my portion was going to be. I spoke first to Walter for about an hour on the phone when we revisited some of the situations that arose in his class. Over the course of the conversation we discussed what we thought, how we felt, and our ideas about what could have helped the situation. This was also the point where Walter helped me begin talking about the topic of our article and I started to feel comfortable with the direction of my portion of the writing.

From our conversation, I started to realize a lot about why he asked me to work with him and Amanda. One would think that in order for a collaborative piece to be successful, everyone in the group would have to have a good working relationship. However, while Walter and I did not begin with such a relationship, based on our conversation, we began to open up to each other's ideas and to understand the other's thoughts. During our initial conversation, Walter never tried to push me in a certain direction, he just asked challenging questions that really got me thinking and helped with my thought process in writing my portion of our piece. He did tell me at the end of the conversation that he wanted me to write what we just spoke about and he wanted it to be portrayed in the same way. It was reassuring knowing that I was not going to have to hold anything back, that I could honestly write about the class without having to camouflage some of my thoughts or feelings.

I remember feeling that it would be more accurate for the reader to see how three different people who experienced the same class reacted to situations in that class and their perspectives on those situations. Similarly, I now believe that the presentation of our differing views, rather than three similar perspectives on the same topic, has also made the piece more interesting for readers.

My conversation with Amanda was more general. Mainly, we discussed what we were going to write about and tried to help each other with details we may have forgotten about certain moments in the class. Talking with Amanda was different than talking to Walter because Amanda and I were in the same boat, trying to figure out what direction Walter really wanted to take the paper and how he wanted it presented. Where talking with Walter gave me insight on what the focus of the paper was going to be, speaking with Amanda gave me the courage and reassurance to include certain aspects into my portion.

As it turned out, Walter meant what he said in our initial conversation about working together. He really did not have any specific direction he wanted the piece to take; he simply wanted us to think and write together openly and respectfully. Never at any point did Walter turn down any of my ideas nor did he ever say, "I think you should write about this and leave this out." Although I did not really know it at the time, working with Walter was just like working with another classmate. All the apprehension I had was for nothing. Walter did not dictate what we should say or how we should write at all during the writing process; he was just another writer sharing his experiences.

We were each then left to write our portion of the article. Once we had finished our first rough draft, we emailed it to one another for review. The first time we reviewed each other's work it was to get a sense of how each of us was approaching our piece and to see what we each really thought and felt. We then had the opportunity to make suggestions to each other about our pieces. The most important part about the suggestions was they were just that—suggestions. We could do what we wanted with suggestions and I chose to see them more as guidance that helped me to think and develop my portion of the article.

This particular process happened at least three or four times. Each time the three of us reviewed each other's work, we made suggestions then reviewed the comments made about our portions. As this process repeated we looked not only for the content to match the flow with what everyone else was writing, we also checked each other's work for grammar and spelling errors on one of the last reviews.

Once each of us finished our final drafts we sent them to Walter who put all the pieces together as they would appear in the paper. We then decided to meet to review the article one last time. Due to the convenience of email and our hectic schedules, most of our previous reviewing had been done via email. However, when it came to the final review, it was important for all three of us to sit down together because when we had a chance to read the paper aloud we also had the opportunity to discuss what we each wrote. In this round of editing, we discussed what each other had written and why we each decided to address those topics and ideas. Even after this review of our final draft, there was still time for us to go back after this meeting to alter any section of our portion if we decided to do so. Although the process of working collaboratively with others can be very overwhelming, I found it to be as rewarding as it is challenging.

Amanda Peel

When Walter first approached me about this project, I was very excited. It had been two semesters since our class, and I still struggled with the experience. The content I was to teach during my student teaching was loaded with issues of race, class and gender. I expected our class to be a place where we could talk about these types of issues and how to address them with our students. However, as Walter mentioned above, this is not what happened. Over the course of the semester I had frequent discussions with him during office hours about what I perceived to be my peers' inability to engage in meaningful discussions about what it means to be a social studies teacher and how the ways in which we teach content affects our students' perceptions of themselves and society.

It was indeed a difficult semester during which I often felt frustrated and isolated. I think it is fair to say that it was a frustrating experience for everyone involved and I thought this project would be a good way to try and make some sense out of my experiences there, to try to arrive at some sense of peace. I also took it as an opportunity to reflect on my teacher education program and how that education had informed the choices that my classmates and I make as teachers and as students.

I was also intimidated. Walter first proposed this project with the intent of presenting it an upcoming conference, and then seeking publication. I have no experience in this arena, have no advanced degree, and was unsure if I was up to the task. While talking about what he envisioned for the paper, Walter suggested that it might be a little bit disingenuous for me to be the only student voice, as I mostly shared his opinions of the class and this was not the majority view. When

Walter suggested that we ask someone who did not necessarily share our views on the class to join us, Carrie immediately came to mind. While I knew that Carrie was frequently unhappy and frustrated in class, I thought that she might be willing to share her views, and that her voice would be representative of a majority of the class. With Walter's encouragement, I sent Carrie an email, although I was not sure she would agree. I was thrilled when Carrie decided to join us because I thought our personal friendship might make the task less intimidating.

As it was very difficult to coordinate three very busy schedules, our interactions were frequently via phone and email, but also occasionally in person. We began the process after arriving at a series of understandings. Our first discussions were about purpose, format, and group dynamic. I understood the purpose of the project to be an examination of our differing experiences of the class and why it was so difficult for each of us. What I felt to be most important was the idea that it did not matter that we have a "happy ending" or try to reach a consensus. What was important was that we all were to have space to voice our experience and how we felt both during the class and at the end of our writing process.

However, things were a little awkward at first due, for example, to differences in our status between Walter (former professor, advanced degree holder, experienced writer, male) and Carrie and me (former students, undergraduate degree holders, inexperienced writers, females). Also, when Walter first approached me about this project and suggested that we invite someone who did necessarily agree with us, he expressed a concern that such a person might feel "ganged up on" during the process. This was an ironic inversion of the dynamic during our course, as Carrie's experience was closer to the majority of students in the class than Walter's or mine. I believe that these factors were mitigated by the format that Walter proposed and to which Carrie and I agreed.

We would each be given uninterrupted space to write about our experience of the class and we would edit each other's pieces for grammar only. We would then each be given uninterrupted space to respond to what the others wrote. In my mind, we were all a little vulnerable in this situation: Carrie because her perspective was different from Walter's and mine, me because my perspective was different from the majority of the class, and Walter because he was obligated to accept whatever Carrie and I wrote about our difficult experiences in his class. Walter would write the beginning and ending sections, subject to Carrie's and my approval. This process was further facilitated by an implicit understanding that we would all be respectful of each other's experience and feelings, and not argue with the content of each person's piece. Rather than rebut, we would simply respond.

As I alluded to above, unsurprisingly, our group dynamic was a little ill at ease, as our classroom had been, at best, an awkward environment; the prospect of revisiting that experience could breed nothing but more awkwardness. This was obviously a different kind of relationship than the student/teacher dynamic I was used to having with my professors. I was also a little nervous about my relationship with Carrie. I considered her to be a valued friend and I hoped that we would be able to disagree without taking it personally.

It was with the above understandings that I set out to write my first section. My initial excitement quickly turned into anxiety and a general sense of malaise. The process of writing about my very difficult semester felt eerily like reliving it. I frequently felt lost in a sea of recollections and frustrations that I was constantly questioning—Is that how it really happened? I was a little surprised at the some of the conclusions I reached and often questioned if this was how I truly felt. Similarly, it was difficult to publicly criticize my peers as I consider many of them to be my friends and most of them had a very different perception of our class.

It felt especially awkward to criticize my teacher education program. I had and still have enormous respect for my professors. The time I spent in their classes was truly an enlightening and paradigm shifting experience. Additionally, while I feel that there are areas where the program fell short, I felt precocious and ungrateful pointing them out. There were many moments where I was said to myself, "Wow. That's a little harsh," or "Are you sure you're not letting yourself off the hook?" Of course, it was also difficult to look at my own actions and see where I could have/should have acted differently. Because it was such a complicated experience, my feelings about the class changed daily which made it hard to commit to words on paper.

At some point, it occurred to me that this was the first thing I had ever written that would not be assigned a grade, and so I was often worried that I was somehow "doing it wrong." Also, I felt that my experience during the course was personal. Did Walter really want me to write about my personal *feelings*? This was intended to be for public consumption? It felt self-indulgent and I could not imagine how anyone would find it interesting or useful. So, it was with great anxiety that I sent my first draft to Carrie and Walter for their response.

Reading Walter and Carrie's sections was also an anxiety-provoking experience at first. I was worried that I had really gotten lost in my recollections, and although I knew there would be differences, I was a little worried that they would tell me they had no idea what I was talking about. Of course they didn't do that, but it was still a little strange to read their accounts.

After reading Carrie's piece, I found there were a lot of areas where we agreed. For instance, we had similar expectations of the course and we both found the workload to be heavy and of questionable value. It was a bit difficult, as her friend, to read about how at certain points in the semester she questioned whether or not she was ready to be a teacher. As her classmate, I often felt the same way, and wished we'd had more discussions along those lines as a class. I also found areas of disagreement, such as Carrie's feeling worn out by all the emphasis on race by the end of the course where I felt frustrated by the lack of discussion of the subject. I still cannot escape the feeling that if the class had only talked more we would have had a less difficult experience.

Of course, it was very strange reading Walter's piece, as former students do not generally get to hear about how a professor feels about the class. It was interesting to read about how Walter perceived my classmates' refusal to talk about race as one of the "make out games" (Foley, 1990) that students play to avoid work. It helped me realize how my own students used similar tactics during my student teaching, and started me thinking about how I would deal with them in the future.

It was while reading Walter's piece that I had the biggest "wow" moment. I was reading his account of a particularly tense class session that I had also addressed in my piece. It was, in my opinion, the closest our class ever came to having a discussion of race. During this particular session one of my classmates made an inflammatory statement, and (in my perception) another student made an equally inflammatory response. I viewed the situation as one student versus the other. However, Walter perceived the response not to be toward my classmate in particular, but to the class' general attitude that they already knew everything they needed to know about race (What?!). I thought about this for a long time. Eventually, after reviewing the class blog and discussing it with Walter, I realized that while my classmate certainly felt he had been wronged in class, I seemed to be the only one who saw it as one student versus the other. This gave rise to the question, "Why did I see it that way?" I eventually arrived at the conclusion that this says more about me than the class, as I tend to take these matters personally.

The one thing we all had in common was the questioning of our teaching methods. Although I wrote less explicitly about my doubts than Carrie and Walter, it was reassuring to know that other people were going through the same process, even the professor.

During this time while we were reading each other's thoughts I had long conversations with Carrie and Walter. Carrie and I talked a lot about how different our education had been. Although we were in the same program, Walter's was the first class we were enrolled in together. Had we not known each other from our mutual volunteer work, we would have been total strangers during this class. While I felt that my professors had challenged me in my beliefs and attitude toward "difference," Carrie seemed to feel that her professors had been more "nurturing" and did not necessarily challenge her thinking in these areas. It became apparent how much of an impact that this had, not only on our experience in Walter's class, but also on our conceptions of what it means to be social studies teachers and how we approached issues of race and class in our student teaching. We also talked about the kind of teachers we want to be and our experiences during student teaching.

These conceptions also influenced how we perceived our time in Walter's class. What I now realize is that Carrie and I had the same goals as teachers, but differed in our opinions on the best way to reach said goals in the classroom. On one hand, this was reassuring because there were times during our class that I felt completely isolated and I realized that I was not alone in my opinions. On the other hand, it made me a bit angry because we were never able to discuss our common goals and varying approaches as a class. I felt we all missed an opportunity to learn from each other. Carrie and I also talked about the difficulty of this process. It was reassuring to know that I was not the only one who found this project challenging.

Walter and I were having somewhat similar discussions during the same time period. As Walter was my former professor, there were times where I looked to him for guidance. However, he was very careful about how he advised me. This was actually a little frustrating for me at the time, as there were moments when I felt I needed his help but he did not want to edit my thoughts or influence what I wrote. At the time, I perceived this as "not help." However, I now think that this was for the best and I was able to arrive at a draft that I was satisfied represented my views.

This is not to say that Walter was not supportive. I recall a particular conversation with Walter about half way through the process at a time when I think he must have sensed my anxiety. He told me that this type of writing is difficult but that he felt it was valuable and that we (Carrie and I) were doing very well. It was very reassuring coming from someone who has actual experience in this area, as I have none. Walter also acted as a sounding board, often listening and posing thoughtful (but not leading) questions as I talked through my ideas to arrive at a coherent thought. Again, he was always careful not to try to influence what I wrote. For example, he would say, "This sentence reads like…is this what you mean to say?" as opposed to challenging my statement. There were times when the answer was yes, and times when the answer was no. Walter always accepted my response. He encouraged me to be honest and helped me to feel more comfortable writing some of my more critical statements. By the time I finished writing my response section and reading Carrie's and Walter's responses, I was more comfortable with the project but still a bit uneasy.

As I write now, after working on this project for a year (off and on), I am much more at peace with our difficult semester. Carrie helped me realize that there were big differences in the way that she and I, and therefore at least some of our classmates, were educated over the course of our program. This helped account for our varying opinions and actions during our student teaching semester. Walter also helped me realize that perhaps my classmates did not possess the requisite language to discuss matters of race, class, and gender.

Participating in this project has certainly given me the space and opportunity to reflect on the choices I made during the course and helped me see how I might have done certain things differently. For example, I could/should have spoken up more often or challenged my classmates in their silence. Additionally, this project has helped me grow not only in my conceptions of teaching but also in my conceptions of what it means to a member of a community and our individual responsibilities to the group. It has helped me realize that we owe it to each other to be honest, especially when it is difficult (from Walter). And at the same time, we owe it to each other to be understanding and patient (from Carrie). While it was a difficult process in many ways, I am glad Walter invited me to write because I think the story of our class is an important one and writing about it in this way with Walter and Carrie really does justice to what was a complicated experience for all of us.

At some point (I'm quite sure when), I stopped feeling so apprehensive about our project and I feel that what I wrote is an accurate reflection of how I felt. I am definitely more comfortable in my relationships with Walter and Carrie, so that writing this chapter has been less difficult. I believe the reason I am able to emerge from this process so positively, is mainly due to the format and the understandings that we reached at the beginning of the process. I was given the space to tell my story uninterrupted, and had the opportunity to respond to Walter and Carrie. We did not feel obligated to reach an agreement, although an agreement of sorts was reached. Our different statuses have become less of an issue as we progress because we made the effort to discuss them and took steps to proceed in as democratic a manner as possible. And, although we never talked about it out loud, we were very careful to be respectful of each other's opinions. At this point in our project, I am very pleased with our work and where we are as a group.

Walter

Spring 2007 was a troubling semester for me as a teacher, largely because of my experiences in the course I shared with Carrie and Amanda. It rubbed against all of my understandings about pedagogy. Practices I thought of as open and democratic in nature, students found to be constraining. Open-ended questions were seen as teacher traps designed to trip students up so that they could be publicly corrected for their lack of knowledge, a conception I unwittingly further confirmed in students' minds by frequently asking for additional possible answers to the questions I posed. Comments that I meant literally ("That's a really good idea. Does anyone else have something they'd like to add to the conversation?") were often misinterpreted by students to be fishing for single, correct answers ("That's not right, would someone else please tell me the correct answer?"). The reason I can speak so clearly to these ideas is that I had several candid conversations with students where we each shared our concerns and frustrations over the course of the semester, all to no avail for either the students or me.

It was my hope that asking former students to write with me would provide some better insight into the semester, a space for further conversation about the content and pedagogy of the course, and an opportunity to think concretely with students about teaching and learning when they are difficult. There is a tendency for educators to write about our successes and find a source of blame for our less than successful experiences. In the P-12 teaching world, successes and difficulties often get boiled down to "what works" and "what not to do." In educational scholarship, studies tend to present successes and challenging educational contexts that detail what went "right" or "wrong." Rarely is it the case that students are active participants as co-authors in the entire process of data collection, analysis, and reporting of findings.

Although these were my thoughts and hopes, I anticipated that our process would be difficult in ways that I had not yet conceived and would most likely amount to a kind of public accounting of our perspectives. Therefore, what was of paramount importance was conceptualizing a framework that would allow each of us the chance to voice our perspectives in an unfettered fashion as well as the opportunity to address one another's thoughts with an equally candid transparency. With this in mind, I approached Carrie and Amanda with the following framework as a springboard for discussion and further modification, including the possibility of its total rejection:

- Each person would be able to write whatever s/he wanted
- What each author contributed would be used in the manuscript
- While I each author would edit the others' work for mechanics, I would not edit their work for content while they could edit my work for content

- After we presented our work at the American Association for the Advancement for Curriculum Studies, we then amended this rule so that I could be more involved in editing the piece for submission to journals with an understanding that those changes needed to be checked and met Amanda and Carrie's approval
- Each author would have an opportunity to respond to their co-author's thoughts in a similarly edited fashion
- Carrie, representing the majority view, would go first, followed by Amanda as representative of the next largest group; I would be last
    - This was also done in an effort to purposefully not foreground the teacher's perspective
    - Carrie and Amanda asked if I would frame the piece and that I also write the conclusion based on our conversations over the few months when we put the piece together
- Any questions or concerns would be addressed openly via email, on the phone, or when we met in person.

In addition to this framework, I also did not initiate the possibility of our working together until a good six months after the semester had ended.

Because of the tensions that began during the lesson briefly described in the introduction, tensions that lessened but did not abate over the course of the semester, I had some trepidation about working with Carrie. My concerns were more about how we would be able to work together given both the history of tension between us and because I did not want to inadvertently build upon those tensions. As Carrie shared with me during one of our conversations, regarding her participation in our manuscript one of Carrie's friends asked her, "Isn't that the guy you thought was such a jerk all semester!?" Given Carrie's genteel nature, I'm fairly certain that "jerk" was a substitution for a much stronger noun.

I also wondered about two seemingly contradictory concerns. On one hand, I was unsure how candid any of us would be able to be. Writing about difficult contexts and your difficulties with others is hard enough without knowing that those you are writing about are going to read and respond to those thoughts and feelings. On the other hand, I was not certain if the writing would be anything other than the equivalent of a "brain dump" of venting, talk that would leave little room for further discussion or response. Then there was the perfect storm concern: we would all dance around the difficulties we faced except for moments of rather explicit expressions of displeasure to which there could be little response other than an apology. As Amanda and Carrie's former professor, I also understood that there was the distinct possibility, if not the likelihood, that such displeasure was likely to fly in my direction.

Despite these concerns, our process felt to me to be transparent, organic, and collaborative. We communicated in pairs and as a group. Our emails ranged in topic from ideas on how to approach our writing process to questions of authorship. We also spoke on the phone in pairs but shared the concerns, questions, and praise we had for one another with whomever was not present. On a few occasions, we met in person over coffee, drinks, or meals to hang out and talk about our manuscript and its progress.

Our manuscript mirrored our interactions as we worked together to write the paper. I felt it was a strong combination of not pulling any punches yet was truthful without being malicious. It also seemed as though all three of us generally felt free to write what we believed was important to bring to the collective table and worked hard to try and hear the others' perspectives instead of trying to defend our actions, thoughts, or feelings.

This was aided in no small part by our mutually agreed upon process. Knowing that I would have an opportunity to respond to Amanda and Carrie's sections, I found it easier to be critical and to receive their equally frank, critical presentations of their perspectives on our semester together. An understanding that we each would be provided the space to write without interruption; that our constructions of past events or their meanings did not need to be either reconciled; and that we did not need to arrive upon some kind of consensus as to what a "correct" vision of those occasionally disparate constructions meant, similarly contributed to my comfort in writing in such a critically candid fashion.

Furthermore, that I wrote to these understandings with the two women whom I was writing about felt more forthright and just. There was no chance that either Carrie or Amanda would not hear what I wrote and they would have an opportunity not only to tell their own side of the story but also respond to my constructions of events—a level of critical transparency and opportunity for response often missing in qualitative research and researchers' accounts of teachers and something I have found problematic in my own work (cf. Cohen, 1990; for talk about this tendency, see Erickson, 2006). Although I do not have time to address this point in detail in the space allotted to this chapter, my argument is not that there are not times when reporting to those one studies is either inappropriate or contextually challenging, for such discussions are always frought with questions of appropriateness and power (cf. Nespor, 1997; Page, Samson & Crockett, 2000). Rather, I mean to note that an effort to include those "researched" in the processes of qualitative research or reporting of pedagogy are more often than not instances of talking *about* rather than speaking *to* or working *with* those whom one studies.

While I was quite pleased with how collaborative both the process and our finished manuscript felt, what surprised me most about the manuscript were the understandings we gained along the way. I had neither intended nor expected that we would arrive at some kind of mutual understanding of each other's perspectives. Yet, as we reached the end of our manuscript, I found that we had engaged in the very kinds of open, respectful, and generally democratic (its open, critical, and responsive aspects) I had hoped to foster yet fell so short in facilitating during our time together in the classroom. As an added bonus, I was able to better conceive of how students had used talk about race as a semester-long "make out game" (Foley, 1990, p. 112) to avoid both discussions of race and complex conversations about the socially constructed nature of Social Studies.

Although there were other collaborations in which I was and am engaged that lead to the construction of what has become collaborative discensus, the work with Carrie and Amanda described in this chapter was quite central to its construction.

In our working together, our different perspectives unburdened by a need for consensus became our strength. The ability to write without being concerned that our perspectives would be sublimated and an understanding that we would be able to respond as candidly and critically to our collaborators' perspectives freed us to speak more directly. Finally, the space to allow meanings to emerge rather than feeling a need to arrive upon some mutually agreeable conclusion was crucial to our collaboration. Because we were not concerned with having our individual perspectives compromised out of a need to draw some kind of singular conclusion, it enabled us to present a much more complex vision of what conspired during our time together and a richer discussion of those perspectives.

REFLECTING AND RESPONDING

Carrie

The thought of reflecting back on a process that I have already reflected on (twice, once in the original manuscript and a second time in the previous section of this chapter) seemed like a challenge. How do you sum up a process that has already been picked apart and explained in detail? I then realized it was much more than simply writing about the process of working with a former professor and classmate. For me, this whole process was about self-growth. Once our first collaborative paper was done and we had submitted our final draft, I felt a sense of accomplishment. I was proud of the work that I had done and of the work we composed together—I felt a little liberated about what had occurred between Walter, Amanda and me. I had learned a lot about myself and about why Walter did or said the things he did while I was in his class. Although I thought I learned a lot as we wrote our first manuscript together, it was not until I was asked to participate in writing this chapter and this reflection portion was almost finished that I have come to an understanding of what had really occurred the first time Walter, Amanda, and I wrote together.

While the process of writing the first article was hard for me on many levels and I often found myself wondering if I had made the right decision, I learned so much about myself in the end. For example, I learned it was okay to have differing views from one another and that it is possible to disagree with someone and still get along with that person; having a conversation about race with Walter is no longer a situation I try to avoid.

Walter, Amanda and I met the other night to review our work and discuss our reflections and conclusions. If this were a year ago, there was no way that I would be able to discuss so openly how I felt or even share experiences I have had since then. When we met at the conclusion of our original manuscript, I was still hesitant to share my thoughts openly, while I had no problem putting them in writing, discussing them out loud with others was a different story. However, when we met together this time, I found myself willing to share my thoughts and feelings openly without any hesitation. It was at this point that I realized that I had changed for the better. It was refreshing to have a conversation with Walter and Amanda and not worry about how I was going to be judged or how it was going to come out. I look back now and wonder what it would be like if I had never have had this opportunity to write with Walter and Amanda. I don't think I would be as open-minded nor would I be as willing to discuss the topic of race with others who share different views from me.

Amanda

After reading Carrie's and Walter's sections, I am struck by a number of similarities. We all seem to be pleased with the process (collaborative discensus). Everyone felt accurately and equally represented in our manuscript. Despite our mutual concerns about our qualifications to write this paper, Carrie and I are both comfortable that we were not influenced by Walter or our ideas of what he would want us to write. Although we were all concerned about potential conflict within the group, our freedom to respond to each other, and the respectful way in which we chose to do so, prevented any such conflicts. Our group has emerged from this process not only intact, but in a more positive place than we started.

What is most striking to me is the evolution of our relationships, especially Carrie and Walter's. What began as an ungainly pairing at best has evolved into a strong working relationship based on mutual understanding and trust. Both began unsure of how their tense relationship in the classroom would affect the group and, therefore, our writing. It is to both of their credit that, while it was awkward at first, both persevered and were able to arrive at a mutual understanding of each other's point of view. For Carrie, at some point Walter ceased to be Professor Gershon, and became Walter. This was true for me as well. However, while I definitely consider Walter to be a friend, he still remains my former professor. I still looked to him for guidance during this process, although he was as careful about advising me here as he was during our initial process, I'm not sure these differences will ever go away. Carrie and I discovered that we can disagree and still get along. As Carrie points out, when we met to discuss this piece, the conversation was much easier and more relaxed.

Reading Walter's piece reminded me that when we first set out to write, we had no idea where we would end, or if our writing would result in anything valuable. As he points out, this process could have been little more than a "brain dump" or venting that, while it might have been valuable to us as participants, would have little value outside of our group. I don't believe this is what happened because we all made a commitment to the project and to be honest. We were able to learn from each other's experiences. We were able to question our actions as teachers and as students and emerge with new ways of looking at the world.

This is what I wanted for my class all along, as did Walter. I also believe that the story of our class is valuable to others, because I suspect that it's not unique. I suspect that there are many awkward classrooms struggling to discuss issues of "difference," and it is my hope that perhaps our experience can help others navigate theirs with a little more grace and understanding.

Walter

Reflecting on this process now, over a year since we began working and thinking together, my thoughts run on two parallel planes. To one side, I find myself yet again re-examining what this still evolving process means to me as an educator. To the other is the consideration of what our collaboration has contributed to the development of a research methodology that has enabled me to work in a more collaborative, reflexive, just, and critical manner. This section, then, is split accordingly, first addressing how my relationship to Carrie and Amanda has evolved as we continue to work with one another then moving to a discussion of how our work together continues to inform my research practices.

From students to collaborators. On the evolving nature of working with students.
In many ways, I am as surprised to still be working with Carrie and Amanda as I was when began working together during our initial process. When I asked them if they would like to write another reflexive piece on our process, I was again filled with some degree of concern that they would have had enough of working together and would politely decline. Yet, again, both women immediately agreed and began asking questions about our approach and timelines for producing this chapter.

What strikes me now is that Amanda and Carrie may not know how important our working together has been to my life as an educator and a researcher. Had either Carrie or Amanda elected not to work with me, what was a difficult semester for me may well have been swept under my mental rug. It would have been easy to chalk the semester up to either a purposefully disengaged student culture or a bad programmatic fit, a point to which I will return shortly. What would not have happened is that I would not have been able to understand how I was complicit in the difficulties we faced as a class and would not have come to understand the difficulties that Amanda and Carrie experienced.

In light of Carrie's comments both in this chapter and our evolving manuscripts, it is perhaps not surprising that I have learned much from working with her. For example, through our discussions over the past year, Carrie has helped me better conceptualize how to approach talking with the undergraduates I teach about the relationship between sociocultural precepts such as race, class, and gender and education.

What may not be as clear from the similarities of our perspectives is how Amanda has also strongly contributed to my growth as an educator. In our working together, she has helped remind me how difficult it can be for students to gravitate towards ideas that go against the tide of the status quo of their local norms and values—that what we as educators hope our students to achieve over the course of a semester can feel like an albatross around their necks.

As Carrie's section above explicitly demonstrates, the nature of our relationship is continually evolving. Neither Amanda nor Carrie have slipped into calling me Professor Gershon for at least the past nine months, they are much more free in pointing out what I misunderstand or missed altogether, and are continually revealing more of their lives to me as I am of mine to them.

Yet I wonder at some level if we will ever be true collaborators. What event might it take for us to achieve this level of collaboration? At what point will our initial teacher/student dynamic retain its history yet not be circumscribed by those roles? Is such a change of roles possible?

Along similar lines, I think about what a unique situation this process has been. While Carrie and I have become friends on some level and honor and respect each other's ideas, it has taken us a year and a half of continued discussion, writing, and thinking together to arrive at this point, a luxury I will likely not have again with any future preservice teachers who feel about me as Carrie did when she was my student.

In some ways, I feel the teacher/student divide stronger with Amanda than I do with Carrie. When we went to present our manuscript at the annual meeting of the American Association for the Advancement of Curriculum Studies, Carrie was unable to go with us at the last minute so Amanda and I presented without her. In spite of how positively she talks about her time at the conference, this experience in some key ways may have reaffirmed my status as "professor" and Amanda's as "non-professor/student." Similarly, Amanda tends to turn to me more often as a friend/mentor than Carrie, a role that while I am honored to play, also may be reifying a professor/student binary.

However, in spite of such questions, there is little doubt about the ever-changing nature of my relationships with Carrie and Amanda. We are immeasurably more comfortable in engaging each other on a host of topics, thinking with one another, and, perhaps of greatest importance, candidly and respectfully disagreeing. In my mind, they have already moved from students to collaborators and from working partners to friends.

Finally, before addressing the role Amanda and Carrie played in the development of collaborative discensus, I wish to make two brief programmatically related notes. First, in response to difficulties that students and instructors had similar to our concerns about the workload given students during their semester of student teaching, my program decided as a whole to move the majority of that load to a mandatory course offered the semester prior to preservice teacher's student teaching experience. Carrie and Amanda and their peers in all four academic disciplines that semester, language arts, mathematics, science, and social studies, were the last to have the course designed in this fashion.

Second, to date, I have never taught this course again. There are two reasons for this. When it became clear that the semester was not going well, I asked our then chair not to be considered to teach this course the following year; it seemed like an awful fit at the time. Since then, we have hired another professor of social studies education and my services are no longer needed in that respect. What has happened is that I am able to utilize much from the insights gained in working with Carrie and Amanda to the courses I do teach for our undergraduate, preservice teachers. What Amanda and Carrie have taught me has helped me better mitigate students' relative lack of life experience with others unlike themselves and, I hope, more adequately prepare them as future teachers.

Collaboration and the emergence of theory. I am also uncertain if Carrie and Amanda realize how our working together has impacted my development as a scholar. My desire to work with them in as egalitarian, candid, and just manner as possible was in many ways the catalyst for putting what had then been my ideas into action. Until we began writing together, I was unsure if what had seemed like a rather straightforward idea would be possible. To be honest, until I received their portions of this chapter, I was not completely certain that my characterization of our process was either adequate or accurate. That is, until they wrote in this chapter reaffirming their belief in our process and their growth through it, I was not certain how much of my perception of their experiences was truly what they thought and felt.

It was not an easy thing to convince Amanda and Carrie that they would indeed be able to voice their perspectives in an uninterrupted fashion and that they would also have an opportunity to write directly in response. The difficulty lay not in the concept itself but in their belief that it would truly happen. Over the course of our first few weeks writing together, their calls often came down to the same two well-founded concerns: Can I really write what I think and feel? Will you really not change my ideas? Although I answered their questions as transparently as possible, I felt that the only true answer to such concerns lay in my actions. To those ends, I tried my best not to shape their perspectives but ask questions that might help them explore their ideas for themselves, just as they began helping me shape my thinking through their thoughts and comments when we talked.

It wasn't until we had begun to work together in earnest that I began to truly grasp that I was theory-building. Yes, I had an idea that if we all wrote in an uninterrupted fashion, responded to one another's ideas, and were not burdened with a need for compromise or consensus our findings would be necessarily more robust and complex. Our commonalities would emerge and our differences would more accurately represent the complexities of our context. Similarly, I also had been thinking about pushing at the researcher/researched divide, a desire that came from feeling less than comfortable with a disconnect between a central line of inquiry in my scholarship about the roles of students in educative contexts and my research practices in studying about rather than with students. Not that I thought or think that there are not times when either students do not wish to collaborate or that such collaborations are not necessarily helpful methodologically, for those research contexts certainly do exist. Nor do I wish to imply that student voice is not an essential and often underrepresented aspect of studies of classrooms (cf. Erickson & Schultz, 1992; Gershon, 2007). Rather, I was concerned that I might again be addressing the questions I had about what students did in classrooms, in this case my own room, without working closely with students themselves.

At the same time I was wondering about how to work with Carrie and Amanda, I was collaborating with a colleague in Cyprus, utilizing videoconferencing software for our respective groups of preservice teachers to discuss how they conceptualize teachers' roles in their country, culture, and society (Christodoulou & Gershon, 2008). Although Dr. Christodoulou and I use complimentary research methodologies, narrative inquiry and ethnography, we needed a way so that we could each analyze and report data without compromising on language or methodology and that allowed us to respond to each other's findings. Similar concerns surrounded a project with a colleague in physics as we began to think together how we might begin to conceptualize mapping students' movements in classrooms over time; planning for my current research agenda involving working with students and teachers in all stages of research from data collection to reporting of findings also required thinking along similar lines.

Yet it was with Amanda and Carrie that I first put these methodological possibilities into practice and in our working together that I was able to see them come to fruition. Because this process is meant to be malleable and fluid, iterative and recursive like many other qualitative methodologies (cf. Agar, 2004; Denzin & Lincoln, 2005), I was less concerned about any possible need for adjusting the framework. Instead, my main concern was working to ensure that my co-authors found this process to be both concrete enough to provide guidance as they worked and open enough that they could express their perspectives. As they describe in this chapter, it was the method's central combination of being provided the space for voice and the lack of need for consensus or compromise that most enabled our collaboration to be as meaningful as it has been to all three of us.

In sum, I cannot conceive of my work with Carrie and Amanda without thinking about how it has helped my growth as an educator and scholar. I remain grateful to them for their willingness to work with me in writing on such an often-overlooked aspect of teacher-student relationships as well as their continued thoughts in reflecting on this process here.

CONCLUSION

Carrie

Working collaboratively with others does not mean that those who work together must share the same ideas about a topic or share the same education or career. However, I feel it is a common misconception that in order for a piece of writing to be successful, everyone involved needs to share the same ideas and have common backgrounds. It is a somewhat rare opportunity to read an article or a piece of writing where the reader has the chance to read multiple perspectives about a single topic. Walter could have written the first manuscript on his own and included his accounts of what he thought that Amanda and I experienced and how we felt. Instead, he elected to include Amanda and me; Walter wanted our voices to be heard in the paper, not from his suppositions of our point of view but our own perspectives in our own voices.

I have thought about what the paper would have been like had Amanda and I not participated. While I have little doubt that it would have been a generally good piece of writing, it would have lacked the personal touch that Amanda and I added when we were given the opportunity to write about our experiences in our own words.

Our collaborative writing processes have certainly been challenging, due to both personal struggles with the topic as well as the ability to coordinate our busy lives. However, we remained dedicated to this project and worked hard to see it come to fruition. Reflecting on our process now, I am proud of what we accomplished. I am also hopeful that collaborative work like ours in this chapter becomes more commonplace in education as I believe it holds a good degree of promise for those involved in education, students and teachers alike, to work together to discuss ideas and situations they found otherwise difficult to express.

Amanda

One of the issues we struggled with in writing this chapter is the comparative lengths of Walter's response section to Carrie's and mine. There was a concern that this might be viewed as "professor takes up more space than former students." However, I do not see this as a problem. Walter's purpose in this piece is somewhat twofold: he is writing about his experience with Carrie and me as well as the evolution of his theory of collaborative discensus. Carrie and I need only to write of our experiences during our collaboration. It is not an issue for me that Walter writes about that here. Our relationship has evolved to a point where, while I still view Walter as a mentor, I also consider him a friend and fellow collaborator. While he has something to say that I do not, I find his comments to be relevant and speak to our process and history. I am honored that our collaboration has had an impact on him as a teacher and a scholar.

Writing about our experiences in this format has been very effective in doing justice to a complicated experience. It has allowed Walter, Carrie and me to explore our difficult semester together without marginalizing any one person's experience, or taking away any of its complexity. We were able to work together to produce a piece that we are all proud of, despite our different statuses and experiences. Although it was difficult for us personally, we were able to learn and grow as individuals and as a group. The original manuscript we wrote together was quite different from the one Walter would have written by himself. In inviting Carrie and me to join him in this project, Walter has provided us the opportunity to speak in our own voices about our own experiences without having them filtered through the professor. I feel this is important, as student voices are not often heard in educational research, and students have much to offer in educational conversations. Our work to date is one example of how students and teachers can write together on as equal footing as possible.

REFERENCES

Agar, M. H. (1996). *The professional stranger: An informal introduction to ethnography* (2nd ed.). San Diego, CA: Academic Press.

Apple, M. W. (1990). *Ideology and curriculum* (2nd ed.). New York: Routledge.

Apple, M. W. (1999). *Official knowledge: Democratic education in a conservative age* (2nd ed.). New York: Routledge.

Austin, J. L. (1961). *Philosophical papers*. Oxford: Oxford University Press.

Bailey, D. (1993). *Improvisation: Its nature and practice in music*. New York: De Capo Press.

Carrick, R., Mitchell, A., & Llyod, K. (2001). User involvement in research: Power and compromise. *Journal of Community & Applied Social Psychology, 11*, 217–225.

Christodoulou, N., & Gershon, W. S. (2008, March 25). *International crosstalk: Videoconferencing, belief systems, and preservice teachers.* Paper presented at the American Educational Research Association, New York.

Clandinin, D. J. (Ed.). (2007). *Handbook of narrative inquiry.* Thousand Oaks, CA: Sage Press.

Clandinin, D. J., & Connelly, F. M. (2000). *Narrative inquiry: Experience and story in qualitative research.* San Francisco: Jossey-Bass.

Clifford, J. (1988). *The predicament of culture: Twentieth-century ethnography, literature, and art.* Cambridge, MA: Harvard University Press.

Cohen, D. K. (1990). A revolution in one classroom: The case of Mrs. Oublier. *Education Evaluation and Policy Analysis, 12*(3), 311–329.

Denzin, N., & Lincoln, Y. (2005). *The Sage handbook of qualitative research* (3rd ed.). Thousand Oaks, CA: Sage Press.

Erickson, F. (2006). Studying side by side: Collaborative action ethnography in educational research. In G. Spindler & L. Hammond (Eds.). *Innovations in educational ethnography: Theory, methods and results* (pp. 235–258). Mahwah, NJ: Erlbaum.

Erickson, F., & Schultz, J. (1992). Students' experience of the curriculum. In P. W. Jackson (Ed.), *Handbook of research on curriculum: A project of the American educational research association* (pp. 465–485). New York: Macmillan.

Foley, D. E. (1990). *Learning capitalist culture: Deep in the heart of Tejas.* Philadelphia: University of Pennsylvania Press.

Gershon, W. S. (2007, September 1). *Overlooked: Curriculum and students in classrooms.* Unpublished Dissertation, University of California, Riverside.

Gershon, W. S. (2008, May 28). *Collaborative discensus: Research at the nexus of interpretive methodologies, urban school partnerships, and curriculum.* Invited presentation, Centre for the Study of International of Curriculum Studies, Centre for Cross-Faculty Inquiry, Noted Scholar Lecture Series, University of British Columbia, Vancouver, B.C.

Gershon, W. S. (2009, May 26). *Towards a theory and practice of collaborative discensus.* Paper presented to the Canadian Society for the Study of Education/Canadian Society for the Foundations of Education.

Gershon, W. S., Peel, A., & Bilinovich, C. (2008, March 23). *Sorting through the pieces together: A teacher and two students' perspectives of a challenging social studies class.* A paper presented at the American Association for the Advancement of Curriculum Studies.

Given, L. M. (2008). *The encyclopedia of qualitative research methods.* Thousand Oaks, CA: Sage Press.

Hammersley, M., & Atkinson, P. (1995). *Ethnography: Principles in practice* (2nd ed.). New York: Routledge.

Kumashiro, K. K. (2002). *Troubling intersections of race and sexuality: Queer students of color and anti-oppressive education.* New York: Routledge.

Kumashiro, K. K. (2008). *The seduction of commons sense: How the right has framed the debate on America's schools.* New York: Teachers College Press.

Lakoff, G. (2004). *Don't think of an elephant!: Know your values and frame the debate.* Chelsea Green.

Lincoln, Y. S., & Guba, E. G. (1985). *Naturalistic inquiry.* Beverly Hills, CA: Sage.

Mehan, H. (1978). "What time is it Denise?": Asking known information questions in classroom discourse. *Theory into Practice, 18,* 285–294.

Miller, J. H. (1998). Literary and cultural studies in the transnational university. In J. C. Rowe (Ed.). *"Culture" and the problem of the disciplines* (pp. 45–68). New York: Columbia University.

Nachi, M. (2004). The morality in/of compromise: Some theoretical reflections. *Social Science Information, 43*(2), 291–305.

National Council for the Social Studies/Creating Effective Citizens. Retreived May 2, 2009, from www.socialstudies.org

Nespor, J. (1997). *Tangled up in school: Politics, space, bodies, and signs in the educational process.* Mahwah, NJ: Erlbaum.

ODE-Ohio's Educator Standards. Retrieved May 2, 2009, from http://education.ohio.gov/GD/Templates/Pages/ODE/ODEDetail.aspx?page=3&TopicRelationID=521&ContentID=8561&Content=61814

ODE-Social Studies Academic Content Standards. Retrieved May 2, 2009, from http://www.ode.state.oh.us/GD/Templates/Pages/ODE/ODEDetail.aspx?page=3&TopicRelationID=1706&ContentID=852&Content=59094

Page, R. N. (2001). Reshaping graduate preparation in educational research methods: One school's experience. *Educational Researcher, 30*(5), 19–25.

Page, R. N., Samson, Y., & Crockett, M. (2000). Reporting ethnography to informants. In B. Brizuela, J. Stewart, R. Carrillo, & J. Berger (Eds.), *Acts of Inquiry in Qualitative Research*. Cambridge, MA: Harvard Educational Review.

Pugh, A. (2005). Selling compromise: Toys, motherhood and the cultural deal. *Gender & Society, 19*(6), 729–749.

Shircliffe, B. J. (2000). Feminist reflections on university activism through women's studies at a state university: Narratives of promise, compromise, and powerlessness. *Frontiers: A Journal of Women's Studies, 21*(3), 38–60.

Varenne, H., & McDermott, R. (1998). *Successful failure: The school America builds*. Boulder, CO: Westview Press.

Wills, J. (2006). Authority, culture, context: Controlling the production of historical knowledge in elementary school classrooms. In J. L. Pace & A. Hemmings (Eds.). *Classroom authority: Theory research and practice* (pp. 33–62). Mahwah, NJ: Lawrence Erlbaum.

Weis, L., & Fine, M. (2005). Beyond silenced voices: Class, race, and gender in United States schools (Rev. ed.). Albany, NY: State University of New York.

Ziarek, E. P. (2001). *An ethics of dissensus: Postmodernity, feminism, and the politics of radical democracy*. Stanford, CA: Stanford University.

DIANE CONRAD, KIM MCCAW AND MATTHEW "GUS" GUSUL

9. ETHNODRAMATIC PLAYWRITING AS COLLABORATIVE WORK

DIANE: INTRODUCTION

In the spirit of collaboration, this is a collaborative piece of writing. It is an intertwining of the personal journals of its three authors, engaged collaboratively in a process of ethnodramatic playwriting—a collaboratively written piece about collaboration based on collaborative research.

For me, Diane Conrad, the "playwright" who will introduce and conclude this chapter, this collaborative project is the culmination of an academic research project, the arts-based dissemination of my three-year funded research (Social Sciences and Humanities Research Council of Canada) which involved doing participatory drama with youth in an Alberta jail. Tragically, a majority of incarcerated youth in Alberta are Aboriginal—a symptom of systemic racism within the Canadian justice system. My research was set within the Centre's Native program that is reflected in the play. I mention this here because Aboriginality does come up in the text that follows.

Kim McCaw is the project's dramaturg, faculty member in the Department of Drama at the University of Alberta and Director of the newly founded Canadian Centre for Theatre Creation housed there. I am honoured to have this opportunity to work with him and the Centre. Kim's introduction follows mine. Our other collaborator, Matthew "Gus" Gusul, is a research assistant on the project, completing his master's program in the Department of Drama. Gus also worked with me in spring and summer 2008 as a research assistant with my work at the youth jail. Our shared experience doing work at the jail is valuable to me at this dissemination stage of the process in that it provides a reality check.

Theatre is so much a collaborative art form that for the three of us, all thoroughly steeped in the culture, collaboration feels natural. Playwriting, like all the other dramatic arts, is from the outset a collaborative undertaking. In this way, my playwriting project is significantly different from other academic writing projects I have undertaken, even for co-authored academic papers. In academic writing authorship is straightforwardly accredited to each individual based on the extent of their contribution. In playwriting the fact that many individuals will have contributed to the finished product is taken-for-granted. While each participant is acknowledged for their role in the process of dramaturgy and/or work-shopping, authorship goes to the playwright—with the understanding that a director and an entire cast and crew will ultimately engage in further interpreting and disseminating the "product" to its audience. Theatre is and always has been truly and thoroughly, from start to finish, a collaborative art.

In the spirit of collaboration I need to give credit to all the collaboration that lead up to the playwriting process, the research upon which the play is based. I have spent the last three years making weekly visits to the youth jail. These youth are also primary collaborators on the project. Without them, their generous participation, their performances and insights, the project would not have been possible. Thanks are also due to the coordinator of the Native program at the jail who invited my drama-based research to collaborate with her program, to the administration and staff at the jail, and the Alberta Office of the Solicitor General who granted me access. Other collaborators included the two undergraduate and six graduate research assistants that I employed over the three years, whose participation contributed significantly to the work.

The following describes a brief period of collaboration around our ethnodramatic playwriting project from the perspective of its three collaborators engaged in the process of playwriting and dramaturgy. Gus and I wrote our journal entries after each meeting. Kim provided his entries orally in response to our journal entries at the end of the collaboration period, which Gus audio recorded and transcribed for inclusion here.

KIM: INTRODUCTION

I am currently a professor in the Drama Department and the Director of the new Canadian Centre for Theatre Creation (CCTC). I have been with the Drama Department since 1997. I teach directing, acting, and I also teach dramaturgy—primarily new play dramaturgy as opposed to production dramaturgy which is a whole other story. I came to the University with 20 years or so of professional theatre experience. I am not a conventional academic. I do not come from a university background and primarily my work in the profession was as a director, artistic director, and dramaturg of new Canadian plays. I ran a theatre company in Winnipeg called Prairie Theatre Exchange with a history of developing and producing new work and I was also the director and chief dramaturg for the Banff Playwrights' Colony for a number of years. I have continued to be active working as a dramaturg with playwrights across the country as part of my creative activity as a professor. Most recently I was the guest dramaturg at the Playwright's Atlantic playwrights colony in Sackville, New Brunswick, last summer and will be back there next summer.

I was excited to work on this project because it promises to be a different type of play development process in that Diane is not a conventional playwright. She is a professor, an academic, and a theorist who also has a creative writing background. But the actual writing of a play is a relatively new experience for her, and I am glad to be a part of that. It is also notable that it is a play that is coming out of a research model, as she puts it, and is the culmination of a three-year research project. She is building on the research she has done working in the youth jail, case histories and observations that she has made, and theories that she have developed over that time. It is interesting to be working on a play that has this kind of germination point which is not necessarily where other playwrights start.

This is also an initiative that involves the CCTC, a new venture at the University designed to explore theatre creation processes and to create new pieces of theatre.

DIANE – JANUARY 16, 2009

I'm on sabbatical this term to write a play based on my funded research entitled *The Transformative Potential of Drama in the Education of Incarcerated Youth* for which I facilitated weekly drama sessions with inmates at a local youth jail over the past three years. I'm on faculty in Secondary Education at the University of Alberta. My scholarly field is drama/theatre education. Several years of teaching drama at the high school level showed me that drama can be an effective pedagogical approach with "at-risk" youth. It's also great to be able to put my undergraduate degree in playwriting to use.

I had a few preliminary meetings with my dramaturge Kim McCaw last term to make arrangements and toss around some preliminary ideas . . . Today was our first official meeting with the dramaturgical team. I really appreciate Kim's willingness to take this on. It's also great to have Gus on board as he understands the kids and the context of the research so he'll be able to help me keep it real.

It's almost too good to be true to have all this support to write my play. While collaboration is a vital element of drama/theatre practice and dramaturgy and workshopping script is common in the process of developing a new play, it is not, in my experience, common to scholarly writing which is more often than not a very solitary process. As the work proceeds, the intention is to employ a few youth to help us develop the youth characters and dialogue. I'm excited to be combining my art and scholarship in this process.

Our collaboration, at this first meeting scheduled just two weeks into my sabbatical, has really pushed me to get some ideas for the play sketched out and to get something substantial down on paper, to give us something to talk about. In this sense, the collaboration is already proving a valuable vehicle to move this process forward in a timely fashion.

I had an outline of the entire play, tentatively titled *Athabasca's Going Unmanned*, and a draft of the first act ready to share with my collaborators today. I was excited to be able to share my ideas with them, my first audience, and get their feedback. They were quite open to my ideas and supportive—at this very early stage—elaborating on some of my themes, providing me with new insights. Our combined wisdom will no doubt be a great asset. My limited experience in theatrical production, my focus is more on applied theatre, will be compensated by Kim's considerable experience in this area. My idea of a series of "alternative endings" for the play was met with curiosity—not sure if that had ever been done before in theatre. My idea for integrating technology media as an integral part of the action will need some further exploration. Kim said he'd be getting "up to speed" on possibilities in relation to that.

I also consulted with my former supervisor Dr. jan jagodzinski, a leading theorist in Lacanian psychoanalysis, regarding points of character development.

The work I've done in this area is proving invaluable for understanding my characters' unconscious motivations. For me, the integration of theory in my thinking about the play is inevitable. Theory that so much underpins my research is coming through in the playwriting.

GUS—JANUARY 16, 2009

I am sitting down to write this entry three days after my initial introduction to this project. Dr. Diane Conrad of the Department of Secondary Education at the University of Alberta, Prof. Kim McCaw of the Drama Department at the University of Alberta, and I started work at the Leva coffee shop on campus. I am the junior member of this team as Master's of Arts graduate student of the Drama Department. I am very grateful for the opportunity to work on this project. As I said the meeting was three days ago and I still have much excitement about what took place on that day.

I feel as the junior member of this team it would be useful for me to highlight what qualities I bring to the table of the discussions we will be having. Diane will be writing a play based upon her experiences working in the Young Offenders Centre. Kim is acting as her Dramaturg. We decided in the meeting on Friday if I were to have an official title it would be something like Assistant to the Dramaturgical Process. I think this title makes sense for what I can bring to this project.

I had the opportunity last summer to work with Diane teaching drama at the Young Offender Centre. I have also done two other projects over my career which involved working with Aboriginal communities throughout Alberta doing a muralism project and story-telling workshops which both focused on expressing Aboriginal spirituality. These experiences offer me a perspective of a white man working with Aboriginal communities in a creative capacity. I believe this causes me to be somewhat of a bridge between the two other members of our team. Being a Graduate student in the Drama Department I have acted as a Dramaturg on several new scripts and on two productions. Of course the two members can communicate fine without me there but I will bring the language of each area of study in my understanding of this project, which should be of significant help to the end result.

I want to include a small section here about the idea of this project being an interdisciplinary collaborative project. This aspect of the project seems natural. Diane, in her goal of writing a play dealing with her experience at the Young Offender Centre, is engaging in an interdisciplinary project. The more I work in our academic system I see a greater need for a realization that most projects we engage in are interdisciplinary. No matter which department we study in there is a need for cross-pollination of ideas and work. I read in an article for a course I took last semester the term *post-disciplinary.* I believe this idea is where academy is headed. We are beyond disciplines and reaching a more holistic understanding of the world in the academy. I feel the collaborative we are doing in this project is an example of what is happening on a larger scale throughout the academic system through the Western world.

I have yet to read the script. I only have my initial responses to what Diane told us about the script and the small amount of reading I was able to do during the meeting. There are a number of elements that I am very excited about. Diane is very interested in not committing to a singular ending but to use technology to show many possible endings. There is a quote in her writing that jumped off the page at me when I first read it. She writes, "...possible outcomes to the potential choices." I really like this idea because to me it sounds like the staging of a forum theatre. In forum theatre the actors present a scenario to the audience and the audience works to provide different endings to the scene. To me Diane's idea sounds like a version of doing the same thing where the playwright has control over the images portrayed onstage. I think this could be a very effective form for the script to take.

There is strength to forum theatre as a model for community based theatre in that the answers come from the community that is watching the scenario presented by the actors. But what often occurs in these situations is only a few willing people in the audience participate. The people in the audience of the subaltern point of view often remain silent in these sessions just as they do in society. With Diane taking on the responsibility of representing community she can ensure that this viewpoint is represented onstage. This means that at some point in the process of the writing of the script we need to include this viewpoint. I know that we are going to include some of the boys in a reading of the script and this will be an important part of the process.

One thing that I think is a nice inclusion inside of any incarceration story I have seen is the idea that any person can place them in custody of their corporeal reality but not over their mind and their imagination. I think that I will push that this idea is used as some sort of metaphor in the script. In theatre I believe it is important to think in terms of images and metaphors and when dealing with Aboriginal spirituality in any way there is a great opportunity to find beautiful imagery. If there is anyway to tie these ideas together it would be very helpful for the audience to relate to the situations presented onstage.

KIM – JANUARY 16, 2009

The first session we had was on January 16th and it took place at Leva, a coffee shop near the University. My first observation from that session was that while Leva is a terrific coffee shop, it is a lousy place to have a dramaturgical conference. It was really noisy and crowded. The kind of intimacy and reflective, quiet conversation that one is looking for in a dramaturgical session was a little bit more strained. We were wrestling with the environment so I made the suggestion at the end of the meeting that we look for an alternative and quieter place in the future.

My first reaction in that session was delight but also shock at the sheer volume of material that Diane brought with her. She had character sketches, and a detailed scene breakdown all the way through the whole play which gave a very thorough picture of the story that she had in mind. She had also drafted an entire first act! This was all within the first few weeks of her sabbatical beginning. It is a remarkable pace. I do not know any writers who write that fast. One problem was that we had not been able to read any of the material prior to the meeting, so we were looking at it, admiring it, but weren't able to offer any comments on it simply because we did not know what was there. One thing we could determine was the ambition Diane has for this project. We were also able to see that she imagines a fairly significant role for video in the piece which is going to be an interesting thing in terms of cost. Diane is operating with a lot of optimism that cost does not have to be a negative factor in this case. I am also aware that there are aesthetic challenges that come with video in theatre. I do not have much personal experience with this so I will have to learn to open my mind up a bit in order to avoid being in a position where I say, "Oh, no. I don't think we can do that."

What was becoming clear is that she has done a lot of thinking about the three foundational questions I think are important: Who are these people? What is the story? What is at stake? I think that Diane is on the road to identifying all of those things.

It is worth talking about collaboration at this point. As Diane mentions in some of her notes, on the one hand virtually all theatre is collaboration, so in some ways we are not doing anything that is particularly radical. One of the reasons we choose to work in the theatre is because we flourish in collaboration. We do not want to work in isolation. This is by no means saying that one is better than the other, but it simply does not work for us to go off in a room and paint a painting or write a poem, although some of us may do that for fun. But in terms of the serious work that we need to do, we need to engage with a few other people in some way. We are drawn toward that sort of work. In this particular project, in many ways we are not doing anything particularly radical, but in others it is different. Diane is not a conventional playwright. She is coming with a different background, I am coming from a very traditional dramaturgical tradition, and Gus is a student who has his own interests in theatre which are unique to him. It is community-based theatre, popular theatre, and intergenerational theatre with a different aesthetic and a different socio-political agenda. Also, Gus's background with Diane as an assistant to her with the work with the young offenders brings another set of tools or perspectives that should be of great interest as the project develops. Finally, I think Gus's age difference is significant. I am a middle aged guy and he is not, and Diane is somewhere in the middle. The differences are notable and potentially very useful.

We set a time for our next session and determined we would meet in a more friendly environment. One thing that I did stress was that Diane would attempt to send us material in advance of the next working session, so that we had the opportunity to read it before we got together. That way we could have useful comments, which is what has now happened on a regular basis.

DIANE—JANUARY 30, 2009

We had our second meeting of the dramaturgical team today. I'd sent Kim and Gus a complete first draft of the play prior to our meeting, so they had a chance to read through it. I think I caught them a little off guard having so much writing completed already. It just exploded out of my brain—after a three year gestation period, I reminded them. Kim commented that writing something and handing it over to someone to read is a "courageous" act. True, it's a bit nerve-wracking to have one's creative work scrutinized, though I'm somewhat used to it via my undergraduate degree in creative writing which was completely workshop based, and my graduate studies and academic publishing career where one's scholarly writing is always dissected. I've learned that it goes with the territory. I've developed the prerequisite thick skin—and honestly, I'm more grateful to have them working with me than I am concerned about receiving their critique. I got some excellent preliminary feedback, which will inform my writing of the next draft.

This sort of focused attention on my writing at this early stage of the process is quite exciting—to hear the ways in which their readings correspond to or deviate from my intentions. Some comments were expected—details that had also struck me, upon which I needed some feedback in order to proceed. The help that Kim and Gus provided here was very welcomed. Other comments caught me by surprise and sent me off on new exciting directions. Such constructive reading of the work is invaluable to the playwriting process—to get a more objective perspective of the whole, which as a writer, being so close to the process, gets lost.

I particularly appreciated the very different perspectives that Kim and Gus were able to provide. As we're each coming from different backgrounds and experiences. Kim brings his considerable experience dramaturging new work to the process, which is much appreciated. He offers tried and true advice about playwriting, learned by those who have been there, which I have no doubt will be of great benefit to my ongoing writing process. Gus's perspective as a younger reader—with fresh eyes, currently immersed in the theoretical aspects of theatre taken up in his grad studies, is quite refreshing. Also the fact that Gus knows the context, that he worked with me at the youth jail for a while, is proving very useful in confirming my perceptions of certain details.

I talked about what I'd been reading: applied theatre practitioner Baz Kershaw's *The Radical in Performance.* Kershaw makes a distinction between theatre and performance claiming that there is no room for the radical in theatre, because it's so highly commodified. If there is radical potential, he says, it is in performance which might happen in the theatre, but more likely in other locales such as protests, prison theatre, etc. One of my challenges is to see if I can hold onto the radical performativity that I value in my applied theatre practice and perform that in the context of theatre—the play.

Kim cited a quote from Shaw—something like "If you're not radical at 20, you're an idiot. If you're not conservative at 40, you're a fool." I guess that makes me a fool. I said, "Oh no, then I'm in trouble." Gus said, "You're just 20 at heart." Which is precisely the point!! I wonder if political differences will be something to negotiate along the way—perhaps more so in the production than the writing. In any case, for this reason, and others, I'm glad that Gus, twenty something, is joining us. That we're a trio. Three perspectives, I think, will avoid getting into any binary opposition of opinions and open the possibility for more diversity. Gus will be in a strategic position to unsettle points on which Kim and I agree on and perhaps mediate the points on which we don't.

Along with the writing, I introduced some of my ideas about staging the play that were met with less enthusiasm. Some of my ideas are perhaps not all that practical? I'm trying to test the limits of what is customary or possible onstage in a traditional theatre setting. This comes from my location regarding this work focused more in applied theatre than theatre production per se. This is perhaps a source of potential conflict as we continue to negotiate the integration of my applied theatre sensibilities with the world of theatre production. It will be interesting to see how this works out.

By all accounts I have the seeds of a workable little play here. Based on their feedback, I think I've managed to capture the major elements that I was after with regards to my research findings. I look forward to working through the play's overall structure and individual scenes in more detail in coming sessions.

GUS—JANUARY 30, 2009

I am writing this entry three days after our first meeting where Diane had written a first draft of her script. It was very impressive how quickly Diane wrote all of this. It felt like I had only started reading act one when suddenly act two was in my email box and before I had a chance to even start working on act two act three was in my inbox. I like seeing this kind of output. Diane has a huge passion for what she is writing and it is very exciting to work in this type of atmosphere.

We met on Friday in the Drama Department and the meeting was productive. I think we are developing a working structure in our discussion. This is naturally occurring and I like where it went. Kim needed to provide the meeting with structure. I had never sat in a room before to critically examine a script that was in process of being written. What really engaged my thinking was when Kim spoke about the idea of there being two stories. He brought in the idea from a script analyst from cinema. The idea hinges on there being an "A" story and a "B" story. The A story is the main driving point of the plot and the B story is the subplot. In Diane's script the A story is the escape plot that the boys are coming up with and the B story is Eileen's program time with the boys. There is also a C story, which would consist of the love story between Val and Randy.

Breaking up the story into different areas helps our ability to communicate about the script. After bringing this idea in, Kim talked about the concept of the dramatic question. He defined the dramatic question as the single question that gets answered in the action of the script. He used the example of Romeo and Juliet saying that the question for that play is: Can two people fall in love if they are from two feuding families? I find this useful for when we are talking about our three different stories. The stories have not been solidified yet but I have my impression about what they are in my mind. If I had to state the three questions they would be as follows:

A Story – Will the boys follow through with their escape plan?
B Story – Do Eileen's efforts working to teach the boys life skills by using Aboriginal spirituality and drama skills have effect in their decision making skills?
C Story – Can Val fall in love with Randy?

It is very helpful to consider these questions when we start to work forward. I think this will help Diane write the story in a way that can show the complexity of the three areas she is attempting to cover in this play. It is a complex story that is being woven together and we need to be able to make sure that we can keep it all straight.

I believe we need to really work out what is being shown in the B story. That is where Diane's passion lies. I share this passion as well. The A story is in place to keep the action moving but it is in the B story that the theme is carried. I would love for the answers of these three questions to be yes in all three cases, but with the Val and Randy story to define a parameter of love that would be ethical considering Val's professional position and the age gap between the two.

I brought a few points to this meeting to which I believe we will pay attention. I believe the character of Val needs to be stronger. At this time she is a pushover to anything that Eileen desires. I understand that there could be a tendency towards this for Val's character because she is white and Eileen is Aboriginal and this could be a sign of white guilt, but I believe it would be more dramatically stimulating if she were strong in her opinions.

I also believe we will need to be constantly vigilant about the language in the script. There needs to be a difference between the language the adults are using and the boys are using. I mentioned to Kim and Diane about Jean Racine, a writer during Restoration France. He wrote his plays based upon the Greek tragedies. In writing the plays he limited the words he would use. In a famous play of his *Pheadra* he used only a limited vocabulary for his characters. This helped the grand nature of the tragedies. The characters would encounter such huge obstacles and emotions but they only had very simple language to describe themselves. I believe this same idea could be used in this script. Some of the monologue the boys have would benefit from this technique. I am specifically thinking about when one boy describes killing his mother.

Also, one thing I noticed in reading the play was how Randy changed his speech when he spoke with Val. With the other boys he would speak in the same crude colloquialisms but when he speaks with Val his language is more like an adult. In the next draft I believe that Diane should go further with this.

KIM—JANUARY 30, 2009

January 30th, our next working session, we met in a seminar room in the Fine Arts Building at the University. It is a little bit of a bunker. There are no windows in there but it is quiet and there is a large table. For me, it is much more conducive to the thoughtful work that we want to have.

Something I have become aware of in my work with playwrights as a dramaturg is that I find it is important where you meet with them. Early in the process I suggest that we get together in a restaurant or a coffee shop or a bar or whatever, in an informal kind of a session. It is usually a favorite place they like to go to, a place they like for lunch or a coffee shop, so I find out more about them. Then we will tend to meet there regularly as the project develops and it gives then an ownership of the process. I have also realized is that it is a little bit like dating more than one person. Which means I never take a playwright to a place that another playwright goes to. I do not want to be seen with Ian Ross at a restaurant that I go to with Patrick Friesian. They know I am seeing other people but I do not want to flaunt it. It becomes crucial to me where we are meeting.

By this time Diane had now completed the whole play, which at the moment has a three act structure. This is a remarkable amount of writing in a two-week period. After that session that Gus is currently playing a low status role, which is interesting and useful because the comments he offers are insightful and have a keen perspective. As I mentioned earlier, I think that our generational difference is proving to be important. He is closer in age to the young people in the play, and while Gus is not a young offender, he has spent time with them. In knowing these kids, or at least the kind of kids that are in this play, better than I do, I think it adds a valuable layer to the team's discussions.

I find it continually fascinating that Diane as a scholar, a theorist and an academic has approaches that are so new to me. Specifically, prior to this meeting she had been reading Baz Kershaw's book *The Radical in Performance* and was now actively trying to see how the theories and the comments coming out of the book could impact her process in writing the play. This is new to me that a playwright would so consciously and openly be attempting to use critical theory as a direct tool in writing the work. I find it intriguing because I am not a theorist, and both Gus and Diane have far more theoretical underpinning than I do.

One thing that I noted was that Diane is trying to stage some aspects of the play as she writes it and so is trying to address theatrical problems, perhaps earlier in the process than she should. I feel there is still a great deal of work to be done on the story itself: on the depths of the story, the complications of the story, of the dramatic potential of the story, without worrying about staging possibilities or theatrical problem solving. I am encouraging her to keep focusing on the story itself and not on theatre stuff.

I did bring up in that session, in terms of breaking down the story, something that I had learned from a book on being a story editor in film, but which definitely translates to the theatre. The book is called *Making a Good Script Great* by Linda Seger, and in it the writer, who is a very successful Hollywood story editor, talks about the A stories and B stories in film. Her analysis is that the A story carries the action of the film and the B story carries the theme. She also made the comment that if you ask a writer what their film is about they will always describe the B story as opposed to the A story, which is very interesting. We spent some time breaking that down and discussing what those stories were in Diane's play. We did, in fact, come up with a third story, and I think that was useful and will continue to be a useful tool to reference.

In a way this particular session became a playwrighting fundamentals session. We backed up and thought about things a playwright should think about as they are working on their play. Now that we had the whole story of the play in an early draft stage, we need to know where it begins and ends and what happen along the way. We can now start doing some analysis. I brought the concept of the dramatic question into play because what you are trying to do is sum up what is the central dramatic problem of the play. I used a *Romeo and Juliet* example and we started to talk about what the dramatic questions or question could be for this play. I think it will be helpful as we identify where the strengths of the piece are and where work still needs to be done.

As a dramaturg I need to find out where the dramatic spine is for the play in order to keep looking for ways to increase and maintain interest and to raise the dramatic stakes for the piece. The dramatic question is a way of finding out: what does everything hang on in this play?

Gus had some very valuable observations about Val and Eileen's relationship. It started to introduce the roles of Aboriginal characters in the piece and how it is a delicate issue and something about which we will need to be constantly vigilant as we continue, since none of the three of us are Aboriginal ourselves. It is a potential mine field that I think we are all aware of but are intent on addressing in an interesting and responsible way.

DIANE—FEBRUARY 4, 2009

I had lunch with Gus today. It gave us an extra chance to chat some more about the play. I sure appreciate that he took the time to go through it again in quite a bit of detail. It's so useful just to have someone to chat about it with. Talking through things via Gus's questions and prompts, rather than just talking to myself, is really helpful, forcing me to articulate ideas and to find new direction. And again, it's so useful that he also knows the context. I can check in with him regarding how my perceptions of the details compare with how they read to others. To get outside of my head a bit—that distance and a different point of view really opens up possibilities. It's very useful to the process. With Gus's confirmation on many points I'm confident that these aspects of this first draft of the script are solid. His suggestions regarding other points will help me focus and go deeper where more depth is needed.

DIANE—FEBRUARY 13, 2009

We had another very valuable meeting today. It's wonderful. I feel more supported in this writing process than I have ever felt before. In fact, it's a little uncanny to think that ultimately, as is usual in the playwriting process, I will receive authorship credit for this play, while Kim and Gus will get credit as dramaturges. Already, just in these initial stages of draft 2, this play would not be what it is without their feedback. Perhaps that's the difference between an academic article and a work of art.

The suggestions that Kim and Gus offer are things that I would never have arrived at on my own. They are able to see things at a greater distance. And they've been very good about giving me honest feedback, which I much appreciate—e.g. This scene is too much like a social history lesson, not adversarial enough. . . These characters need to be more gritty. . . The dialogue needs to be more reflective of the changing context . . . . Kim is fantastic at providing tidbits from his arsenal—the tried and tested playwriting strategies and wisdom from those with whom he has worked in the past. At every meeting he comes out with suggestions that make so much sense, that I would never have thought of: His point about "The dramatic question;" about the various storylines that, A carry the action of the piece, and B, carry the central theme. And what he shared today about tragedy:

How the tragic character must make a choice, and that the choice they make must be the wrong one. Complementarily, Gus offers details and insights that are fresh and exciting from his perspective as young(er) audience member, director, actor and budding dramaturge.

The second draft is coming along more slowly as I struggle to work out the fine details of dramatic structure, plot line, themes, character development, relationships, etc. Nevertheless, with all the support I'm receiving I'm confident that it will come together.

GUS—FEBRUARY 13, 2009

This is great. I enjoy this work a great deal and I feel lucky to be working on this project. I am writing this entry four days after our last meeting. We met on Friday, February 13, and had about a 90-minute discussion about Diane's script. There are a few ideas and thoughts that I have coming out of this meeting and I also want to discuss some of the topics we chatted about in the meeting in this entry.

I am learning a great deal about the juggling act that takes place in a collaboration effort like this project. An illuminating experience of this happened in this meeting. Kim is representing a purely theatrical/dramatic point of view where his efforts are working towards putting a script together that will be entertaining for an audience and have a strong dramatic form. Diane's efforts are angled more towards writing a script that is an arts-based research project that will accurately reflect her experiences working with the boys in the Centre. I believe that this is the dynamic relationship we are working with on this project. Our goal is that in the end each side will be satisfied with the end result, which would be a script that is playable for an audience and can act as a truthful expression of Diane's research at the Young Offender Centre.

There are two instances in our last meeting that cause me to think about the juggling act we are working with. The first was what Kim called his main message for the meeting. He believed that the boys in the script should show their nasty and mean side to help the script. He believes that if the boys in the script have scary sides it will help raise the stakes and the risks for all the characters. If the boys are dynamic characters that have both a terrifying and a sweet side it will improve the script. The issue that I see from Diane's perspective would be that it is not reflective of her experience to include this in the nature of her characters. In my experience with the boys that we worked with at the Centre, I never felt at risk for even a brief moment. The boys that we work with are the well behaved ones that earn the right to participate in the program, therefore they are, for the most part, calm natured and happy to be involved.

I agree with Kim that there needs to be risk and high stakes in the script but I also believe it needs to be reflective of Diane and my experience. I think in may be better to have a new character that gets kicked out of the program or maybe some uprising in the jail while they are working in the program. My memories of working with this population have been that there is very little apparent risk despite the negative perception of these youth. Perhaps this may be a useful place to use the news clips like those already in the script. The news reports of how the boys got into jail could be shown and there could be a Crime-Stoppers style dramatized version of the scenarios presented. It could work to show the perceived nature of the boys and juxtapose it with their calm nature.

The other question that came up was about the dramatic function of the scene between Val and Eileen where they discuss making dream-catchers and sending them to Afghanistan. What purpose to the action of the play does this scene serve? At this moment it seems as though it does not serve any purpose to the dramatic structure except to show a bit of dysfunction between the two. Kim suggested that something should occur from this scene that would change the nature of the path of one or both of these characters because as the scene is now it feels like a history lesson. I agree with this sentiment but I also feel that it is important to include some of the facts that come out in the scene about Aboriginal Canadians' history with armed forces. I do not believe that this is readily known and if there is a moment in the script that can expose some of these facts, it should be included.

Coming out of the meeting I am really interested about the symbols that are in the play. When I direct, act, or study a play I also pay close attention to the important symbols and what they represent inside the world of the play. So far I have identified six symbols in Diane's script. They are: car keys, Val's fingernails, a band-aid, dream-catchers, and the evidence board.

I think it is useful to pin down what each of these symbols represents in the script and if the audience's relationship to the symbols will change throughout the playing of the script. The keys are a clear symbol of freedom for the boys. If they get the keys and escape they can be free from the jail. For Val they represent something different. In the hands of the boys they represent her possibly losing her job and doing the unethical act of helping the incarcerated youth escape.

Val's fingernails represent her dedication to her work as being unhealthy because she loses her ability to care for herself. This is something that many people who work in non-profit organizations will be able to identify with, elements of their life falling apart because of their dedication to their cause. The band-aid she uses on her finger is representative of the band-aid solutions that governments and aid-organizations place on the Aboriginal issues in Canada. Her work caused the fingernails to grow and now she is using a band-aid to cover up the injury, but the actual problem of her overworking herself is not dealt with. This parallels what goes on between Aboriginal people and the system of aid organizations that work to help.

The dream-catchers represent the commodification of Aboriginal culture into mainstream culture, especially since these are going to be used to help show solidarity with Canadian soldiers in Afghanistan. This symbol is a powerful spiritual symbol in Aboriginal traditions that has lost some of its power because of its prevalence and use by non-Aboriginal Canadians.

Val's evidence board shows the growing nature of the problem of Aboriginal youth's role in the justice system. Throughout the play there will be more and more objects on the board and this will show what is happening in Canada.

I think it will be useful to think of these symbols as we continue to work forward and also it is worth some consideration to add to this list. I believe it is useful to have a multitude of images and symbols that an audience can attach meaning to, especially in theatre. Right now, with how most of our culture perceives the world around, them it is important to have easily identifiable images in any work of art. It helps the audience attach meaning to the work. It can be effective because the audience gets to have a relationship with the work that can stick in their mind and they can attach their own meaning to the symbols that can dynamically act against or with the meaning that is attached through the script and the playing of the script.

KIM—FEBRUARY 13, 2009

The next session was February 13th, two weeks later. There was not as much new writing between those two sessions, which was probably a good thing. I seem to spend parts of these sessions telling stories or bringing in anecdotes of things that I have learned or remember from over time. I had just recently sat in on a lecture from a candidate for a theory position in the drama department and he had given us a new definition for tragedy. I found his definition wonderfully succinct, so I shared it with Gus and Diane and they seemed to enjoy it.

After re-reading the play prior to the session, my feeling was that because we are dealing with offenders, because we are dealing with kids who have committed crimes and who have lived difficult, challenging, harsh lives that there is an edge and a toughness that I think we need to explore more fully in the piece. I encouraged Diane to look at situations in ways that would be more dangerous, to consider that there could be the potential for violence and for a lot more trouble. The presence of a guard with a bad attitude towards these young people is more justified because there is the real possibility of physical danger at certain points. Not from everyone and not all the time, but I think it needs to be a bigger reality in the play. It was interesting that that is neither Gus nor Diane's experience. They both commented that they do not feel at risk. That brings up to me what is an interesting challenge: trying to create drama based upon real life. My view is there is a point at which you have to lie or make stuff up because it may not be dramatically satisfying to just show what actually happened. Ultimately, what we are trying to do is create a piece of theatre that moves people, that excites them, that changes the way they see things, and we may have to crank things up in a way that is not just the day-to-day.

That being said I am also getting to a point in a dramaturgical process which is a real danger zone for a dramaturg. I have to be constantly checking myself and making sure that I am not actually trying to re-write the play. That never works. It sometimes is a short term fix but at the end of the day the playwright has to make the final choices and the dramaturg ultimately has to accept them. I think that my job is to constantly be trying to reflect back to the playwright, "Here's what I think you've written. Is this what you want to write? If not, what can change so you can write what you want?" But not for me to come in and say, "This is what I think should happen." That is dangerous and I try desperately to avoid that.

The next step for me is to look at the play as it is still growing and to make sure that every scene directly contributes to the advancement of the dramatic action. In that session we discussed one particular scene with the dream catchers etc. It is a fairly extensive socio-political discussion looking at Aboriginal history and my concern is that it is largely un-dramatic and I am not sure how it moves things ahead. It is useful and interesting information and it's important from a socio-political point of view, but at the moment I am not sure it is dramatically successful.

DIANE— MARCH 1, 2009

I'm just back from spending a week in Vancouver visiting with colleagues George Belliveau at UBC and Lynn Fels at SFU—both in Education with a focus on theatre-in-education.

George assembled a group of his graduate students who were also working in the area of theatre-in-education and exploring ethnotheatre for disseminating research. In two two-hour sessions we read through the play in its entirety and they provided me with feedback. Having them read the script aloud was, in and of itself, a valuable exercise. To actually hear the dialogue spoken gave me a much better sense of what worked and what didn't. The feedback they provided on the storyline, the form(s) and the characters was also most welcomed. One graduate student said that the character of Val, whose struggles echoed those of a friend of hers who worked in corrections, resonated with her. This was good to hear. Another graduate student provided lots of useful insight from an actor's point-of-view. George, as well as another graduate student, raised some important questions around ethical considerations related to ethnotheatre and how we represent others. I've been very careful in my representation of the boys in the script, but haven't even considered how the character of the male security guard is represented rather unsympathetically symbolizing the authority of the justice system.

My weeklong stay at Lynn's house provided us lots of opportunities to talk over, in minute detail, the many nuances of the play including aspects of form, characters and themes. Lynn's post-modern performative perspective helped me open up my thinking around possibilities of form in particular. The many extended talks with Lynn really helped me to consolidate many of the ideas that had been rolling around in my head. I also went to Lynn's undergraduate theatre-in-education class one evening where I talked with her students about my research and the play and had them look at two scenes with which I was struggling. They divided into small groups, read the scripts, in some cases acted them out and provided me with feedback. When I saw one group actually get on their feet and act out one of the scenes for the class, seeing the characters embodied for the first time was quite a thrill. The students gave me some excellent practical ideas, particularly for one of the scenes, some of which I took up immediately in my revision of the scene. Playwriting is indeed a collaborative undertaking.

The week of intensive talking and thinking about the play with others was very useful. This kind of generous collaboration with others who understand drama/theatre-in-education, arts-based research, ethnotheatre and performative inquiry was a real gift for me as playwright.

DIANE—MARCH 5, 2009

Today I presented on my research at a Community-University Partnership Showcase event and read a few scenes from my play. It was well received. I think my passion for the work really comes through when I talk about it and audiences respond to that.

One critical comment came from an Aboriginal woman in the room—the only Aboriginal person at the presentation and the first Aboriginal person to have heard me talk about this playwriting project. Not a great start. Her comment came before I began reading scenes from the script, after I had introduced the characters. Her comment was that by having represented Randy and Wesley, the Aboriginal boys in the play, as having committed the "more serious crimes" (assault, matricide), as compared to Stan, the White boy, who I described as a repeat offender of more minor offenses, that I was perpetuating a stereotype. My response was that while I was aware of her concerns, what I was trying to do in the play by looking in detail at the life experiences of the Aboriginal boys was to invert those stereotypes—and that I wasn't yet sure whether I had achieved that or not.

The character of Randy in particular is the hero of the play, represented as a very ethical and sympathetic character. His story of looking after his siblings and his concern for the welfare of Wesley, Val and Eileen in the play shows his caring attitude towards others. I really want him to come across as a good guy, caught up in the circumstances of his life that led him to crime—gang activity and drug dealing. Others have indicated that he is a sympathetic character. Whether or not this justifies my representing the youth this way is a challenge that I'm confronted with.

I didn't get a chance to speak with the Aboriginal woman after the presentation. I'd be very interested to hear her response; I need to hear these sorts of responses to understand the impact the play may have. The Métis staff person, Doreen, who I worked with at the jail will of course be reading the play and providing feedback. I wonder how Doreen will respond. As a non-Aboriginal person is my representation of Aboriginal kids and/or Aboriginal kids as "criminals" —whatever my intent, justified and ethical? How can I represent my research without representing the youth with whom I worked—Aboriginal and incarcerated for "crimes?" This was the reality, the context of my research. Is there value in talking about these things in the way I do; in raising these issues? I think so. I think these issues need to be spoken about openly, but if it troubles even one Aboriginal person, is this work justified? Should I rather deny or avoid such representations? What perspective does this woman bring that challenges my work? Is this the same attitude as that of the jail administration who don't want me to talk about criminal activity with the kids? Is this about not wanting to confront these issues or about someone like me (non-Aboriginal) not justified in confronting the issues? I/we (non-Aboriginals) are part of the problem and so, I think, must also be part of the solution. I am trying to raise questions about how crime and criminals are constructed, the systemic racism in our justice system, the inadequacies of the justice system in dealing with these issues, of meeting the needs of these youth. Is this a challenge, of a non-Aboriginal representing Aboriginal youth, that I have to be willing to face or one that I should attempt to avoid? I suspect I'll be faced with lots of challenges and critique over this play. There are, no doubt, struggles yet to come.

DIANE— MARCH 13, 2009

At this meeting with Kim and Gus we debriefed some of the feedback I had received from the students at UBC and SFU. The re-write of the scene based upon feedback from the SFU students, it was agreed, was more successful. The issue around the ethics of representing Aboriginal youth was brought up. We all acknowledged that this was a contested area, but the representation of characters is at the very heart of playwriting; there's no way around it. Playwriting as an art form would cease to exist if all the playwright could ever represent were themselves.

We also talked over our plans for the ongoing development of the script. We identified some individuals who we could potentially enlist/consult as actors for workshopping, for creating the videos, for directing the play. The next step will be to engage in a few intensive sessions reading through the script together in detail, scene by scene. We plan to get together to do this intensive close reading in a couple of weeks time at my house as we share some food and drink. Then we'll recruit some actors for a workshop that will ask them to read through the parts on their feet. This stage is vital to give us a chance to hear the script aloud and see the actors move through the dialogue, actions and transitions. It's never quite the same on paper as it is to see it on its feet. I hope that we'll be able to find some youth willing to help us work through this process too.

I have also sent draft two of the play to Doreen, the Native program coordinator at the jail, and to a few of my colleagues at the University including a colleague who identifies as Aboriginal. Their feedback on my work will also be vital.

GUS— MARCH 13, 2009

After our meeting that took place on Friday, March 13, I have a point that I want to write about. I am left with a question: What is the effect of video onstage in the style that Diane is working with? We breached this discussion on Friday and I would like to reflect on some of what we said.

Our discussion stemmed from our talking about some of the directors that could possibly help us stage the video portions in the script. One of the other students in my program has extensive experience with film and would be a very good fit for directing the video sections of the script. He has held some apprehension in using video onstage in the theatre production he has directed.

His opinion, as best as Kim and I can recall it, is that when someone is watching theatre they engage in a different way than when one engages watching a video. Think of the difference of engaging in a theatre production and watching a television show. Theatre audiences are more active. When watching a live show put on by other human bodies in the same space there is not only a shared corporal reality but also a temporal space, the audience of theatre sharing time and space with the performers. A video performance does not share these qualities. The performers in a recording do not share temporality or corporality with the audience. Because of this an audience member can relax when watching a video. There are filters between the experience of watching a video of performers and watching a live performance.

Diane instantly realized the advantage of these parameters of video and live performance. I believe the reason Diane wrote in the video parts was to take advantage of the alienating effect. She can use this to blur how an audience reacts to the characters. The alienation caused by the videos will help to distance the audience from the sections of the scripts that are intended to be dreams or visions. The only sections that are intended to be in reality are staged all the visions are done on the video screen. I believe this convention will work to alienate the audience from the sections that are on the video in comparison to the sections onstage.

Diane just wrote a scene that incorporates a camera onstage that will record an image live to the video screen. This means that the audience will be viewing both the live and recorded versions of the action. This will create a blurred line between the conventions that Diane is working to set up. I think this will have an effect on the audience that will serve to problematize the relationship between the reality-world onstage and the vision-world of the videos. I think this idea is very interesting. This complex relationship will need to be paid attention to throughout the writing process and when we look to staging the play.

KIM—MARCH 13, 2009

Diane had been traveling and had found a number of opportunities to expose the play or parts of the play to a broad range of individuals and audiences. At one reading, she encountered an Aboriginal person who had some very serious objections to what was going on in the piece. This is not a surprise but it is an interesting problem to encounter and, as we expected, is something that will have its challenges. She has expanded the play a lot and has received a lot of feedback. My only concern here is that, playwrights have to be careful in the early stages of a play as to what exposure they are giving it, who they are sharing it with, what they are asking for from those people, and if they are able to tell which things they should listen to and which they should not.

I remember during my time at Banff, there was a wonderful novelist, Adele Wiseman, who was my counterpart as the person running the writing program. At a session where all of the program directors were to introduce ourselves and say a little bit about what we did in our jobs she had a wonderful statement which I have stolen to apply to dramaturges. She said, "My job is to free writers from reliance on the unnecessary opinions of others." That is what I hope to do with playwrights. Show the play to people and get what they think but do not count on what they are going to tell you and really know when you just stop listening.

We had a lot of talk about video work in that session as well. I am realizing that we need some consultation with it, in terms of what is possible, what problems one will encounter when we try do the things suggested with the range of styles that Diane is interested in exploring, what technology would be involved, the kind of time that might be involved in producing that kind of work. There is a graduate directing student I have been working with who is a very experienced video and film director, and who has a complex and sophisticated theory on why video is problematic in live theatre. I find it a persuasive theory because I also have concerns about video in live theatre. It does not mean that we cannot do it, but it does mean that it is a factor that has to be considered.

We then talked about where to go from here. We had been going very fast at this point. The material has been coming out and we had been talking in broad strokes. We had occasionally zeroed in on a particular scene but mostly had kept to a lot of general discussion.

All of this has been good, but now it is time to start focusing on the details. Earlier, we had talked about getting some actors in to read the piece but prior to this meeting I had made the decision I was going to recommend against that at this point. I felt it was too soon to engage actors in the process. We do not necessarily know enough about how this play works moment-to-moment to get the most use out of actors. My suggestion was that we take a couple of sessions where just the three of us get together and read through the play together scene by scene. We will read a scene and ask, "OK. What happened here? What is going on in this scene? What are we finding out?" and engage in a detailed dramaturgical study.

We have committed ourselves to a couple of sessions at the beginning of April to do that. I think that will be extremely useful. I have confidence that coming out of that we will then know what the next step is. There will be some kind of re-writing process that will emerge. I think we will have to determine with Diane what kind of time she wants to take with that and I am going to encourage her to slow down. We need to talk about what kind of timeline would be useful for us. We will determine after the close reading what timeline will be most useful for the next stages of this collaboration.

DIANE—CONCLUSION

With just three months of our collaborative ethnodramatic playwriting journey behind us, we have, and the play has, already come a long way. As draft 2 becomes draft 3 the input from the three of us, as well as the many other collaborators, has added a richness and aliveness to the writing process that I hadn't anticipated. Kim and Gus and I are now engaged in a process of close reading. We have met for two three-hour sessions and have a third session scheduled, where we read through each scene together and discuss the details of character development, dialogue, plot structure, etc. I've also sent the play out to several friends and colleagues to read and they are providing me with feedback from their various perspectives. I am arranging a consultation session with a young man who has some prior street involvement, whom I contacted through a youth organization in town. He will help me further develop the language used by the youth characters in the play—to make the dialogue more realistic.

Based on a wealth of feedback, I look forward to continuing to mould and shape the characters and plot, to finesse the dialogue into workable scenes, to struggle with ethical issues, issues of representation, and to work with others to envision the play that will ultimately be brought to life. As a playwright, I'm coming to realize, I will never be lonely. The journey continues collaboratively . . .

MELANIE GEORGE AND JOAN MEGGITT

10. IMBED/IN BED

Two Perspectives on Dance and Collaboration

INTRODUCTION

Dance makes clear and expands that which cannot be otherwise articulated, be it through language, image, or sound. The creation and the watching of dance are powerful and intimate exchanges that inform participants in ways that are both immediate and vast. Similar to a handshake, when someone witnesses another person moving, there is an immediate sense of knowing, to some small degree, who the other person is. Likewise, the witness' response informs both individuals' understanding of the other. Dance seeks to finetune these understandings, to embolden them, and to engage in community exchange that informs both the participants and the witnesses alike.

The ways and means of scholarship in dance are varied, particularly as they relate to the creation of dance. In this text, the scholarship of creativity and creativity within scholarship are championed as fundamental to research. The creation, analysis, and evaluation of artistic processes determine ways of knowing and critiquing artistic mediums, as well as heavily influencing the curricula and methodology for teaching dance theory and practice in the academy.

In this chapter, the authors will specifically address the creative scholarship of dance making, including their respective research methodologies, practices, and outcomes, as well as ethical concerns that arise out of the process of making dance within a larger framework. Further, we will discuss the ways in which we conduct our research and the effect that has on how choices are made, how the end product is crafted, and, consequently, how further research is accomplished. Ultimately, the scholarship of each choreographer is determined, to a relatively significant degree, by the collaborators with whom they engage.

We begin with the premise that the creation and realization of dance is, by its very nature, collaborative—it is inherent in the framework of dance making, regardless of whether or not the choreographer makes this explicit at any point during the process. While dance can be undertaken as a solo endeavour—more specifically in the creation and performance of dance by a single individual—it is most often practiced by a community of people a process in which the ultimate completion of the work (usually in a formal performance) is utterly reliant upon the individuals within that community. The choreographer may choose to operate from a tacit understanding that the dancers will contribute to the final outcome by their very participation in the rehearsal of the dance. On the other hand, the choreographer may address the creation of the work as a distinctly overt collaboration that involves the dancers more directly in the making of movement.

Composing dance is action-based research in which the choreographer serving as both researcher and immediate co-participant with the dancers. The materials of the dance only come into being through the work of the choreographer and dancers. The research and the subject of said research are one and the same; the choreographer creates and/or facilitates the creation of data (the movement material of the dance) and assesses the outcome (the rehearsal and performance of the dance). In other words, the methodology of dance making is arrived at through the dance making itself. This specific form of research yields a much more intimate relationship between the researcher and the subjects, namely the choreographer, the dancers, and the dance.

There are additional avenues of research that directly affect the work and which the choreographer must address that include music, stage elements, costuming, and lighting. While these elements are often designed by separate artists/designers, the manner in which they work with the dancework as a whole must be considered from early on in the process. Among the aforementioned elements, music and stage elements (sets, props, multi-media) require the most attention from the choreographer. The choreographer must have an intimate understanding of the music that can be clearly passed on to the dancers. In some cases, the music may itself be the result of a commission or collaboration. Set design and props must be a part of the rehearsal process so that all possibilities may be fully explored, and both functional and aesthetic concerns can be fully addressed. Again, a commission or collaboration is often the means by which these elements are secured.

Finally, there are a number of widely accepted terms in the field of dance that we use interchangeably. The term choreographer refers to the authors, both as specific individuals and more broadly as creators of dance, and is synonymous with creator, dance maker, and director. Dancers may also be referred to as movers and performers. When addressing the outcome, the terms dance, dancework, piece, and performance will be utilized. Finally, the work or labour itself is the creative process and the dance is choreographed or composed. Related to said work, the term rehearsal refers specifically to instances when the choreographer is working directly with the dancers, a process by no means limited to rehearsals.

IMBEDDED: IMPLICIT COLLABORATION MELANIE GEORGE

Collaboration is imbedded in the making and presentation of all dances, whether intended or not. To be sure, collaboration frequently occurs in an overt manner. There are many well-documented methods for these approaches, some of which are discussed in my co-author's portion of this chapter. Those methods frequently involve two or more artists of somewhat equal stature and experience in their respective fields engaging in a premeditated venture for the purpose of creating art. Some of my choreography was created in that manner. However, my approach to collaboration in this text reflects my role as artist within the academy. My collaborators are my students.

As a dance teacher in higher education, I am regularly called upon to create new works on students. These young artists are more than mere vehicles for the production of my art. My work serves as one of many models through which they will shape their dance manifestos. As their instructor, my chief aim is to cultivate articulate movers, thinkers and speakers of dance. Process is valued, with an understanding that product will inevitably result, and that the success of the product is tied to a process in which student performers feel validated.

To produce strong art on student dancers, I must be concerned with their level of comfort and comprehension and prepare them to be active participants in the dance. While this is true of most choreographers, there is an added responsibility because the dancers in these works are students, not professionals. The student/teacher dynamic is therefore always present. We are not peers. Our relationship is timely (conception, gestation and birth typically occur in a three month period), our dances have an expiration date (most dances will not be performed after the end of the semester), and students are put in a position of vulnerability with an expectation or desire to please me because I am in a position of authority.

I choose to engage in a collaborative relationship with student dancers to cultivate their performance and composition skills. In this context, collaboration is a tool for teaching a hidden curriculum, as well as facilitating a productive choreographic process. Students are active contributors to the work, though they often do not realize the extent to which they contribute and their growth over the course of a semester.

VALUES

My approach to composition, and movement in general, is filtered through the lens of Laban Movement Analysis (LMA) (cf. Laban, 1971; Bartenieff & Lewis, 2002). LMA is a system of observing, understanding, and notating movement. LMA is organized into four interrelated categories: body, effort, shape, and space. The principles of LMA establish that change is inherent in all movement experiences and consideration of movement without context (person, place, circumstance, intent) has little meaning. From this the following values emerge in my work:

—Dance making involves a four-stage process of attending to intent, content, execution, perception. Each of these stages requires inclusion of the performers in the creation of the work.

—A focus on inquiry and problem solving with the understanding that there is no one correct answer, truth is often defined by the individual, and discovery will be revealed from the contributions of everyone involved in the piece.

—Guided discovery as educational and choreographic tool: Instead of imposing my will, I encourage the individual journey of each dancer in the learning and interpretation of choreography. Dancers are responsible for their own learning and must take ownership of their role in the pedagogical cycle.

—An expectation of transformation: The dance must be allowed to evolve into what it will become based on the choices the collective makes while creating the dance. As choreographer and director, I cannot stay "married" to an idea if it ceases to be relevant.

—Process over product: The final piece is an artifact of the experience of making the work. The process has as much if not more value than the piece itself. The making of each dance presents an opportunity to learn about dance making which informs the making of the next piece. The dance is the research tool and the outcome of the research.

WHY COLLABORATE?

Dancers are called to work with others regularly. Whether creating work that is literal or abstract, of motion or emotion, the dance maker is accustomed to employing other bodies to bring her vision to fruition. In the case of my own work, I am concerned with making dances about existence and relationship. In my experience, the human condition is best explored in consult with other humans. In short, dances about people demand the input of those who will perform the dance. I discovered my dances were more effective when I did not premeditate every moment or movement. When I made all the decisions in advance, simply using rehearsals to stage the work, the logic of the dance was apparent, but it lacked vitality, a two dimensional dance in a three dimensional world. In these dances, everyone moved, but the dancers had little interaction with each other. In the moments where interaction did occur, it lacked authenticity because it was imposed on the performers rather than arising in an organic manner. Over time, I learned to leave room for the dancers to respond to the work. Instead of "you are feeling this emotion" it became "what are you feeling?" Through this process, my work became less didactic, more cooperative, and better for the change.

My choreography is a physical manifestation of research and inspiration. As a visual learner, concepts and theories are hypothetical until I see them in time and space on human bodies. This physicalization imposes temporal reality on ephemeral thoughts, musings, and seemingly brilliant ideas that may not be best realized through dance. It is through collaboration that I grasp what ideas are relevant to the dance.

New choreography is greatly affected by the mover on which it is created. When conceiving movement, I visualize who will perform it in addition to how it will be performed. A nameless sequence of movement is only given meaning, direction, clarity, and context when it becomes "Nealya's solo," "Dave's entrance" or "Leah's phrase." In this instance, the dancer is both conduit and container. The movement must "pass through" the dancer for it to be developed in the greater framework of the piece, but without "Leah's" existence the movement has little value and, by extension, does not "exist" in the world of the dance. Without the dancer, there is no dance, but the world of the dancer is only defined by the work of the dance maker.

In Laban Movement Analysis, we recognize this as the theme of self/other, an organizing principle of the way we experience movement and relationship in our environment. Self/other recognizes the duality or continuum inherent in the choreographic process. In the above example, the composer and the performer are not separate entities, but two sides of the same coin. It is a process of delineation that also addresses the sum of the process. For choreographers working with dancers other than themselves, the question is not "do I choose to collaborate," but "will I acknowledge the exchange inherent in the process." The dancer always brings something of herself to the work regardless of whether it is intended or not. All dancers contribute, though not all choreographers collaborate. The implicit collaboration model requires wilfulness on the part of the composer to utilize the dancer's contributions as they arise; the perfunctory must be made functional. By recognizing this at the onset of composing, I can use it to aid the creation of the dance.

My work primarily takes the form of jazz or modern dance compositions. My choreography reflects the values of jazz dance (individual virtuosity is defined within the group context) and post-modern compositional methods (choreography is developed by the collective). The roots of modern and jazz dance value the creative capacity and self worth of the individual as fundamental to the art form. These values are embraced by the academy and form the basis upon which dance curricula in higher education is drawn. Individual self-expression can be seen as an artistic manifestation of democracy. By extension, allowing for the individual voices(s) within the work of a choreographer elevates the dancer's role to one of active citizenry in the world of the work. Though some choreographers seek to create dancers in their own image, I have little interest in working with dancers who think my thoughts and mimic my movements. I do, however, actively seek dancers who think like me, meaning they exercise their proverbial voices regularly in the creation and sculpting of content and embrace their right to make choices in the execution of performance. This is the imbedded model for collaboration in dance making. And it is through this method that autonomy and cooperation can be simultaneously developed.

METHODOLOGY

Successful collaborative relationships emphasize process over product, with the knowledge that product is inevitable. Moreover, inquiry is at the root of the process. The decision to foster collaboration is, chiefly, a method to explore the questions that spur the need to make a new dance. Out of this inquiry will develop a process that is idiosyncratic to a particular work. From these methods, tools emerge that form the foundation of an individual's approach to collaboration within choreography.

The process for making each dance is not identical, but, as choreographer, I identify patterns that recur within the making of a dance and refine or reconfigure them for a specific piece. At the start of the process, there is copious note taking, usually a combination of brainstorming and research on a theme. After the initial flood of inspiration, I review the text and images, listen to the accompaniment if it has been identified, and begin to organize the information into categories of what is known and unknown. From this process, questions emerge. Among these are questions pertaining to casting. Who is an ideal dancer for this work? What is his movement profile? When working with students, one may have ideals, but casting is often a democratic process among colleagues. After a cast is established, the vision for a dance may change based on who will actually perform the piece.

First rehearsals always begin with a discussion of theme, procedure, and the expectation of the dancers' responsibility. This information is discussed in hypothetical terms, as the piece does not yet exist. I enter early rehearsals with short phrases, beginnings or ending positions, text, etc. Through experimentation, guided discovery, and problem solving activities, I lead the dancers in filling in the blanks. Like throwing clay on a pottery wheel, the dance begins to reveal itself. I then set about sculpting the structure of the piece (reordering sections, determining duration etc.), with the knowledge that I will have to turn to the cast again and again to refine relationships and transitions. This back and forth between the dancers and myself repeats until we reach performance.

In general, the dancers are keepers of the work, but not makers of the work. More often than not dancers are manipulating my phrase-work as opposed to creating their own. Decisions regarding the crafting of the piece lay firmly at my feet. In those rare moments I call upon dancers to create phrases, those sequences are usually kept intact. I categorize this activity as overt collaboration and consider it separate from the method I am discussing here. Implicit and explicit choreographic methods can and do occur simultaneously, but require different processes and are used for different ends.

Improvisation is often employed to develop my movement. Dancers are given a score from which to work. This score establishes the conditions under which the dancer can "play" with material with consideration to body, effort, shape, space, motivation and theme. As some students are unfamiliar with experimentation in rehearsal, early scores are stricter than later in the rehearsal process. Structure is a catalyst for the initiation of risk taking. Dancers are given the widest berth regarding body and shape choices (the what and how). I tend to be more didactic in relation to effort and space (the how and where). As a result of the improvisation, themes and motivation grow or change.

The way a dancer executes a phrase often gives it new meaning. Frequently, dancers will perform movement based on my guidelines, but the result will be different, and more interesting, than the expected outcome. This may arise from a mistake on the part of the dancers or different interpretations of directives by the dancers and myself. Noticing these "happy accidents" is an important function of my role. Recognizing the opportunity mistakes provide is a tool for welcoming the dancers' perspective in the work. Additionally, these moments validate the students as worthy and needed contributors. For those that seek approval, this can be a watershed moment, allowing for further risk taking.

Collaboration with the dancers is of most import when the piece is formed into some semblance of beginning, middle and end. Once we pass the stage of simply executing the sequence of events, performers begin to attune, adapt, and accommodate each other and the dance. I observe the manner in which they engage with each other as the piece begins to gel. Characterization begins to develop and patterns of behavior will repeat themselves. From this point, notes and directives are based entirely on what happens in rehearsal. I believe this is the deepest moment of imbedded collaboration, as I am dependent on the dancers choices and responses to continue to guide the piece. At this stage, inquiry always involves consideration of relationships because the movements of the cast define such questions.

Though collaboration is actively occurring there is little formal discussion of it in rehearsal, further emphasizing the implicit nature of this work. Collaboration is a means of communication for all involved, but we do not engage in a deconstruction of methodology as a mode of inquiry. After the piece is completed, I will reflect on the process in a more explicit fashion with students, but while the dance is occurring the focus is on completing the work.

Part of my role as rehearsal director is creating a healthy environment for the free exchange of ideas. Assuming the role of active contributor places students in a vulnerable position. As choreographer, I assign value judgements to their contributions as I determine what choices are appropriate to the piece. I choose to divert attention from dissecting the process. Instead, I focus on the construction of relationship during the making of a dance. My aim is to alleviate the weight of expectation to prevent the dancers from becoming so preoccupied with outcomes that they become disengaged from the process.

OWNERSHIP

When considering ownership in this context, two themes emerge: 1) Figurative ownership as a synonym for the agency of the performer within the work; 2) Literal ownership, i.e. who lays claim to the rights to the work? These are two distinct, yet intertwined, issues.

Early in their education, young dance makers are instructed on the importance of developing an individual voice—to create work that is distinct from that of others with the indelible signature that says "I, me, mine." When confronted with the notion of imbedded collaboration the inevitable question of ownership arises. It goes something like this: "By inviting dancers to contribute, is it still my work?" And, perhaps, more to the point, "is my individual voice weakened by including the contributions of others?" The traditional pre-postmodernist model promotes constructions of choreographer-as-container and dancer-as-conduit. However, when collaboration, such as that detailed previously, becomes part of the process, a new paradigm arises that recognizes that the fluid nature of creating and the lack of fixed identities in the rehearsal process. The "choreographer" and "dancer" may rotate between the roles of composer, teacher, director, assessor—each has opportunity to create, interpret, sculpt, edit, and critique. For performers who are accustomed and, perhaps, comforted by the caste system in dance, the upset of this balance of power can be unsettling. If I, as the choreographer, put the power in a dancer's hands, the dancer has to 1) accept yourself as powerful and 2) wield the power with prudence. This is often a new and frightening experience for young dancers in college.

When dancers co-sign on the making of the dance is the piece still mine? I believe that it is. In the same manner that jazz composers create music, I leave room for the performer to contribute, but the foundation, structure, and arrangement of the work emanates from me. Moreover, my process and phrase work values a need for structure and context. During rehearsals, I give dancers as much information to inform their choices as is possible. In the making of my piece *Shiny Exteriors (and visible strings)*, dancers were given "dossiers" on their roles detailing character origin, motivation, archetypal images and a list of references. From this, dancers were instructed to conduct their own research, and choices emerged. From these choices, more questions emerged which continued the process of refinement by the dancers and myself. In less character driven work, choices exist within a movement score that dictates the parameters of body (initiation, sequencing, organization, patterns), effort (time, flow, space, weight), space (kinesphere, intent, geometry), and shape (modes of shape change, shape qualities). In imbedded collaboration, dancers are not expected to provide the content for the piece.

At the start of a new piece, my ultimate goal is to allow the dancers to "own" the dance. Agency is used as a metaphor for investment. Ideally, they will be freed from the preoccupation of being "right," which is often code for a desire for my approval. This is particularly relevant to student dancers. Choreographers may refer to this as "turning the work over to the dancers," where movers are free to make choices and are so steeped in the process they are confident their choices are prescient, with little need for affirmation. In the best of circumstances, agency produces a sense of security. Again, this is democracy in action.

One can track the cultivation of agency in my work through rehearsal notes. Early on, my language is peppered with words such as "fix" "change" and "try," with many questions posed to myself about the arc of the piece; during this stage the dancers are quite liberal with questions that often demand specific answers I do not yet have. Their questions usually begin with "What should I do when...?" or "Do you want me to...? My common responses to such questions may be "I don't know" or "your questions are too hard" or "I'm not sure yet." I attempt to deliver such statements with light touch, to indicate that I am unconcerned with the lack of clarity in that moment. Humour is often a part of my rehearsal process. A luxury of working with students is that many are aware of this facet of my personality from classroom experiences. While those desiring concrete answers may initially feel uncomfortable with the murkiness of my response, humour often salves the chaffing of indecision.

Later notes pose questions to the dancers. My questions for them become less fixed to encourage a range of responses. Problem solving can and should produce multiple answers. Early notes pertain to structuring the work; later notes address the need for dancers to establish their identity within the piece. I encourage them to engage in "scripting" for the piece. This process, which I learned while performing for Denise Szykula's Dance Nonce dance company, calls upon the dancers to write a narrative (be it abstract or literal) for their journey though the piece. The traditional roles of choreographer and dancer typically demand the dance maker provide the inner monologue for the mover. In this instance, however, instead of providing Autumn a reason for embracing Rachel, I ask her why she does so in that moment. The content is established. She must provide the intent, which will effect the execution. The consideration of the question is more important than producing an answer as if it were a pop quiz. Performers are directed to take the time to discover the answer both cerebrally and viscerally. This process is reflective of dancer/choreographer Daniel Nagrin's (2001) six questions on acting technique for dancers, which requires the performer to address intent (who, what, what, where, and to what end?). This exchange calls upon the dancer to be present and to *effect* the outcome of the time before and after any given moment, rather than employ *affect* to produce manufactured meaning.

When dancers begin to identify personal intent, they also begin to make subtle changes to the execution of content. When the performer questions the work, the nature of the work changes. This highlights another moment of imbedded collaboration, where dancers begin to unconsciously re-choreograph movement phrases. I regularly allow this to happen, though I rarely, if ever, comment on it in rehearsal or performance. I allow dancers to execute movement that may not mechanically be in keeping with the given phrase work, but proves to be generated from such pure authenticity of intent that accuracy takes a backseat to artistic license. In these moments, the piece belongs more to the cast than to me. During performances, I limit my notes as much as possible (generally focusing on blocking, timing and music cues) to aid the dancers, rather than me, to be responsible to themselves, each other, and the work.

It is important to note when confronted with the question of "why" in rehearsals, most young dancers are not only unprepared to answer, but are also made uncomfortable by nature of the question. Many students are not taught the value of questions in their training. They are often so preoccupied with *what* they are supposed to be doing that the question *why* has never occurred to them. This is one of the many services the academy provides to the artist in training. Guided discovery promotes self-direction while reinforcing the value of inquiry. In my work, when dancers began to offer suggestions about characterization, instead of movement vocabulary, inquiry has become imbedded in their process (at least in the context of the piece we are creating). I am reminded of a dancer in *Shiny Exteriors (and visible strings)* who explained during dress rehearsal that she would remove the mask from her face as she exited the stage, because "it seems like that's what my character would do." This was a pivotal moment not only because she made choices based on her deep understanding of her character, but also because she felt she had something relevant to contribute. She offered an effective choice that, frankly, never occurred to me. Part of the hidden curriculum is the dancers' recognition that it is to their benefit that I do not hold the ultimate truths of the piece.

Dance is an art of moveable space that, video aside, exists only in the moment. My awareness of the timeliness of dance is reflected in my stance on the possession of the piece. My need to put the dance in the "hands" of the dancers is imperative because when they are on stage I have limited capacity to affect the outcome. Ultimately, agency in this context champions the dancer as stakeholder in the work, while recognizing the limits of the choreographer beyond rehearsal.

OUTCOMES

The creation of a fully realized work that the performers and choreographers are satisfied with is, obviously, a primary concern. Indeed, the choice to collaborate is the fulfilment of that end goal. In my experience, imbedded collaboration yields dividends that enhance the final product in performance. My choreography centers on relationships. Frequently, these relationships are imposed on a dancer by the context of the work. Dancers' contributions to a piece facilitate the development of organic interaction among performers as themselves and their characters; this, in turn, facilitates the portrayal of relationship in the work. Moreover, it initiates intelligent dialogues among the dancers about the work, further defining and refining the portrayal of relationship in the piece.

Inevitably, as the performers begin to engage in inquiry about identity, they collectively discover answers and questions (in that order) about the work. I am pleased when feedback sessions during rehearsals include phrases such as "we were discussing our duet and..." or "we have a question about...," as this is an indicator that the dancers are considering the work from the perspectives of others in the piece. When dancers form their own web of knowledge about existence in a dance, familiarity is established which, ideally, produces an exhibition of authenticity through movement. In such moments, dancers are self-actualised rather than apologetic (literally and figuratively) to themselves, each other, the audience and me.

Making work within a college setting is quite different from creating dances in a professional environment. Unlike work with a dance company, I do not have the luxury of sustained, evolving relationships. Every semester, each cast is different. There is great variety among ability, and interests, as well as personal and professional relationships with me. Casting is often dictated by circumstance and the needs of the dancer, rather than the dance. As choreographer, educator and mentor, I strive to provide a host of dance performance experiences, with multiple choreographers, that will contribute to the student developing into a well-rounded dancer capable of performing many kinds of dances. While Stephanie may be a wonderful muse for my work, it is inappropriate to have her in every dance I create; it would be unfair to her and her fellow students. Though each dance differs, the expectation of the quality of the product is the same. Incorporating the dancers into the work aids in the creation of a level playing field, which is particularly helpful with students at different stages of their training. Collaboration often establishes community in spite of the transience of casting, creating a parallel if not identical experience to a dance company.

Imbedded collaborative work is especially helpful in the restaging of an existing piece on a new cast. By design, my dances are created for the dancers in the piece; their individual idiosyncrasies and talents are incorporated into the dance as it evolves. This can be problematic when reproducing a dance on a new cast. Engaging in the process of inquiry reshapes the work for the new cast, allowing for the transfer of ownership from the previous cast to the current dancers. To a certain extent, the dances must be malleable to allow for changes that will result when the new dancers claim the work. These changes affect body, effort, shape and space, meaning and intent.

Like our bodies, the dance has dynamic alignment[15]. When one aspect of the piece changes, everything changes; it is a different dance. I do not expect a dancer to try to perform like anyone other than herself. Casts are comprised of individuals and that must be honored. To that end, my collaborative choices are contingent upon a specific cast for a specific piece. As my casts change with each piece, understanding about the piece, and process in general, evolves. The truths that emerge from inquiry are timely and specific to the moment. The dance would form differently with a different cast at a different time. Each version of each piece is unique.

If education is at the heart of the exchange between the choreographer and dancer in higher education, the most prescient question is: what have the students learned? Because dance is a kinaesthetic art form, there are clear psychomotor objectives that can be measured in the physical performance of the piece. Affective growth is tied to a sense of agency in the piece. Students will differ in their level of success in these areas; that is to be expected in an educational environment. One facet of my role is to provide appropriate challenges that may be met over time, but not necessarily within the timeframe of the piece. There is also cognitive growth from this process. When dancers engage in inquiry, they are better equipped to speak articulately about the process, relationship and craft. Moreover, they attend to these areas in the making of their own work. They evolve from movement organizers to composers, and tend to be more responsible to the needs of their casts.

CONCLUSION

Ultimately, my choice to collaborate reflects my commitment to forming strong, productive interpersonal relationships with dancers. Student engagement with the work facilitates the craft of choreography. It also provides an opportunity for me to learn about students' dispositions and learning styles, which affects my mentorship, advising, instruction and compositions for them in the future. Each student, regardless of knowledge or ability, has something valuable to offer. Ideally, the rehearsal/classroom is a cooperative environment—student learning from teacher, student learning from student, teacher learning from student—transcending traditional student/teacher roles and interacting as human beings.

My identities as artist and educator are intertwined out of necessity. In fact, my philosophy of teaching and approach to imbedded collaborative choreography are essentially the same. I expect a high level of commitment and focus, and support of peers. I appreciate reliability, open minds, and a strong work ethic. When assessing progress, participation and intent weigh equally with apparent skill and technical improvement. In return, I endeavour to create a safe harbour that encourages exploration and risk taking and strive to balance integrity, passion, patience, and humour. Embracing the roles of mentor and friend, I try to always be mindful of the needs and desires of the individual as well as the group when making decisive choices. Furthermore, I count myself as a member of that group. Dancers should be fearless explorers, open to the possibilities. This cannot be willed or forced; it requires a conducive environment.

To be sure, I would not engage in this process if it did not produce successful results. Theinclusion of imbedded collaborative methods has changed my choreography for the better. My dances morphed into work that speak to audiences on an emotional and visceral level in ways they never did before. The experience of the viewer is as important as that of the dancer and dance maker. Indeed, the exchange between the watcher and the watched is another collaboration of sorts. Dances are transformative for the maker, the doer and the observer and I relish the opportunity to assume all three roles when creating my art, for they yield information on separate aspects of craft.

As a dance maker in higher education, I am at the service of many masters, the performers, the observers, the dance program, the dance, and myself. Engaging in the imbedded collaborative process allows me to attend to all stakeholders in a mutually beneficial manner. Change inevitably results from the experience, which always informs my future work.

IN BED: EXPLICIT COLLABORATION
JOAN MEGGITT

As an educator, I recognize the many ways in which teachers and students engage in collaborative learning and that such endeavours are inherent in the educational process. This mutual exchange extends to creative work as well. While I do choreograph for students and involve them in the process beyond the mere replication of choreography, the bulk of my creative work is carried out as Artistic Director and principal choreographer of my professional dance company, Antaeus Dance. Working in these specific capacities, I engage in collaborations with the dancers in the company, as well as with artists from other disciplines, including music, visual art, and film.

The premise that the creation and realization of dance is, by its very nature, collaborative was established in the introduction and elucidated in my colleague's writings. I will expand upon this assertion by addressing the more explicit nature of my collaborations with and through Antaeus Dance.

In my work, collaboration is a distinctly overt phenomenon. I will specifically speak to the work that I conduct with my professional company: what the work is and how it is carried out; the specific nature of our collaborations; briefly, how said collaborations compare to those with individuals outside of the dance field; how decisions are made and thereby affect the evolution of choice over the course of the collaboration and beyond; and, finally, how outcomes are assessed.

Prior to going into the studio with the company, regardless of whether or not it involves collaboration, I engage in a significant amount of preparatory research. Following the initial impulse behind any new work—which could arise from a content idea, a string of words that catch my attention, a piece of music, a movement I witness or experience, a response to recent work—there is a considerable period of reflection. During this time I seek out any and all related ideas and materials (such as movement, images, text, and music) that could potentially inform the dance making process. All materials are kept in a portfolio dedicated to the project—everything from notes and musings, to drawings and collected images, to music notations and scores, are chronologically organized in their respective categories. The project portfolio will eventually include rehearsal and showing notes, a video log, notes from meetings with collaborators, and responses to the formal performances. In addition, contributions of inspirational material from the dancers are also included.

The initial phase of the creative process is somewhat indulgent, allowing me to be wildly expansive in my exploration of the dance's potential. I inevitably collect more material than is finally utilized; however, this makes for a much richer process and also offers more points of entry and engagement to the dancers. Ultimately, the preliminary research helps to focus my ideas and the resultant materials (movement and otherwise) that I will bring to the dancers and any other collaborators. Frequently, this process begins long before the in-studio work commences, and often while I am in the midst of another project. I prefer to let ideas simmer for some time before acting upon them. By giving myself time to reflect openly, rather than focus intensely, I find that more ideas and possibilities arise.

In due course, I arrive at the first rehearsal with an extensive collection (an assemblage in and of itself), an evolving identity for the dancework, a plan of action that will further clarify my intention(s), and specific assignments/assignations for the dancers.

THE WORK

Practical Components

Traditionally, a choreographer makes the work—more specifically, she choreographs the dance—and the dancers perform it. This is a time-honoured practice that has been augmented through the centuries by dancers who also choreograph, whether because they begin to compose dances at a relatively young age, or because they extend their performing careers to serve their own creative work. Even so, dancers have still been largely responsible for the learning and performing of material generated by the choreographer, whether she is one of them or not. This is not to say that dancers are not an integral part of dance making, or that they do not contribute greatly to the creation of the work. What it does mean, however, is that the roles of choreographer and dancer remain clearly delineated, even when they are one in the same person. Collaboration as an explicit phenomenon is most clearly seen in the work of post-modern dance artists during the 1960s and 70s; individuals worked within collectives that recognized everyone as a creative force (be they dancer, musician, visual artist, or writer) and no one person as a distinct leader. The most well known of these was Judson Dance Theatre, a performance collective that developed out of a composition class hosted by Merce Cunningham and led by composer Robert Dunn. The remnants of this egalitarian way of dance making are still at work in many dance companies today, though there is frequently an established director who leads and facilitates the involvement of the dancers. Today, dance companies such as Gina Gibney Dance, Urban Bush Women, and Pilobolus engage the dancers in movement exploration and invention toward the realization of the director's choreography. In the case of Troika Ranch, artists from three different disciplines engage in what they call "cooperative interaction," with each discipline (dance, music and media) given equal weight.

For my part, I have developed from a choreographer who has been solely responsible for the creation of dances, to an artist who is active in larger endeavours that involve numerous and varied perspectives, all of which contribute to the making and witnessing of dance. I am equally comfortable in both roles; however, I have found that the latter is much more rewarding. The principal work of my professional company is to create and perform original danceworks in the modern dance idiom. Even though we are a formal dance company, versus a collective that features a uniform structure with respect to direction and creation, there are works within the repertory that have been created in a much more collective or collaborative fashion.

While I have collaborated with numerous artists from across a wide range of disciplines, I collaborate most frequently with the dancers in my company. Antaeus Dance is comprised of six dance artists who have been working in the same region for nearly two decades and who have been dancing with one another for roughly eight years. Prior to our working together, we had similar dance experiences in our respective training, participated in master classes and workshops together through the years, and watched one another in countless performances. In short, there is a shared base of knowledge and an understanding of our individual movement strengths and propensities. The watching of dance is a kinaesthetic experience; for dancers this contributes to proprioception, or the awareness of the body in the moment, and often elicits physical responses not commonly found in the average audience member. In witnessing one another move, we have learned a great deal; and we came to know and understand facets of one another before ever working together as a discreet community. While this shared knowledge, in part, defines our community, it by no means limits us to one way of perceiving, executing, or creating movement.

In collaborations wherein the dancers are called upon to contribute to the dance through significant movement invention, the parameters are made clear from the beginning. I present the overall concept of the piece, initial ideas to be explored, specific materials related to the piece such as images, writings/text, and music, and the extent to which the dancers will serve as co-creators of the dancework. The dancers are accustomed to speaking freely, asking questions, and making suggestions during rehearsals. Occasionally, I may ask them to solve a movement problem on their own. This behavior is characteristic of a productive rehearsal, both with my company and with students; however, it does not constitute a comprehensive collaboration. Again, there is a tacit understanding between choreographer and dancers that, within widely accepted parameters, both parties will actively contribute to the rehearsal process. An explicit collaboration acknowledges the creative roles of the dancers at the onset and includes clearly established expectations of all participants.

By agreeing to participate in the dance making and performing, the dancers accept their role as collaborators and mine as collaborator, principal choreographer, and director. They understand that their movement inventions will be integrated into a complete and singular dancework that will be included in the repertory of the company and will bear my name as principal choreographer and director. They will be credited as collaborators and I include a separate program note that details the process and their specific role(s) in the creation of the work.

The dancers and I are involved in a regular rehearsal process that extends over roughly a five-month period for any given dancework. Improvisation plays a significant role in the creative process, through which the dancers explore ideas I present, and from which I gather movement ideas for incorporation into the piece. I also provide strictly choreographed movement, sometimes but not always arising from improvised material. The rehearsal process is a constant dialogue. After every improvisation there is discussion during which the dancers and I share our observations with one another and from our respective perspectives as participants and witness. I will frequently ask them to explore something again based on insights gained from previous explorations.

In most cases, I utilize improvisation to generate the initial material for the company's dance collaborations. I outline the parameters of each improvisation, based on specific ideas I want to explore. In some cases, the improvisations attempt to solve functional physical problems, such as: What happens if four dancers physically overwhelm one dancer? What if one dancer is constantly supported above the floor by the other dancers? In other cases, the explorations seek to concretise more esoteric subject matter, for example: How is alienation reflected in the individual/solo form? How does one shed bad habits? All improvisations are recorded on video, watched repeatedly, and then culled for material. I shape this material further and distil it into choreography—set movements which, in the long run, are not subject to change within the final performance, versus sections within the final performance that are designated as malleable and can be performed differently every time. Additional movements are taken back to the dancers for further exploration. Some of the original material is kept intact and worked directly into the final dancework.

I take copious notes while observing the improvisations and still more when watching them again on video. Potential material is meticulously logged in a journal that includes the date, originator(s) of the material, specific movement to be utilized, duration, potential use for and placement of the movement within the overall piece, and an informal name to identify the movement/phrase. Later, notations will include further description, drawings, space maps, and the assignment of specific dancers to particular movements and roles. These notes are part of the aforementioned project portfolio.

Video is an important tool in this process. While I can easily learn and teach the material with which I want to proceed, the recording allows the dancers to see themselves moving and reminds us all of who originated which movements and what performative qualities make them unique. Frequently I will not have the dancer who originated the movement perform that movement in the final performance. This cross-pollination of movements contributes further to the collaborative process. The dancer/collaborators are thereby exploring and embodying the movements of everyone involved in the process.

Methodology

My individual methodology has developed significantly since establishing the dance company eight years ago. Through consistent creation and performance with an established group of dance artists, I have been able to explore different ways of creating dance, evolving my practice from a somewhat autocratic approach to a fully collaborative process (while still maintaining my authority as director and principal choreographer). While I have not concerned myself with how others go about creating work, I have drawn from what I see as successfully methods. For example, after collaborating with another dance maker wherein we improvised extensively prior to choreographing any movement, I began incorporating that into my own practice with the company. This particular way of working has yielded some of my best work to date.

Beyond the concrete practice of movement invention, there are many other avenues that inform the work. For me, creating danceworks includes the extensive use of visual elements (photographs, paintings, sculpture, sketches) to help set the tone for the work and provide potential shapes and movements for integration into the work. These images are always shared with the dancers as part of the rehearsal process. They provide the dancers with a sense of what I am thinking/feeling beyond the actual movement itself and, ideally, providing them with an entry into the work before it even begins. From there I go directly into the teaching of movement phrases and the structuring of the work at large. While there is always room for input from the dancers, a more traditionally choreographed dance features a very direct line of teaching from choreographer to dancer. The utilization of visual components as groundwork for the dance is the same in the collaborative rehearsal process, and the material has grown to include articles, short essays and poems, most of which come from the dancers. Through their substantive contributions, the dancers have expanded the foundational materials from which we all draw during the collaboration.

One of the challenges that I face is finding new frameworks for the company's improvisational work. Improvisation is a means of exploring new ways of moving and experiencing the body, without the pressure or concerns about "getting it right." Mistakes are frequently the best thing that can happen, leading the individual into new territory, requiring her to problem solve and think on her feet (or head, hands, back, hip, side, etc.). By the same token, improvisation also allows the company members to freely indulge in the movement that she most enjoys, thereby reinforcing idiosyncratic movement patterns. While the dancers are a creative and vastly inventive set of individuals, they are equally capable of indulging their preference as they are of pushing their boundaries. The longer a group works together, the more easily they fall into movement together, the better they recognize and anticipate one another's choices, and the more staid the work becomes. This situation requires me to push them beyond that sense of ease to get to something raw and far enough outside of their expectations that, in those moments, they surprise themselves and one another.

Improvisation is a mainstay of my collaborations with the dancers; but it is not the only means of movement invention. Another way in which I develop movement is by giving the dancers very specific assignments that they usually complete during the rehearsal period. In some cases I will utilize images to directly create movement sequences. For example, I will provide each dancer or pair of dancers with a group of images and the following instructions: order the images; distinctly replicate each image in posture and/or movement; string the postures/movements together in the same order as the images; expand this into a more fulsome phrase. In other instances I have given the dancers movement conundrums or challenges that I ask them to work out in duets or trios; such as, the dancers must stay in contact at all times, or one person must stay in the same place at all times regardless of what she and/or the other dancer(s) does. This has proved to be a very effective way of working, providing the dancers a clear sense of ownership of the material since it came directly from their individual ways of moving and expressing themselves.

Explored for their own sake, or within a larger context, these examples are very basic yet fruitful ways to generate movement. In all of these instances—improvisation, video capture and exploration, and assignments—the dancers are responsible for a significant portion of the original movement invention. Everything that occurs after this exploratory period either builds upon or is directly affected by that preliminary work. This raises questions about ownership and formal attribution.

Ethical Concerns

When so much has been determined by the dancers, one might ask at what point the choreographer ceases to be the creator of the dance and is more accurately described at the facilitator or director. Is the choreographer merely imposing her will upon the dancers and taking credit for the work which she did not create herself? For my part, I am extremely clear with the dancers about my expectations from the start. When I am seeking to engage them fully in movement invention and to collaborate with them in the crafting of that movement, I present the project in so many words. The program lists the dancers as participants in the dance making and, in the instance of several of my evening-length danceworks which featured extensive improvisation and problem solving on the part of the dancers, I detail the process and the roles of everyone involved in a program note. Other citations also include the dancers as collaborators; for example, the company website, relevant publicity material, and even my curriculum vitae, credit any and all collaborators.

My hope is that any individual in the company who felt that she was not appropriately represented and credited would make their feelings known to me. I assume that an individual who is unhappy with the modus operandi would either decline to work on a project or choose to leave the company.

For me, involving the dancers is a natural extension of the world in which I live. I am reliant on others, at every turn, for survival, community, enrichment, and evolution. At the same time, I experience conflict and the desire to resolve it. Both of these aspects of living within a large society—enrichment and conflict—are inherent in the creative process.

THE NATURE OF DANCE COLLABORATION

Collaboration is, at once, a wonderfully risky and intensely rich undertaking. The choreographer, typically the recognized leader of the creative process, becomes a co-creator with the dancers. The rehearsal process is a distinct discourse; in collaboration this exchange is much more complex and extends beyond traditional boundaries. This collaborative process requires a mutual recognition of ideas and concepts and a weaving of these directly into the work at hand. While the dancer is most typically in the hands of the choreographer—receiving instruction and feedback—in a collaboration she is now in a position of being responsible for the co-creation of the work. Her movement invention is therefore subject to assessment by the choreographer. In agreeing to participate in a collaborative process with the choreographer, the dancers give the choreographer permission to assign value to their creative efforts. Such assessment is customarily usually limited to the rehearsal and performance of someone else's work (namely the choreographer's).

There are several assumptions inherent in my collaborative work with the company members: the dancers have something valuable to offer the process and the product; their individual movement propensities inform the dance; so-called mistakes are inherent in the process and provide options that might not otherwise present themselves to the choreographer alone; both choreographer and dancer(s) are responsible for making decisions; and shared decision-making expands the possibilities for the work.

My reasons for collaborating have evolved significantly and in conjunction with my perspectives on dance, choreography, and the creative process. In working with a dedicated group of individuals for an extended period of time, I have developed a great desire to make dances *for them and with them*. This has affected how I engage with dancers with whom I am less familiar, such as students and other professional companies. While the creation of concert dance is largely driven by individual ego, requiring significant self-motivation, it has the potential to be so much more expansive. Both the creation and viewing of dance engages the individual in the realization of collective truths, as dance did when it was a communal activity in which everyone within a local context engaged. In learning more about myself and the dancers, I have found that their ways of knowing are vastly different than my own. They possess understandings that I can only imagine. If our work is to be of any value, it must acknowledge these different ways of knowing and utilize them toward a collective expression, albeit one that is ultimately guided by a singular vision to which all have agreed to subscribe. It is the collaboration that allows a singular vision to expand beyond its initial limitations.

Collaboration enlarges the statement that I am trying to make, through dance, about the human condition. My interests in exploring the intersection of individual expression and collective experience are more fully realized through the collaborative process and more accurately represented by dancers who are an active part of this process. Bringing their individual expression into the process, whether through the creation of movement or the contribution of additional materials, is the first step in creating a collection of experiences from which the work will be drawn. Even as the dancers engage in their individual movement invention(s) they are interacting with one another, forming distinct statements about where and how they relate to the collective whole.

The capacity to facilitate the realization of a singular vision out of numerous, and sometimes disparate, perspectives is one that the company has allowed me to cultivate. Beyond that, working collaboratively with the company has challenged me to expand my own vision and remain open to possibilities. Most often I feel that my own voice is not enough. While I may possess the initial ideas and the resources to develop them further, they are not enough. Dancers exponentially expand the world of the dance far beyond my own knowing and imaginings. It is the desire to know more, to be more, which drives my work with others. The dancers, through their different ways of knowing, are at once the catalysts for and the realization of a larger vision.

I firmly believe that collaboration, most especially those with the members of my company, has made me a better human being. When directing a collaboration that ultimately puts forth my personal vision, there is the incredible responsibility to appropriately utilize the dancers' contributions. Their time and energy, ideas, and movement exploration are invaluable components of the work. Furthermore, the additional materials the dancers provide supports the collective inquiry, thereby yielding further inspiration, dialogue and movement.

Collaboration is more than simply the sharing of ideas and/or a sharing of the creative load. For me, a fully inclusive collaboration is about being in the moment together. The rehearsal process is a subtle negotiation and, in collaboration, that negotiation comes more clearly to the forefront of the process. Individual artists, making separate work on their own, no matter how closely tied they may be in intention, are not in an active collaboration; rather they are coordinating their parts at different points along the way. When the collaboration includes a guided rehearsal process, decisions are made together on a moment-by-moment basis—choreographer and dancers alike are informed by one another's work and perspectives. Every moment of the practice of dance making is in itself a collaboration. Ideas are exchanged in real time and, specifically, through the medium of movement/dance.

The burden of responsibility resides firmly with the choreographer to organize and document all movement and relevant support materials. While the dancers are joint originators and repositories for the work, the choreographer preserves everything else. She is a participant/witness who initiates, directs, records, assesses, augments, and concludes the process.

COLLABORATING ACROSS DISCIPLINES

My collaborations with artists outside of the company have been marked by much more independent creative work on the part of the lead artists. This makes for a much different kind of collaboration. Similar to the work that I do with Antaeus Dance, the collaborative process begins with a full discussion of the intended project, the respective roles of the lead artists, and how the elements will ultimately fit together. We, as collaborators, agree to work toward a composition that brings together our respective work/creations into a singular, fully integrated work. In most cases, I am the initiator of the project and set the tone for the project. I am also very specific about my personal desires regarding how, specifically, we will collaborate. Finally, depending upon the discipline, the manner in which the elements will work together is usually self-evident.

After dancers and choreographers, the most fundamental collaborations are between choreographers and composers. Dance and music are natural partners. There are a great many ways in which they can work together in performance. The music can be live or recorded; if live, the musicians can be in the pit, on the stage, or moving about with the dancers; the music can be highly traditional, contemporary or experimental. In all instances, and regardless of what the audience might think about the music on its own merits, the combination of music and dance will nonetheless make sense to the viewer. Therefore, the parameters of the final music performance play a significant role in determining the nature of the collaboration.

The same is true of stage elements created by a visual and/or multi-media artist. A visual element that serves purely as an identifier of time and place (backdrop, hanging element, immobile set) is much different from one that is both an identifier and an integral part of the choreography. The latter category refers specifically to interactive sets that the dancers move or, in the case of certain technologies such as sonar and touch pads, are responsive to the movement of the dancers. The artist creating the set elements will, likewise, have a different relationship to the making of both the dance and the set based on its role.

Stepping away from the company to collaborate is a distinctly different experience because I am entering into a process with someone who does not necessarily speak my language, express themselves in the same way and through the same means, and/or have the same investment in the outcome of the dance itself as I do. While we are all working toward the same project outcome (successful completion and integration of the elements), all of our passion, expertise, and creativity is focused toward our respective disciplines. At the same time, I am presuming to tell them what and how to create, and dictating its specific utilization.

For example, when I worked with an electronic-media artist to create a dance and dance film to be presented together in performance, we agreed that the creation of the film would be a shared responsibility, while the choreography would remain mine (and the dancers'). We had collaborated on two previous projects, in which he and I participated fully in all aspects of the work, including: movement generation, story boarding, filming, media generation, and performing. Based on those experiences and their respective outcomes, we proposed a new model for collaborating that suited both our individual preferences and strengths. Ultimately, this allowed for both the process and the outcome to be successful and satisfying for everyone involved.

After our initial discussions and planning, the choreographic process began first. Once a significant amount of movement had been generated and crafted, the material was presented to the electronic-media artist. Together, we chose particular portions of the movement to be filmed and spent countless hours in the lab going through footage, choosing specific segments, editing, and ultimately crafting the film. That work in the lab led to further movement invention and also affected the performance of the existing choreography. The crafting of the film and dance continued together to their joint completion. In this collaboration, decisions about the film were made together; although he did an immense amount of preparatory work and video sampling that organized the material and allowed us to make decision with ease. I greatly appreciated the artist's willingness to allow me such a significant role in his work. In turn, his viewpoints about perspective, which translate to staging or directional facings in dance, vastly informed my way of crafting, structuring, and performing the movement. He was never in the studio with the dancers, aside from the filming; however, he had a profound affect on the dance. In this project, the collaborative spirit was strong and clearly executed.

In contrast, when I have worked with composers, initial planning has been followed by extended absences from one another, during which time we are each working on our respective elements. In many cases the collaboration has ended up as more of a negotiation between relatively complete works, with my work taking the lead role and the music being responsive to it. This more closely resembles the commissioning of a score since there is not a mutual exchange wherein both elements are directly affected by the other throughout, or at least at various points during, the process. My hope is that, in the future, I can orchestrate a collaboration that will allow the choreographer, composer and dancers to work together, in the moment, to create a truly collaborative dance/music project.

Finally, my collaborations with visual artists tend to be loaded at the beginning of the process. The bulk of the visual designs are interactive set elements with which the dancers work during the creative process. An object in the space will profoundly affect the movement, regardless of whether or not it is manipulated by the dancers. Ideally, the dancers have the opportunity to work with set pieces from the very first rehearsal. Because the dance will be created in response to the functional and aesthetic possibilities inherent in the set, the visual design must move ahead of the choreographic design. As with previously-detailed collaborations, both artists engage in significant discussion, evaluate numerous renderings, and ultimately make a decision together regarding the best design for the project. If the design proves unsuitable, both must be willing to go back to the drawing board and rebuild as needed. Similar to the problem-solving movement inventions, set elements provide the dancers with challenges they would not otherwise face in the dance space; especially because most dancers are accustomed to a completely bare stage with an even, uninterrupted surface. In reflecting upon the company work with interactive set elements, I have found that the visual elements haves been the most provocative for the company's creative process. While the collaborations are much briefer, they are no less rich than those with other dance artists and composers, and have profoundly affected my view and use of space.

DECISION-MAKING & THE EVOLUTION OF CHOICE

By utilizing improvisation as a basis for movement invention and as the foundation of any given work, the choreographer and dancers share in the decision-making process. Looking back at the idea that an active collaboration requires that the work takes place in the moment, and for choices to also take place in those moments, one must consider the ways in which decisions are made and by whom.

In order for such a process to be successful, both the autonomy of the individual dancer and the cooperative spirit of the group must be present in equal parts and fully supported by the choreographer. In addition to developing the piece, the choreographer must be aware of emergent qualities which the dancers clearly present during movement exploration. She must also be equally committed to cultivating those that are nascent within each dancer, willing to allow for these often complementary developments and be prepared to let go of preconceived notions of who the dancers are or should be. Ultimately, the rehearsal process seeks to integrate different qualities present within the individual in such as way that both the individual and the dance are appropriately served. There is a fine balance to be struck between keeping the original intention present in the process and following the course that the work is taking on its own.

There is also the concern of presenting apposite challenges so that the work does not languish. While mature dancers possess the awareness to develop performance qualities in the moment and make appropriate choices individually and in relation to one another, it is the role of the choreographer to challenge and shape them. Consistent dialogue encourages an organic development that honors both the participants and the emerging work, not to mention the choreographer's intentions. It is only later, in the crafting of the material, that the choreographer imposes her own will on the work; even then, it is ultimately informed by what she has witnessed and is thereby influenced by the dancers, the originators of the movement. In doing so, the choreographer must be willing to say no, many times, and to do so in a way that does not discourage further input.

Ironically, at the beginning of such a process, when I have the least amount of control, I tend to refer to the work as mine. Regardless of the clarity of my intentions, the work is wide open and entirely mutable. Relationship is important in the beginning and most of the work is about exploring and establishing the universe, if you will, which the dancers inhabit, as well as their roles in it. As the work progresses, my language shifts and I refer to the piece as ours. This reflects our evolving roles as collaborators. Having identified who they are, where they might be going, and how they relate to one another, the dancers are best suited to make decisions that affect the outcome of the work. Finally, as the dance approaches completion, I call it theirs. Even as I make more specific decisions regarding the crafting of the dance, it moves further away from me and more firmly into the domain of the performers. It is at this point that I am most fully in the traditional role assigned to the choreographer, making decisions for the group and guiding them with a firm hand. The work has come full circle; the command that I gave over to them in the beginning has been returned to me.

OUTCOMES

From a formal perspective, the performance of a completed dancework is seen as the final outcome. However, there are many small outcomes that are apparent and acted upon during the creative process. As a result, the collaborators are able to constantly practice outcome assessment and implement resultant insights. As stated earlier, the methodology for any given dancework is created in the process of creating the dance. Naturally, there are many similarities from dance to dance; but collaborators bring new ideas, concepts, and practices to the work. Essentially, the creation of a dancework is one extended process of outcome assessment.

For any assessment to be productive there must be at least a modest sample from any given method. For example, an improvisation that does not yield the anticipated outcome is often revisited at another point. Failure to produce an agreeable movement series at the onset is not grounds for a completely new approach. Because there are so many variables in a single improvisation, repeated practice is necessary to effectively address ways and means of movement. Conversely, a wonderfully successful improvisation—both experientially and with regards to the resultant material—is sometimes a signal to move right on into the next thing without attempting to repeat the experience. A less successful repetition of an engaging exploration can sour the process. Again, there is a balance to be struck. The choreographer's ability to read the dancers, to know when to push them and when to back off, is a vital part of effectively utilizing improvisation as a tool for dance making.

The manner in which the individual dancer approaches the explorations is also subject to assessment. The very manner in which she engages with the other dancers and makes choices could be either an impediment to or a catalyst for the process. For example, a dancer who constantly works outside of the established parameters could be the spark that launches everyone forward, moving them beyond their assumptions to a new understanding. On the other hand, that person could be a disruptive element that throws off the entire improvisation. The group dynamic is very fluid and improvisation requires that everyone be willing and able to make decisions for themselves, adjust to what is happening around them in the moment, and not get caught up in their personal desires or preferences.

One of the frustrations of formal performance is the clear separation between performers and audience. Audience members who know the artists will frequently speak with them at length about the performance. Hosting a talk-back at the end of each performance encourages audience members to comment on their experience, as well as to ask questions of the participants, thereby illuminating aspects of the process and the performance. Audience surveys are usually included in programs to poll statistical data for grant purposes, and can also include room for comments about the work. Out of all of these possibilities, live dialogue between a pure witness and a participant, be it immediately following the performance or several days later, is the best way to assess the outcome from a formal perspective.

While this does not necessarily influence the methodology per se, such input does address issues such as: clarity of intention, what speaks and what does not, what went untapped, what if anything was the audience left wanting, and so forth. The biggest question is whether or not the audience has a right to determine if, when, how, and by whom the next work is made. A product-oriented project places a great deal of power in the audience's hands, without attention to responsibility. A project that seeks to honor those who create it, with attention to how it can inform participant and witness alike, asks more of the audience. It requires that an investment be made, that awareness and thought be a part of the witnessing, and that witnessing is, in its own right, a process to be honored. There is a responsibility to thoughtful response, regardless of whether it is in support of or opposed to the work.

CONCLUSION

Of utmost importance to me as a choreographer and director is the individual experience and how that can be clearly manifest within the larger context of community and performance. I am particularly interested in the fundamental process of exploring and mining these shared experiences. Realizing authentic and dynamic human connections in a way that enlarges perspective and provokes the imagination is the impetus for my choreography. To this end, I find that individual expression toward a collective understanding is essential, and I seek out performers who can contribute to the group dynamic while remaining true to themselves. While many of my danceworks are inspired by larger events in the world, they are ultimately investigations of much more intimate exchanges that address basic concerns of human interaction and relationship. I am ultimately seeking a balance between the subtleties of individual expression—the simple poetry of motion—and the passion, or drama, of the human experience.

Collaboration that fully and openly engages the dancers in the creative process makes all of this possible. Consistent practice cultivates greater awareness and responsivity among the dancers. Through an economy of movement that breeds potency, and a commitment to being in the moment, the dancers create a genuine space inside which they and the viewer are no longer separate.

In keeping with this focus on the responsivity inherent in relationship—more specifically the call to takes risks and trust in that which is not yet fully known—I am further committed to significant collaborations with other artists, including other dancers, composers and visual artists. Cultivating our mutual awareness and reciprocity to further the audience's experience of these very things in their own mind/bodies is an important aspect of collaboration.

REFERENCES

Bartenieff, I., & Lewis, D. (2002). *Body movement: Coping with the environment.* New York: Routledge.

Laban, R. (1971). *The mastery of movement* (3rd ed.). Revised and Enlarged by Lisa Ullmann. New York: Plays Inc.

Nagrin, D. (2001). *Choreography and the specific image: Nineteen essays and a workbook.* Pittsburgh: University of Pittsburgh Press.

RENEE T. COULOMBE

11. IMPROVISATION AND COLLECTIVITY

Practical Applications for Research

INTRODUCTION

In *The Sublime Object of Ideology* Slavoj Zizek (1989) articulates unusual cultural abstractions, a sort of forced indirectness and retrospectivity that any analysis requires.

> The Lacanian answer to the question: From where does the repressed return? is therefore paradoxically: From the future. Symptoms are meaningless traces, their meaning is not discovered, excavating from the hidden depth of the past, but constructed retroactively—the analysis produces the truth; that is, the signifying frame which gives the symptoms their symbolic place and meaning. As soon as we enter the symbolic order, the past is always present in the form of historical tradition and the meaning of these traces is not given; it changes continually with the transformations of the signifiers's network. Every historical rupture, every advent of a new master-signifier, changes retroactively the meaning of all tradition, restructures the narration of the past, makes it readable in another, new way. (p. 56)

While it may seem at first somewhat incongruous, I believe that Zizek articulates a particularly resonant construct for those who conduct musical research. Music engages the symbolic directly and, thus, its praxis is fundamentally abstract. Therefore, by definition, it cannot be described, analyzed or taught directly. Traditional modes of musical research require a constant "quilting," to borrow again from Zizek, between the symbolic and syntactic, but the quilting can never be complete—no absolute meaning can be determined, as the quilting process itself requires responsive mutability because meanings are retroactively constructed. We can of course teach and engage music theory, literature and history, and carefully instruct or learn instrumental technique; indeed, these disciplines have developed complex linguistic and notational systems for that purpose. But we cannot, in the end, routinely engage music *directly* with our students or peers in musical language collectively in real time with one notable exception, improvisation.

The unique nature of improvisation—spontaneous expression in the act of performance itself—has no "translation" from abstraction into metaphor and therefore no language, no syntax. Other than a few notable exceptions (cf. Bailey, 1993; Lewis, 2002), this abstract nature also explains the relative lack of theorization and documentation in comparison to other performance disciplines. This does not diminish, however, the vast community of improvisers and improvisational genres in culture, or the burgeoning quantity and quality of scholarship in the area. Nor am I positing that improvisation is the only form of collective qualitative research conducted in music. Rather, primarily through detailed examples from my own practice, this essay widens current inquiry, engaging the unique praxis of collective musical improvisation as artistic research in order to articulate both the aspects of improvisation present in collective qualitative research as a methodology as well as the aspects of this methodology inherent in improvisational praxis. Additionally, the collective research examples presented here go further, in articulating the unique modes of production and performance only achievable within the collective qualitative research framework that "restructure the narration of the past" both within the methodology and the work itself.

While the issues arising from collective research with peers only and in combinations of peers and students overlap significantly, they are not identical. Thus, I will begin with a discussion of several examples of collective improvisational projects in which students have been active co-participants before moving on to those focused primarily on peer collaboration. This classification is by no means offered as cut-and-dried, for most collective artistic research associated in some way with the academy or academic artists contains aspects or layers of student collaboration. However, there are separations in focus that are helpful particularly in outlining some significant pedagogical aspects and potentials of collective qualitative research.

NEW MEDIA/NEW WORK

As a Free Improviser who creates large-scale, collaborative intermedia performance works, collective qualitative research is my essential methodology. A central aspect of this praxis is the cultivation of ongoing research collaborations with artists and scholars of many disciplines in order to create opportunities for those collaborations to mature and formulate results in the form of performance events. Although my understanding of performance theory and history, facility with digital an interactive technologies, and performance techniques are all integral to this research, they do not represent its substance, which is quite impossible to articulate outside the performance itself. Conducting such research within an academic setting quickly revealed both difficulties and opportunities after I joined the Music Faculty at the University of California, Riverside, in the Fall of 2000. Other performance departments were geographically distant on campus; there were no facilities and few opportunities to meet and explore each other's research; interdepartmental research and performance collaborations were somewhat rare. In 2001 these departments moved to a new Arts building on campus, sharing performance and research facilities. While this new neighborliness had extremely varied results, the possibilities for new collective artistic research in shared spaces with shared resources sparked an outpouring of new research projects.

Taking advantage of the new performance facilities and positive research climate, I began recruiting artists at all levels for a new performance project loosely organized around the integration of emergent digital technologies with performance and the concomitant merging of many performance practices into new hybrids and forms. The collaboration included composer and artist Sean Griffin, dancer/choreographer Susan Rose, the members of our professional Free Improvisation collective, *Erroneous Funk*. All these artists were fluent in multiple performance modalities and most were producing work in multiple formats. In addition to these professional performers, the ensemble featured student members of the UCR Free Improvisation Ensemble including undergraduate and graduate student musicians, dancers, visual artists, writers, technologists and theatre artists.

The project was conceived around several central research questions arrived at communally: what new kinds of performance could be generated through an ongoing dialogue among technologies, practices and practitioners? What kinds of performance works emerge from ongoing collective research dialogues and performance workshops among engaged artists? Including students of various levels, what indigenous advances in performance practice emerge in interactions among artists whose methodologies and techniques were still evolving rapidly? Given the desire on the part of all collaborators (not to mention funding sources) to generate work of the highest quality, when was it appropriate both artistically and pedagogically for students to take the lead? To follow? And finally, how might this work developed among a specific collaborative group and set of facilities travel to other venues and across new groups of collaborators to demonstrate the viability of such performances beyond one's home institution.

The format of the collective research was equally fluid in order to capture the nuances of each artist's native methodology in improvisation yet allow room for new methodologies to arise within the group. At first casual, then weekly, and finally daily conversations exploring artistic mutual responses to workshops, discussions and rehearsals occurred among the professional members of the collaboration. We visited each other's working spaces and studios, viewed and exchanged work, discussed inspirations and our own current research formally and not-so-formally. Slowly we coalesced around a number of performance pieces, some of which predated the collaboration, but most were developed in workshop, and all encompassed a variety of media, deploying more than one performance or technologic modalities. All members of the group wanted to dedicate strategic sections of the performance to real-time improvisational responses to more structured pieces, in effect to present simultaneous layers of research developed in individual praxis through collaborative teams to a collective performance unit.

As the ultimate goal of the project from the beginning was a performance event, the parameters of which were to be determined by the group, the task of setting research goals was a relatively dynamic process. Collaborative improvisation research requires that no single artist, even the director of a research group, exert control while maintaining a high level of internal critique as the work develops. Negotiation and conflict resolution must be accomplished both within critical dialogue *and* the artistic expression of each member. To such ends, the structure, form, even auditory and visual language of the final performance could not be predetermined, and were up for increasingly detailed discussion.

Unlike many research groups, most of us preferred to begin our negotiations artistically—in free improvisation sessions where we could explore, experiment, and even work through frustrations with pieces and other collaborators. These sessions, sometimes lasting the entire planned meeting time, were some of the few opportunities many of us had to express ourselves completely in artistic language with colleagues, blending rather than bridging disciplinary gaps. We were free to integrate all our research modalities, undertaking modes and means of expression without thinking first about discipline. As we were in those moments—subject, object and means of production for the work—this process had to be supplemented with rigorous critique. However, the climate of openness and engagement lingered long after our collective improvisation sessions and indeed our critical work was faster, more focused and effective. We planned our collaboration schedule so that the bulk of our critical decisions for the performance event would be considered after months of intense artistic and critical exchanges. We did this in a very real sense in order to allow the group personality to fully emerge and provide the space for that personality to fully express itself in the final performance.

This performance, as previously noted, included works by each individual collaborator, including video works by Sean Griffin, choreography by Susan Rose, musical compositions by the author and performances by *Erroneous Funk*. Selecting pre-existing works from individual collaborators kept individual voices strong, creating a layered counterpoint with new pieces—solo, collaborative, or collective. As a group, we interrogated our own spectres, literally creating a digital séance with mouse serving as planchette and video/audio effects controller. As the mouse swept across the Ouija board at the fingertips of the performers, student performers secreted about the performance space (including, because of this particular facility) under the seats of the audience, haunting the space, the performance, and the other performers. This work, which contained pre-recorded audio and video from historic séances by Rosemary Brown and others, presented the work of the collaboration most directly. It was simultaneously a real-time interrogation of our pasts and futures as artists, the powerful immateriality of our work, and the presence-absence of previous improvisations in current work. While Derrida's (1994) name was not mentioned during the work, it was a powerful mediation on the concept of hauntology at the disciplinary level, a space where invoking new media in performance also invoked old ghosts lurking in the performance genres and methodologies themselves.

As the students of the UCR Free Improvisation Ensemble were a powerful feature in this work, separate student workshops and joint sessions with all performers supplemented the ensemble's regular meetings. Each of the major collaborators conducted master classes in improvisation and contemporary performance practice with the students. These included performance with interactive audio and video technologies and the use of live digital processing as well as the integration of visual art practice into performance settings. Students, in turn, often hit upon simple, original, and effective performance solutions in workshops that shaped the research in unanticipated ways.

After its initial performance in the Performance Lab at UC Riverside, several collaborators left the group before subsequent performances at the California Institute of the Arts. The second performance incorporated new artists, including video installation artist Marsia Alexander-Clarke, added new pieces into the collaboration, and necessitated shifts working methodology and research goals. The collective "personality" of the group adapted seamlessly, in large part because the core of undergraduate and graduate performers constituted a powerful collective memory from one event to the next. While the goals shifted, the collective personality of the research remained as new members quickly extended or transformed that personality but never eclipsed it. In essence, the research had established its own personality, one that could adapt to new input because it originated within the spirit of artistic openness, interactivity, and collectivity.

Several audience members, primarily visual artists and sculptors, from the first performance asked to join the ensemble for subsequent events. When asked later about why they joined, the response from each was the same: they could see within the framework of the performance itself "room" for their work, their personality, and their own desire to work interactively and collectively. Indeed, within their own discipline they saw interactivity as something they stood apart from (they created work and then stood back while others interacted with it). This project therefore offered something they could not find within their own disciplines. They understood intuitively and immediately how they could at once join the collective spirit, and contribute unique individual perspectives and pieces. Indeed, during the subsequent performances they constructed sculptures live on stage during collective improvisations, the sounds of their power tools and hammers joining with the instruments and their movements becoming dance in a joyous collective experience.

Thus, the research can be seen as challenging separations commonly found in other forms of artistic research: between past and present, students and professsionals, performers and audience, process and product. Research results were in real time, and presentations of research results were powerfully shaped by the methodology—even at the level of the constituent researchers. Attracting dedicated future researchers through the presentation of results is also an endorsement of any methodology, as is the ability to design research protocols that can more easily adapt to their presence.

UCR IS IMPROVISING

Capitalizing quickly on the successful methodology of *New Media/New Work*, and desiring to expand the methodologies of collectivity, I sent out an email in the summer of 2003 to the students who had participated in the UCR Free Improvisation Ensemble during the previous academic year. Recognizing the collective memory they represented from the previous project, I called an exploratory meeting for those who might be interested—in the oppressive heat of a Southern California summer—to discuss the idea of organizing an international festival of improvisation at UC Riverside during the following academic year. Calling a meeting in July is a risky, if quick, way of determining real interest in an idea. Many of the students on the UC campus are commuters, and need to work toward college costs over the sweltering Riverside summers, and most are already active working artists; it is not a moment when students generally undertake major new projects.

This core group of approximately fifteen students was engaged in the work of the ensemble, begun just a few years earlier when I joined the faculty in the Music Department of UC Riverside, and they had already begun to recognize the lack of improvisational resources on campus. This is not to say they experienced a lack of instruments, materials or facilities, but rather they did not have the powerful resource of other high-level improvisers in their lives. I had been fortunate enough to engage a modest number of professional improvisers for workshops with my students and performances on campus since joining the faculty, and each visit sparked enormous growth in the students. Workshops with Pauline Oliveros, Phil Gelb and Dana Reason ("The Space Between Trio"), or Nels Cline and "Acoustic Guitar Trio," and spontaneous master classes with violist Mary Oliver, jazz tabla master Badal Roy, or violinist Mark Menzies seemed to set the work of the group on fire and generate new work of considerable quantity and high quality. The opportunities to perform at other institutions and festivals had equally strengthened and transformed the group's work in their ongoing collective improvisational research. This work had for years consisted of weekly, two-hour sessions in which students engaged in dynamic and diverse improvisational exercises and had fostered in them a new understanding—that their own research and practice benefited most from interactions with other improvisers.

Still an interdisciplinary group, we quickly formulated a list of musicians, technologists, dancers, visual artists, poets, theatre artists and others that we wanted to bring to campus. Determining funding sources was a massive undertaking, as was designing the structure or format of the Festival proper in order to foster the kind of collective improvisational research we wanted to accomplish. How best to adapt previously successful models of collective research over extended periods to research completed over several days—with artists with whom few of us had ever worked? If the presentation of the results of this research were also different from previous projects (multiple performances by groups and solo artists, rather than continuous collective undertakings), would the results be as significant? And, given such an interdisciplinary nature, could it be funded? Given the far looser nature of this collective research coupled with the far more intense structural and facilities considerations, could the festival serve as a viable model for the presentation of collective improvisational research in the academy? And ultimately, given the emphasis of most research on reproducibility and peer review, how could artistic impact be assessed in the circumstances of this Festival?

Moving production into the center of the collective research, we nonetheless captured aspects of improvisational work that are central to praxis of improvisation in the broader culture, if difficult to capture within the pedagogical framework of the academy. Speaking "disciplinarily" for a brief moment, musical free improvesation, both as a practice and pedagogy, is a relatively recent discipline in the West and is relatively rare as a course of study. The abstract nature of the art, spontaneously creating music within no particular discipline or genre, but free to draw from any and all, prevents the direct instruction of students in "what to play" or "what to create." As this is the focus of much instrumental or ensemble work, and a central aspect of musical instruction in general, free improvisation in particular is most often tangential to mainstream western art music pedagogy.

Nonetheless, professional free improvisers often represent both the most innovative and technically accomplished among contemporary musicians, reflecting a desire to engage with artistic research—to literally create new works, with each performance. As much of the musical academy and industry is occupied with reproducibility as a fundamental aspect of music analysis, criticism and study, Free Improvisation represents a counterpoint to many of the ideologies of western art music. Entrepreneurship is of the essential here. Improvisers must be creative not only in their art but also in creating networks for new collaborations, performances and events, challenging their techniques with new performance modalities, and new ways or contexts for their work. Many are artistic chameleons, honing their abilities in diverse genres and modalities.

Communicating such skill sets to students and collaborators became central to the success of the Festival. Raising funds from a variety of foundations and campus groups, student and faculty collaborators "sold" the Festival to funding organizations based on the successful track record they could demonstrate through previous events (like *New Media/New Work* and or at Festivals like *Teknika Radika* in La Jolla), and a first-hand understanding of the benefits of this work in their own research. It was not coincidental that the growing number of collaborators on campus were experiencing considerable productivity in their own creative and scholarly work and that the experience gained in these projects was furthering their individual artistic careers in many important ways. As a research collective, we frequently discussed how to articulate the work of the group as well as how our own work or other projects were influencing, or being influenced by, the work of the group. As we attended each other's openings, showings, and concerts, and kept an active research schedule in attending concerts by fellow improvisers and experimental artists, we maintained a rigorous critical dialogue about the process, its progress, and our own praxis in light of this research. Each member of the collaboration was responsible for carrying this critical dialogue inward to his or her own practice; only with intense individual *and* collective foci could the research attain the high quality results to which we committed early.

The Festival itself centered around three fundamental "layers" of spontaneous research. The first was a series of performances (seven performances over three days) by professional improvisers of many disciplines and genres that was open to the general public. As participants were encouraged to attend each other's concerts, these performances also served as research showings that could serve to generate discussion among artists during workshops and free time. In order to encourage this interaction and discussion more directly, the Festival also had open sessions scheduled in the performance space when public concerts were not scheduled. As a small discipline, Free Improvisers are frequently geographically distant from one another. There are few opportunities for artists living in New York to collaborate with artists in Tokyo, or those from Los Angeles to jam with artists from Madrid.

Our Festival recognized the research value in spontaneous collaborations with fellow participants, to generate new networks, collaborations and work. Scheduling free time in performance spaces was all it took—they were literally never empty. One might stumble in on students playing with bassist Tetsu Haitoh and flutist Jane Rigler, leave the room only to return and find them joined by dancer Valerie Metiver or guitarist Rod Poole. These sessions had no audience save those participants in the room and went completely undocumented or reproduced. Like improvisation itself, they had no stated goal or desired outcome. In that regard, they represent pure, spontaneous collective research in an environment designed for that purpose. As such, they were instances of the performative nature (Austin, 1961) of the performing arts; the research resided not in the documentation of the event but in its enaction. While this may not have been a central aspect of the Festival's publicity, it was a primary consideration for the organizers.

Some artists, especially the Festival artist-in-residence Karl Berger, led master classes with improvisers during the three days of the event. All participants, from presenters to students, were welcome at these sessions, so the constituency was completely self-determined. A third central occupation of this Festival was to present this research within the context of the Festival as well; the closing performance featured the participants in these Master classes. This final performance recognized that the intimacy of exchange and the enormously creative outpouring of the previous events represented a major opportunity for high-level exchange at the close of the Festival: to "physicalize" through performance the collective undertakings of the event. While this did not represent the collectivity of *New Media/New Work*, after months of collaboration, the intensity and immediacy of the Festival nonetheless fostered a similar research climate. The diversity of approaches was represented primarily in the artists participating—from new media improvisation collective *SoNu*, to duos like Wade Matthews (multi-instrumentalist) and dancer Valerie Metiver, solo artists Jane Rigler and Rod Poole, to innovative trios like Phil Gelb (shakuhatchi), Tetsu Haitoh (bass), Shoko Hikage (koto) trio to Dana Reason (piano), Alex Cline (percussion) and Lisle Ellis (bass). The *Erroneous Funk* performance on Saturday evening[16] featured a visual art installation by UC Riverside Artists and invited guest artist Wade Matthews to take the stage with them for an impromptu set. Similarly, guest artist Karl Berger, a multi-instrumentalist and founder of the Creative Music Studio, conducted workshops with his partner, poet Ingrid Sertso, creating a genre-defying performance on the final day. The largest performance event with regard to participants and performance genres referenced, it was nonetheless one of the most unified, with large-scale intermedia improvisations constituting the bulk of the performance.

Groups can be difficult to negotiate without considerable previous experience both professionally and artistically. However, in this instance performers of differing experience and technique levels from multiple genres blended in a relatively seamless fashion easily slipping between numerous modalities and approaches. Both performers and audience felt no hurry to leave afterwards, as the lively engagement of the event spilled over into the reception after, the many dinners hastily organized to continue conversations, and the active email chatter that continued long after the event.

This leads directly to a feature of both events outlined above, the considerable informal and interpersonal component of such work heretofore unarticulated but central to this aspect of collective research. Free improvisers, who represent an integrated research unit as individual artists, deploy a number of informal techniques to increase their understanding of fellow artists and their work. Conversations as informal sessions and exchanges are not coincidental to this research but rather a central aspect of its methodology. To be exposed to other improvisers is to be exposed to their work, and although this exposure can be manifested implicitly or indirectly, the benefits to one's own practice are often remarkable. While there may be no direct pedagogic or artistic value to such informal exchanges, they represent potential future collaborations, inspirations for future solo research, context for existing practices or impetus for new, hybrid ones. Collective research of this type requires large blocks of unscheduled time with unfettered access and contexts that encourage free exchange. As such, it necessitates geographic and intentional proximity as well as both the will and the means to engage.

It is in response to these kinds of requirements that the production of such Festivals and events serve as a primary means of research reporting for collective improvisational research, in reflection in manuscripts such as this one and enacted musically in the improvisations themselves. This, in turn, meant that venues for such work needed to be self-created, mutable, and highly collaborative in-and-of themselves. They require continued commitment not only to the practice of one's discipline but also the shaping of its venues and evolving contexts. In this instance, it required acquisition of appropriate spaces, funding for travel, lodging, and documentation, publicity and press releases, coordination and careful planning.

With few ongoing opportunities of this type in academia, each event at the Festival became an experiment representing research, its collation and presentation and required grants, administrative volunteers, academic collaborators, facilities and publicity staff, and the like. The skill set for publication in this area of research is considerable and therefore impossible to undertake as a solo project. For these reasons, those engaging collaborative improvisational research must continuously adapt to new opportunities for presentation, capitalizing on new networks and facilities whenever possible.

In years subsequent to the 2004 Festival, collaborators went on to incorporate new emphases and collaborators. A theater director who attended a performance by Festival participants expressed a desire to create a new collaboration with theater artists. The 2006–2007 Free(style) Theater Project, funded in part by a grant from the Andrew W. Mellon Foundation, was a series of collaborative workshops exploring innovations in performance within a narrative theatrical context. The goal was similar to previous collaborations, to create a series of intermedia improvisational performance events. However, this iteration of collaboration engaged narrative, set, and sound installation elements of theater, with works emphasizing sound, movement and installation. Lacking the funds to engage artists across a disparate geographic area, we concentrated our efforts on local artists, but took advantage of a new institutional collaboration with the Open Fist Theatre in Los Angeles, an active performer-led theater in Hollywood dedicated to the nurturing of new theatrical works and projects.

In this instance, the theater represented an opportunity both to present in a venue of considerable quality and cultural relevance, as well as the opportunity to share work developed among academic collaborators in a professional context. It was also within driving distance of the majority of the participants and could accommodate the lengthy technical set-up and rehearsal required. As musicians and dancers had represented the core members of many previous collective research units, the opportunity to expand into theatrical performance was gratifying and greatly desired by participants. The collective nature of the workshops, performance creation and its execution adapted easily to the new focus, as did the modality of event production alongside artistic production during performances in Hollywood, as participants dealt with transportation, scheduling, publicity and press issues while preparing the performance works.

STATE OF THE ART: DEMONSTRATION

But while all these evolving research collaboratives, projects and contexts represented a constellation of contemporary artistic practices, none completely engaged all practices and, indeed, as the primary mode of research expression had heretofore been performance, the research collaborations had centered on performing arts. While installation artists integrated into a performance modality rather easily, other forms of visual art and new hybrids between scholarship and performance had been difficult to include in the ongoing collaborations. New collective modalities would be required for successful collective research emphasizing all contemporary art practice and modes of scholarly discourse usually held outside the bounds of traditional conferences and meetings.

The UC Institute for Research in the Arts, a Multicampus Research Unit originating in the office of the President at the University of California, is one of a very few examples of how such spaces can be generated within the umbrella of the academy. Charged with fostering high-quality, interdisciplinary research in contemporary arts both within the UC system and beyond, the organization hosted an annual research exchange highlighting UC artists and their practices. Historically, this event had solicited artists for presentations and thus relied on established networks to solicit artists and projects. For the 2008 event, however, the board wanted to fundamentally change the nature of the event in order to create more opportunities for collaborative research and dialogue that reflected, rather than limited, the possible artistic exchanges. Having conducted research events in the past that were enormously successful in this regard but lacked the opportunity to engage artists outside traditional performance disciplines, I solicited the co-directors and board for the opportunity to employ this collective methodology in producing State of the Arts.

As I had hoped, the collective methodology developed over previous research groups was the perfect solution for UCIRA's event transformation. Because all previous research collaborations required the cultivation of a polyvocal working method, collective decision making, and event production at the heard of collective research, this methodology was particularly well suited to the goals of UCIRA. The research questions set forth by the co-directors and board of UCIRA were far more complex and interdisciplinary than any undertaken by a research collective before in that they needed to encompass all aspects of artistic practice and scholarship currently undertaken on all UC campuses. But the goal here was similar to previous events: to foster a collective experience among participating artists and scholars so that there was sufficient "room" within the event for audience members to contribute their own perspectives and envision their own place within the collective. The event needed to foster a communal experience without the benefit of lengthy collaborations or artistic relationships, and thus it needed a methodology for continually opening to new questions and perspectives.

How could performances and presentations by a variety of artists be integrated with scholarly presentations and administrative discourse? The co-directors and board of UCIRA began by soliciting a dedicated group of faculty coordinators from various disciplines, secured necessary campus support in funding, participation and facilities, and began activating the established network of UC artists across California. We formulated and distributed a call for participation, to open up the pool of participating artists beyond the system, and to create a level of community commitment to the event in the months prior to the event. Once the proposals had been reviewed and chosen, the schedule was augmented with keynote speakers who could address contemporary artistic practice and scholarship from highly divergent fields and perspectives. Ultimately scheduled to coincide with the meeting of the UC Arts Deans, this access to senior Arts administrators from across the system presented another opportunity to widen the inquiry. Taking advantage of the unique nature of this opportunity, a Deans' panel was scheduled as a central feature one afternoon of the event.

The inclusion of new arts practices and diverse formats for presentation meant that scheduling and technical issues were of paramount importance because the collective methodology would here not be expressed by months of intense collaboration or a concentrated event encouraging collective performance but rather between and among presentations of diverse origin and genres. The collectivity was at once a by-product of the event and its goal. Reflecting the idea of "entering the symbolic order" in real time, which opened this essay, here the by-products of our working method were also the ultimate goals of our research. Creating a truly polyvocal event without hierarchies either in approach or methodology required rigorous planning, both from a technical and critical perspectives. Facilities needed to accommodate solo artist talks and group performances, scholarly presentations and media installations. Moreover, with the stated goal of bridging University and community artists, the facilities were significant symbolically as well. They had to bridge University and community facilities in a very real sense, and thus the event was scheduled around them—in the Life Arts building, an historic, independent, building in downtown Riverside that currently serves as community event space and artist studios. Although well-suited for our layered needs in a theoretical sense, this choice meant considerable difficulties for it lacked facilities the University can provide, such as state-of-the-art technology, including those wired for interactivity with flown projectors and multi-channel audio playback.

What the location lacked in technology it more than made up for in other ways. The working studios in the building created an easy way to network with established community artists, and integrate our event with its premiere event, the downtown Riverside Arts Walk. To foster a real University-community partnership, all the individual (non-academic) artists renting spaces within the Life Arts building were invited to participate in the conference free of charge, including receptions, meals and performance events. In exchange, several artists opened their studios during the three days of events for casual conversations and showings with the visiting UC participants. The building's communal spaces, usually employed for weddings and quinceaneras, lent some of that celebratory feeling to State of the Arts, encouraging active dialogue among participants and presenters, conversation, laugher and friendship. Rooftop terraces on the upper floors held impromptu performances and interventions, as well as private conversations over coffee or sandwiches. Large meeting rooms held scholarly presentations, intermedia performances, rants, structured dialogues, and screenings. Painters set up in the main room to create new works during panel discussions and local photographers set up impromptu studios to take portraits of participating artists in the upper floors.

The final evening of the event brought the entire building alive, with events crammed into all event and studio spaces throughout the massive space. Featuring screenings by local filmmakers, performance pieces and improvisations by UC and community artists, theatrical works, a creative fashion show with local artists as models, dance and video installation, all culminating in DJ performances and dancing in the main reception space. Artistic expression was once again subject, object and means of production in that no single collective performance or series was the goal here. Rather, capitalizing again on the Zizekian "transformations of the signifier's network" that became the hallmark of so many previous collaborations, the central methodology was one of collectively entering the symbolic network in real time, which therefore stretched to include participants from all contexts and disciplines, at all levels of collaborative commitment, from bystanders to coordinators. Our stated goal, capturing the vitality and diversity of contemporary arts practice both within a university system and community beyond in a weekend-long event was quite impossible if attempted as individuals or singular small groups of artists. Only by agreeing to organize and work collectively could we achieve the stated goals of the research/event.

This collectivity was improvisational at its very heart. The demanding technical requirements and scheduling meant that obstacles were not likely, they were guaranteed. An ad hoc collective of organizers responded in real time; they offered last minute tech fixes, ran for supplies, did repairs or worked on other disasters. They engaged young artists after presentations or danced with graduate students and community members after evening performances. The vitality and complexity of contemporary arts practice were captured in these moments, the disasters averted and the schedules shuffled. Each of us were required to draw on all our skill sets in the creation, production and criticism necessary to fully engage in the work of the event. The ways in which we all became individually and collectively responsible were brought powerfully beyond the confines of our own practice in real time and with real colleagues both established and new from the University and beyond. For a moment, we were contemporary arts practice in its purest form, a benefit of the collective research methodology and something unachievable directly and intentionally but emergent to those of us willing to undergo the process.

CONCLUSION

The preceding examples, while representing collaborations across time as well as divergent disciplines, practices and approaches, have one central aspect in common. They collectively enter the symbolic order in real time, within the context of artistic practice, in order to consciously and deliberately rewrite the "narration of the past" as central research protocol. This rewriting is far from a by-product of the collective research. Rather, it is fundamental to capturing the dynamic and mutable aspects of improvisation as praxis and the extension of those aspects beyond the boundaries of explicitly improvisational music to the improvisatory nature of all performance and research disciplines. Deploying collective improvisation as methodology beyond performance to research events allows *both* participants *and* audience members to themselves enter the symbolic order in real time, broadening the conscious rewriting of signifiers and narrations of the past and allowing new meanings to collectively emerge. This eliminates what has been a fundamental dissociation of artistic practice—the separation of process and product, in which the negotiation of meaning has traditionally occurred apart from the work itself, hidden from the audience and sometimes even from participants themselves. At a time in which new critical approaches, hybrid disciplines and emergent technologies exert a powerful interdisciplinary influence on new work and scholarship, such merging of process and product has profound benefits. Collective research does not suppress individual critical inquiry or the broadening of individual artistic practices; instead, it encourages both the group and the individual artist/researcher in the ongoing negotiation of new meanings through a focus on the emergent. Creating opportunities for new modes of inquiry collectively invites "the repressed" to return from the future, in real time, to take its rightful place at the heart of the research.

REFERENCES

Austin, J. L. (1961). *Philosophical papers*. Oxford: Oxford University Press.
Bailey, D. (1980). *Improvisation: Its nature and practice in music*. Ashbourne, England: Moorland Press.
Cut for recorded samples, live electronics, live video feed, live-action drawing, and dancer. With Vuslat and Ilknur Demirkoparan, and David Horvitz and members of the UC Riverside Free Improvisation Ensemble. Refereeed Selection at Teknika Radika Festival, La Jolla, CA, January 30, 2004.

Derrida, J. (1994). *Specters of marx: The state of debt, the work of mourning & the new international.* New York: Routledge.

Free(style) Theater Project, with co-director Rickerby Hinds. A one-hour experimental theatrical event combining, original music, collaborative dance, media installation (live and pre-recorded video, live-action projected drawing, sculpture) and narrative elements. Research completed in the "Free(style) Theater Project workshop group. Premiered June 3, 2007, Arts 157, UC Riverside. Free(style) Theater Project @ Open Fist Theatre, 6209 Santa Monica Blvd, Los Angeles. July 10 and July 11, 2007.

Jenkins, T. (2005, Summer). Highly recommended: Erroneous Funk. *Signal to Noise: The Journal of Improvised and Experimental Music, 38,* 12.

Lewis, G. E. (2002). Improvised music since 1950: Afrological and Eurological perspectives. *Black Music Research Journal, 22,* 215–246.

New Media/New Work a concert-length, collaborative, digital-intermedia performance work for 15 performers. players. Performance Lab, UC Riverside, Riverside, CA. April 5, 2002. Roy, O. Disney Hall, California Institute for the Arts, on October 9, 2002.

State of the Arts: *Demonstration* UC Riverside, November 6, 7 and 8, 2008. Schedule and proceedings. Retrieved from www.ucira.ucsb.edu

UCR Is Improvising: Festival of Spontaneous Art, Dance and Music, April 2, 3 and 4, 2004.

Zizek, S. (1989). *The Sublime Object of Ideology.* London: Verso.

CONTRIBUTORS

Paris Banks is in his sophomore year at Roberto Clemente Community Academy High School, a Chicago Public School, in downtown Chicago. He grew up in the Cabrini Green 'hood and now lives on Chicago's Southside with his mom, dad, and six sisters. He spends a lot of his free time footworking—just dancing and moving his feet real fast. He recently recorded a CD with his rap group, *Cash Out Boys*. Paris is really interested in reading because likes to challenge and push himself to learn new things. He hopes to someday get a record deal, but also has a backup plan to become a teacher and live up to some of his own expectations of what teaching could and should be.

Carrie Bilinovich resides in Clinton, Ohio. She graduated from Kent State University with a degree in Education in 2007. During her collage career, she spent time working with students in East Cleveland at a Life Skills Center and completed her student teaching in an eighth grade classroom in Akron Public Schools. Carrie also volunteers for Buckeye Girls State hosted by the American Auxiliary where she mentors and educates young women about state and local government through mock government scenarios.

D. Jean Clandinin is Professor and Director of the Centre for Research for Teacher Education and Development at the University of Alberta. She is the author of many books, book chapters and articles. Her most recent book is the H*andbook of Narrative Inquiry: Mapping a Methodology*, published in 2007 by Sage. She is also the co-author of *Narrative Curriculum Making as Identity Making: Intersecting Family, Cultural and School Landscapes*. She is winner of a number of awards and honors including AERA's Early Career Award, Divison B's Lifetime Achievement Award and the Canadian Educational Association Whitworth Award.

Diane Conrad is Associate Professor of Drama/Theatre Education in the Faculty of Education at the University of Alberta in Edmonton, Alberta, Canada. Her research program combines critical pedagogy, applied theatre and participatory research with high risk youth. Her most recent project *The Transformative Potential of Drama in the Education of Incarcerated Youth*, funded by the Social Sciences and Humanities Research Council of Canada and won the 2006 SSHRC Aurora Prize. Her recent publications include "Rethinking At-risk in Drama Education: Beyond Prescribed Roles" in *Research in Drama Education* and "Drama, Role Theory & Youth: Implications for Teacher Education" in *Theatre Research in Canada*. www.ualberata.ca/~dhconrad.

Renee T. Coulombe is a composer, improviser, and theorist, and Assistant Professor of Music Theory and Composition at the University of California, Riverside. She writes on an array of subjects in music and culture, media and theory; from female punk and blues music to the Anglo-Indian electronica, feminism and embodiment

Buffy the Vampire Slayer (Ashgate and Cambridge University Presses), to critical interrogations of dissonance in Western discourse. She is a contributing Editor for *Open Space* Magazine, and an Associate Editor of *Perspectives of New Music*. Her music has been performed and broadcast throughout the United States, Europe, Asia and Oceania.

Denise Gastaldo is an Associate Professor at the Faculty of Nursing, University of Toronto. Her academic work is organized around four main areas: gender, migration, and other social determinants of health; poor relations in health promotion, nursing, and health care; nursing and international health theoretical development; and qualitative methodology. Teaching projects include introducing global health as a core component of graduate nursing curriculum, doing international capacity-building for health research, and coordinating the International Nursing PhD Collaboration (INPhD) which involves nursing faculties from Canada, Spain, Mexico, and Australia. Professor Gastaldo currently has a grant to research the topic of Latin American workers as caregivers in relation to globalization, health promotion, and access to health care.

Melanie George holds a BA in dance from Western Michigan University, an MA in dance and Graduate Certificate in Secondary Teaching from American University, and is certified in Laban Movement Analysis through the Laban/Bartenieff Institute of Movement Studies. Ms. George has an extensive teaching history, including administrative and instructing positions with The Roeper School for the Gifted and Talented, and the Washington School of Ballet. From 2004–2008, she was an Assistant Professor of Dance and Dance Education Program Coordinator at Kent State University. Her performance history includes Dance Nonce Dance Company, Boris Willis Moves, and the Kennedy Center Honors. Her choreography includes works in concert dance, theater, musical theater and voice. Ms. George has presented her research on jazz dance improvisation and pedagogy in the United States, Canada and Scotland. Currently, she is a full time faculty member at American University, Curriculum Specialist for the Dance Institute of Washington, and serves on the National Dance Education Organization's Board of Directors.

Walter S. Gershon is an Assistant Professor in the School of Teaching, Learning, and Curriculum Studies at Kent State University. His scholarly interests include questions about the relationship between curriculum and students, the ways that sociocultural precepts inform educational contexts such as classrooms, connections between the arts and education, and the exploration of qualitative research methodologies. Prior to his time in higher education, Walter taught students of all ages in urban and rural settings in North America and Japan. In addition to serving as the editor of and a contributor to this book, his most recent work can be found in *The Handbook of Public Pedagogy: Education and Learning beyond Schooling* (Routledge, in press) and *The Teaching Paradox: Creative Improvisation in the Classroom* (Cambridge, in press). Walter's ethnographic account and scoring of students' classroom interactions, "Collective Improvisation: A Theoretical Lens for

Classroom Observation," won the 2007 Outstanding Narrative Theory Article from the Narrative and Research SIG of the AERA.

Amoaba Gooden is an Assistant Professor of Diaspora Studies in the Department of Pan-African Studies at Kent State University. Dr. Gooden has numerous research interests which include the life experiences of African Caribbean people living in Canada and the United States. Her current research focuses on Migration, Gender and Identity among African Caribbean immigrants living in Canada and Social Networking as a Determinant of Health among African Caribbean people and immigrants in general. Dr. Gooden's research can be seen in numerous publications including the *Journal of Black Studies, Wagadu: Journal of Transnational Women's and Gender Studies* and *the Canadian Woman Studies Journal.* Dr. Gooden may be reached at Kent State University, Department of Pan African Studies, Oscar Ritchie Hall, P. O. Box 5190, Kent, Ohio, 44240, 330.672.0149 (o), agooden@kent.edu.

Matthew "Gus" Gusul is a Master of Arts candidate at the University of Alberta in the Drama Department. Gus came to Edmonton after doing his undergraduate degree at Augustana University College in his hometown of Camrose and spending time living and working in rural Mexico. He has been active using theatre with diverse community groups throughout Western Canada, in the Arctic, and in rural Mexico. He has worked with Alberta Council for Global Cooperation, Canada World Youth, Taking it Global, and Change for Children Association, where he is currently on the Board of Directors. He is also currently working as the Assistant director for the intergenerational theatre group *GeriActors and Friends*.

Robert J. Helfenbein Jr. is an Assistant Professor of Teacher Education at Indiana University-Purdue University Indianapolis and Associate Director for Community Engagement in the Center for Urban and Multicultural Education in the School of Education. He studies urban education and curriculum theory. He regularly teaches qualitative research methods and curriculum in the context of instruction. In addition to publication in multiple journal articles and book chapters, he is also the co-editor of *Unsettling Beliefs: Teaching Theory to Teachers* (Information Age).

Janice Huber is Associate Professor in pre-service and graduate teacher education at the University of Regina. She is a former elementary teacher and teacher researcher who, with Karen Keats Whelan, coauthored a paper-formatted doctoral dissertation exploring the contextual, narrative, temporal and relational aspects of teachers' and administrators' diverse identities. Questions of the meeting of children's, families, teachers' and administrators' lives, which weave across Composing Diverse Identities, continue to shape Janice's teaching and research.

Marilyn Huber is currently seconded to the Alberta Ministry of Education. She has been a secondary teacher for many years in both urban and rural settings. Marilyn was recently awarded AERA's Narrative and Research SIG 2009 Outstanding Dissertation Award for her dissertation, *Narrative Curriculum Making* *as Identity Making: Intersecting Family, Cultural and School Landscapes*. In addition to being a co-author of Composing diverse identities: Narrative inquiries into the interwoven lives of children and teachers, Marilyn has collaboratively published articles in *Curriculum & Teaching Dialogue, Journal of Educational Research and Development, Reflective Practice* and *Teachers College Press*.

Janice Kroeger is an Associate Professor in Teaching, Leadership, and Curriculum Studies, Kent State University where she teaches qualitative research, contemporary issues and trends in early childhood education, home-school-community-partnerships, and integrated curriculum for young children. Janice's research and teaching interests are focused on issues of power and identity in schooling, early years teacher development, early childhood policies and practices, and qualitative research methodologies. Janice has researched and written scholarly work about social action, agency, culture and cultural and identity change in diverse communities as well as the impact of pre service teacher's work on classrooms. She tends to works at the intersections of social justice work, activism, school formation and the formation of schooled subjects. Her published work has appeared in such journals as *The Journal of Early Childhood Teacher Education, the Journal of Educational Change* and *The Urban Review*, and she has contributed to or co-authored other works.

Patti Lather is a Professor in the Cultural Foundations Program, Ohio State University, where she teaches qualitative research and feminist methodology. She has authored three books, *Getting Smart: Feminist Research and Pedagogy With/in the Postmodern* (1991 Critics Choice Award), *Troubling the Angels: Women Living with HIV/AIDS*, co-authored with Chris Smithies (1998 CHOICE Outstanding Academic Title), and *Getting Lost: Feminist Efforts Toward a Double(d) Science* (2008 Critics Choice Award). Her in-process book, *Engaging (Social) Science: Policy from the Side of the Messy*, is with Peter Lang. She is a 2009 inductee of the AERA Fellows.

Kim McCaw is the Director of the newly-formed Canadian Centre for Theatre Creation, housed in the University of Alberta, where has been a professor of drama since 1997. He has also been Director of the Banff Playwrights' Colony and Artistic Director of Winnipeg's Prairie Theatre Exchange. For more than thirty years, he has been engaged in the development and production of new Canadian plays.

Joan Meggitt is a choreographer, educator, and dancer. She is the founding Director of Antaeus Dance, a modern dance company based in Cleveland, OH. Active in the field of dance education, Meggitt has been a guest artist and lecturer in modern dance at colleges and universities throughout the United States and internationally. She is currently Visiting Professor in the Dance Division at Kent State University. Meggitt's impressive repertory explores the intersection of individual expression and collective experience and has been performed by Antaeus Dance and numerous other dance artists and companies, both nationally and abroad. Meggitt began studying dance at Allegheny College (B.A. Economics), and earned her M.F.A. in Dance from Case Western Reserve University under the instruction of Kathryn Karipides and Kelly Holt. Her training has been devoted to the modern dance technique of Erick Hawkins, which she has studied under numerous company members, most notably Kelly Holt, James Reedy, and Cynthia Reynolds.

Shaun M. Murphy is an Assistant Professor in preservice and graduate teacher education at the University of Saskatchewan. His research program focuses on narrative inquiries into the ways curriculum and identity are shaped in relationship with each other. He has co-authored a number of papers with diverse colleagues. Co-authoring *Composing Diverse Identities: Narrative Inquiries into the Interwoven lives of Children and Teachers*, continues to be a significant event in his life.

Joe Norris is a professor in Drama in Education and Society in the Department of Dramatic Arts, Marilyn I. Walker School of Fine and Performing Arts, Brock University. Underpinning all of his work is a deep sense of the epistemology of form. Spending his formative years in the 60's, Joe was immersed in McLuhan's concept of the interrelationship between form and content and has spent his life playing with multiple ways of understanding self and the world. Looking back, it is no surprise that his 1989 doctoral dissertation has four hours of VHS videotape bound to it. Joe advocates the use of the arts as a way of knowing, doing, and being, has spent a number of years pioneering research methodologies and instructional and assessment strategies that are based in emancipatory pedagogy and the arts. 'Duoethnography', co-created with Rick Sawyer, also experiments with form as the script like format disrupts the metanarrative created by single-voiced texts. He has taught courses in integrating the arts in the curriculum, playbuilding, learning through drama, curriculum theory, qualitative research, arts-based research, community literacy, and principles of learning throughout Canada and the United States. His book, *Playbuilding as Qualitative Research: The Mirror Theatre Process'* explores how data generation, its interpretation, and how it can be disseminated through theatrical means, further expands our understanding of the embedded meanings in form.

Marie-France Orillion is a researcher at the University of California, Riverside Graduate School of Education. She is currently working on two projects: (1) a collaborative study of veteran teachers' implementation of inquiry-based science curriculum in elementary school classrooms and (2) beginning teachers' experiences with action research in the context of induction. Her interests include interpretive research methods, the social and cultural construction of classroom knowledge, and teachers' professional learning.

Anne Murray Orr is an Associate Professor in pre-service and graduate teacher education at St Francis Xavier University in Nova Scotia. Narrative inquiries into how teachers, children, families, and administrators experience life in schools, specifically around topics such as assessment, cultural diversity, and identity making, are the focus of Anne's research program. She has been fortunate to collaborate in creating *Composing Diverse Identities: Narrative Inquiries into the Interwoven lives of Children and Teachers*, and in other writing.

Marni Pearce works with Alberta Education as Director of Cross Ministry Services. She has over twenty years of teaching experience ranging from primary school to pre-service teacher education. Marni has also been a school counselor and community based researcher. She has collaboratively published several journal articles and is a co-author of the book, *Composing Diverse Identities: Narrative Inquiries into the Interwoven lives of Children and Teachers.* Marni continues to be interested in the intersections between children's and families' lives on and off the school landscape.

Amanda Peel received her B.S. in Education, Integrated Social Studies, from Kent State University in 2007. She completed her student teaching in a 10th grade United States History Class in a suburban high school in Northeast Ohio. Amanda volunteers with the American Legion Auxiliary in their Buckeye Girls' State program where she mentors and teaches young women about state and local government in a mock government setting. She resides in Boardman, Ohio.

Richard D. Sawyer's research focuses on curriculum theory in the promotion of social justice. He has published studies of how curriculum itself can act as a fulcrum to promote teachers' and students' awareness of and actual construction of social justice, not only in the classroom, but more broadly in society. Lately his work has taken an international perspective with research in Mexico to examine the impact of NAFTA on lives of Mexicans living near the U.S. border. Much of this work has been advocacy research intended to challenge instrumental and dehumanizing implications of large-scale, neo-liberal reform policies. He has worked to develop the research methodology of duoethnography has a context for collaborative empowerment. Furthermore, Richard chairs both a teacher preparation program and an Ed.D. Program at Washington State University Vancouver.

Brian D. Schultz is associate professor of education, honors faculty, and the associate chair of the Department of Educational Leadership & Development at Northeastern Illinois University in Chicago. His research focuses on students and teachers theorizing together, developing integrated curricula based on students' priority concerns, and curricula as social action. Prior to his role at Northeastern, Brian taught fifth grade in Chicago's Cabrini Green. His book, *Spectacular Things Happen Along the Way: Lessons from an Urban Classroom* (Teachers College Press, 2008) details a school year in which he and his students (including the co-author of this chapter, Paris Banks) developed an emergent curriculum to solve an authentic problem. The book received the 2008 Critics' Choice Award from the American Educational Studies Association and the 2009 Outstanding Book Award in Curriculum Studies from the American Educational Research Association. He is currently editing with Jenny Sandlin and Jake Burdick, *Handbook of Public Pedagogy: Education and Learning beyond Schooling* (Routledge, in press). Brian is the recipient of early career awards from the American Educational Research

Association in both Narrative & Research and Critical Issues in Curriculum & Cultural Studies.

Janet Siltanen is a Professor of Sociology at Carleton University in Ottawa, Canada. Her book publications include *Gender Relations in Canada: Intersectionality and Beyond* (OUP, 2008), *Gender Inequality in the Labour Market* (ILO, 1995), and Locating Gender (UCL Press, 1994). She has published articles in *Citizenship Studies, Work, Employment and Society, Royal Statistical Society Series A (Statistics and Society), International Journal of Sociology*, the *Canadian Journal of Sociology, Theory and Society*, and the *International Journal of Social Research Methodology*.

Joshua S. Smith is an Assistant Professor of Educational Psychology at Indiana University-Purdue University Indianapolis and Director in the Center for Urban and Multicultural Education in the School of Education. He studies educational transitions including the transition from middle school to high school and the transition from high school to college. Dr. Smith also works with schools and community-based organization to evaluate educational programs on student and organizational outcomes. He regularly teaches Educational Psychology in the undergraduate teacher education program and research methodology courses in the graduate school.

Chris Smithies has a PhD in counseling and is a middle school counselor at the Columbus School for Girls in addition to a private practice. She began organizing women and HIV/AIDS support groups in 1988.

Pam Steeves is an adjunct professor at the Centre for Research for Teacher Education and Development at the University of Alberta. She has over twenty five years diverse teaching experiences ranging from the primary classroom to graduate Teacher Education. Pam's research evolves from inquiries with self, diverse children, teachers, administrators and pre-service teachers as they compose lives in transition. She has collaboratively published numerous articles. She considers the co-authoring of *Composing Diverse Identities: Narrative Inquiries into the Interwoven lives of Children and Teachers* a profound learning experience.

Alette Willis is a SSHRC Post-doctoral Research Fellow in the School of Health and the Social Sciences at the University of Edinburgh. Her PhD—which she received from the Department of Geography and Environmental Studies at Carleton University in Ottawa, Canada—explored reading and environmental ethics from a narrative therapy perspective. She believes that how we work as academics is as important as what we research. To move in the direction of survivable futures for all requires that we learn how to work together non-hierarchically, collaboratively, and with shared purpose.

ENDNOTES

[1] As this point has been made by multiple scholars elsewhere (see for example, Agar, 1996; Behar, 1996; Clifford, 1988; Eisner & Peshkin, 1990; Erickson, 1986; Minh-ha, 1989; Rosaldo, 1993; Spindler, 1982), I do not pursue this line of inquiry further here.

[2] Both Spindler & Hammond, 2006 and Springgay et al., 2007 are examples of recent works with chapters dedicated to, respectively, collaboration in/through educational ethnography and a/r/t ography.

[3] The original article was published in the Society of Professors of Education's journal *The Sophist's Bane*. Full citation: Schultz, B.D., & Banks, P. (2009). A shorty teaching teachers: One kid's perspective about 'keeping it real' in the classroom. *The Sophist's Bane, 5*(1), 19–24.

[4] Our collective academic homeplace is the Centre for Research for Teacher Education and Development (CRTED) at the University of Alberta. Since the Centre's beginning in 1991, Jean has been its director. It was this space that nurtured each of our beginnings as narrative inquirers as we undertook graduate studies.

[5] Drawing on Trinh's (1989) distinction between "I" and "i" in their collaboratively written doctoral dissertations, Huber and Keats Whelan (2000) have deepened our understanding of "relational spaces." They wrote, [Trinh] moves beyond a limiting and self contained understanding of identity~"I," to one which is fluid, relational, and ever-embracing of their multiple stories that shape our lives~"i." Her work begs us to move beyond a bordered sense of self to a consciously created place where the categorical conventions that so often define us as separate, can leak. (p. 89)

[6] Hilde Lindemann Nelson (1995) has, for many years, inspired our thinking about, and collective efforts to stay at, the work of composing and sustaining counterstories. Later in our chapter we more fully describe counterstories.

[7] We worked with the concept of fictionalization of field texts (Murphy, 2004) in *Composing Diverse Identities* (Clandinin et al, 2006) as a way to represent the layeredness and complexities of tellings and retellings of stories of our research participants and ourselves. One aspect of fictionalization to which we are drawn is the possibility of blurring identities to protect the anonymity of participants with whom we are in relation. Fictionalized is not the opposite of fact, but rather a rendering of the research experience in order to facilitate representation.

[8] The phrase "what we know first," part of our title and last paragraph is taken from Patricia MacLachlan's (1995) book "What you know first." The words of the story resonate with our shared understanding of relational knowing fostered and attended to first as we undertook graduate work at the Centre.

[9] The research discussed in this chapter is from the project "Social Citizenship and the Transformation of Work" funded by the Social Sciences and Humanities Research Council of Canada (#410-199-807). Thank you to Walter Gershon and Liz Bondi for helpful comments, and to each other for an enjoyable collaboration.

[10] This shift is well exemplified by writings of Breuer & Roth (2003), Findlay & Gough, (2003), Mauthner and Doucet (2003), Alvesson & Sköldberg (2000), Marcus (1998) Gibson-Graham (1994), and Calhoun (1992).

[11] The transcript excerpts in this section of the chapter are from a research team meeting called for the explicit purpose of reflecting on and sharing experiences of doing the project fieldwork. Three team members were present at this meeting including the two authors of this paper. Some of the excerpts analyzed here are also in Siltanen, Willis and Scobie, 2008.

[12] These transcript excerpts are from the reflexivity team meeting described in footnote iv – however, at this point in the meeting there were only two team members present - the two authors of this paper.

ENDNOTES

[13] The transcript excerpts in this section of the chapter are from a research team meeting called for the purpose of analysing the first wave of interviews. Four team members are present at this meeting including the two authors of this paper. These excerpts are also in Siltanen, Willis and Scobie, 2008.

[14] In our case, multiple authors and the process of collaborative discensus in which we engaged served as our means of collecting multiple sources of data and member checks, our semester together provided our prolonged engagement with our subject matter.

[15] The term somatic refers to the process of change that occurs in the whole body from any movement.

[16] This performance was also reviewed (Jenkins, 2005) in *Signal to Noise: The Journal of Improvised and Experimental Music*.

INDEX

A

Aboriginal/Aboriginality, x, xxiv, 165, 168, 169, 172, 173, 175, 177, 179–182
Academia, 8, 13, 74, 110, 123, 217
Academy, 101, 105–123, 168, 185, 186, 189, 193, 210, 214, 215, 218, 223
Action-based research, 186
Anti-racist, 74
Artist, x, xxv, 131, 186, 187, 193, 195–198, 200, 203–205, 207, 208, 210–221, 226
A/r/tography, xxii
Art(s), x, xix, xxii–xxvi, 46, 130, 137, 165–167, 175, 178, 181, 186, 187, 189, 193, 195, 196, 212, 215, 216, 218–221
Arts-based research, xxii, 176, 179, 227
Audience, xxiv–xxvi, 17, 41, 43, 44, 46, 90, 112, 128, 132, 136, 137, 166, 167, 169, 176–178, 180–182, 194, 195, 198, 204, 207, 208, 212, 213, 216, 219, 221
Authoritarian, 67
Authority, xi, 38, 39, 43, 59, 113, 179, 187, 200
Autobiography, 11, 129, 134
Autoethnography, xviii, xxiii, 127, 128, 134
Awareness, ix, 129, 132, 193, 198, 206–208, 228

B

Believe/belief, xx, 35, 38, 39, 42, 43, 49, 50, 60, 62, 79, 94, 97, 122, 127, 129, 130, 138, 139, 147, 149, 151, 152, 157, 160, 162, 168, 169, 173, 176, 177, 182, 190, 191, 203, 209, 225, 229
Boundary(ies), x, xi, xviii, xix, xxi, 42, 46, 61, 200, 202, 221

C

Canada/Canadian, xxi, xxiv, 22, 57, 68, 71–85, 87, 135, 165, 166, 177, 223–227, 229, 231n9
Caregiver, 73, 224
Catalyst/catalytic, 9, 142, 145, 160, 190, 203, 207
Choreograph/Choreographer, x, xxv, 185–189, 191–208, 211, 226
Co-construction, 40–41, 110, 114, 118
Collaborate, xi, xviii, 8, 35, 36, 83, 96, 107, 160, 166, 188–189, 193, 195, 198, 201, 204, 216, 228
Collaboration, ix–xi, xiii, xvii–xxii, xxiv–xxvii, 3–51, 55–68, 71–87, 89–101, 105–123, 127–139, 141–162, 165–221, 224, 231n2, 231n9

Collaborative
  relationships, xi, xii, xxv, 36, 38, 58, 59, 62, 64, 68, 93, 143, 147, 187–189
  research, ix–xiv, xvii–xxvii, 3–51, 55–68, 71–87, 89–101, 105–123, 127–139, 141–162, 165–221, 223–229, 231n4, 231n7, 231n9, 231n11, 231n13
  writing, ix, xxii, xxiv, 38, 55–62, 64, 65, 128, 161, 162, 165, 196
Collaborative discensus, x, xii, xiv, xxiv, 141–162, 232n14
Collaborative inquiry, x, xiv, 93–94, 96
Collective, x, xx, xxiii, xxvi, 35–51, 67, 71, 76, 80, 81, 83, 93, 105, 106, 108, 109, 115–123, 155, 187, 189, 197, 198, 202, 203, 208, 210–221, 224, 226, 231n4, 231n6
Collective memory, xx, 35–51, 213
Collectivity, 209–221
Colonial/colonialist, 38, 138
Communication, 35, 75, 91, 93, 98, 130, 191
Community, xi, xiii, xxii, xxv, 5, 46–48, 58, 62, 65, 67, 68, 71, 73–75, 77, 78, 84–87, 91, 92
Community-based research, 74
Company (dance), 192, 194, 196, 198–200, 224, 226
Complex/Complexity, ix, xi, xii, xviii, xxiii, xxiv, xxvi, 25, 33–36, 39, 41, 64, 90, 97, 110, 117, 118, 130, 131, 134, 143, 145, 155, 156, 160, 162, 172, 182, 183, 202, 210, 219, 220, 231n7
Complicated, 17, 35, 39, 44, 121, 122, 136, 142, 150, 152, 162
Context, x, xvii, xviii, xxi, xxiii–xxvi, 40, 44, 57, 60, 68, 71, 75, 86, 89–101, 105, 108, 110–113, 121–123, 130, 131, 133, 134, 137, 141–145, 153, 154, 160, 167, 171, 175, 180, 187–189, 191, 193, 194, 201, 202, 208, 215–218, 220, 221, 224, 225, 227, 228
Contextuals, xx, 81, 142, 155, 225
Consensus, xi, xxiv, 143–145, 149, 155, 156, 160, 161
Conversation, x, xiii, xiv, xx, xxv, 11, 12, 15, 30, 33, 40, 41, 49, 56–60, 63, 64, 80, 84, 99, 105, 108–110, 112, 113, 116, 119, 128, 131–135, 138, 141, 142, 146, 147, 151–157, 169, 211, 217
Cooperative, xix, 188, 195, 197, 206
Co-researchers, 65, 112
Counterstory(ies), xxi, 56–59, 61, 67, 68, 231n6
Create, x, xix, xx, xxiii, 3, 25, 27, 42, 45, 57–59, 61, 64, 66, 78, 81, 82, 91, 92, 94, 95, 99, 105, 111, 112, 116, 119, 127, 131–135, 138, 146, 167, 178, 182, 186, 187, 189–191,

233

INDEX

194, 195, 198, 201, 204–208, 210, 213, 215, 217–219, 227
Creation, xxiii, xxv, 58, 72, 92, 115, 119, 127–139, 165–167, 185–187, 189, 193, 194, 196–198, 200, 202–204, 207, 218, 221, 226
Creative, 46, 86, 110, 114, 128, 136, 166, 168, 170, 186, 189, 196–203, 205, 206, 208, 215, 216, 220, 224
Critical, ix, xii–xiv, xxi, xxiii, xxvi, 36, 37, 42, 74, 77, 82, 95, 98, 116, 117, 123, 127, 129, 145, 152, 155, 156, 158, 172, 180, 211, 212, 215, 219, 221, 223, 224, 229
Critical theory, 74, 174
Critique, xii, xiii, 81, 92, 99, 127, 128, 171, 181, 191, 211, 212
Culture/cultural, xii, xxiii, xxvi, 22, 30, 38, 60, 75, 77, 78, 82, 83, 93, 94, 123, 127, 129–131, 134, 136, 138, 158, 160, 165, 177, 178, 209, 210, 214, 218, 223, 226, 227, 229
Currere, 129–131
Curriculum
    null, 130

D

Dance, xxii, xxv, xxvi, 77, 154, 185–208, 213, 220, 224, 226, 227
Dancer, x, xxv, 185–208, 211, 214, 216, 218, 226
Dancework, 186, 197–201, 206–208
Dialectical, 128, 129, 132, 133
Dialogic, ix–xi, xxiii, 59, 61, 94, 101, 105, 110, 114, 119, 127, 128, 130–132, 134, 137, 138
Dialogue, xxiv, xxv, 35, 40, 45, 57–59, 61–67, 94, 99–101, 108, 110, 112–116, 118–122, 128, 129, 131–135, 137–139, 143–145, 167, 175, 179, 181, 183, 184, 194, 199, 203, 206, 207, 211, 215, 218, 220, 226
Discensus, x, xii, xxiv, 141–164, 232n14
Discipline(s), xxv, 36, 85, 130, 138, 159, 168, 196–198, 203–205, 209, 210, 212–215, 217–221
Discourse, ix, xiii, 76, 79, 80, 83, 106, 107, 115, 123, 131, 135, 202, 218, 219, 224
Discussion, xviii, xxi, xxii, xxv, 13, 17, 21, 38, 39, 41, 45, 75, 77–80, 84, 95, 106, 108, 110–112, 114–116, 118, 119, 121, 128, 131, 137, 141–143, 148–151, 153–156, 158, 159, 168, 172, 174, 176, 179, 181, 183, 190, 191, 199, 203–205, 210, 211, 215, 220
Dissonance, 145, 224
Diverse/diversity, xx, 5, 17, 31, 40, 56, 57, 60, 74, 76, 83, 84, 92, 95, 109, 119, 122, 129, 139, 171, 214–216, 219, 220, 225–229, 231n7
Dominant, xiii, xiv, xxi, 56–58, 65, 67, 68, 79, 107, 115, 123, 128, 129, 135, 144
Dramaturg, xxiv, 165–168, 173, 175, 176, 178

Duoethnography, xxiii, 127–140, 227, 228
Education
    multicultural, xxii, 89, 95, 225, 229
    urban, 38, 100, 101, 225

E

Educator, ix, xxv, 35, 39, 60, 67, 91, 101, 141, 143, 153, 158, 161, 194–196, 226
Element(s), 167, 168, 172, 177, 186, 200, 203–205, 207, 217
Emerge/emerging, xi, xii, xviii, xix, xxii–xxvi, 5, 7, 11, 14, 16, 18, 19, 25, 36, 58, 65, 74, 89, 93, 105–123, 127–139, 141–162, 165–221
Emergent
    nature, 11–19
    themes, xii, 25, 137, 191
    ideas, 65
    data, 12, 14, 17, 18
Engage/engagement, xi–xiii, xx, xxi, xxiii, 5, 18, 33, 38–40, 42, 44, 57–62, 64, 68, 75, 76, 82, 86, 90, 92–95, 97, 98, 100, 106–108, 110–112, 114, 116, 119, 121, 127, 128, 130, 134, 137, 138, 143–145, 148, 155, 165, 166, 168, 170, 172, 181, 183, 185, 187, 190–192, 194–197, 201, 202, 205, 207–209, 211, 212, 214, 215, 217, 218, 220, 221, 225, 226, 232n14
Ethics/ethical, x, xxiv, xxv, 35–51, 95, 127, 143, 145, 173, 179–181, 184, 185, 195, 201, 229
Ethnodrama, xxiv, 165–184
Ethnography/ethnographic, ix, xii, xviii, xxiii, xxvii, 15, 47, 96, 132, 136, 138, 160, 224, 231n2
Ethnotheatre, 179
Evolve/evolving, xxii, 11–13, 66, 74, 106, 157, 158, 162, 187, 194, 195, 197, 200, 202, 206, 211, 217, 218, 229
Experience(s), xi, xiii, xiv, xix, 25, 28, 31, 32, 35, 37, 39–42, 44, 46, 47, 50, 51, 55, 60, 61, 63–65, 67, 68, 71, 74–77, 79, 81–86, 91, 92, 95, 99, 105–109, 111–115, 117–123, 127–129, 134–136, 141, 143, 146–153, 156–162, 165–168, 170, 171, 176, 178, 180–183, 186–188, 191–196, 198, 201, 202, 204, 207, 208, 213–216, 219, 225–229, 231n7, 231n11

F

Family, 4, 21, 36, 47, 50, 65, 72, 73, 75, 76, 78, 80, 128, 223, 226
Feminism/feminist, xix, xxii, xxvi, 3, 5, 6, 11, 13, 26, 74, 105, 115, 223, 226
Fieldnote, 107

INDEX

Focus group, 75–82, 84, 85
Framework, xii, xiv, xix, xxi, xxiv, 18, 89–91, 96, 101, 109, 117, 138, 143–145, 153, 154, 161, 185, 188, 200, 210, 213, 214
Free improviser, 210, 215, 217

G

Generative, x, xi, xiii, xiv, 94, 101

H

Hermeneutic, 20, 35, 36, 39, 47, 133
Heteroglossia, 128, 131, 132
Homeplace, 55, 68, 231n4
Hybrid/hybridity, xxiii, 127, 135, 211, 217, 218, 221

I

Ideals, xxiv, 101, 138, 144, 189, 192, 194, 195, 200, 205
Ideas, ix–xi, xvii, xx, xxi, xxiv, 9, 11, 12, 15, 18, 19, 30, 36, 39–41, 43–47, 49, 55, 57–60, 62–67, 78, 89, 91–94, 98, 100, 101, 109, 116, 117, 121, 131, 134, 138, 142–144, 147–150, 152–154, 157–162, 167–169, 171–173, 175, 176, 179, 182, 187–189, 191, 192, 194–199, 202, 203, 205, 207, 213, 214, 219
Imagination/imaginings, 37, 55, 56, 58–61, 64, 65, 169, 203, 208
Immigrant, xxi, 71–87, 225
Improvisation
  free, 210–215
  collective, 211, 216
Improvisatory
  process, 58, 62, 64
Individual/individualism, x, xiii, xviii, xx, xxvi, 5, 26, 55–68, 73, 76–78, 80, 83–85, 93, 94, 96, 98, 107–111, 113–115, 117, 119, 122, 123, 127, 128, 131, 134, 135, 138, 152, 156, 162, 165, 172, 181, 182, 185–187, 189, 191, 194–204, 206–208, 211–213, 215, 217, 220, 221, 226
Inquiry, x, xiv, xviii, xx, xxiii–xxvi, 39–41, 43, 46, 57, 58, 60–66, 68, 80, 89–93, 95, 96, 98, 100, 101, 105, 134, 136, 141, 144, 145, 160, 179, 187, 189–191, 193–195, 203, 210, 219, 221, 223, 226–229, 231n1, 231n4
Institution, xxi, 57, 67, 68, 74, 211, 214
Institutional, xx, 55–68, 111, 218
Intent, x, xii, 74, 97, 148, 175, 180, 187, 192–195
Intentionality, 99
Interdisciplinary, 57, 76, 168, 214, 218, 219, 221

Interpret, ix, xvii, xviii, xxiv, 35, 41, 67, 68, 75, 83, 85, 105, 108–110, 112–122, 127, 129, 144, 145, 165, 187, 190, 191, 227
Interpretive, ix–xi, xvii–xix, xxii, xxv, 40, 46, 105, 106, 108–110, 114, 116, 121, 122, 227
Intersubjectivity, 127
Interviews, xii, xx, 19–21, 40, 77, 95, 107, 108, 111–116, 118–122, 232n13
Irony, 37

J

Jazz, xxiii, 136–138, 189, 191, 214, 224
Journal, xxiv, xxvi, xxvii, 47, 79, 90, 100, 101, 108, 119, 154, 165, 166, 199, 225, 226, 228, 229, 231n3, 232n16

K

Knowledge(s)
  situated, 108, 109

L

Laban Movement Analysis (LMA), xxv, 187, 188, 224
Labor, 23, 72, 106, 107, 116, 122, 123
Layered/layers/layering, x, xi, xx, xxi, xxiii, xxiv, 8, 12, 17, 24, 30, 60, 64, 119, 128, 130, 134, 135, 137, 174, 210–212, 215, 220, 224, 231n7
Liminal/liminality, xx, 58, 64–67

M

Marginal/marginalized/marginality, xvii, xxiv, 38, 67, 143, 162
Mess/Messiness, 43, 58, 61, 63, 117, 119, 122, 226
Methodology/method, ix–xi, xiv, xvii–xxvii, 3–51, 55–68, 71–87, 89–101, 105–123, 127–139, 141–162, 165–221, 223–229
Music, xxii, xxv, xxvi, 137, 186, 191, 196–198, 204, 205, 209, 210, 214–216, 221, 223, 224, 232n16

N

Narrative, ix, xviii, xx, xxi, xxiii, 35, 36, 39, 41–46, 55–68, 106, 107, 109–113, 115–119, 121, 123, 127, 128, 136–139, 145, 192, 217, 223, 225, 227, 229, 231n4
Narrative inquiry, xviii, xx, xxiii, xxvi, 39–40, 57, 61, 63, 68, 105, 144, 160, 223, 226–229, 231n4
Negotiation/negotiate, xxiv, xxvi, 12, 17, 23, 24, 33, 43, 57, 60, 108, 171, 172, 203, 205, 211, 212, 216, 221
Norms
  & values, 144, 158

INDEX

O

Objectivity, xiii, 42, 43, 93, 94, 127
Organic, 11–19, 28, 131, 138, 139, 154, 188, 194, 206

P

Paradox, xviii, 80, 209, 224
Parallel, xx, xxv, 7, 37, 41, 97, 113, 114, 137, 158, 177, 194
Participant, x, xii, xiii, xviii, xxi, xxiii–xxvi, 24–34, 66, 68, 71, 75–86, 89, 92, 93, 99, 107, 108, 110, 115, 122, 127, 129, 136–138, 144, 153, 157, 165, 185, 187, 198, 199, 201, 203, 206, 207, 215–218, 220, 221, 231n7
Participation, xii, xxi, 37, 38, 71, 77, 86, 112, 136, 146, 154, 166, 185, 195, 219
Participatory Action Research (PAR), xxi, xxvi, 71–87, 94, 95, 144
Participatory drama, xxiv, 165
Partner/partnership, vii, xvii, xxii, xxiii, 3, 6, 22, 33, 71–87, 91–93, 95–97, 99–101, 116, 118, 136, 138, 143, 144, 159, 180, 204, 216, 220, 226
Pedagogy(ical), ix, xii, xiii, 47, 89, 91, 139, 143, 153, 155, 167, 187, 210, 211, 214, 215, 217, 223, 224, 226–228
Performance, ix, xii, xxiii, xxv, xxvi, 136–138, 166, 171, 174, 182, 185–187, 189, 190, 193–195, 197–200, 202, 204, 206–221, 224, 232n16
Performative, ix, xii, xiii, xix, xxiv, 145, 179, 199, 216
Perspective(s), x, xi, xii, xxi, xxiii, xxiv, xxvi, 11, 35–41, 44–46, 66, 71, 75, 83–84, 93, 94, 97, 98, 105, 108, 110, 116, 127, 128, 133, 135, 138, 142–147, 149, 153–156, 158, 160, 161, 166, 168, 170, 171, 174, 176, 179, 180, 183, 185–208, 213, 219, 224, 228, 229, 231n3
Photo(graph), 78, 129, 132–134, 200
Photography, 130
Photovoice, 76, 78, 80, 82
Picture, xviii, 78, 120, 129, 130, 132–134, 169
Place(s)
    educational, 162
    liminal, xx
    stuck, 18, 20–24
Play/playfulness (v), xviii, xxiv, 40, 59, 62, 114, 128, 131, 137, 146, 150, 159, 165–175, 177–184, 190, 204, 215
Playwrite(ing), xxii, xxiv, 165–184
Plot, 123, 172, 176, 183, 184
Plotline, 57, 67, 117
Polyphonic, x, xix, xx, 3–34, 40, 109

Polyvocal/polyvocality, xxiii, 106, 108–109, 115, 119, 122, 219
Possible/possibility(ies), vii, x, xi, xviii, xix–xxii, xxiv–xxvi, 6, 9, 12, 17, 27, 30, 36–38, 41, 44, 45, 55, 57–65, 68, 77, 80, 82, 85, 90, 92, 99, 100, 105, 107, 111, 113, 114, 116, 119, 122, 128, 132, 136, 141–145, 152–154, 156, 159–162, 166, 167, 169, 171, 174, 175, 177–179, 181, 183, 186, 191, 193, 195, 197, 202, 203, 205, 207, 208, 210, 217, 218, 231n7
Postcolonial, 36, 39, 138
Post-disciplinary, 168
Power, x–xiii, 39, 43, 46, 59, 67, 75, 76, 79, 94, 101, 107, 131, 135, 136, 138, 144, 155, 177, 191, 207, 213, 226
Praxis, 5, 127, 209–211, 214, 215, 221
Problem, xxv, 22, 29, 41, 42, 49, 71, 74, 75, 92, 98, 142, 156, 162, 169, 174, 177, 180, 182, 187, 190, 192, 198, 200, 201, 205, 228
Problematic, 42, 113, 130, 155, 183, 194
Process, vii, ix–xiv, xviii, xix–xxvi, 5, 7, 10–14, 18, 19, 26, 30, 33, 35, 36, 40, 44, 57–59, 61, 62, 64–66, 68, 71, 73, 74, 76, 80–86, 91–95, 97, 100, 101, 105, 107–112, 114, 115, 118, 119, 122, 127–131, 133–138, 143–162, 165–169, 171–175, 178, 181–183, 185–209, 211–213, 215, 221, 227, 232n14, 232n15
Protocol(s), 60, 64, 95, 213, 221

Q

Qualitative, ix, x, xvii, xviii, xix–xxii, xxiv, xxv, xxvi, 3–51, 55–68, 71–87, 89–101, 105–123, 127–139, 141–162, 165–221, 224
Qualitative research, x, xiii, xvii–xxvii, 6, 7, 11–19, 99, 106, 108, 110, 121, 123, 127, 144, 155, 210, 224–227
Question, vii, x–xii, xvii, xviii, xx, xxiii, xxiv, xxvii, 3, 5, 7, 8, 19, 21, 30, 35, 38–46, 51, 74, 76, 79, 80, 84, 89, 90, 92–94, 96, 98, 100, 101, 105, 108, 111, 112, 116, 117, 127, 136, 137, 141–160, 170, 172–175, 177, 179–181, 189–195, 198, 201, 207, 209, 211, 219, 224, 225

R

Reciprocal, 101
Reconceptual/reconceptualize, 129, 130, 132
Reflect, ix, xviii, xx, 29, 30, 35, 39, 41, 61, 62, 89, 90, 97, 108, 110–112, 114, 116, 117, 122, 138, 141, 144, 148, 152, 176, 178, 181, 186, 189, 191, 195, 197, 206
Reflective, xxii, 12, 33–34, 39, 79, 80, 169, 175, 176, 192, 226
Reflexive, xviii, xxiii, 80, 105–123, 127, 158

INDEX

Rehearsal, 112, 137, 185, 186, 188, 190–203, 205, 206, 211, 218
Relational
  place, 60, 61, 67
  space, 55, 59, 231n5
Relationship, xi, xii, xiv, xviii, xix, xxi, xxii, xxv, 6, 8, 12, 22, 26, 29, 33, 36, 38, 39, 41–43, 49, 55, 57–62, 64–68, 74, 78, 93, 94, 101, 107, 109, 110, 116, 122, 129, 134, 136, 141–143, 146, 147, 149, 152, 157–159, 161, 162, 175–178, 182, 186–191, 193–195, 204, 206, 208, 219, 224, 227
Reproduce, 71, 107, 110, 194, 214–216
Reproduction, 38
Research
  methods, xviii–xxiii, xxv, xxvi, 74, 99, 138, 144, 158, 160, 185, 221, 224–229
  practices, xxi–xxiii, xxvi, 97, 105, 107, 109, 115, 123, 158, 160
Researcher, ix–xi, xiii, xiv, xvii, xviii, xxi, xxii, xxiii, 4, 6, 11, 12, 24–34, 58, 60, 64, 65, 67, 71, 73–75, 77–81, 83–86, 89–94, 96–101, 105–116, 118, 120, 123, 127, 128, 131, 134–136, 138, 139, 145, 155, 158, 160, 186, 213, 221, 225, 227, 228
Resistance, 57, 99, 142
Resonate, xi, xii, xix, xxvi, 43, 58, 179, 231n8
Responsibility, 14, 55, 57, 66, 68, 93, 94, 152, 169, 187, 190, 203, 204, 207
Restory, 68, 105–123
Reverberate, 60

S

School, xiii, xxi, 35–38, 40–42, 44–49, 51, 63, 65, 80, 91, 93, 95, 97–101, 120, 129, 130, 133, 136, 137, 167, 223–229
Schooling, 37–40, 90, 133, 224, 226, 228
Script, xxiv, 40, 116, 128, 167–169, 172–182
Sensibility(ies), 38, 117, 172
Shorty, 36–39, 43, 44, 231n3
Social studies, xxiii, 141–143, 148, 151, 155, 159, 228
Spontaneous, xxv, 137, 209, 214–216
Story, xii, xiii, xviii, xxii, xxiii, xxiv, 4, 5, 8, 14, 17, 26, 29, 35–51, 55, 57–64, 67, 68, 78, 79, 105–107, 109, 111–116, 119–123, 127, 128, 130–136, 138, 139, 152, 155–157, 166, 169, 172–174, 178, 180, 204, 231n5, 231n8
Storytelling, 39, 40, 42, 44, 105, 106, 109–111, 114–122, 128
Structure, xi, xiii, 38, 62, 86, 117, 123, 138, 172, 174, 176, 177, 183, 190, 191, 198, 211, 214, 220
Subject, x, xxi, xxiii, 47, 74, 86, 89, 93, 109, 110, 113–122, 145, 146, 149, 150, 186, 199, 202, 207, 212, 220, 223, 226, 232n14

Subjectivity, 110, 127, 135

T

Teacher/teaching/teach, ix, x, xii, xiii, xviii, xx, xxi, xxiii, xxvi, 35–51, 57, 59–61, 64, 65, 67, 68, 84, 89–101, 137, 141–143, 146, 148–155, 157–162, 166–168, 172, 185, 187, 191, 195, 196, 199, 200, 209, 223–229, 231n3, 231n4
Team, vii, xxii, xxiii, 13, 73–76, 79, 80, 85, 93, 95, 97, 105–123, 139, 167, 168, 170, 174, 211, 231n11, 231n12, 232n13
Team-based, xxii, 105, 107, 108,
Technique
  musical, 209
Tension(s), x, xii, xiii, xx, 12, 14–17, 35, 58, 64–67, 73, 101, 110, 116–118, 122, 127, 135, 142, 145, 154
Text
  split, 35, 36, 41, 42
Theatre, xxiv, xxvi, 62, 165–167, 169–172, 174, 178, 179, 181, 183, 197, 211, 214, 218, 223, 225–227
Theatrical, 167, 174, 176, 217, 218, 220, 227
Traditional
  research, xxi, 89, 90, 92, 96
  practices, xxi, 197
Transform/transformation(al), ix, xi, xxv, 36, 80, 105, 106, 131, 137, 138, 187, 209, 219, 220, 231n9
Translate(tion), xxv, 74, 82, 205, 209
Translational research (in practice), xxi, 89–101
Transparent(ly, cy), x, xii–xiv, xvii, xviii, xix, xx, xxiv, 11, 12, 143, 153–155, 160
Trouble/troubling, xix–xxi, 3–34, 36, 37, 48, 89–95, 101, 153, 171, 178, 180, 226
Trust, xiii, xx, 6, 15, 18–19, 26, 62, 66, 68, 74, 93, 99, 134, 136, 157, 208

U

University, xii, xxi, xxii, xxiv, xxvi, 3, 4, 35, 36, 40, 59, 65, 72–74, 76, 84, 86, 89–93, 95, 97–100, 111, 129, 145, 165–169, 173, 181, 210, 218–221, 223–229, 231n4
Urban, ix, xxii, 38, 39, 47, 89–101, 197, 224–226, 228, 229

V

Values
  & norms, 144, 158
Video, ix, 43, 81, 160, 170, 181–183, 193, 196, 199, 201, 205, 212, 213, 220, 227
Voice, x, xiii, xviii, xx, xxi, xxiv, xxv, xxvi, 5, 13, 14, 18, 33, 35, 39–41, 43, 44, 46, 58, 59, 64, 71, 76, 78–80, 82, 106, 109, 112, 113,

INDEX

122, 128, 132, 135, 139, 143–145, 148, 149, 153, 160–162, 189, 191, 203, 212, 224
Vulnerable/vulnerability, x, xii, xiv, 62, 64, 68, 115, 149, 187, 191

W

Word image, xiii, 56–58, 67
Working together, x, xvii–xxvii, 35, 39, 42, 63, 95, 101, 106, 108, 109, 143–145, 147, 154, 156, 158, 160, 161, 198

Work/working, vii, ix–xiv, xvii–xxvii, 3, 35, 55, 71, 89, 105, 127, 141, 165, 185, 210, 223–225
Writing story, 35–51

AUTHOR INDEX

A
Agar, M.H., 144, 161, 231*n*1
Alcoff, L.M., 110
Alpert, H., 93
Apple, M.W., 38, 144
Asher, N., xxiii, 127
Assman, J.L., 36, 45
Atkinson, P., xxv
Austin, J.L., xix, 145, 216
Au, W., 38
Ayers, W., 40

B
Bailey, D., xxv, 209
Bakhtin, M.M., x, 41, 128, 131
Barber, N., 108
Barone, T.E., 35, 39–42, 132, 139
Barry, C.A., 108
Bartenieff, I., 187, 224
Bateson, M.C., 63
Beaulieu, M.D., 93
Beck, U., 106
Behar, R., 231*n*1
Bellack, A.A., xvii
Bilinovich, C., ix, xi, xii, xiv, xvii, xxiii, xxiv, 141–162
Bishop, R., 38
Blevins-Knabe, B., 36, 42, 43
Blumenfeld-Jones, D.S., xxv, 35, 41
Bochner, A., xviii
Bornat, J., xviii
Boyer, E.L., 90
Brandist, C., ix, xi
Brantlinger, E., xiv
Bresler, L., 119
Breuer, F., 109, 231*n*10
Britten, N., 108
Bruner, J., 110
Buber, M., 59
Bulterman-Bos, J.A., 92
Burris, M.A., 78
Butler-Jones, O., 74

C
Cahnmann-Taylor, M., xxii
Cain, C., 135
Calhoun, C., 109, 231*n*10
Callaway, H., xviii
Capps, L., 109, 117
Carrick, R., 144
Cech, S.J., 101
Chamberlayne, P., xviii
Chambliss, M., xviii

Charon, R., 112
Christman, J.B., xvii
Christodoulou, N., 160
Clandinin, D. J., xiiii, xviii, xx, 39, 40, 55–68, 144
Clement, W., 106
Clifford, J., x, xvii, xix, 231*n*1
Cohen, D.K., 155
Cole, A.L., xxii, 91
Coleman, A., 91
Connelly, F.M., xviii, 40, 60, 144
Coulter, C., 36, 38
Creamer, E.G., 43
Crockett, M., xii, 155

D
D'Amour, D., 93
Davies, A., 57
de Cosson, A., xxii
Denzin, N., xvii, xxvi, 36, 38, 139, 144, 161
Derrida, J., 132, 212
Dewey, J., 37, 60, 131
Doucet, A., 107, 109, 231*n*10
Dunn, J.R., 72, 197
Dyck, I., 72

E
Easter, T., 39, 47
Einagel, V., 115
Eisner, E., 231*n*1
Ellis, C., xviiii, 43, 216
Emerson, C., ix, x
Erickson, F., xiii, xvii, xviii, xxv, 145, 155, 160, 231*n*1
Erickson, K., 108, 109, 123

F
Fawcett, B., 109
Fenstermacher, G.D., 40
Ferrada-Videla, M., 93
Findlay, L., 109, 231*n*10
Fine, M., xvii, 38, 144
Flyvbjerg, B., 109
Frank, A.W., 112, 113, 122
Freire, P., 37, 38, 71, 74, 80

G
Gastaldo, D., ix, xxi, 71–87, 144
Geertz, C., xiii, 127
Gershon, W.S., ix–xiv, xvii–xxvii, 3–34, 40, 141–162, 231*n*9
Gerstl-Pepin, C.I., xxvii
Gibson-Graham, J.-K., 231*n*10

239

AUTHOR INDEX

Given, L. M., xvii, 144
Gooden, A., ix, xxi, 72, 73, 80, 85, 144
Gouzouasis, P., xviii
Greenlaw, J., 129, 135
Greenwood, D.J., 94
Guba, E.G., 144
Gubrium, J.F., 110, 115
Gunzenhauser, M.G., xxvii

H
Halbwachs, M., 36, 44, 45
Hammersley, M., xxv
Hammond, L., xxvi, 231n2
Hamre, B., 57
Haraway, D., 109
Hawthorne, L., 73
Hearn, J., 109
Heilbrun, C.G., xx, 65, 66
Helfenbein, R.J. Jr., 89–101, ix, xxi
Hoagland, S.L., 36, 39
Hogan, P., 57
Hølge-Hazeltonk, B., xxvii
Holland, D., 135
Hollingsworth, S., 57
Holmes, D.L., 36, 42
Holstein, J.A., 110, 115
Huber, J., xiii,, xx, 231n5
Huber, M., 231n5, xiii, xx
Hughes, S., 40
Hyman, R.T., xvii

I
Irwin, R.L., xviii, xxii

J
Jenkins, T., 232n16
Jipson, J.A., xvii

K
Keats Whelan, K., 231n5
Kelly, N.H., 109
Kemmis, S., 74
Kennard, B., 57
Kilroy, C., 93
Kincheloe, J., 20, 38
Kiselica, M.S., 36, 41
Kliebard, H.E., 37, xvii
Knowles, G., xxii
Kondo, D., xii
Krøjer, J., xxvii
Kumashiro, K.K., 144

L
Laban, R., 187
Labaree, D.F., 92
Lachicotte, W., Jr., 135
Lagemann, E.C., 92

Lakoff, G., 144
Lareau, A., xiv
Lather, P., ix, xvii, xviii, xix, xx, xxi, xxii, 3–35, 41, 89, 93, 94
Leavy, P., xxii, xxv
Leggo, C., xvii
Levinas, E., 131
Lewis, D., 187
Lewis, G.E., xxv, 209
Liggett, T., 129
Lincoln, Y., xvii, xxvi, 144, 166
Lindemann Nelson, H., 67
Lloyd, K., 144
Lund, D.E., 135, 136

M
MacLachlan, P., 231n8
Maines, D.R., 115
Marcus, G.E., 231n10
Massaquoi, N., 73, 87
Mauthner, N.S., 107, 109, 231n10
Mbaye, B., 72
McCorkel, J.A., 109
McDermott, R., 128, 135, 136, 144
McLuhan, M., 139
McNiff, S., xxii
McTaggart, R., 74
Mehan, H., xvii, 141
Merleau-Ponty, M., 127
Miller, J.H., 143
Miller, J.L., 64
Minh-ha, T.T., 231n1
Mitchell, A., 144
Moleski, S.M., 36, 41
Morson, G.S., ix, x
Moss, P., xviii
Murphy, M.S., xiii, xx, 55–68, 231n7
Myers, K., 109

N
Nabavi, M., 135, 136
Nachi, M., 144
Nagrin, D., 192
Nelson, H.L., 67, 110, 112, 231n6
Nespor, J., 155
Nettl, B., xxii
Noguera, P., 36–39
Norris, J., ix, xxiii, 127–139, 144

O
Oberg, A., xxiii, 127, 134
Ochs, E., 109, 117
Okely, J., xviii
Olson, M., 59
Orillion, M., ix–xiv
Orr, A.M., xiii, xx, 39, 54–68
Oyler, C., 35, 41, 57

P

Page, R.N., xii, xvii, 143, 155
Papademetriou, D.G., 72
Pearce, M., xiii, xx, 55–68
Peel, A., ix, xi, xii, xiv, xvii, xxiii, xxiv, 141–162
Pennycook, A., 137
Peshkin, A., 231n1
Petronio, S., 91, 92
Pike, A., 93
Pillow, W., 110, 113
Pinar, W.F., xviii, 129
Pugh, A.J., 144
Purcell, M., 106
Pushor, D., 39

R

Reihl, C., 91
Richardson, L., 36, 39, 46, 123
Ricœur, P., xx, 35, 36
Rodriguez, L.S.M., 93
Rosaldo, R., 231n1
Rosenblatt, L., 129, 132, 134
Roth, W.M., 109, 127, 132, 231n10
Rubert, P.A., 36
Russell, G.M., 109

S

Samson, Y., xii, 155
Sawyer, R.D., ix, xxiii, 127–139, 144
Schafft, K.A., 94
Schubert, W.H., 38, 40, 41, 51
Schultz, B.D., ix, xx, 35–47, 160
Schultz, J., 160
Schwab, J.J., 37, 60
Schwandt, T.A., 37, 60
Scobie, W., xxii, xxiii, 105–108, 110, 121, 122, 231n11, 232n13
Shalla, V., 106
Shelton, N., 128, 135, 136
Shircliffe, B. J., 144
Shuck, G., 137
Shulman, L., 90, 91
Siegesmund, R., xxii
Siegler, E.L., 93
Siltanen, J., xxii, xxiii, 105–123, 231n11, 232n13
Skinner, D., 135
Smith, F.L., Jr., xvii
Smithies, C., ix, xvii, xviii, xix, xx, xxi, xxii, 3–35, 41
Spindler, G., xvii, xviii,
Spindler, L., xvii, xviii, xxvi, 2, 231n1
Springgay, S., xviii, xxii, 231n2
Steeves, P., ix, xiii, xx, xxi, 55–68
Stevenson, F., 108
Stichler, J.F., 93
Stull, D.D., 108, 109, 123
Sullivan, G., xxii

T

Taylor, C., xxii, 109
Toncy, N., xxv

V

Valli, L., xviii
Varenne, H., 144
Vygotsky, L., 137

W

Wang, C., 78
Wasser, J. D., 119
Weis, L., xvii, 38, 144
Wengraf, T., xviii
Whitney, F.W., 93
Wiggins, A., 40
Willis, A., xxii, xxiii, 105–123, 231n11, 232n13
Wills, J., 141
Wilson, B., xvii
Wilson-Fall, W., 72
Wolcott, H.F., xii, xiii, xvii

Y

Young, M., 60

Z

Ziarek, E.P., 143
Zizek, S., 209
Zoloth, L., 112
Zorn, J., 137

CPSIA information can be obtained at www.ICGtesting.com
Printed in the USA
LVOW01s2221020915

452639LV00006B/17/P

9 789087 909581